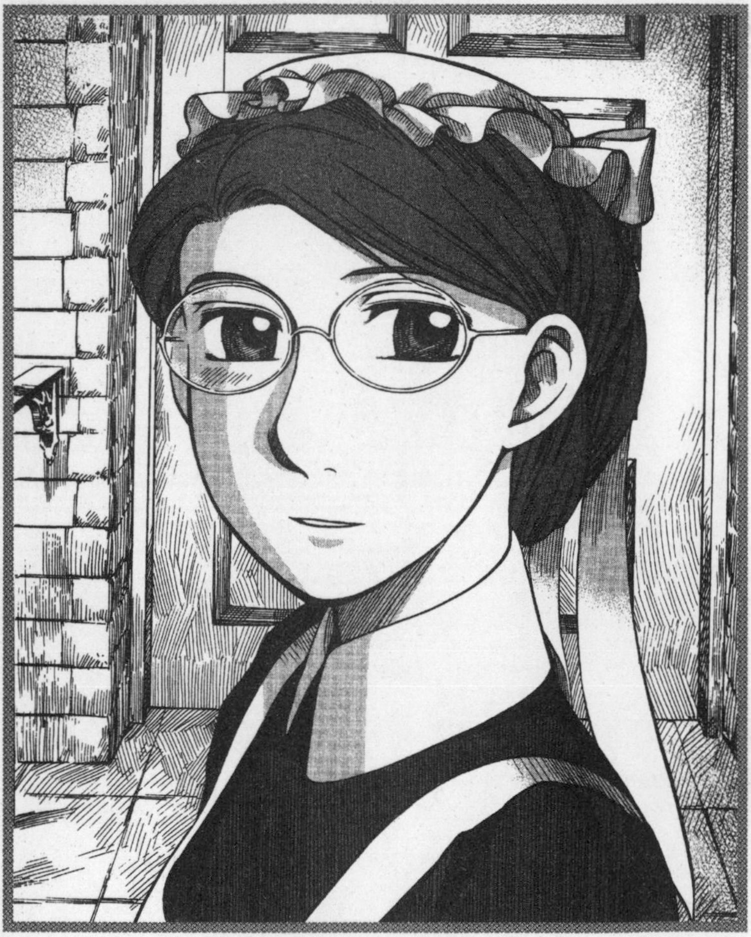

EMMA

Volume 4

By Kaoru Mori

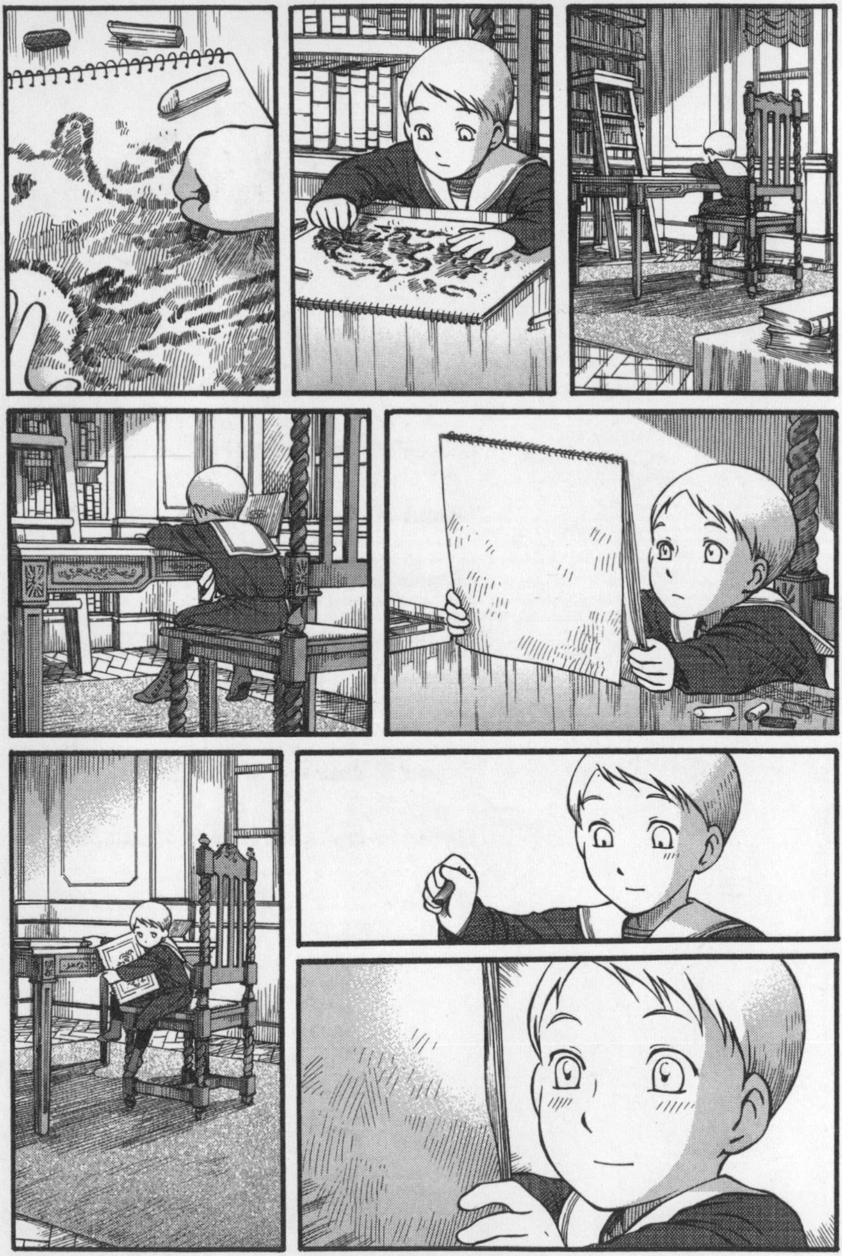

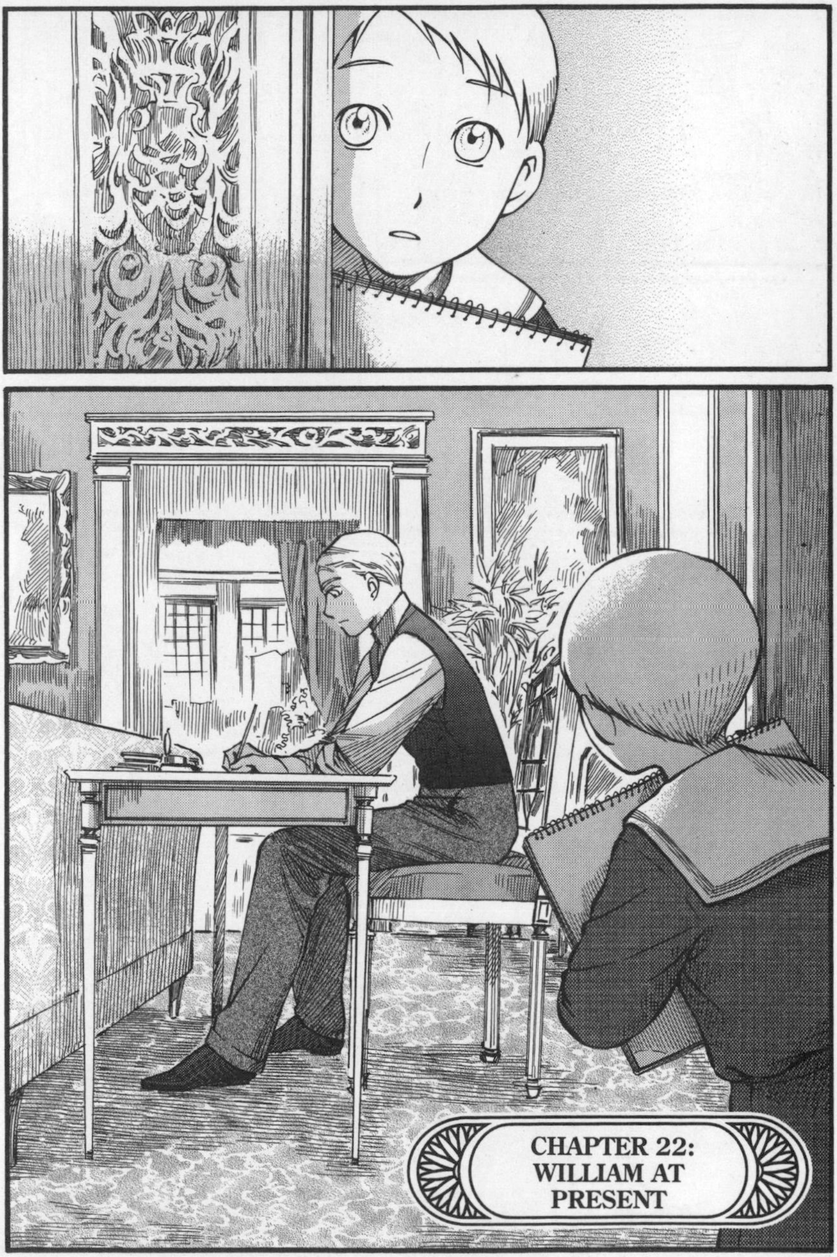
CHAPTER 22:
WILLIAM AT
PRESENT

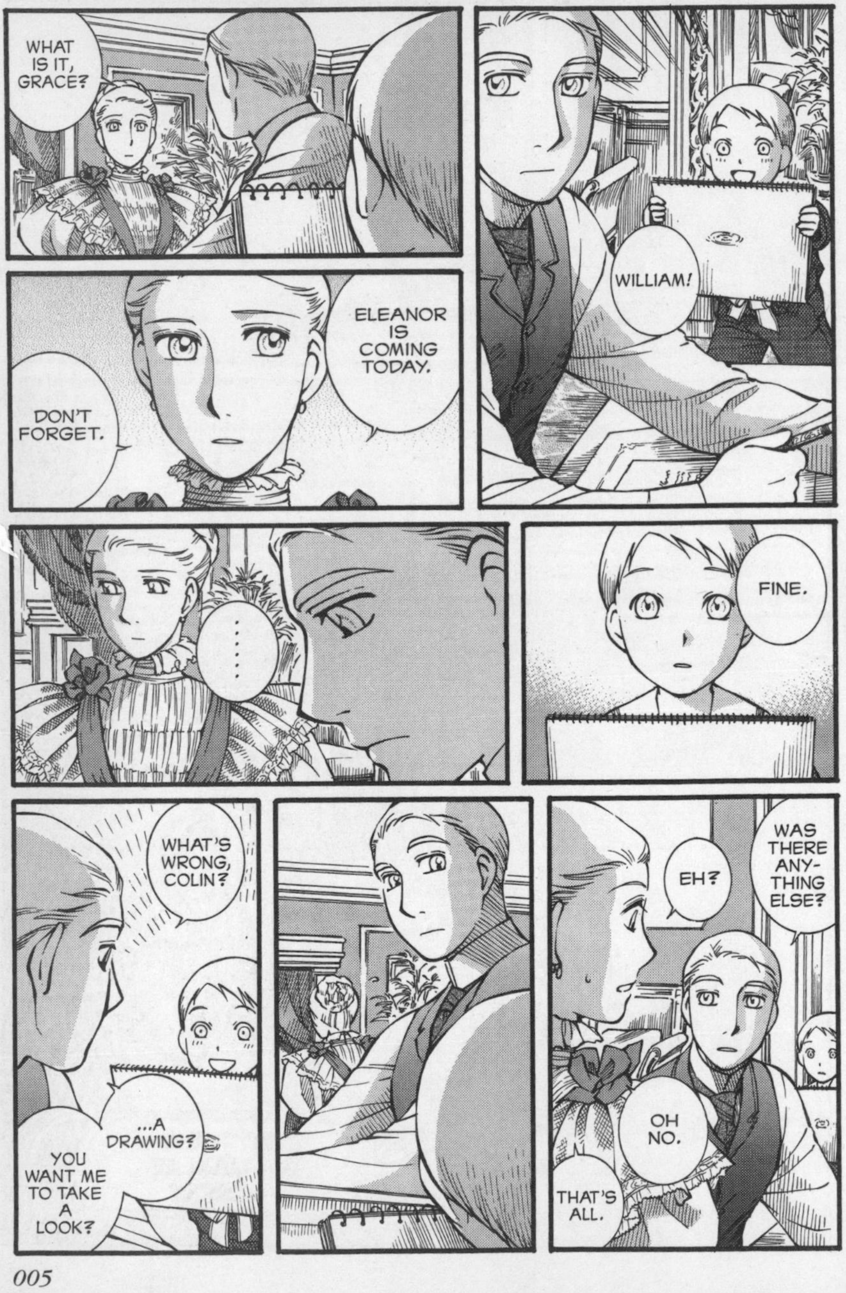
WILLIAM!
WHAT IS IT, GRACE?
ELEANOR IS COMING TODAY.
DON'T FORGET.
FINE.
......
WAS THERE ANY-THING ELSE?
EH?
OH NO.
THAT'S ALL.
WHAT'S WRONG, COLIN?
...A DRAWING?
YOU WANT ME TO TAKE A LOOK?

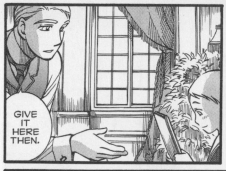

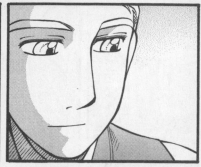

GIVE IT HERE THEN.
MASTER WILLIAM...
YOUR APPOINTMENT...
...HAS ARRIVED.
HAVE HIM WAIT IN THE STUDY.
I'LL BE RIGHT THERE.
I'M SORRY.
I'LL LOOK AT IT LATER ON.

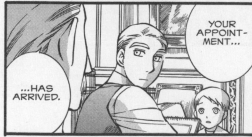

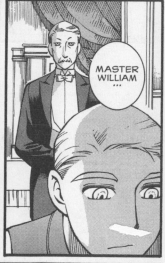

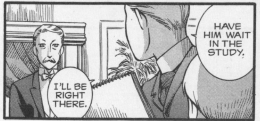

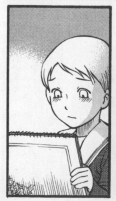

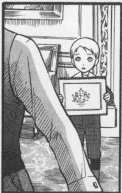

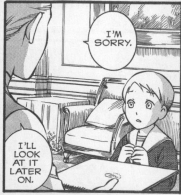

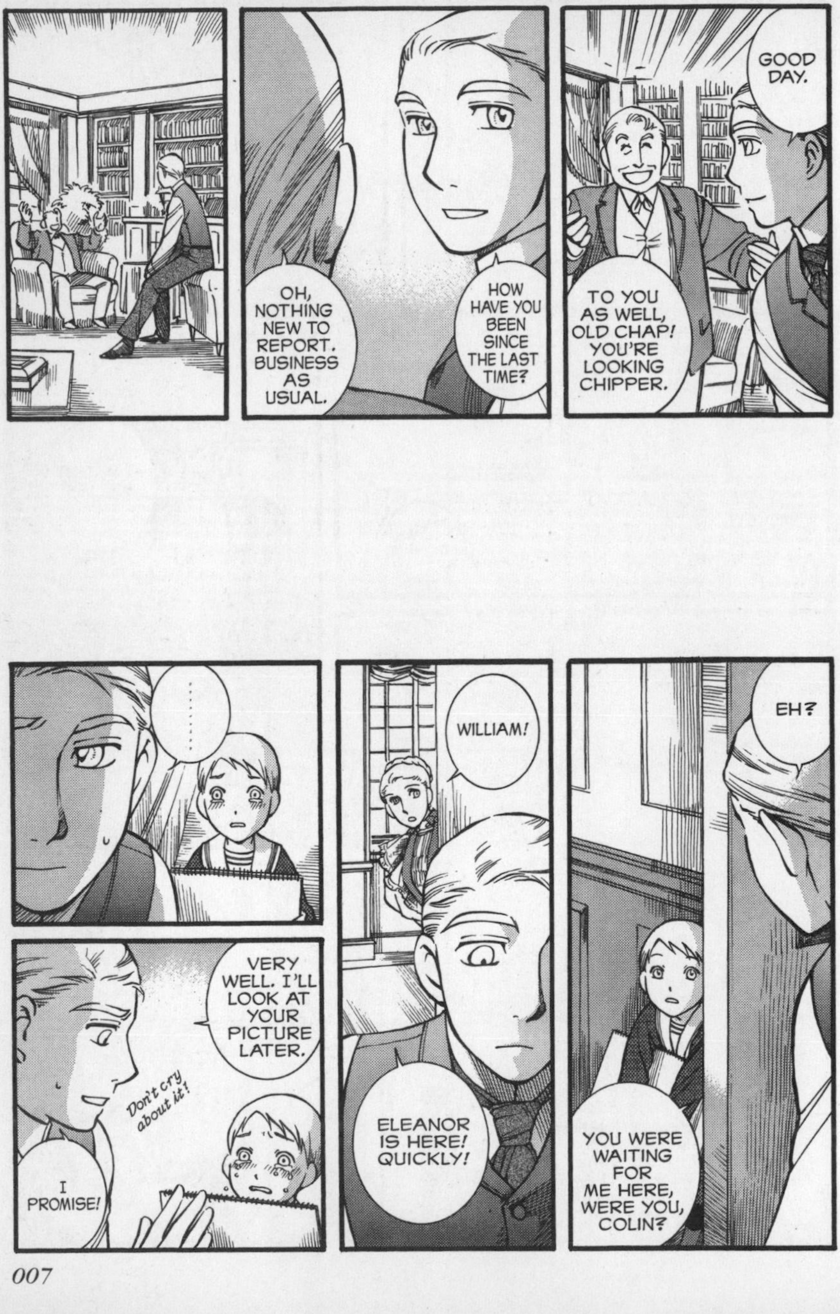
GOOD DAY.
TO YOU AS WELL, OLD CHAP! YOU'RE LOOKING CHIPPER.
HOW HAVE YOU BEEN SINCE THE LAST TIME?
OH, NOTHING NEW TO REPORT. BUSINESS AS USUAL.
EH?
YOU WERE WAITING FOR ME HERE, WERE YOU, COLIN?
WILLIAM!
ELEANOR IS HERE! QUICKLY!
......
VERY WELL. I'LL LOOK AT YOUR PICTURE LATER.
Don't cry about it!
I PROMISE!

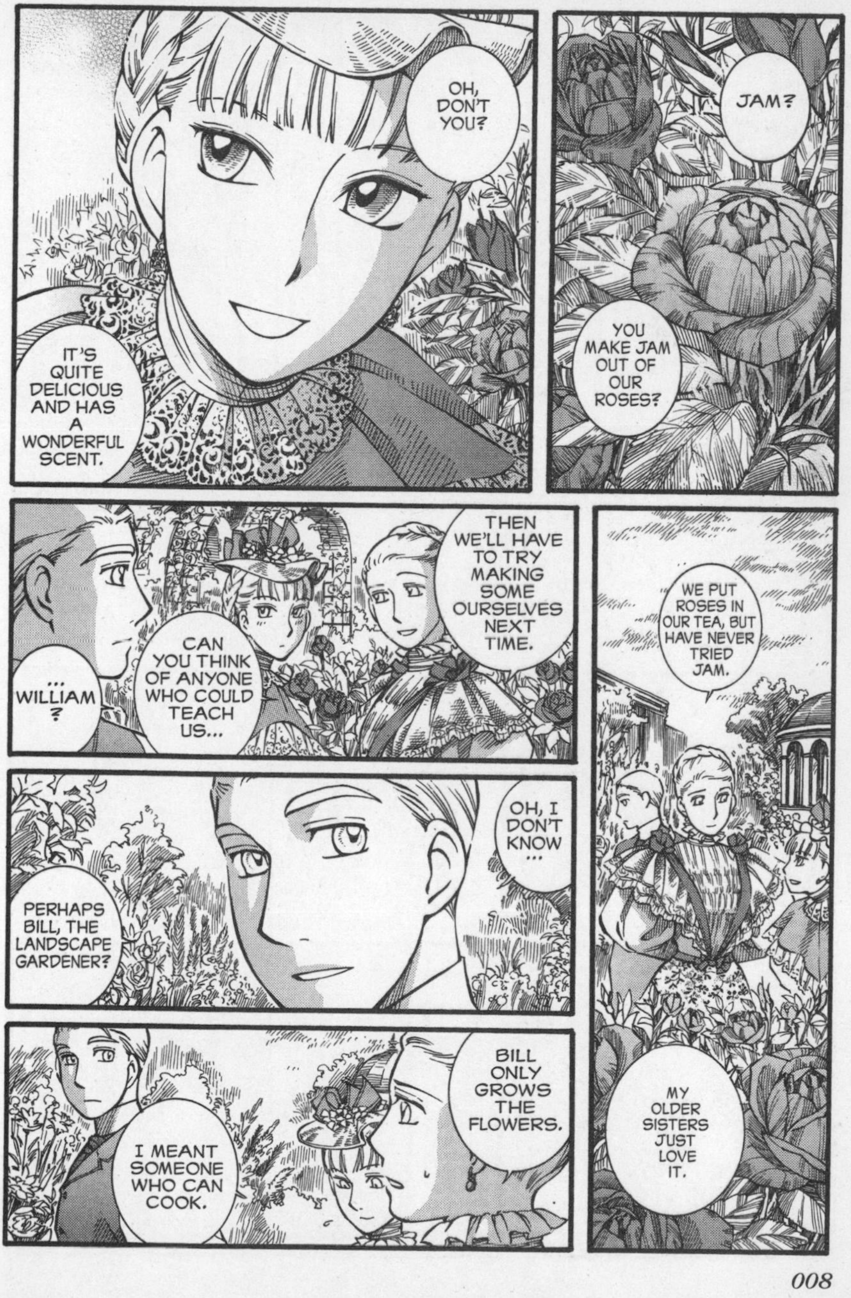
JAM?
YOU MAKE JAM OUT OF OUR ROSES?
OH, DON'T YOU?
IT'S QUITE DELICIOUS AND HAS A WONDERFUL SCENT.
WE PUT ROSES IN OUR TEA, BUT HAVE NEVER TRIED JAM.
MY OLDER SISTERS JUST LOVE IT.
THEN WE'LL HAVE TO TRY MAKING SOME OURSELVES NEXT TIME.
CAN YOU THINK OF ANYONE WHO COULD TEACH US...
...WILLIAM?
OH, I DON'T KNOW...
PERHAPS BILL, THE LANDSCAPE GARDENER?
BILL ONLY GROWS THE FLOWERS.
I MEANT SOMEONE WHO CAN COOK.

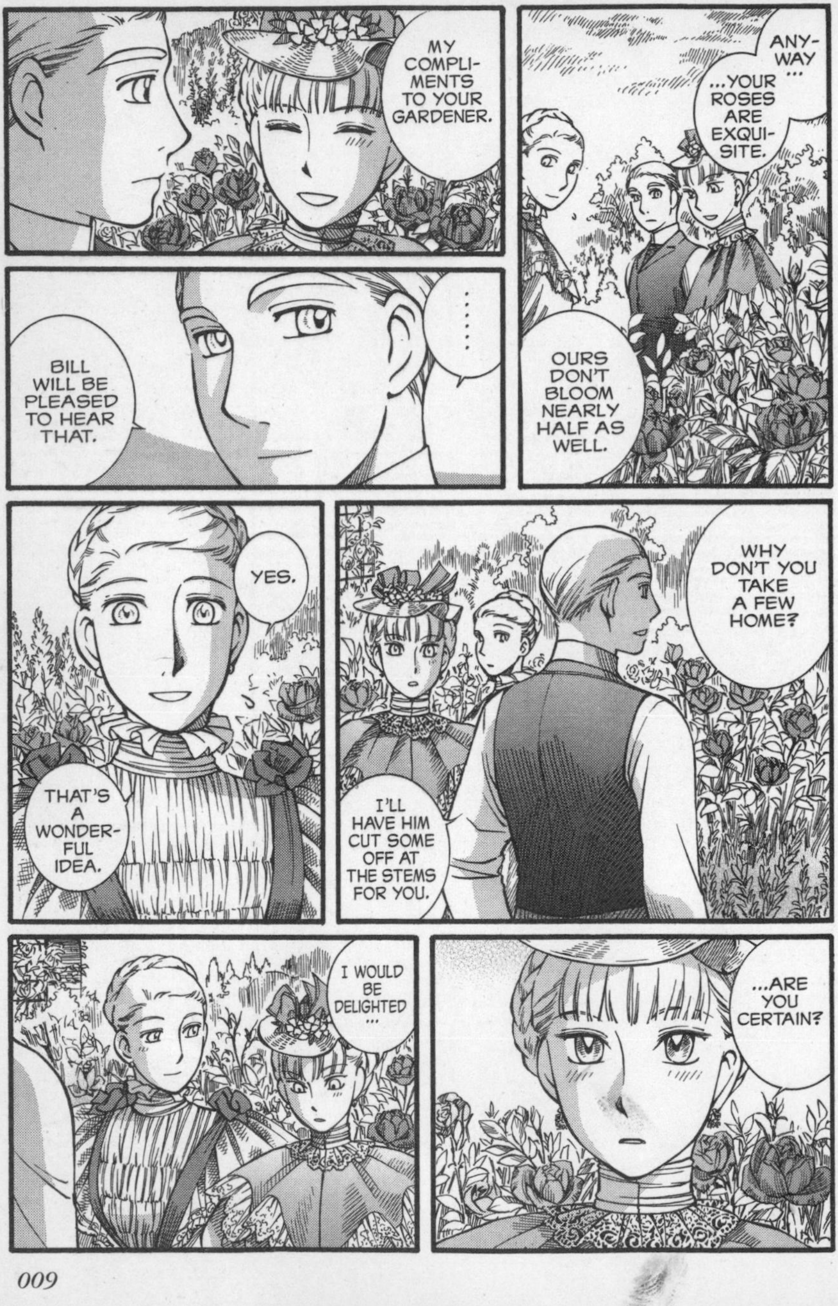

ANYWAY... ...YOUR ROSES ARE EXQUISITE.
OURS DON'T BLOOM NEARLY HALF AS WELL.
MY COMPLIMENTS TO YOUR GARDENER.
......
BILL WILL BE PLEASED TO HEAR THAT.
WHY DON'T YOU TAKE A FEW HOME?
I'LL HAVE HIM CUT SOME OFF AT THE STEMS FOR YOU.
YES.
THAT'S A WONDERFUL IDEA.
...ARE YOU CERTAIN?
I WOULD BE DELIGHTED...

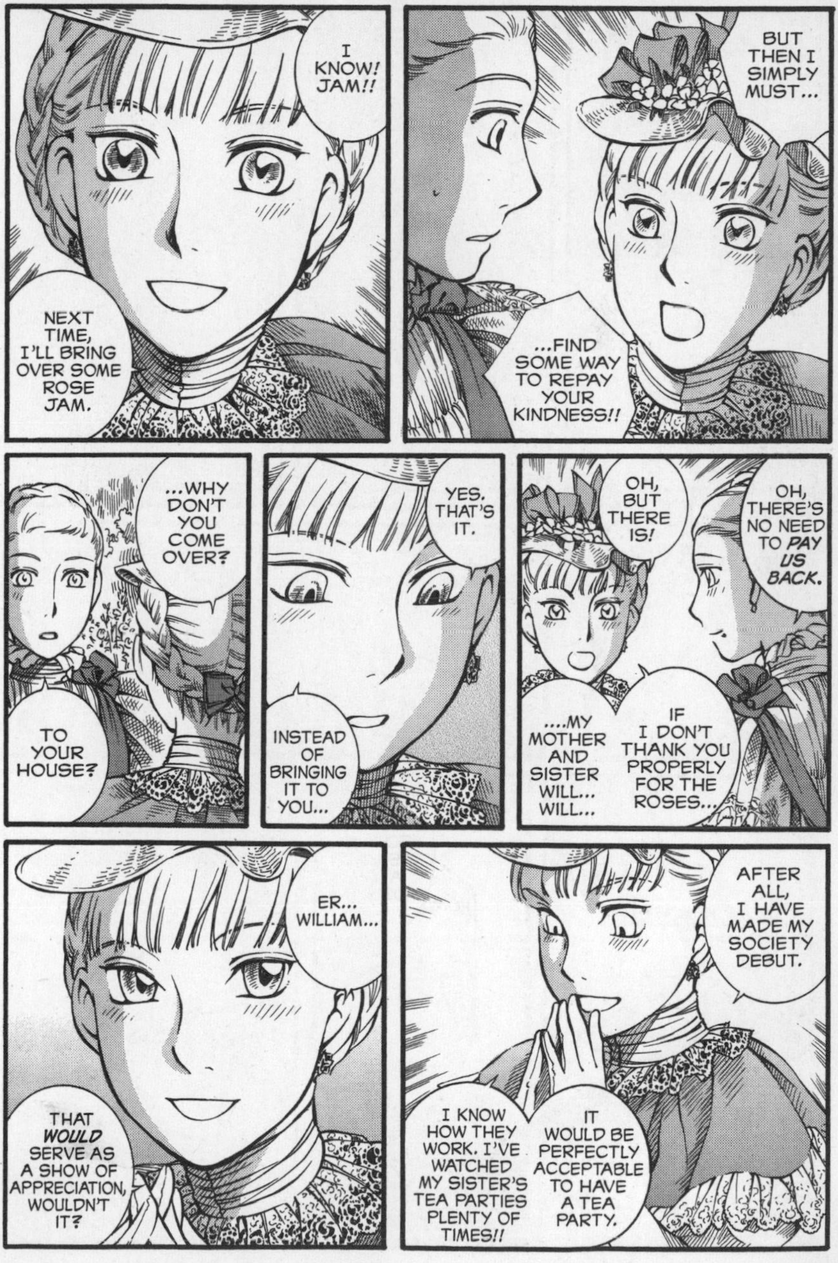
BUT THEN I SIMPLY MUST...
...FIND SOME WAY TO REPAY YOUR KINDNESS!!
I KNOW! JAM!!
NEXT TIME, I'LL BRING OVER SOME ROSE JAM.
OH, THERE'S NO NEED TO *PAY US BACK*.
OH, BUT THERE IS!
IF I DON'T THANK YOU PROPERLY FOR THE ROSES...
....MY MOTHER AND SISTER WILL... WILL...
YES. THAT'S IT.
INSTEAD OF BRINGING IT TO YOU...
...WHY DON'T YOU COME OVER?
TO YOUR HOUSE?
AFTER ALL, I HAVE MADE MY SOCIETY DEBUT.
IT WOULD BE PERFECTLY ACCEPTABLE TO HAVE A TEA PARTY.
I KNOW HOW THEY WORK. I'VE WATCHED MY SISTER'S TEA PARTIES PLENTY OF TIMES!!
ER... WILLIAM...
THAT *WOULD* SERVE AS A SHOW OF APPRECIATION, WOULDN'T IT?

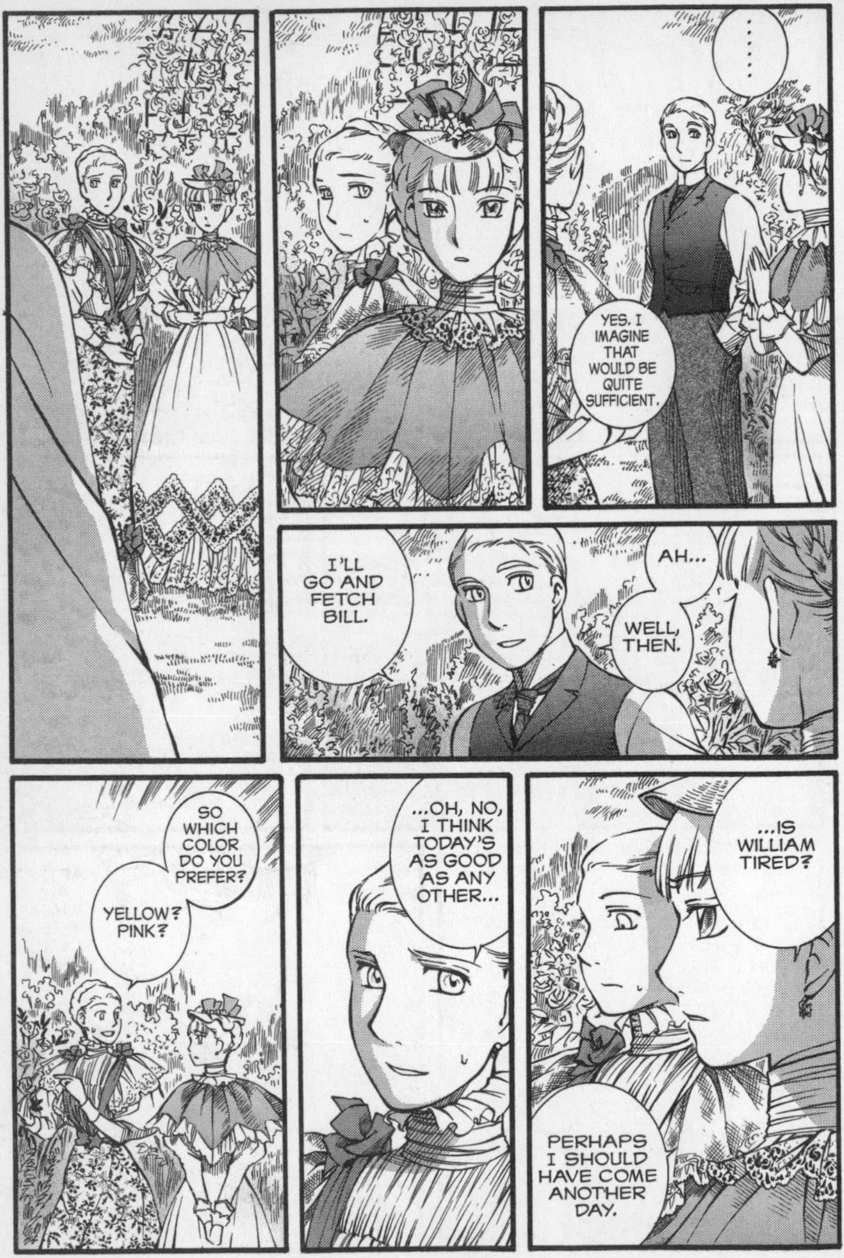
......
YES. I IMAGINE THAT WOULD BE QUITE SUFFICIENT.
AH...
WELL, THEN.
I'LL GO AND FETCH BILL.
...IS WILLIAM TIRED?
PERHAPS I SHOULD HAVE COME ANOTHER DAY.
...OH, NO, I THINK TODAY'S AS GOOD AS ANY OTHER...
SO WHICH COLOR DO YOU PREFER?
YELLOW? PINK?

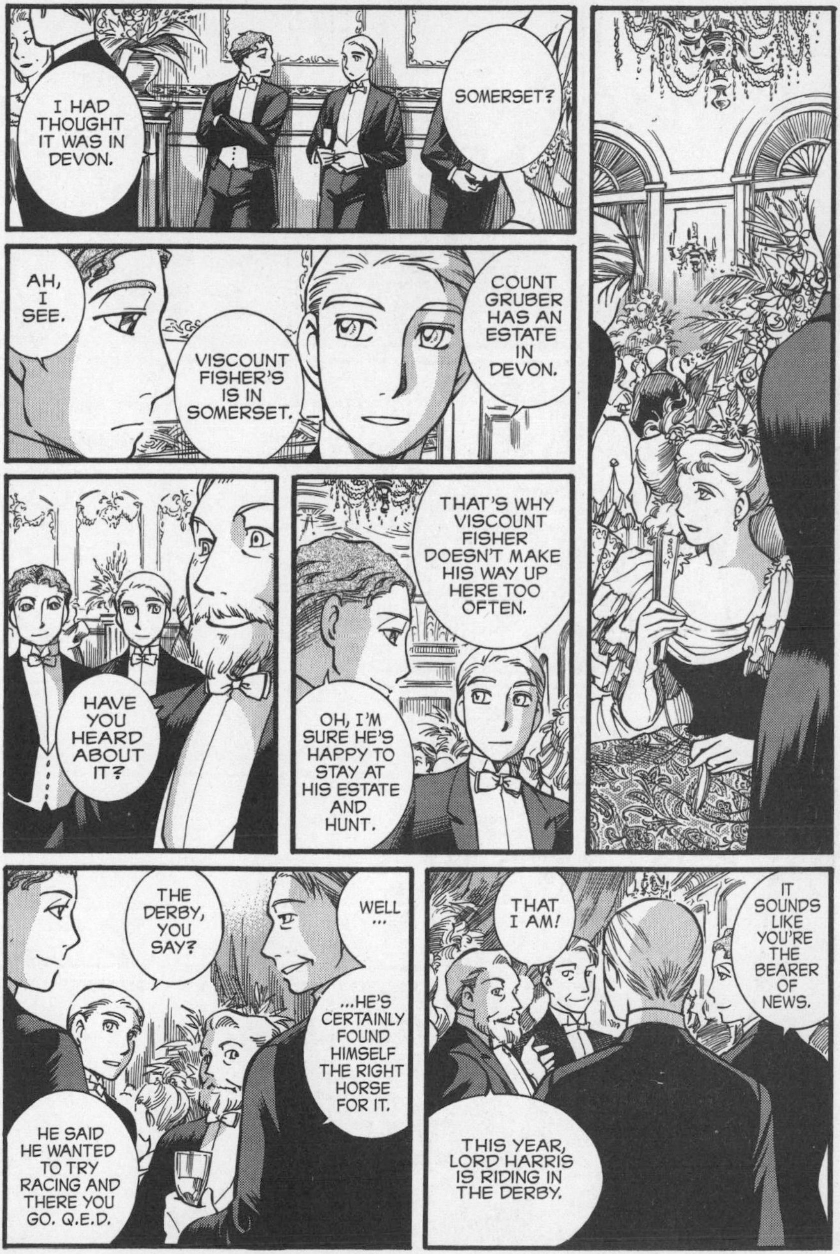
SOMERSET?
I HAD THOUGHT IT WAS IN DEVON.
COUNT GRUBER HAS AN ESTATE IN DEVON.
VISCOUNT FISHER'S IS IN SOMERSET.
AH, I SEE.
THAT'S WHY VISCOUNT FISHER DOESN'T MAKE HIS WAY UP HERE TOO OFTEN.
OH, I'M SURE HE'S HAPPY TO STAY AT HIS ESTATE AND HUNT.
HAVE YOU HEARD ABOUT IT?
IT SOUNDS LIKE YOU'RE THE BEARER OF NEWS.
THAT I AM!
THIS YEAR, LORD HARRIS IS RIDING IN THE DERBY.
WELL ...
THE DERBY, YOU SAY?
...HE'S CERTAINLY FOUND HIMSELF THE RIGHT HORSE FOR IT.
HE SAID HE WANTED TO TRY RACING AND THERE YOU GO. Q.E.D.

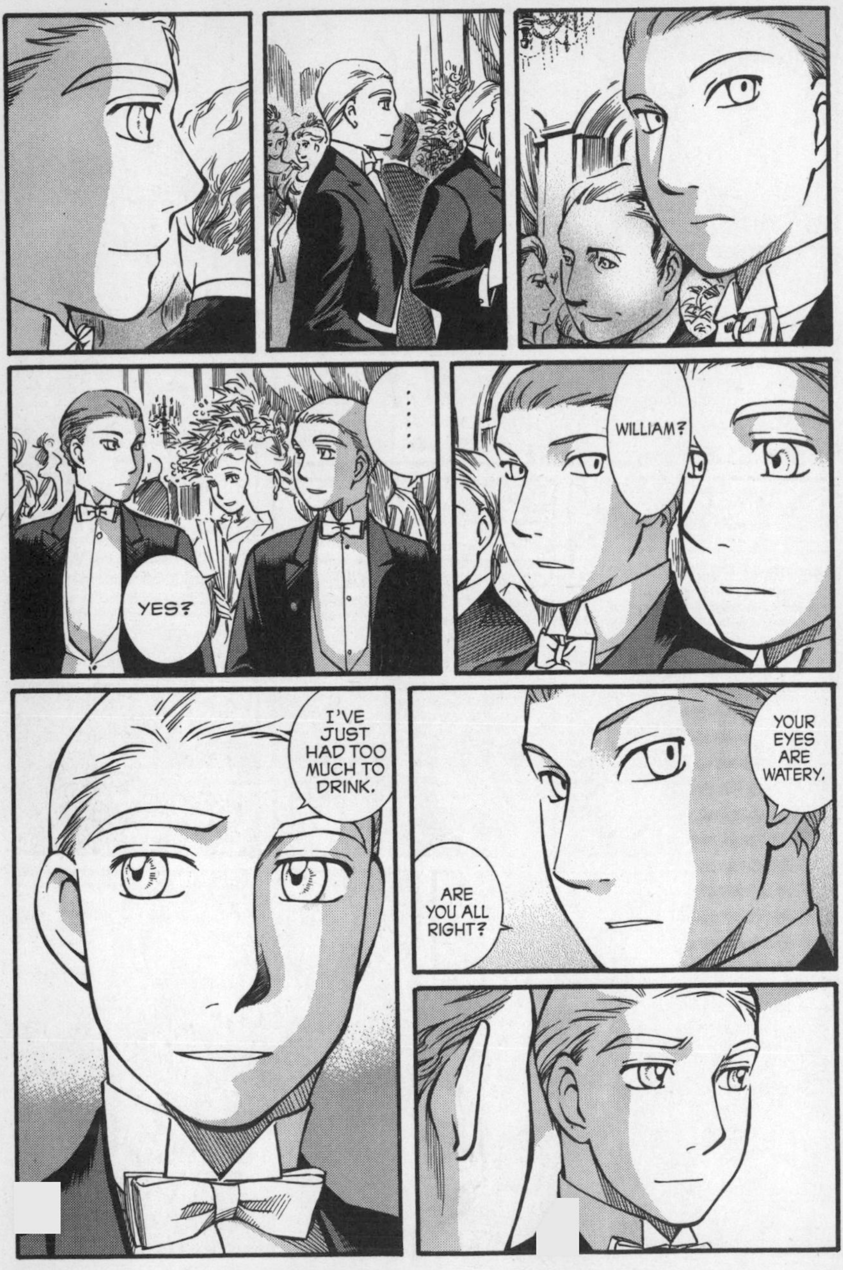
WILLIAM?
......
YES?
YOUR EYES ARE WATERY.
ARE YOU ALL RIGHT?
I'VE JUST HAD TOO MUCH TO DRINK.

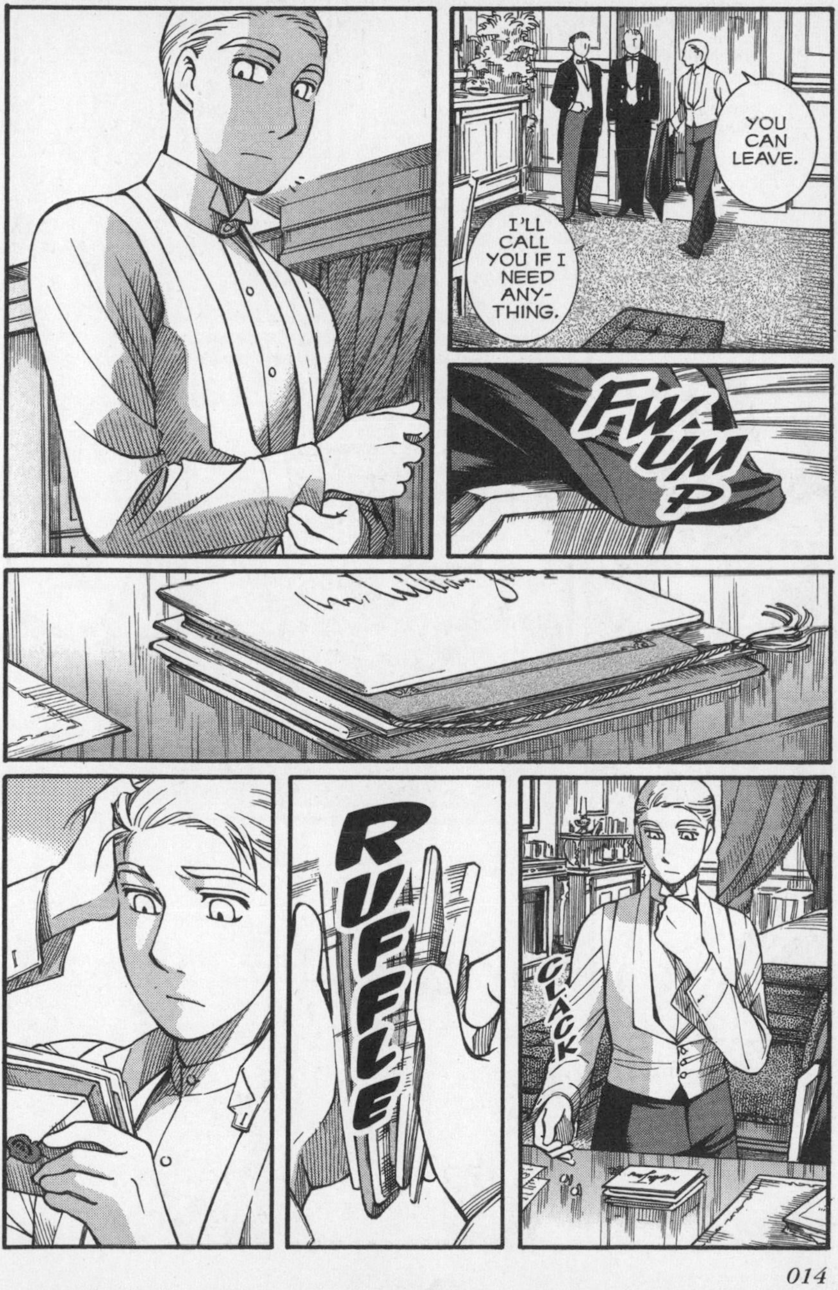
YOU CAN LEAVE.
I'LL CALL YOU IF I NEED ANYTHING.
FWUMP
CLACK
RUFFLE

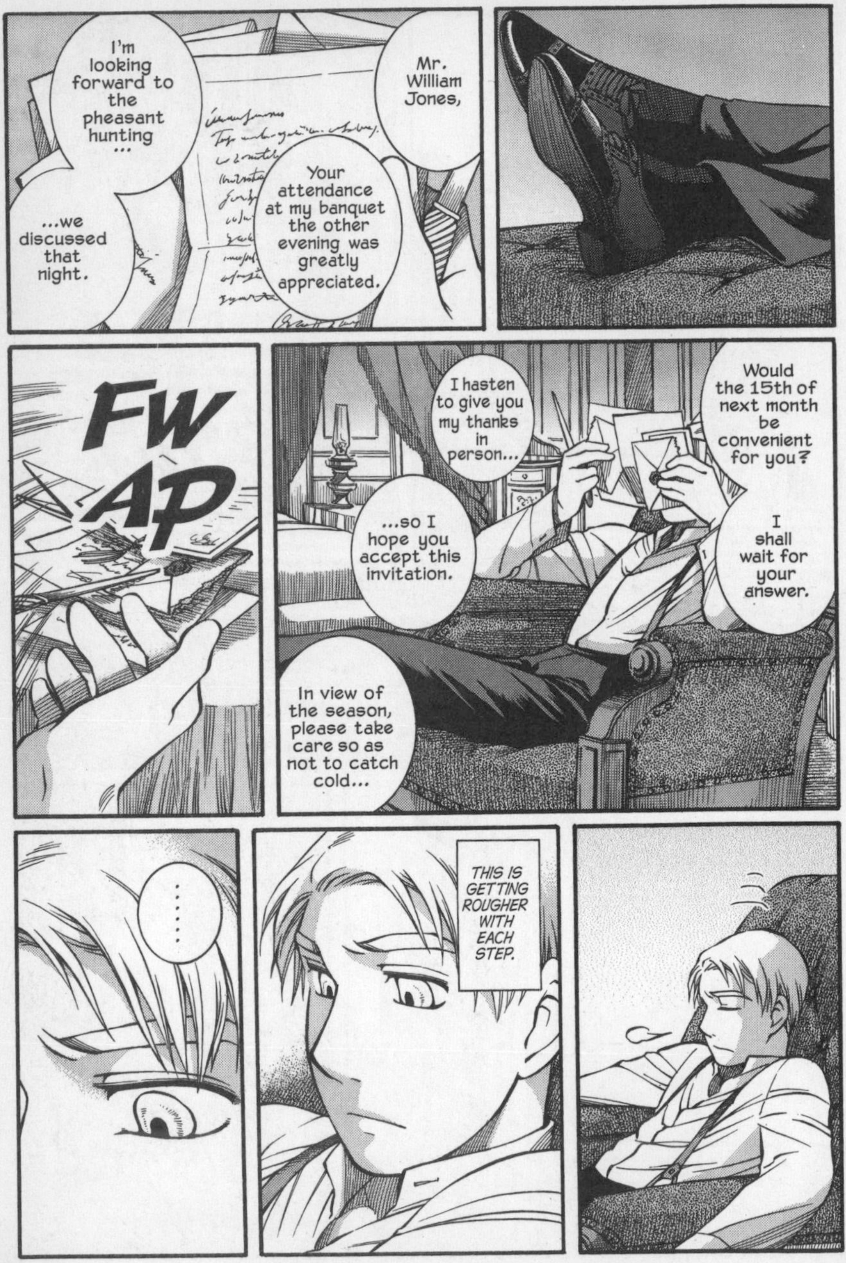
Mr. William Jones,
Your attendance at my banquet the other evening was greatly appreciated.
I'm looking forward to the pheasant hunting ...
...we discussed that night.
I hasten to give you my thanks in person...
...so I hope you accept this invitation.
Would the 15th of next month be convenient for you?
I shall wait for your answer.
In view of the season, please take care so as not to catch cold...
FWAP
THIS IS GETTING ROUGHER WITH EACH STEP.
......

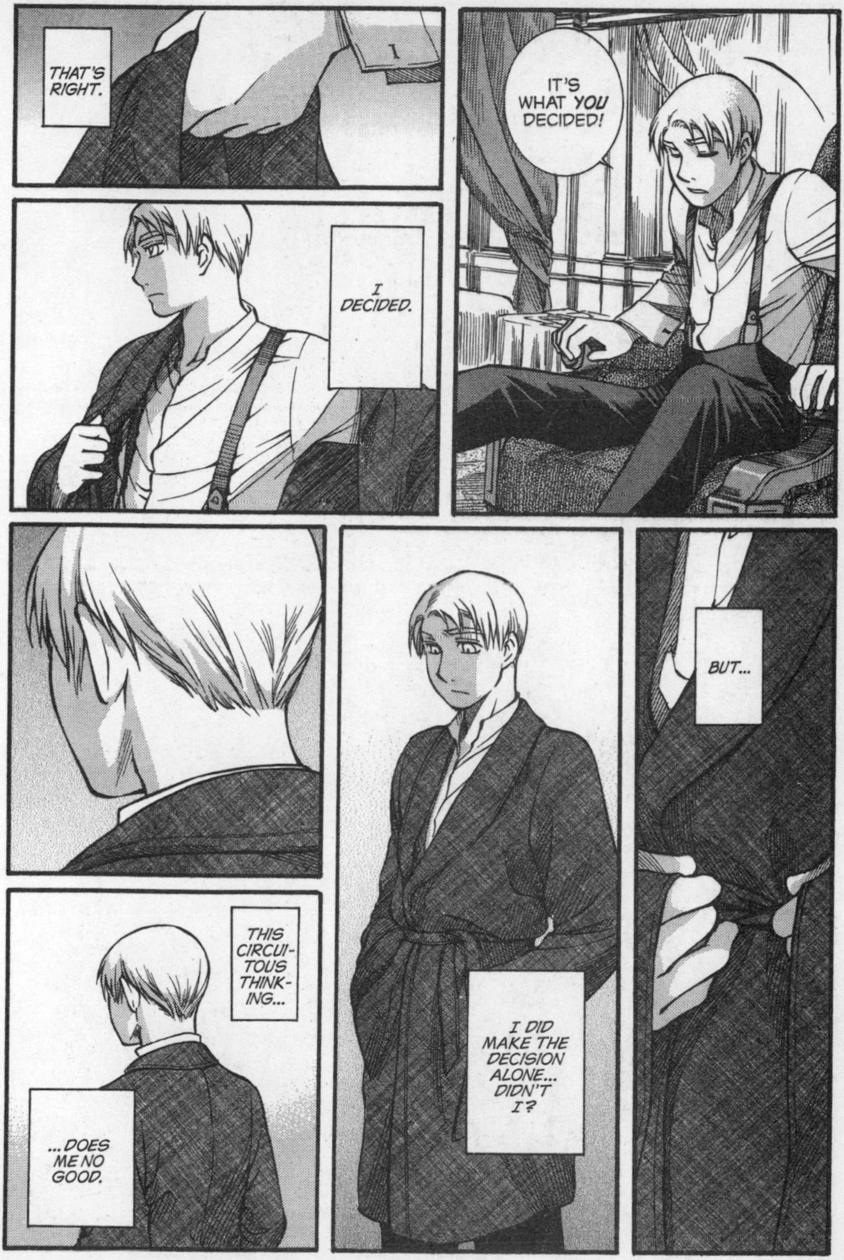
IT'S WHAT YOU DECIDED!
THAT'S RIGHT.
I DECIDED.
BUT...
I DID MAKE THE DECISION ALONE... DIDN'T I?
THIS CIRCUITOUS THINKING...
...DOES ME NO GOOD.

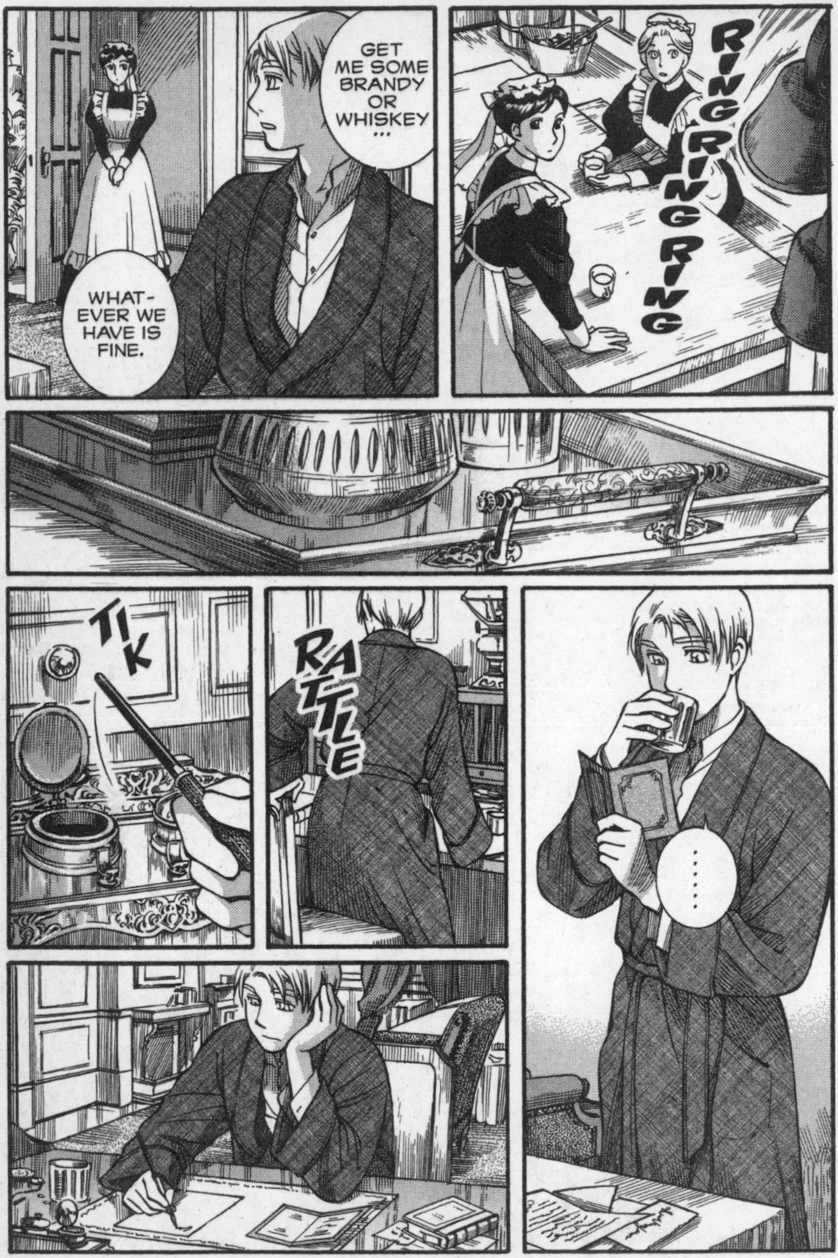
RING RING RING RING
GET ME SOME BRANDY OR WHISKEY ...
WHATEVER WE HAVE IS FINE.
......
RATTLE
TIK

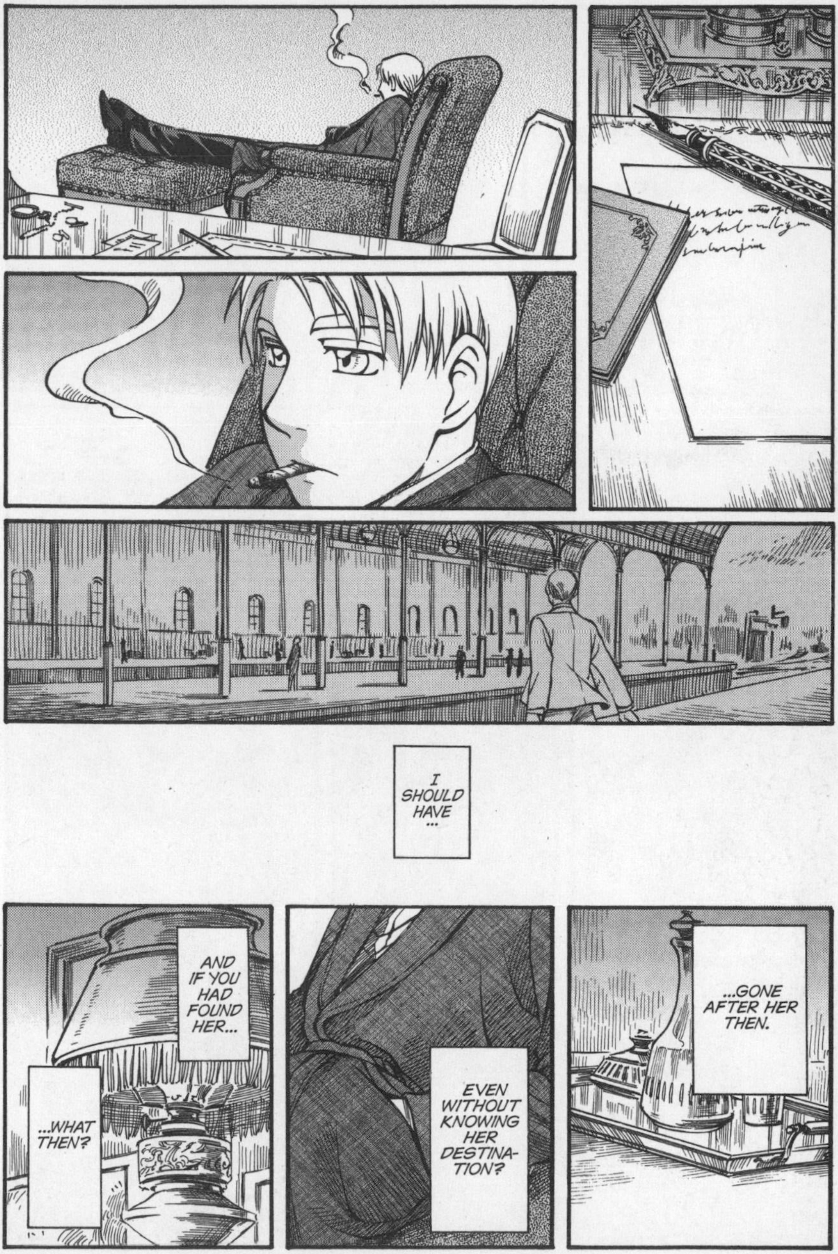
I SHOULD HAVE...
...GONE AFTER HER THEN.
EVEN WITHOUT KNOWING HER DESTINATION?
AND IF YOU HAD FOUND HER...
...WHAT THEN?

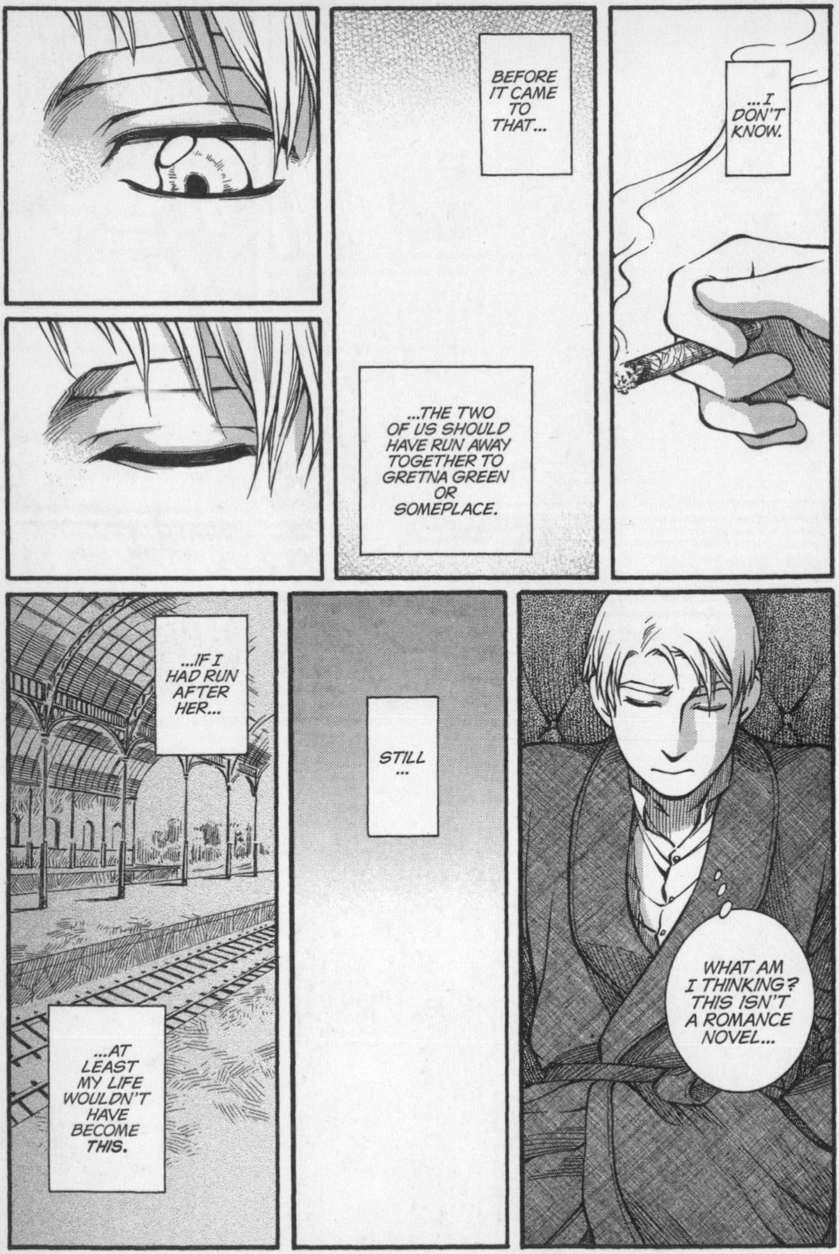
...I DON'T KNOW.
BEFORE IT CAME TO THAT...
...THE TWO OF US SHOULD HAVE RUN AWAY TOGETHER TO GRETNA GREEN OR SOMEPLACE.
WHAT AM I THINKING? THIS ISN'T A ROMANCE NOVEL...
STILL...
...IF I HAD RUN AFTER HER...
...AT LEAST MY LIFE WOULDN'T HAVE BECOME THIS.

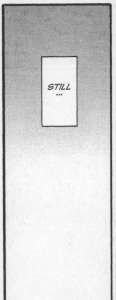

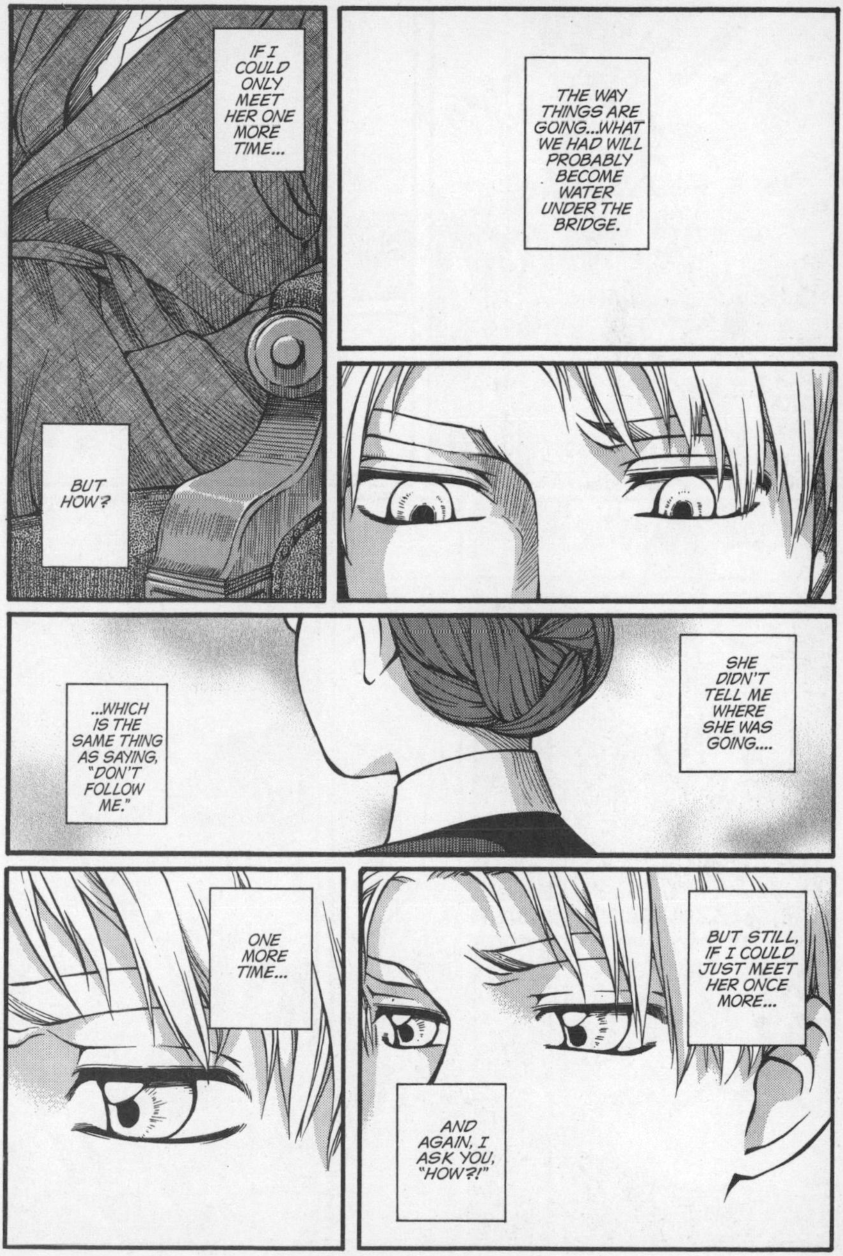
THE WAY THINGS ARE GOING...WHAT WE HAD WILL PROBABLY BECOME WATER UNDER THE BRIDGE.
IF I COULD ONLY MEET HER ONE MORE TIME...
BUT HOW?
SHE DIDN'T TELL ME WHERE SHE WAS GOING....
...WHICH IS THE SAME THING AS SAYING, "DON'T FOLLOW ME."
BUT STILL, IF I COULD JUST MEET HER ONCE MORE...
AND AGAIN, I ASK YOU, "HOW?!"
ONE MORE TIME...

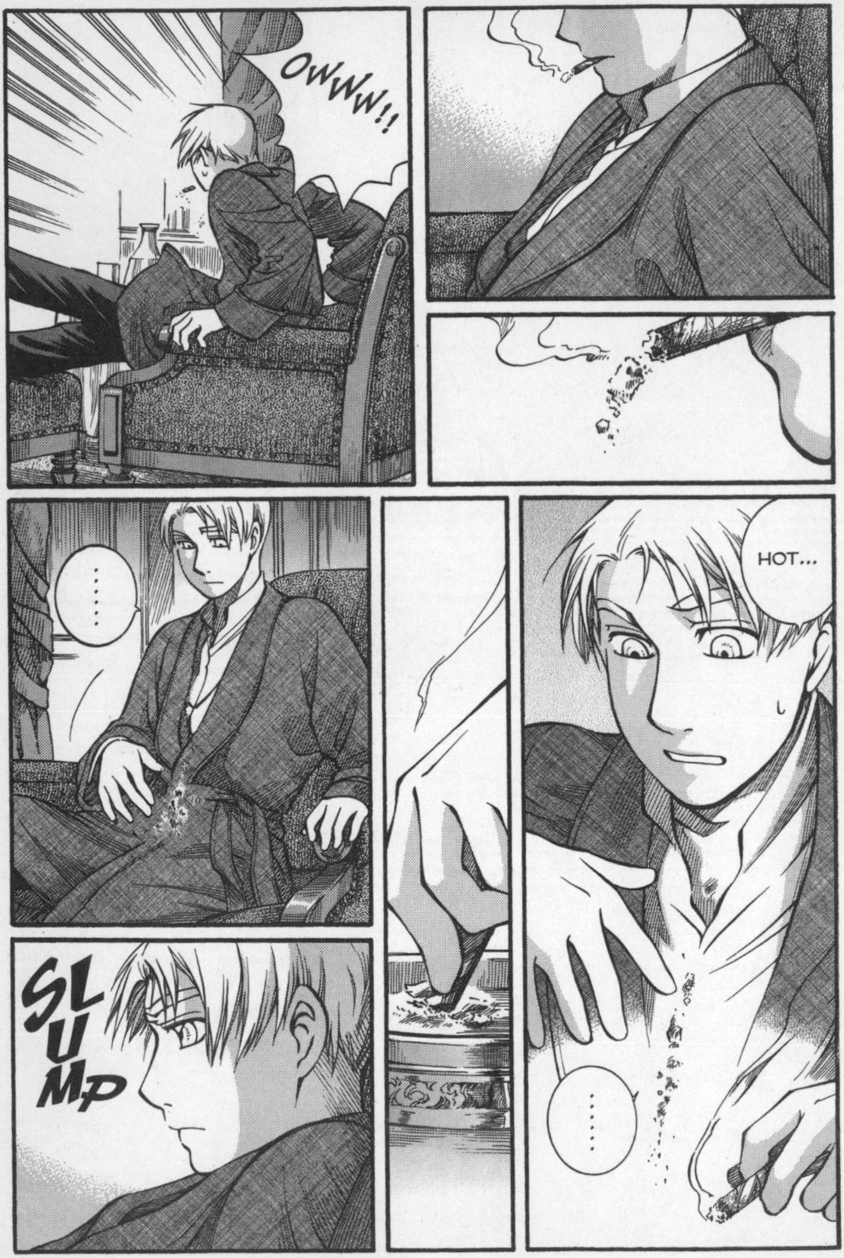

OWWW!!
HOT...
......
......
SLUMP

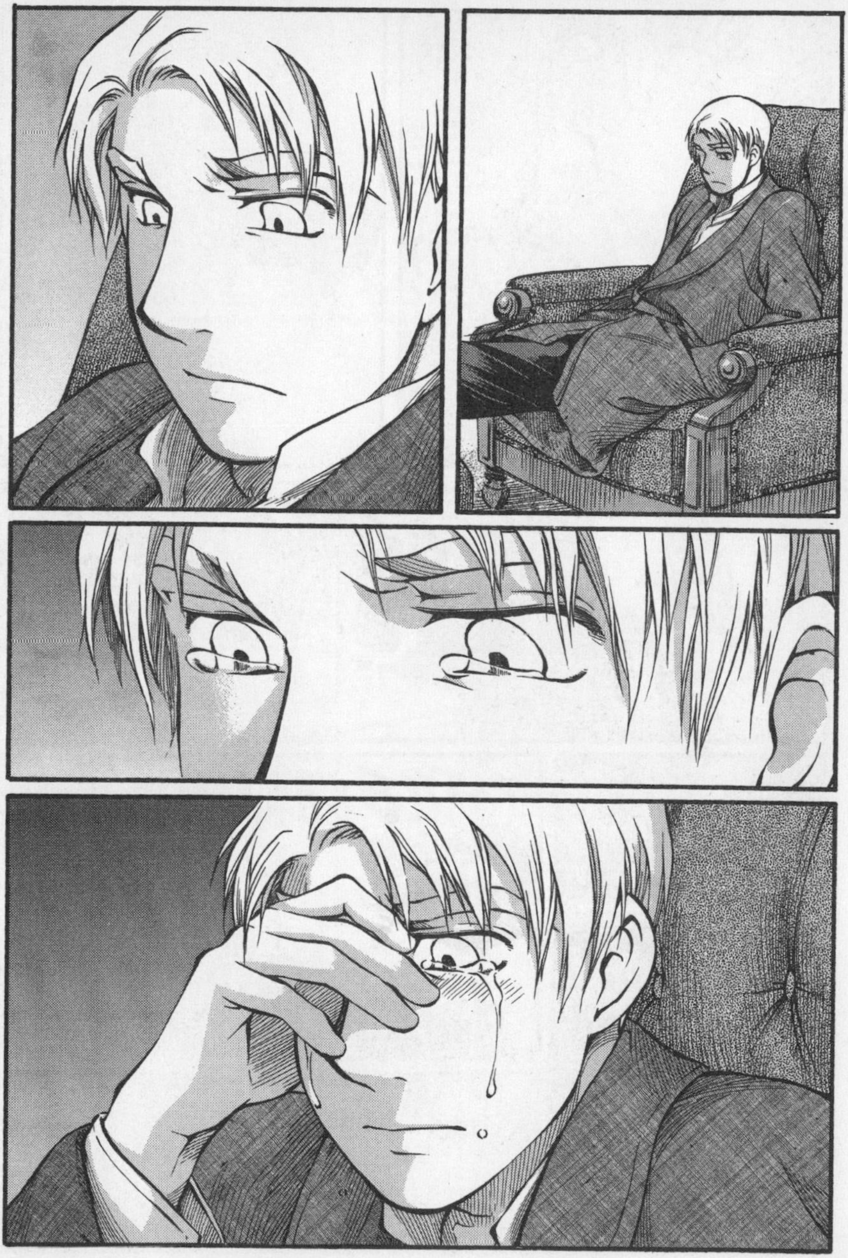

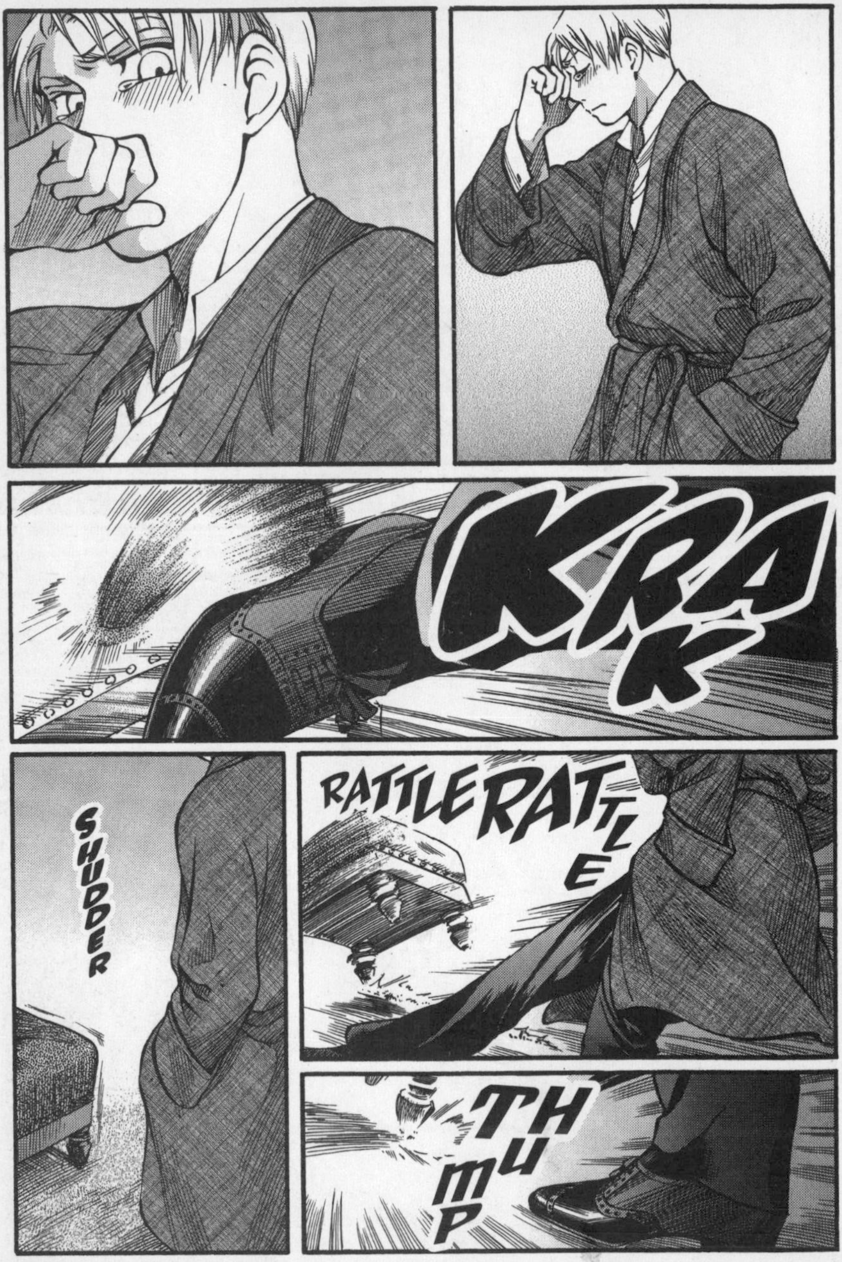
KRAK
RATTLE RATTLE
THUMP
SHUDDER

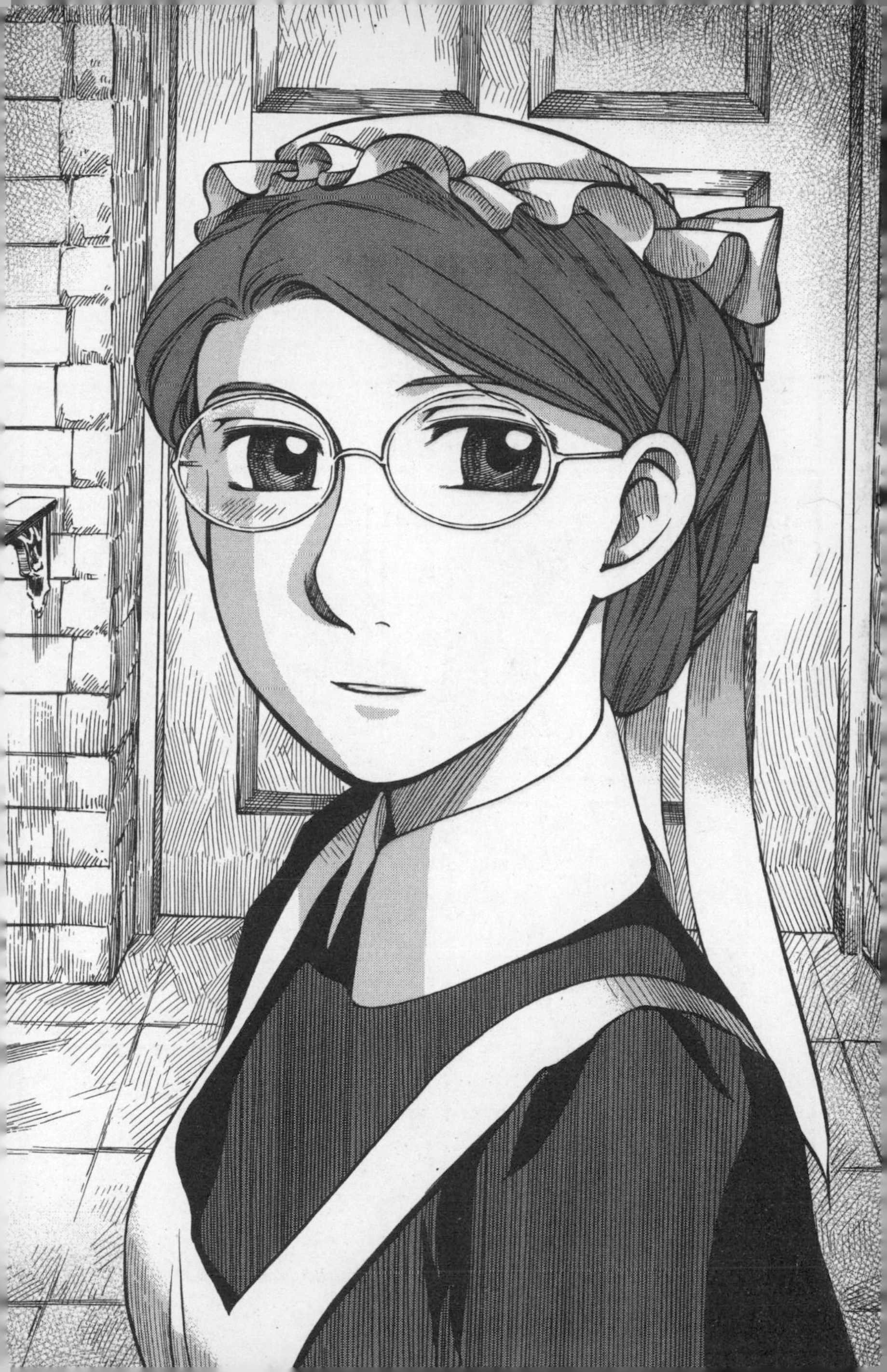

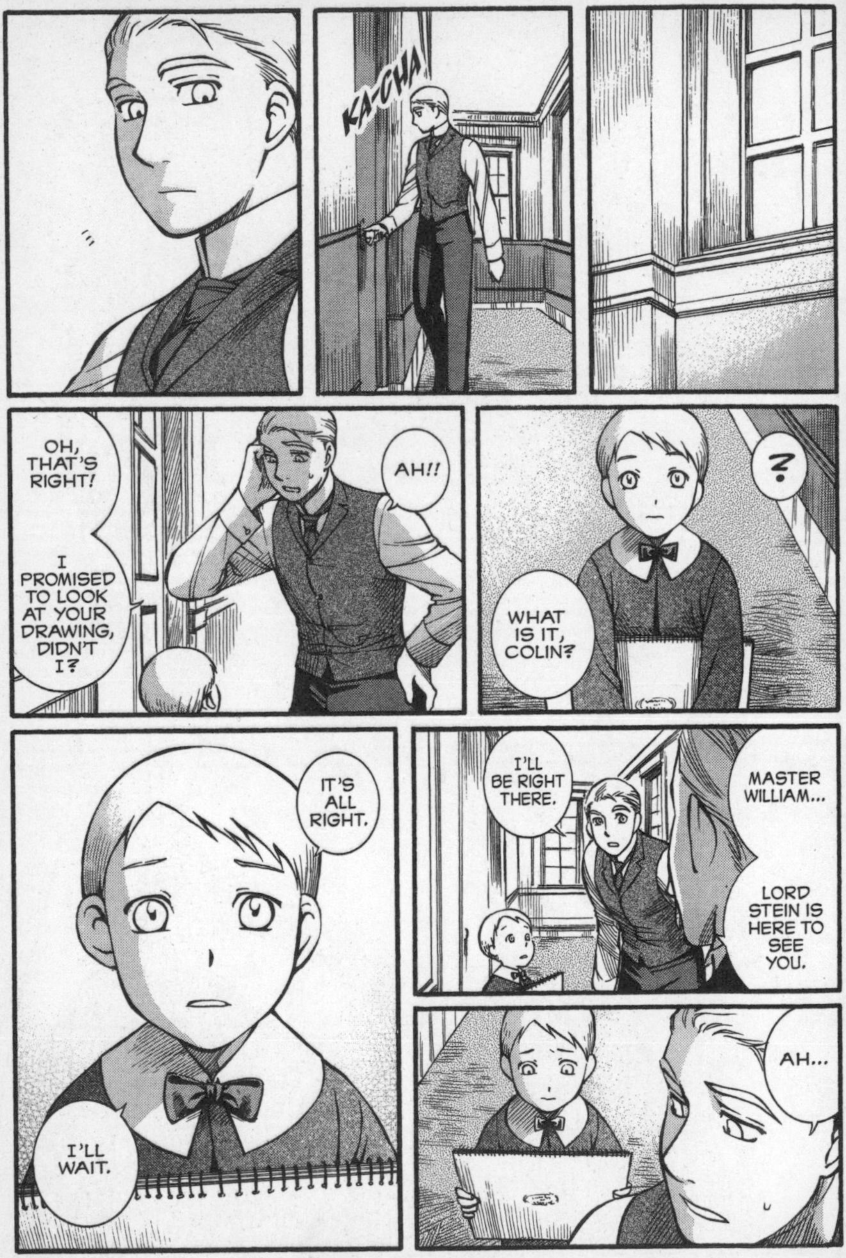
KA-CHA
?
WHAT IS IT, COLIN?
AH!!
OH, THAT'S RIGHT!
I PROMISED TO LOOK AT YOUR DRAWING, DIDN'T I?
MASTER WILLIAM...
LORD STEIN IS HERE TO SEE YOU.
I'LL BE RIGHT THERE.
AH...
IT'S ALL RIGHT.
I'LL WAIT.

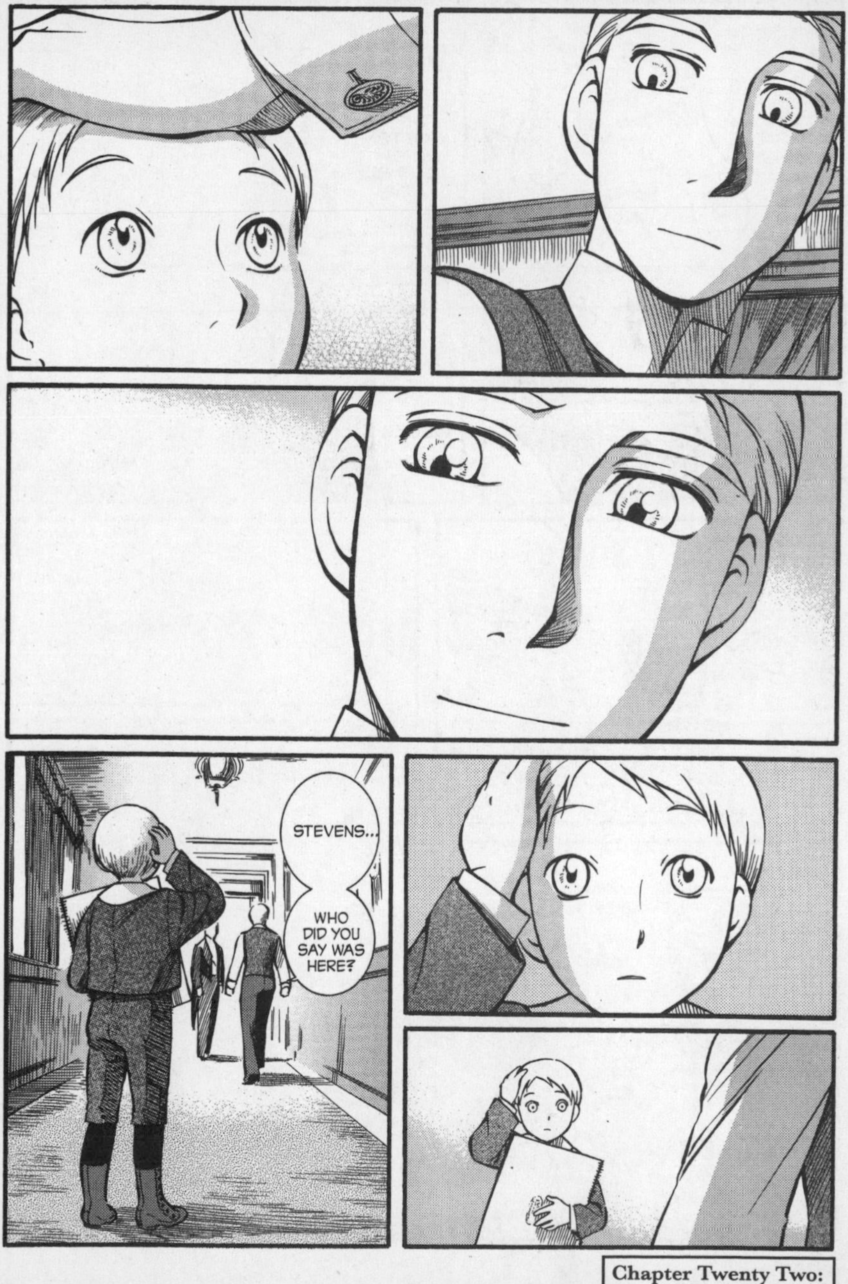
STEVENS...
WHO DID YOU SAY WAS HERE?

Chapter Twenty Two:
The End

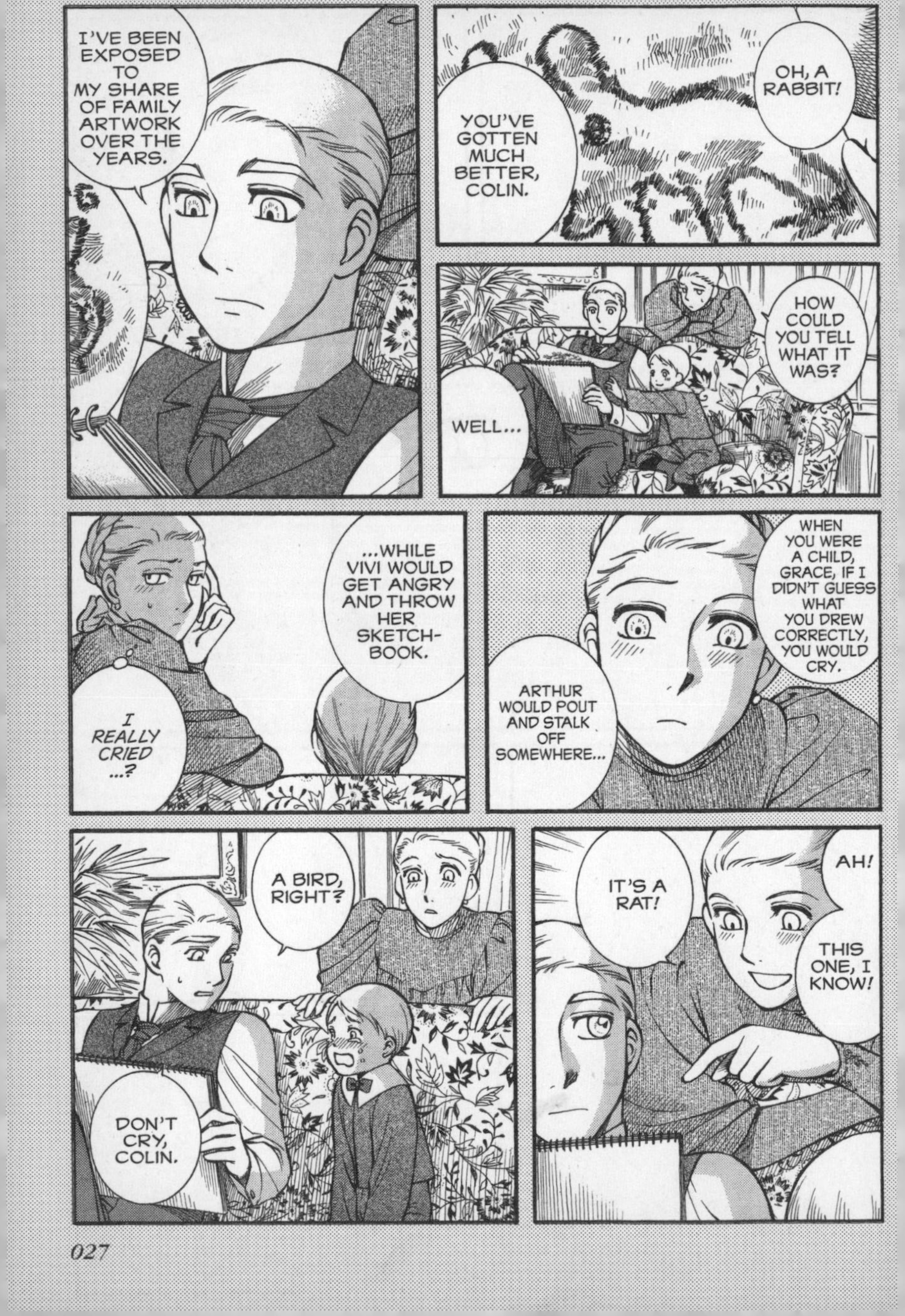
OH, A RABBIT!
YOU'VE GOTTEN MUCH BETTER, COLIN.
HOW COULD YOU TELL WHAT IT WAS?
WELL...
I'VE BEEN EXPOSED TO MY SHARE OF FAMILY ARTWORK OVER THE YEARS.
WHEN YOU WERE A CHILD, GRACE, IF I DIDN'T GUESS WHAT YOU DREW CORRECTLY, YOU WOULD CRY.
ARTHUR WOULD POUT AND STALK OFF SOMEWHERE...
...WHILE VIVI WOULD GET ANGRY AND THROW HER SKETCH-BOOK.
I REALLY CRIED ...?
AH!
THIS ONE, I KNOW!
IT'S A RAT!
A BIRD, RIGHT?
DON'T CRY, COLIN.

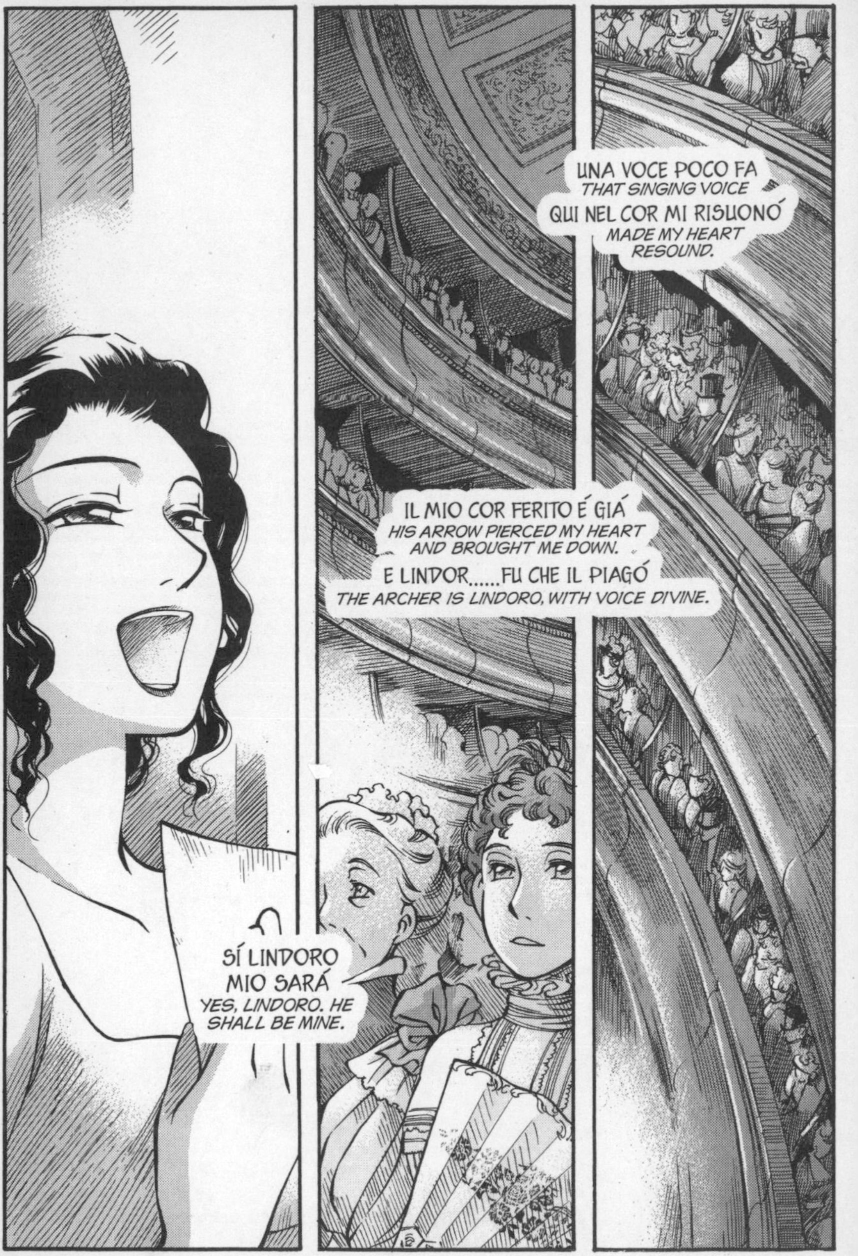
UNA VOCE POCO FA
THAT SINGING VOICE
QUI NEL COR MI RISUONÓ
MADE MY HEART RESOUND.
IL MIO COR FERITO É GIÁ
HIS ARROW PIERCED MY HEART AND BROUGHT ME DOWN.
E LINDOR......FU CHE IL PIAGÓ
THE ARCHER IS LINDORO, WITH VOICE DIVINE.
SÍ LINDORO MIO SARÁ
YES, LINDORO. HE SHALL BE MINE.

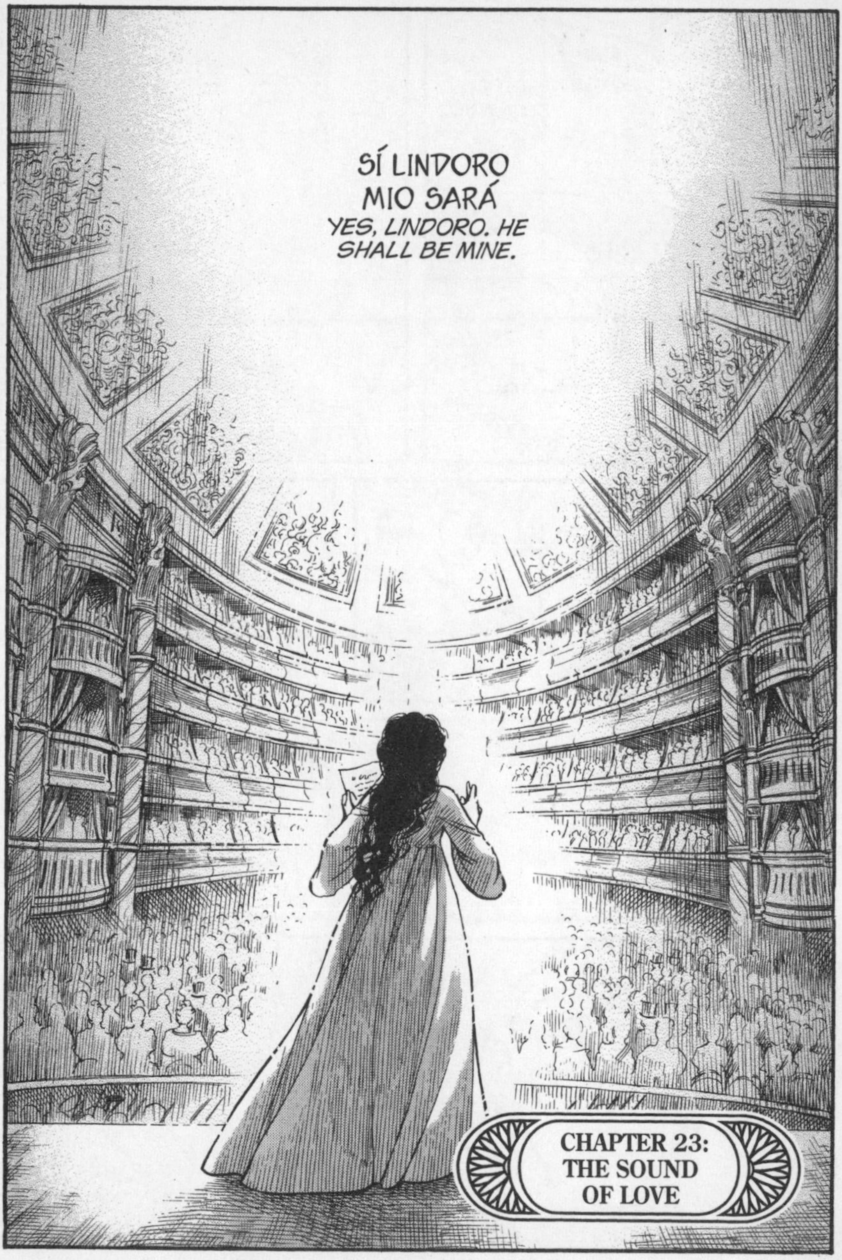
SÍ LINDORO
MIO SARÁ
YES, LINDORO. HE
SHALL BE MINE.
CHAPTER 23:
THE SOUND
OF LOVE

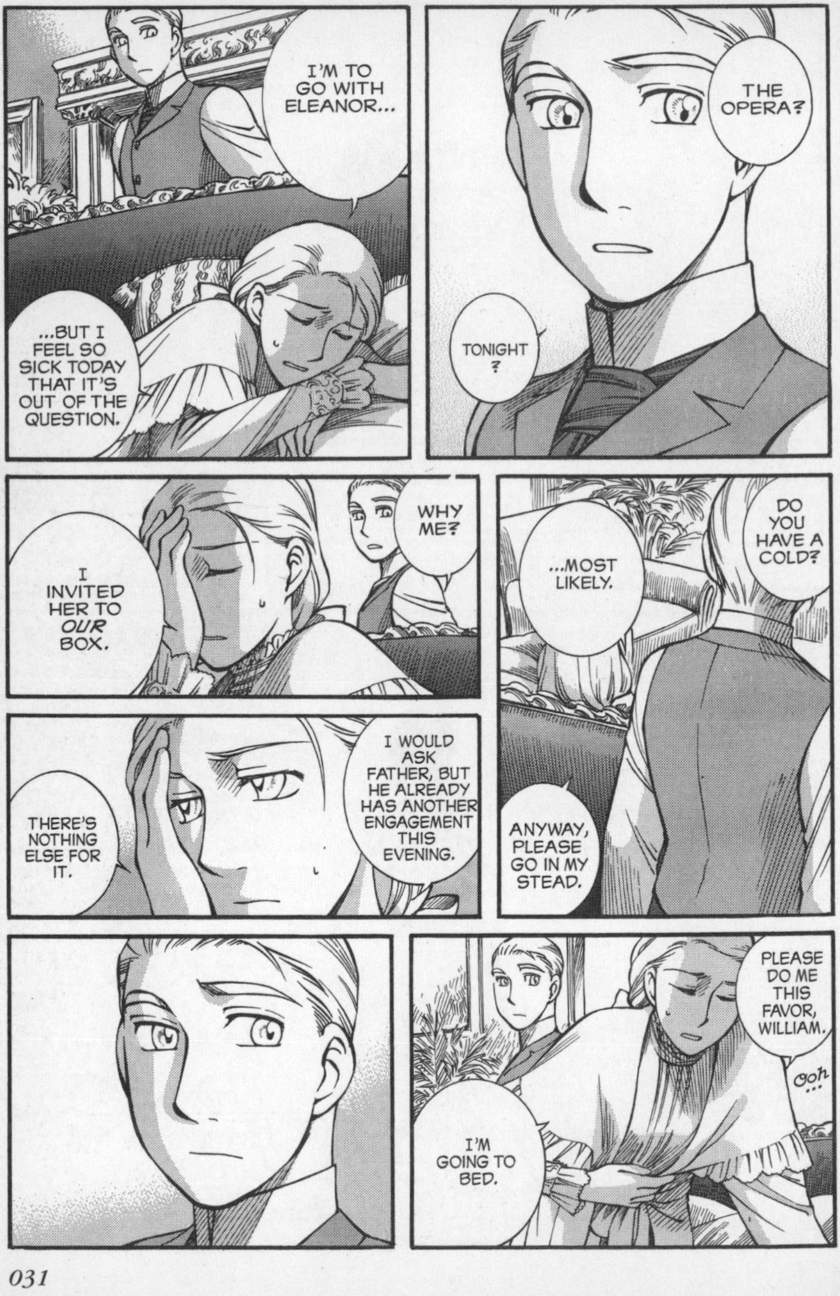
THE OPERA?
TONIGHT?
I'M TO GO WITH ELEANOR...
...BUT I FEEL SO SICK TODAY THAT IT'S OUT OF THE QUESTION.
DO YOU HAVE A COLD?
...MOST LIKELY.
ANYWAY, PLEASE GO IN MY STEAD.
WHY ME?
I INVITED HER TO *OUR* BOX.
I WOULD ASK FATHER, BUT HE ALREADY HAS ANOTHER ENGAGEMENT THIS EVENING.
THERE'S NOTHING ELSE FOR IT.
PLEASE DO ME THIS FAVOR, WILLIAM.
Ooh...
I'M GOING TO BED.

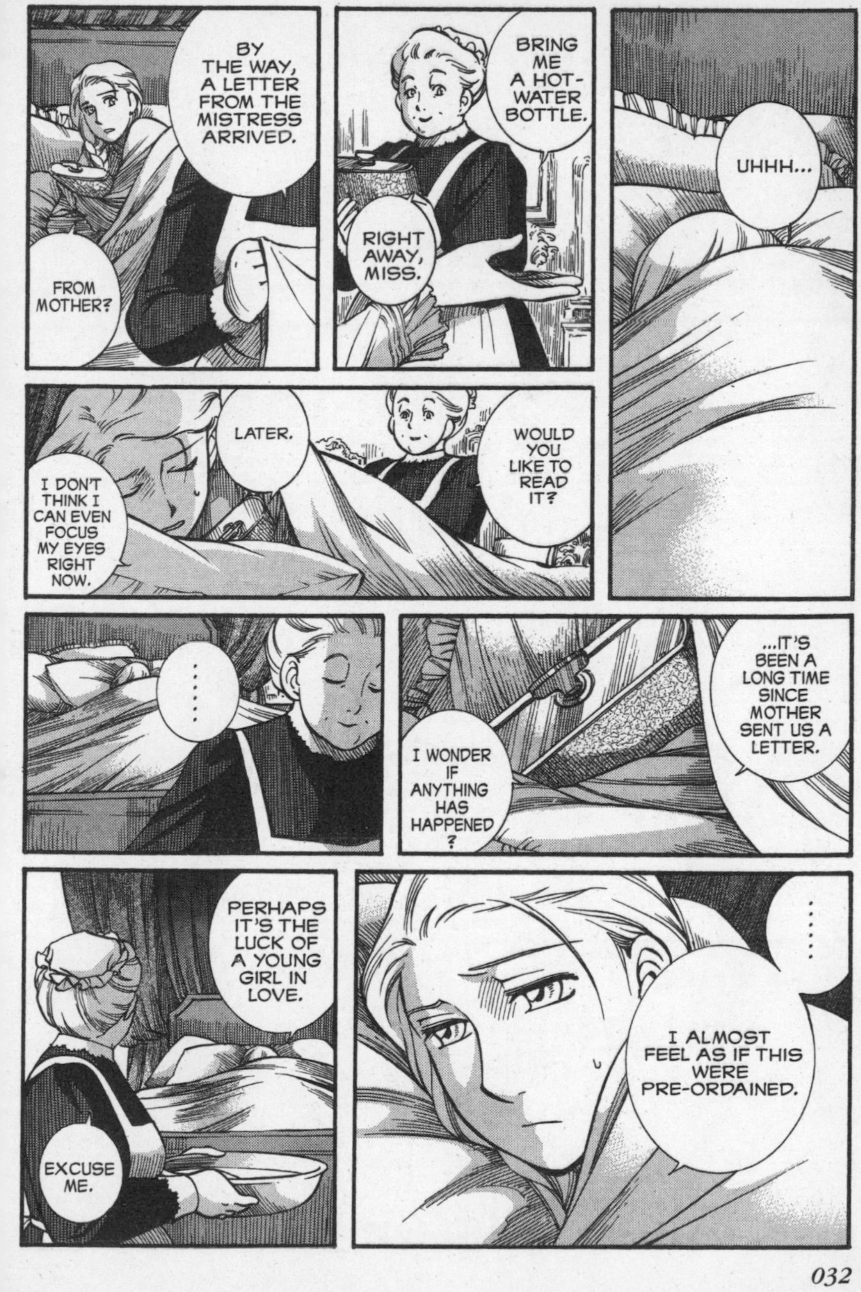
UHHH...
BRING ME A HOT-WATER BOTTLE.
RIGHT AWAY, MISS.
BY THE WAY, A LETTER FROM THE MISTRESS ARRIVED.
FROM MOTHER?
WOULD YOU LIKE TO READ IT?
LATER.
I DON'T THINK I CAN EVEN FOCUS MY EYES RIGHT NOW.
...IT'S BEEN A LONG TIME SINCE MOTHER SENT US A LETTER.
I WONDER IF ANYTHING HAS HAPPENED?
......
......
I ALMOST FEEL AS IF THIS WERE PRE-ORDAINED.
PERHAPS IT'S THE LUCK OF A YOUNG GIRL IN LOVE.
EXCUSE ME.

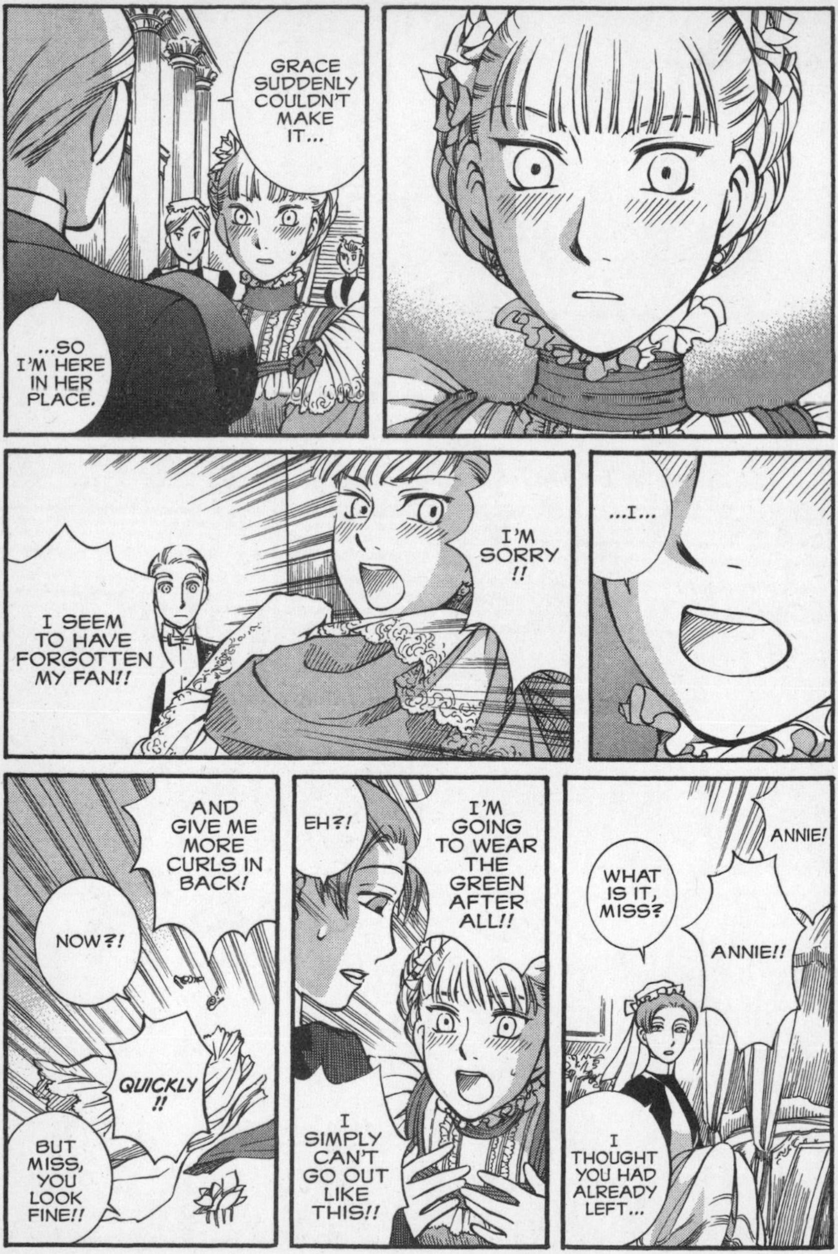
GRACE SUDDENLY COULDN'T MAKE IT...
...SO I'M HERE IN HER PLACE.
...I...
I'M SORRY!!
I SEEM TO HAVE FORGOTTEN MY FAN!!
ANNIE!
ANNIE!!
WHAT IS IT, MISS?
I THOUGHT YOU HAD ALREADY LEFT...
I'M GOING TO WEAR THE GREEN AFTER ALL!!
EH?!
I SIMPLY CAN'T GO OUT LIKE THIS!!
AND GIVE ME MORE CURLS IN BACK!
NOW?!
QUICKLY!!
BUT MISS, YOU LOOK FINE!!

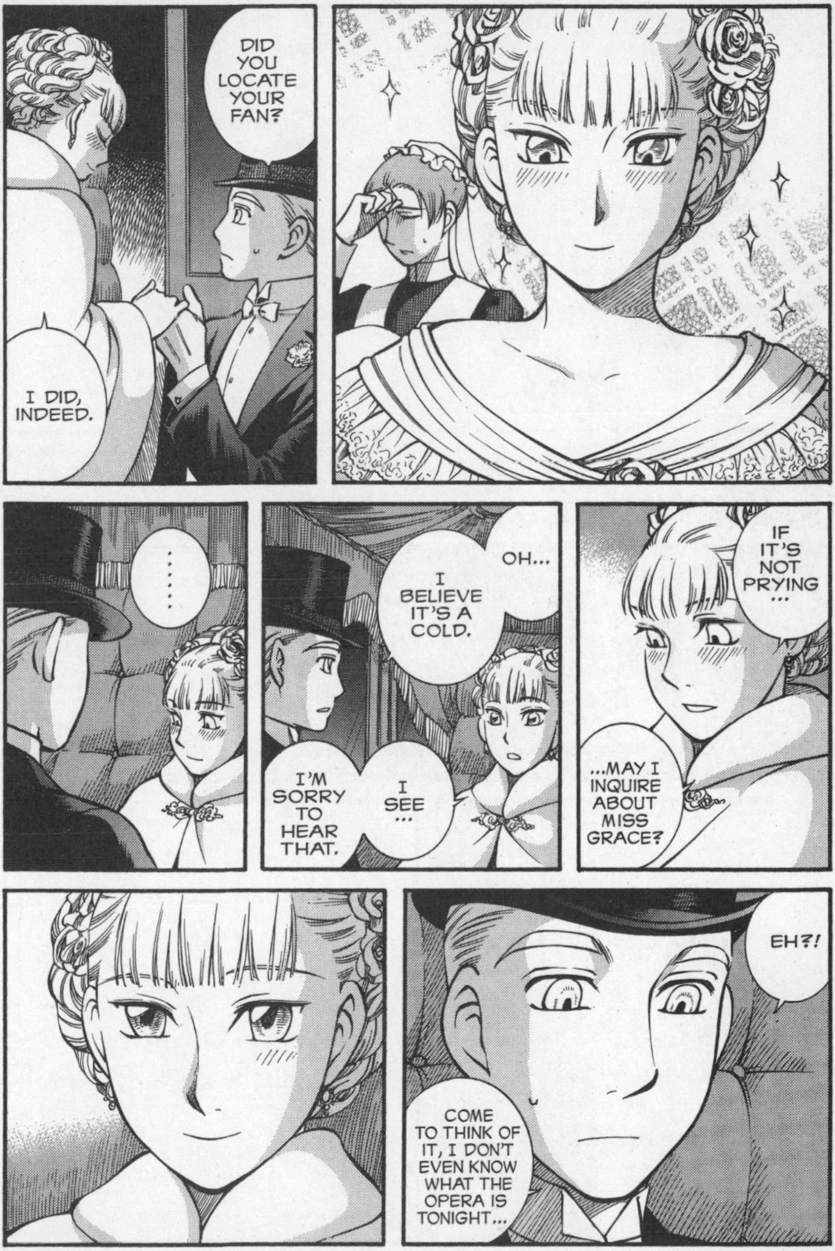
DID YOU LOCATE YOUR FAN?
I DID, INDEED.
IF IT'S NOT PRYING...
...MAY I INQUIRE ABOUT MISS GRACE?
OH...
I BELIEVE IT'S A COLD.
I SEE...
......
I'M SORRY TO HEAR THAT.
EH?!
COME TO THINK OF IT, I DON'T EVEN KNOW WHAT THE OPERA IS TONIGHT...

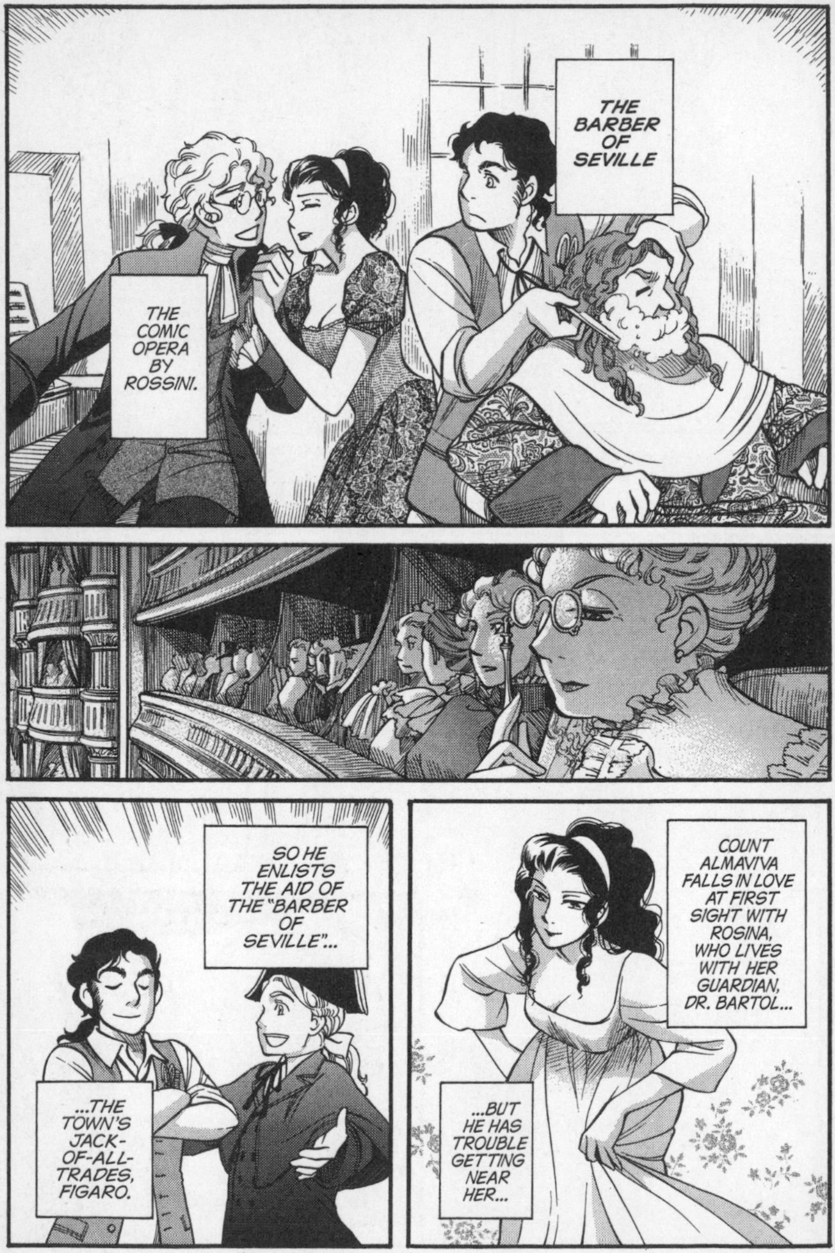
THE BARBER OF SEVILLE
THE COMIC OPERA BY ROSSINI.
COUNT ALMAVIVA FALLS IN LOVE AT FIRST SIGHT WITH ROSINA, WHO LIVES WITH HER GUARDIAN, DR. BARTOL...
...BUT HE HAS TROUBLE GETTING NEAR HER...
SO HE ENLISTS THE AID OF THE "BARBER OF SEVILLE"...
...THE TOWN'S JACK-OF-ALL-TRADES, FIGARO.

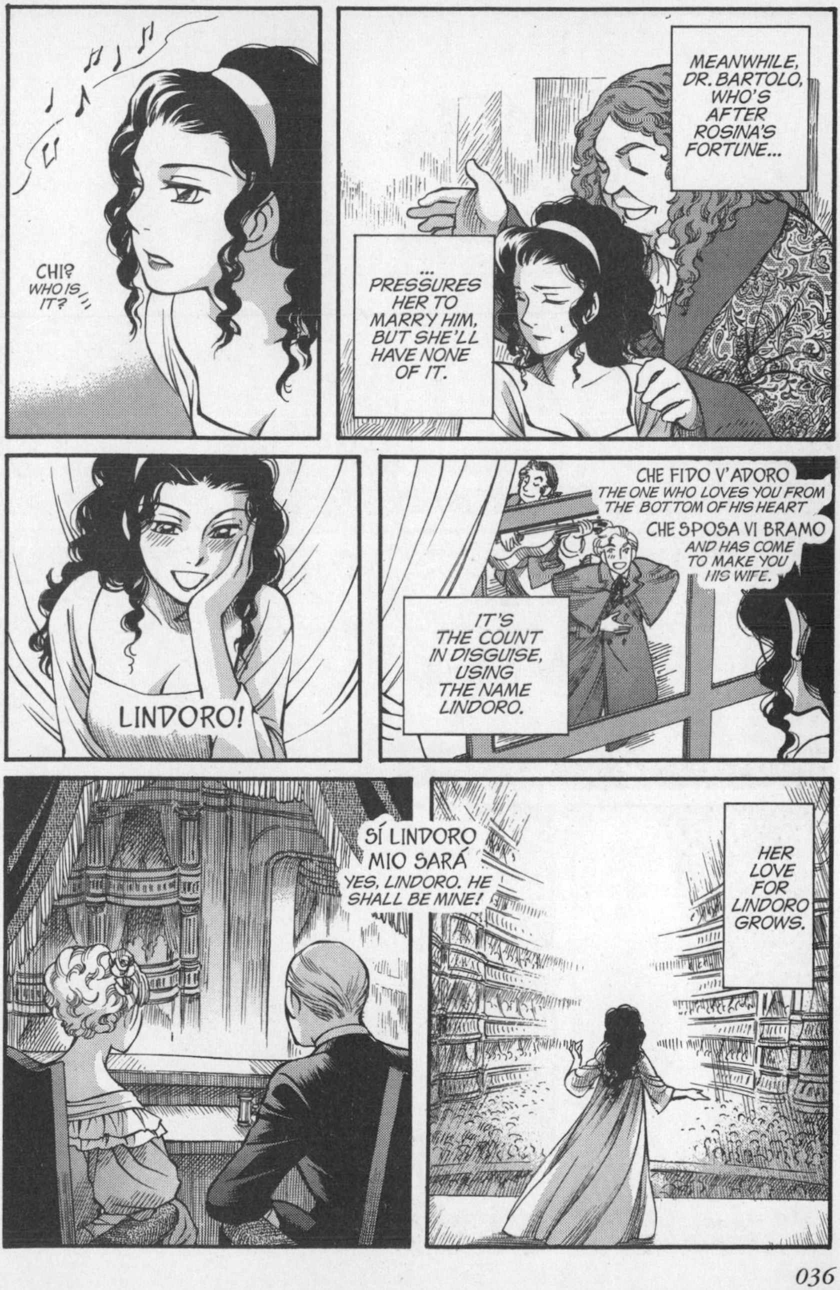
MEANWHILE, DR. BARTOLO, WHO'S AFTER ROSINA'S FORTUNE...
... PRESSURES HER TO MARRY HIM, BUT SHE'LL HAVE NONE OF IT.
CHI? WHO IS IT?
CHE FIDO V' ADORO
THE ONE WHO LOVES YOU FROM THE BOTTOM OF HIS HEART
CHE SPOSA VI BRAMO
AND HAS COME TO MAKE YOU HIS WIFE.
IT'S THE COUNT IN DISGUISE, USING THE NAME LINDORO.
LINDORO!
HER LOVE FOR LINDORO GROWS.
SÍ LINDORO MIO SARÁ
YES, LINDORO. HE SHALL BE MINE!

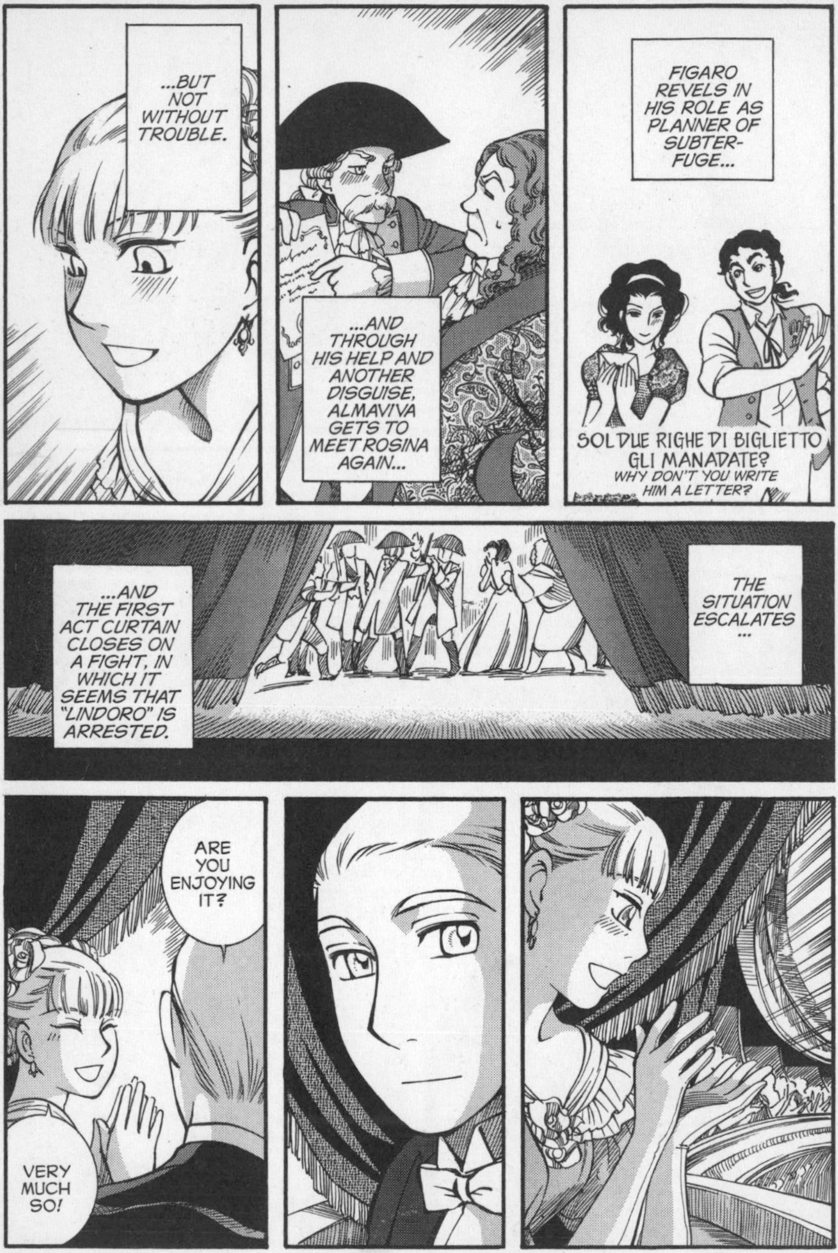
FIGARO REVELS IN HIS ROLE AS PLANNER OF SUBTER-FUGE...
SOL DUE RIGHE DI BIGLIETTO GLI MANADATE?
WHY DON'T YOU WRITE HIM A LETTER?
...AND THROUGH HIS HELP AND ANOTHER DISGUISE, ALMAVIVA GETS TO MEET ROSINA AGAIN...
...BUT NOT WITHOUT TROUBLE.
THE SITUATION ESCALATES...
...AND THE FIRST ACT CURTAIN CLOSES ON A FIGHT, IN WHICH IT SEEMS THAT "LINDORO" IS ARRESTED.
ARE YOU ENJOYING IT?
VERY MUCH SO!

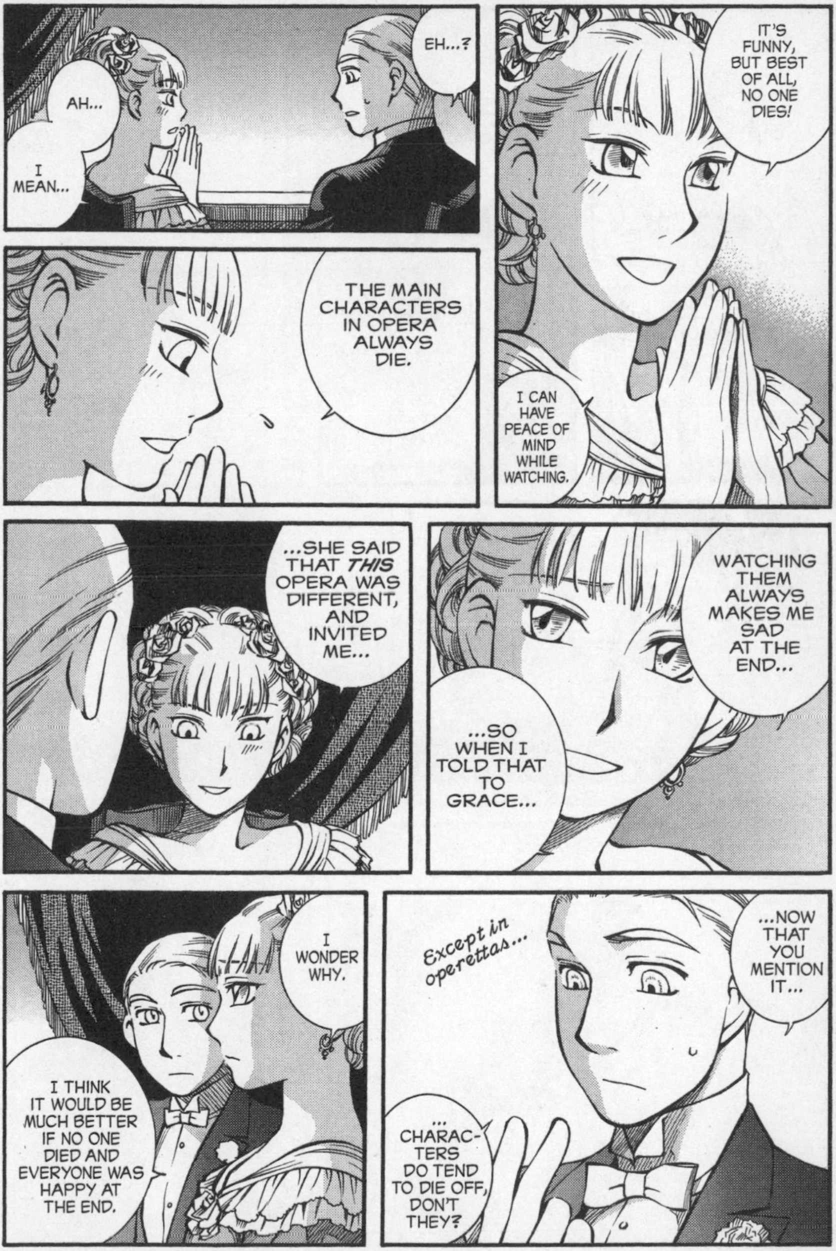
IT'S FUNNY, BUT BEST OF ALL, NO ONE DIES!
I CAN HAVE PEACE OF MIND WHILE WATCHING.
EH...?
AH...
I MEAN...
THE MAIN CHARACTERS IN OPERA ALWAYS DIE.
WATCHING THEM ALWAYS MAKES ME SAD AT THE END...
...SO WHEN I TOLD THAT TO GRACE...
...SHE SAID THAT *THIS* OPERA WAS DIFFERENT, AND INVITED ME...
...NOW THAT YOU MENTION IT...
Except in operettas...
...CHARACTERS DO TEND TO DIE OFF, DON'T THEY?
I WONDER WHY.
I THINK IT WOULD BE MUCH BETTER IF NO ONE DIED AND EVERYONE WAS HAPPY AT THE END.

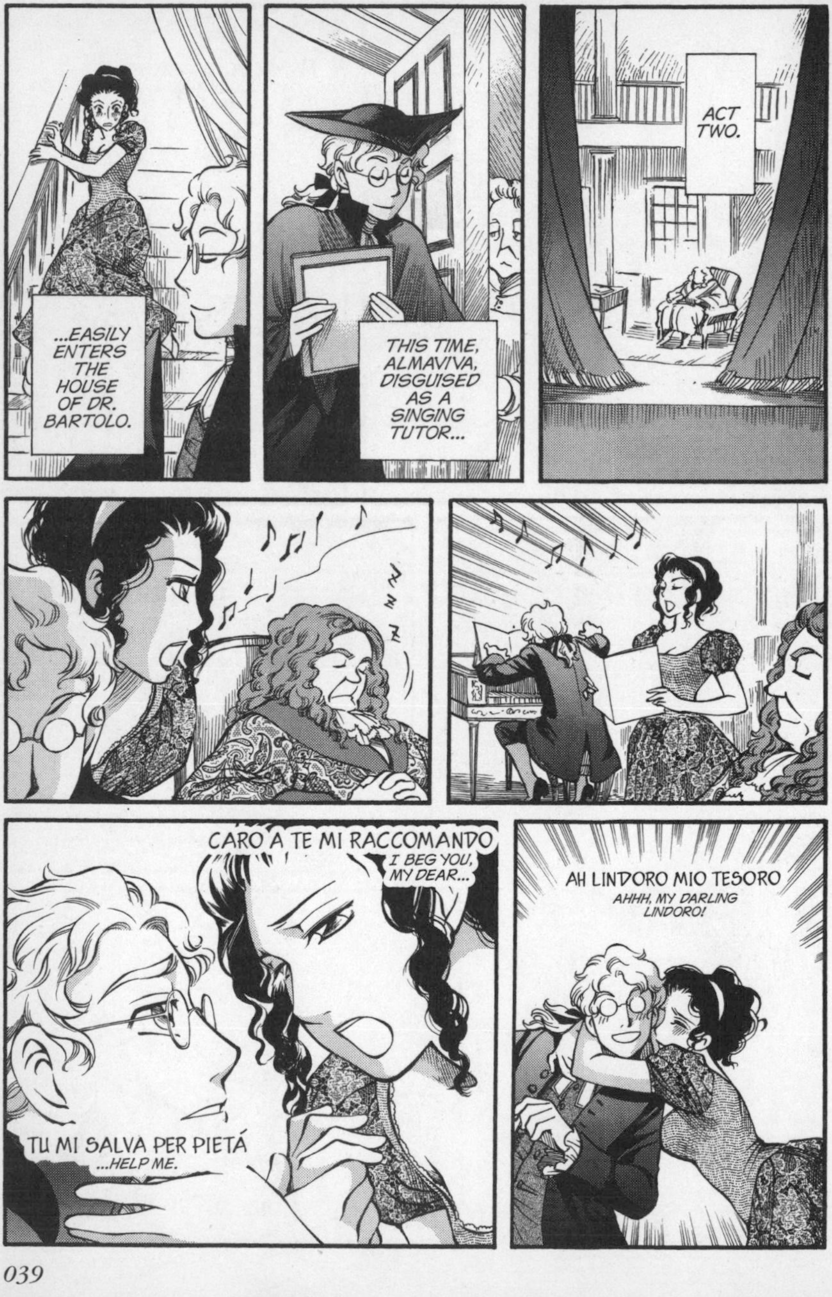
ACT TWO.
THIS TIME, ALMAVIVA, DISGUISED AS A SINGING TUTOR...
...EASILY ENTERS THE HOUSE OF DR. BARTOLO.
ZZZ
AH LINDORO MIO TESORO
AHHH, MY DARLING LINDORO!
CARO A TE MI RACCOMANDO
I BEG YOU, MY DEAR...
TU MI SALVA PER PIETÁ
...HELP ME.

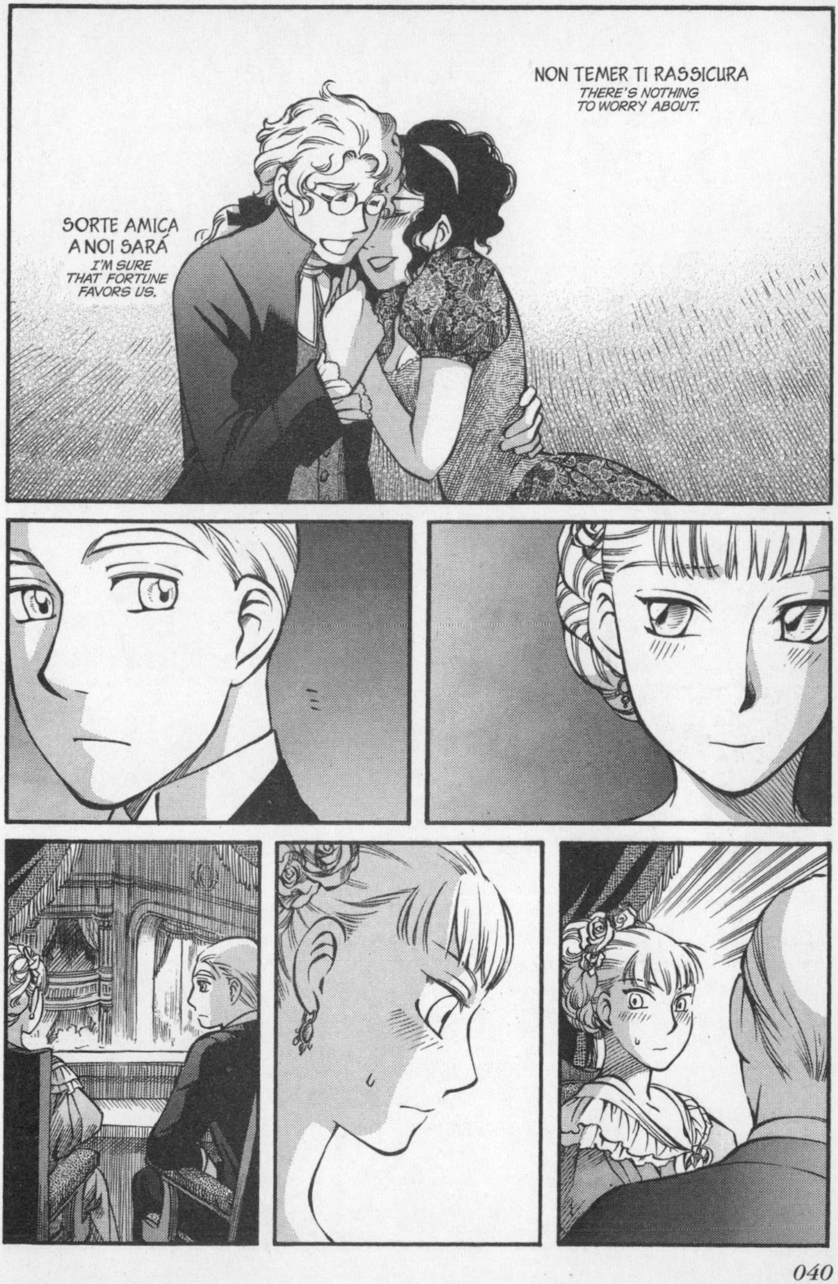
NON TEMER TI RASSICURA
THERE'S NOTHING TO WORRY ABOUT.
SORTE AMICA A NOI SARÁ
I'M SURE THAT FORTUNE FAVORS US.

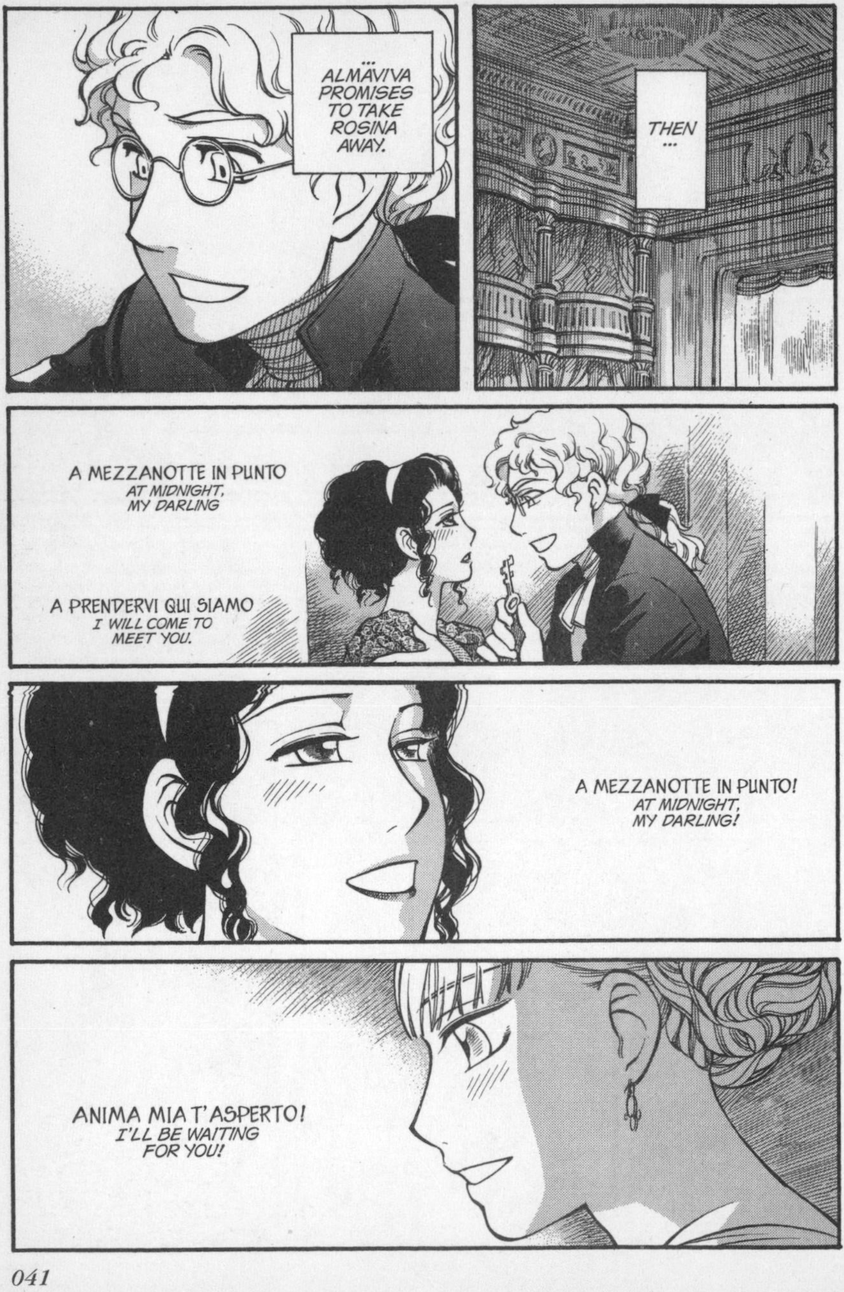

THEN ...
... ALMÄVIVA PROMISES TO TAKE ROSINA AWAY.
A MEZZANOTTE IN PUNTO
AT MIDNIGHT, MY DARLING
A PRENDERVI QUI SIAMO
I WILL COME TO MEET YOU.
A MEZZANOTTE IN PUNTO!
AT MIDNIGHT, MY DARLING!
ANIMA MIA T'ASPERTO!
I'LL BE WAITING FOR YOU!

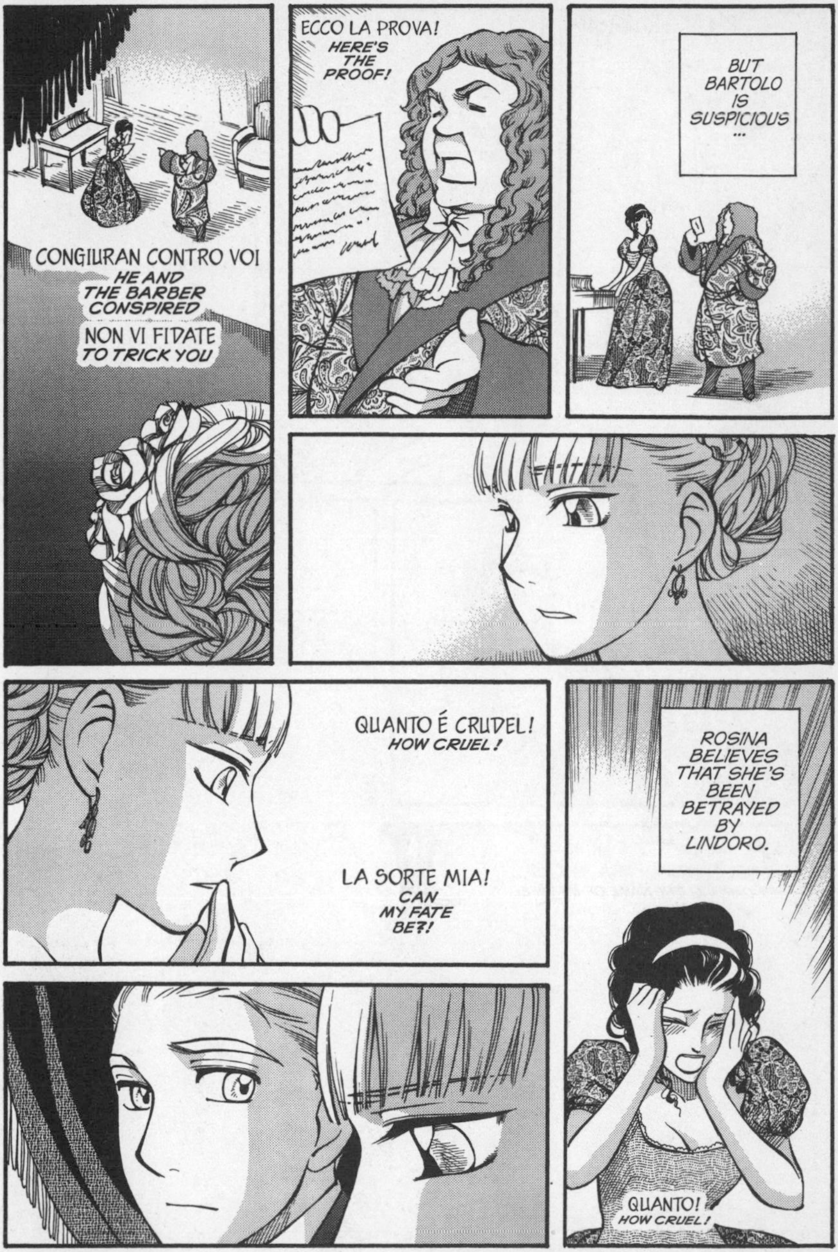
BUT BARTOLO IS SUSPICIOUS ...
ECCO LA PROVA!
HERE'S THE PROOF!
CONGIURAN CONTRO VOI
HE AND THE BARBER CONSPIRED
NON VI FIDATE
TO TRICK YOU
ROSINA BELIEVES THAT SHE'S BEEN BETRAYED BY LINDORO.
QUANTO!
HOW CRUEL!
QUANTO É CRUDEL!
HOW CRUEL!
LA SORTE MIA!
CAN MY FATE BE?!

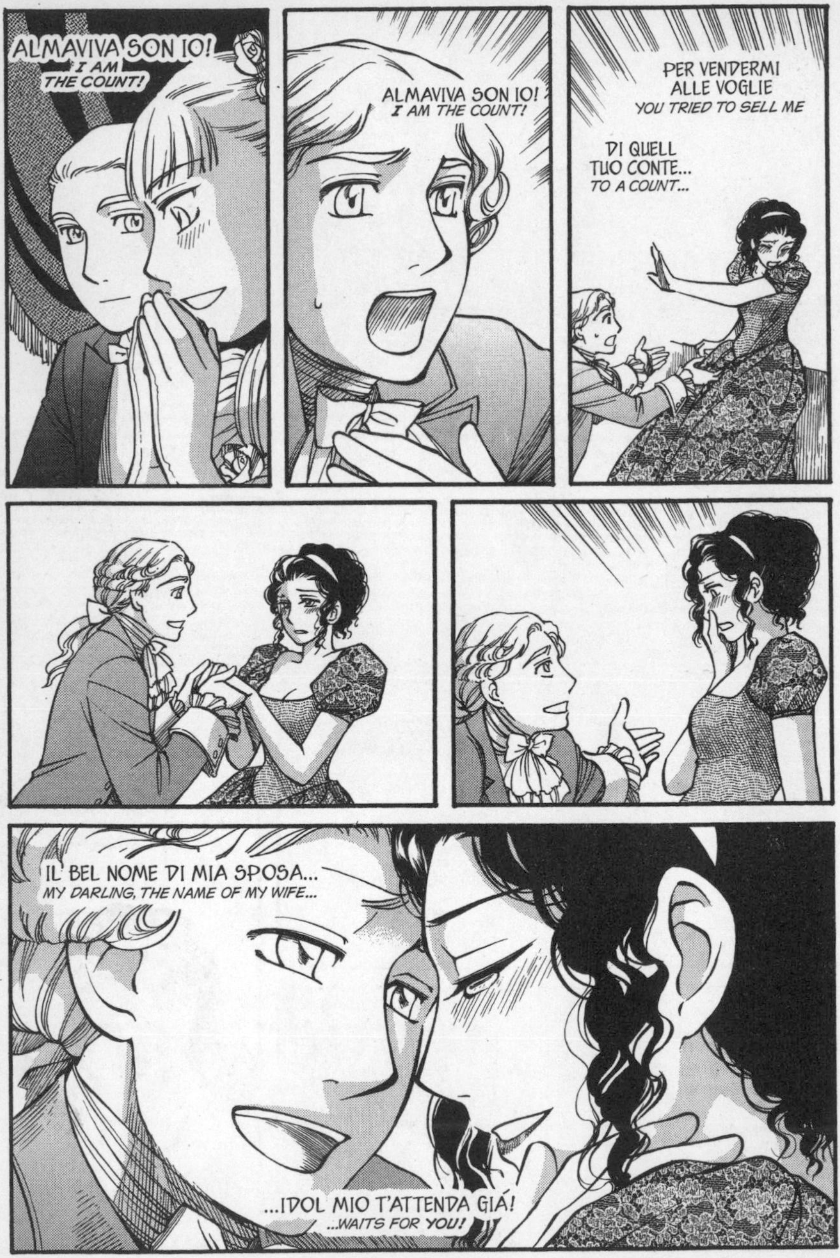
PER VENDERMI ALLE VOGLIE
YOU TRIED TO SELL ME
DI QUELL TUO CONTE...
TO A COUNT...
ALMAVIVA SON IO!
I AM THE COUNT!
ALMAVIVA SON IO!
I AM THE COUNT!
IL BEL NOME DI MIA SPOSA...
MY DARLING, THE NAME OF MY WIFE...
...IDOL MIO T'ATTENDA GIÁ!
...WAITS FOR YOU!

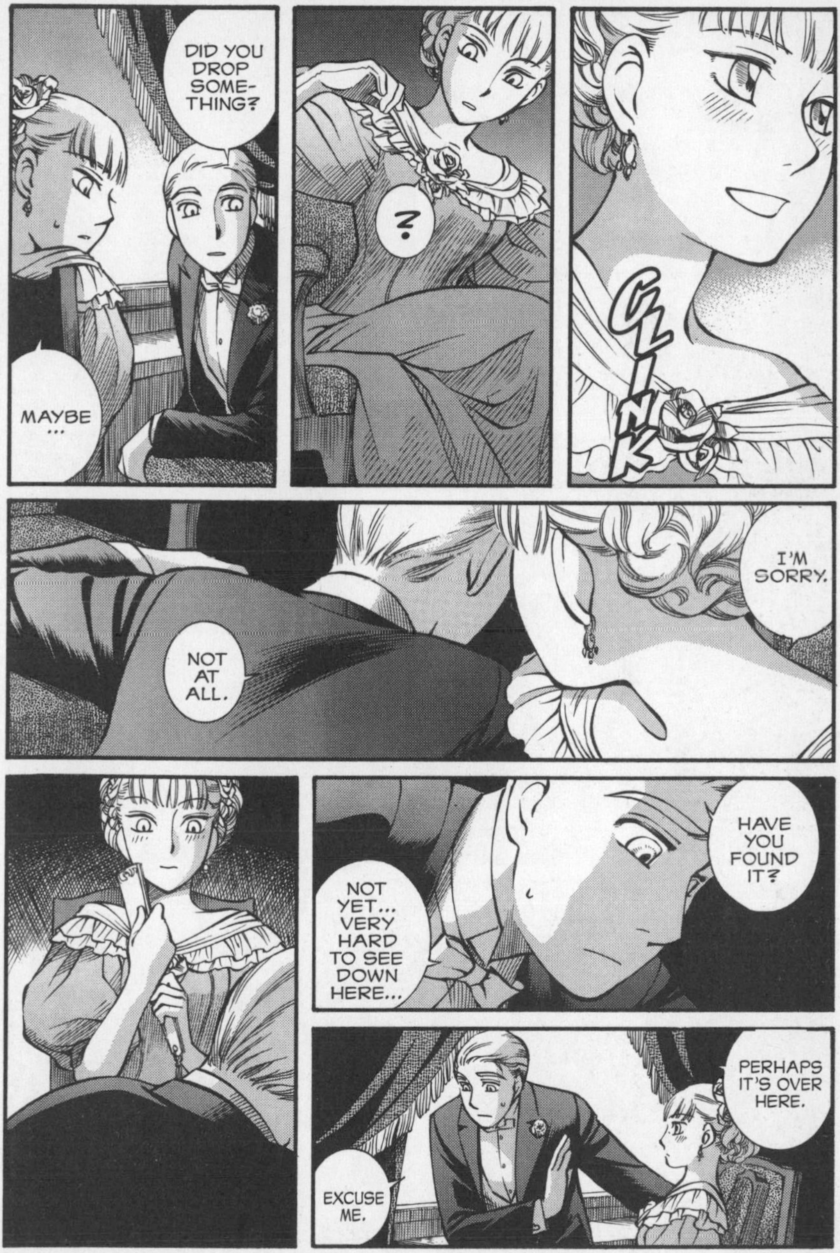
CLINK
?
DID YOU DROP SOMETHING?
MAYBE...
I'M SORRY.
NOT AT ALL.
HAVE YOU FOUND IT?
NOT YET... VERY HARD TO SEE DOWN HERE...
PERHAPS IT'S OVER HERE.
EXCUSE ME.

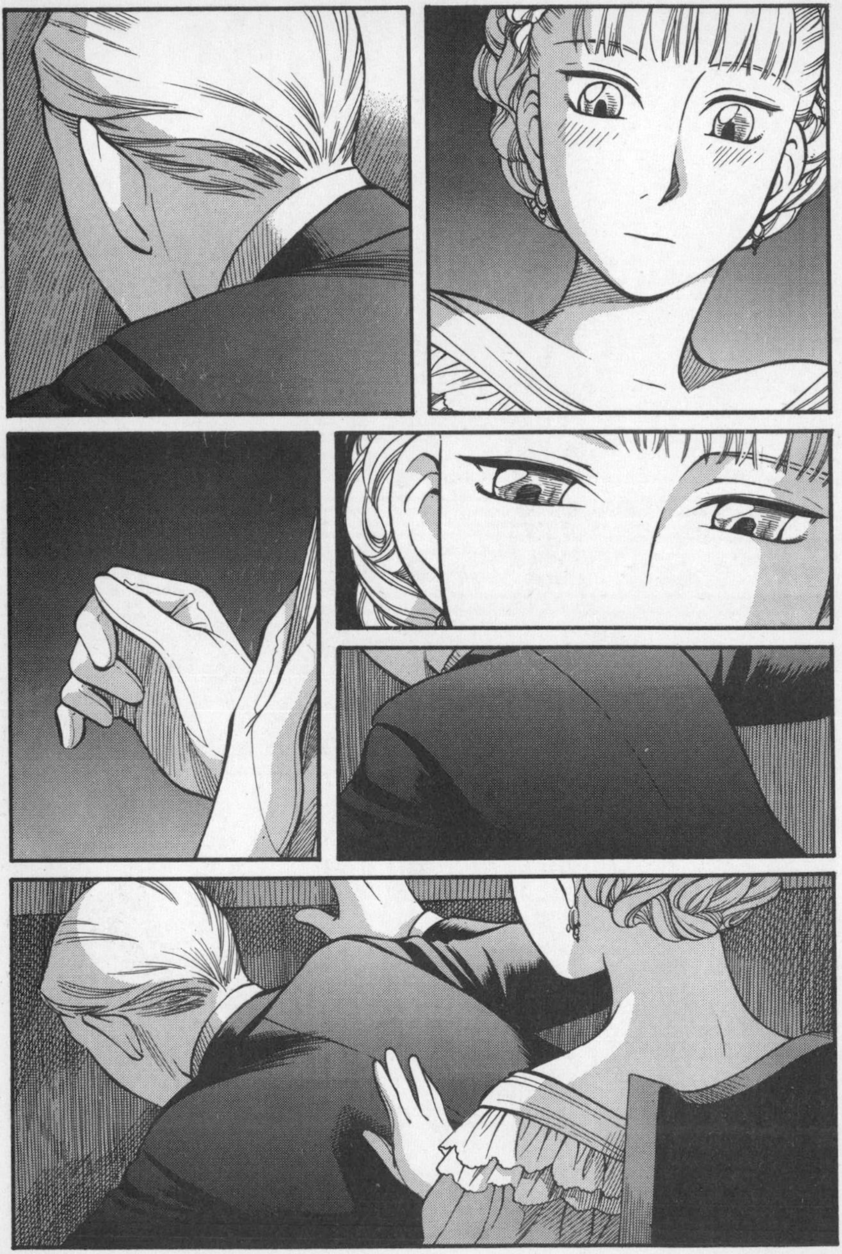

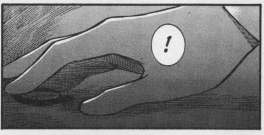

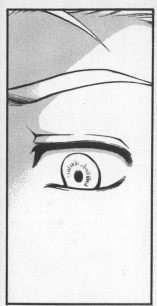

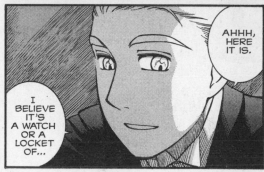

AHHH, HERE IT IS.

I BELIEVE IT'S A WATCH OR A LOCKET OF...

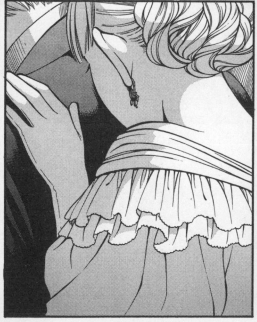

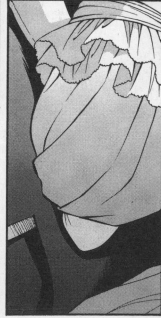

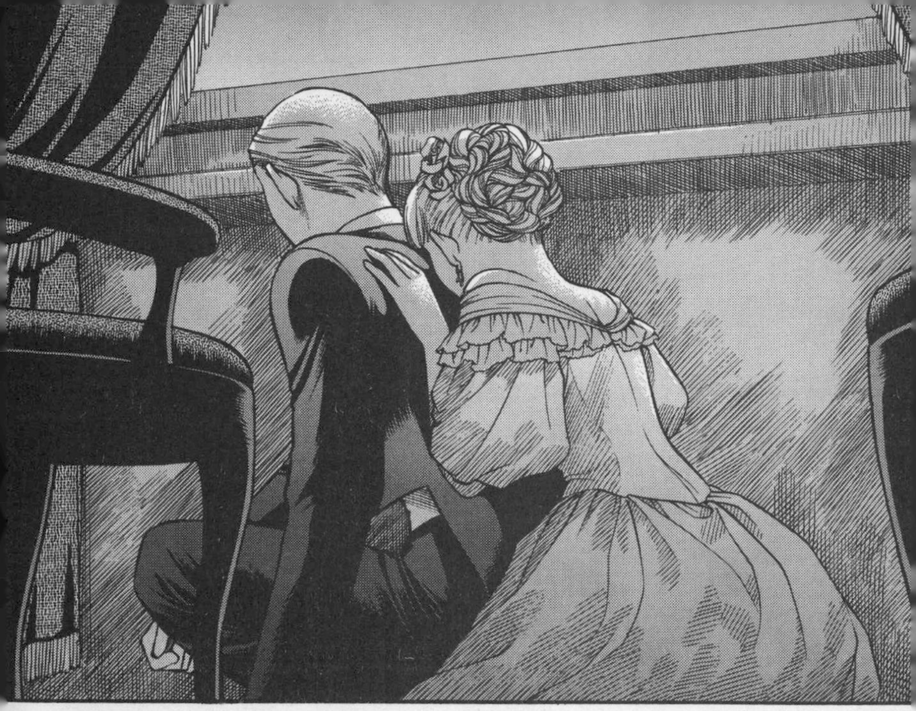

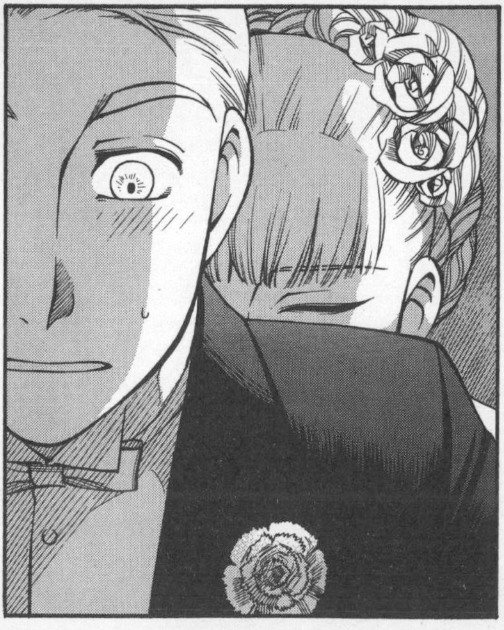

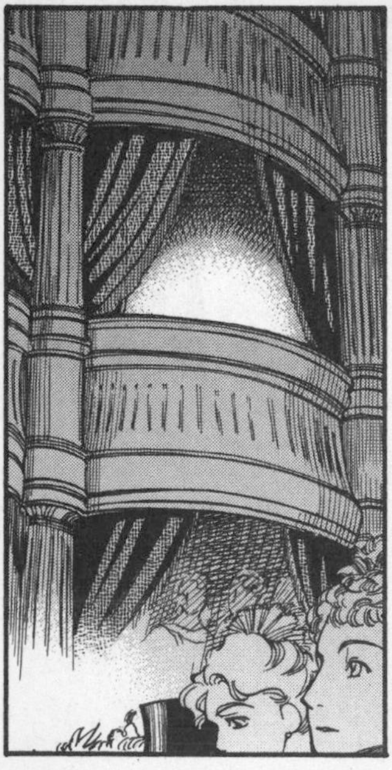

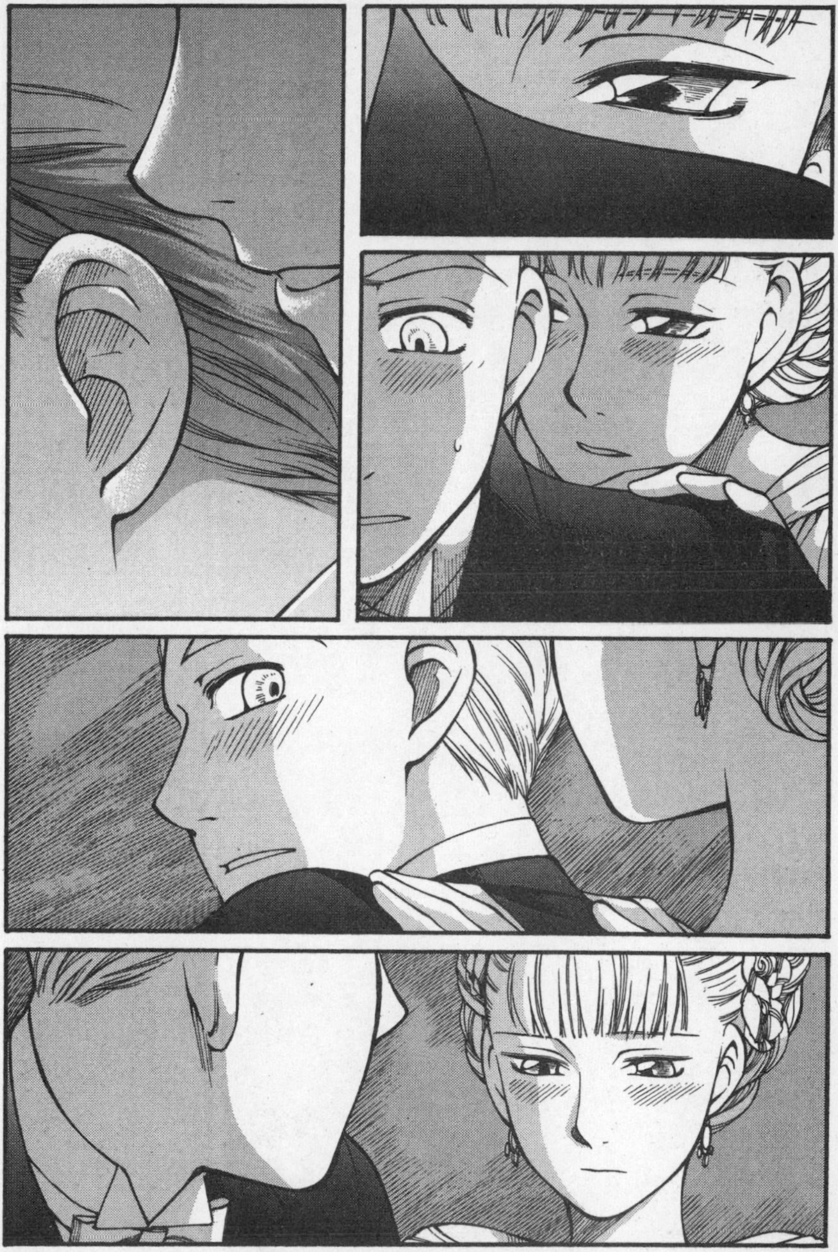

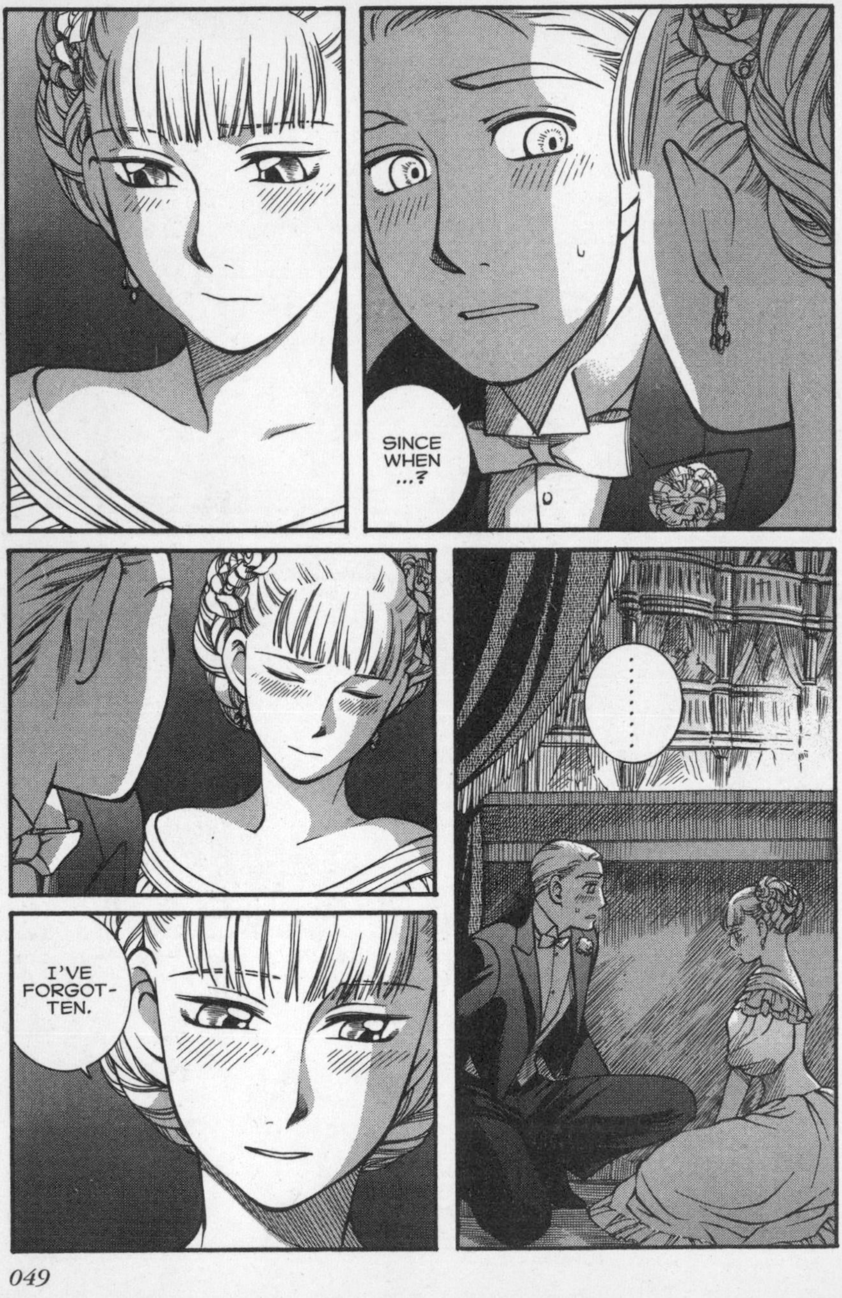
SINCE WHEN ...?
......
I'VE FORGOT-TEN.

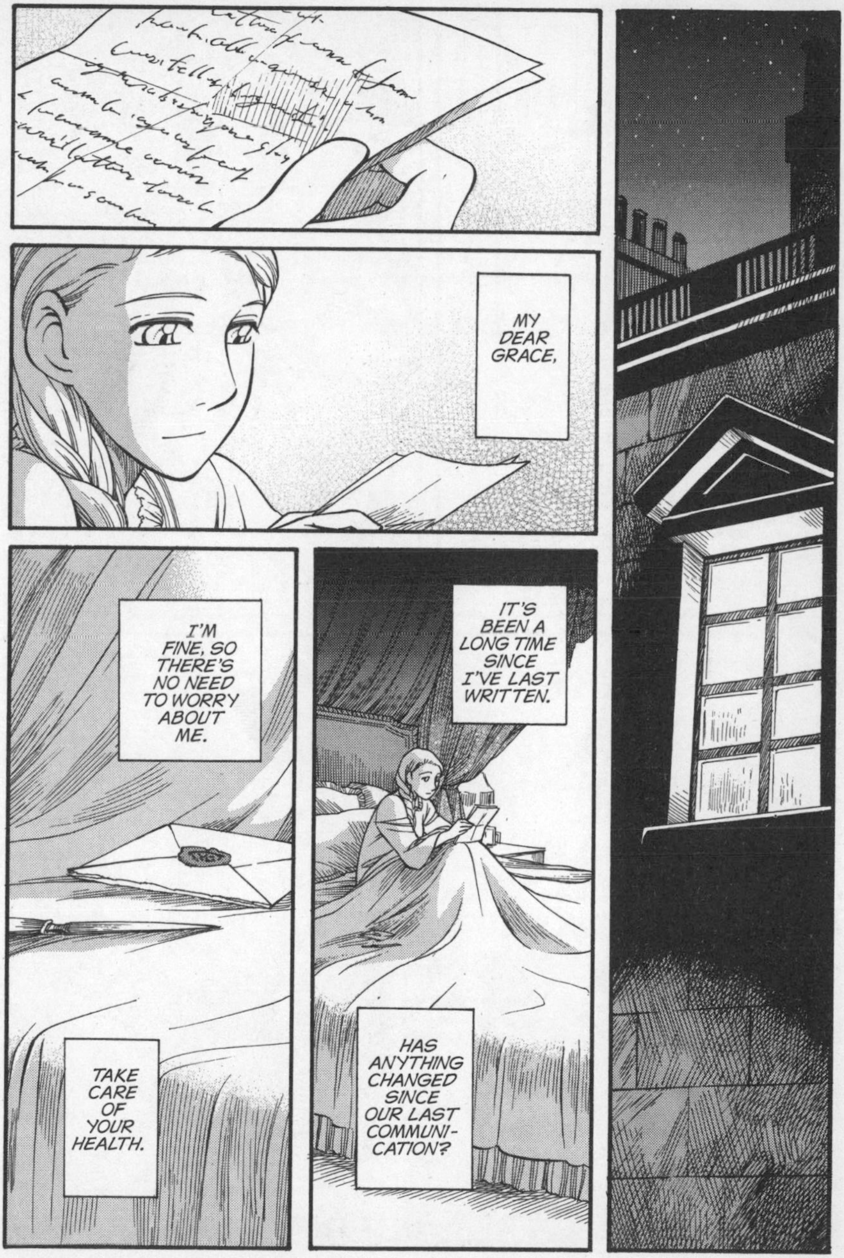
MY DEAR GRACE,
IT'S BEEN A LONG TIME SINCE I'VE LAST WRITTEN.
HAS ANYTHING CHANGED SINCE OUR LAST COMMUNI-CATION?
I'M FINE, SO THERE'S NO NEED TO WORRY ABOUT ME.
TAKE CARE OF YOUR HEALTH.

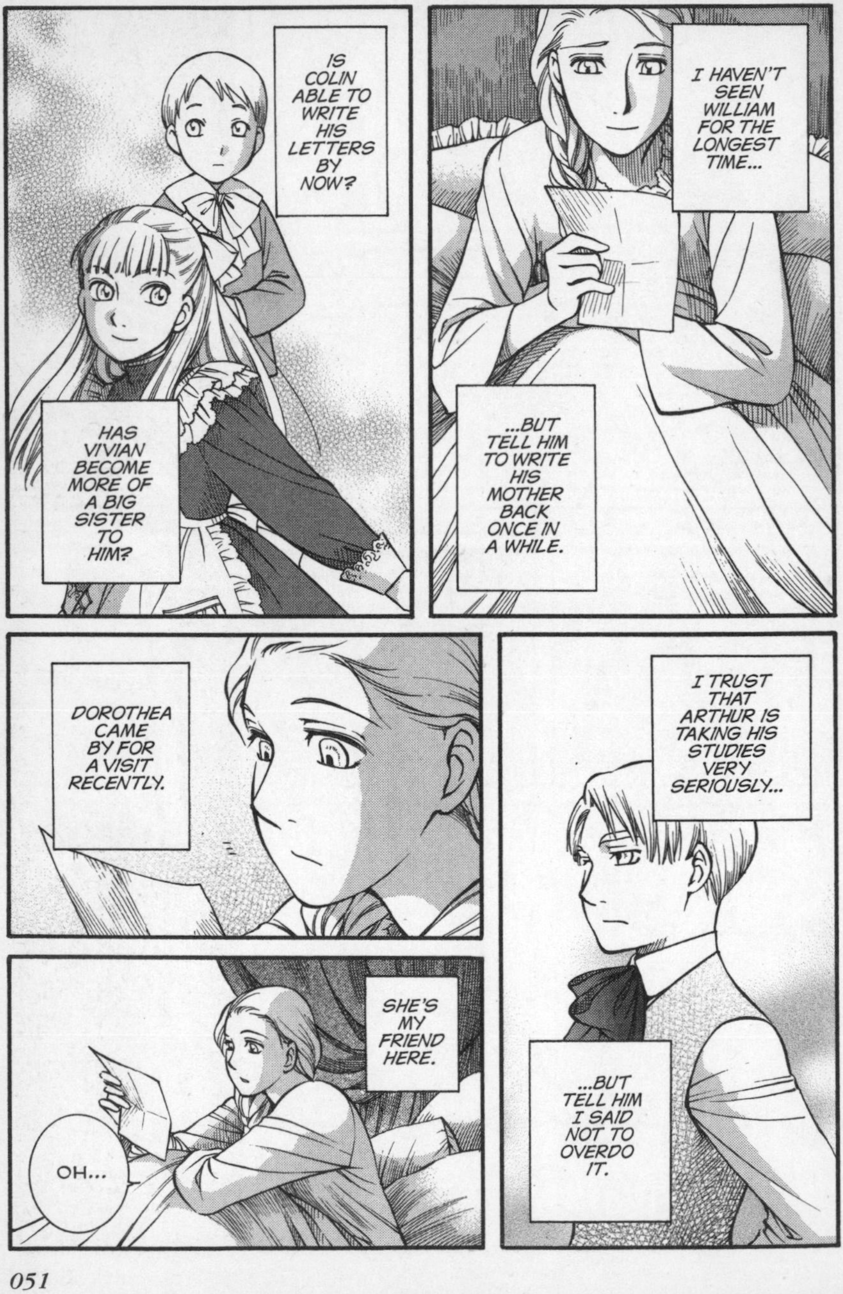
I HAVEN'T SEEN WILLIAM FOR THE LONGEST TIME...
...BUT TELL HIM TO WRITE HIS MOTHER BACK ONCE IN A WHILE.
IS COLIN ABLE TO WRITE HIS LETTERS BY NOW?
HAS VIVIAN BECOME MORE OF A BIG SISTER TO HIM?
I TRUST THAT ARTHUR IS TAKING HIS STUDIES VERY SERIOUSLY...
...BUT TELL HIM I SAID NOT TO OVERDO IT.
DOROTHEA CAME BY FOR A VISIT RECENTLY.
SHE'S MY FRIEND HERE.
OH...

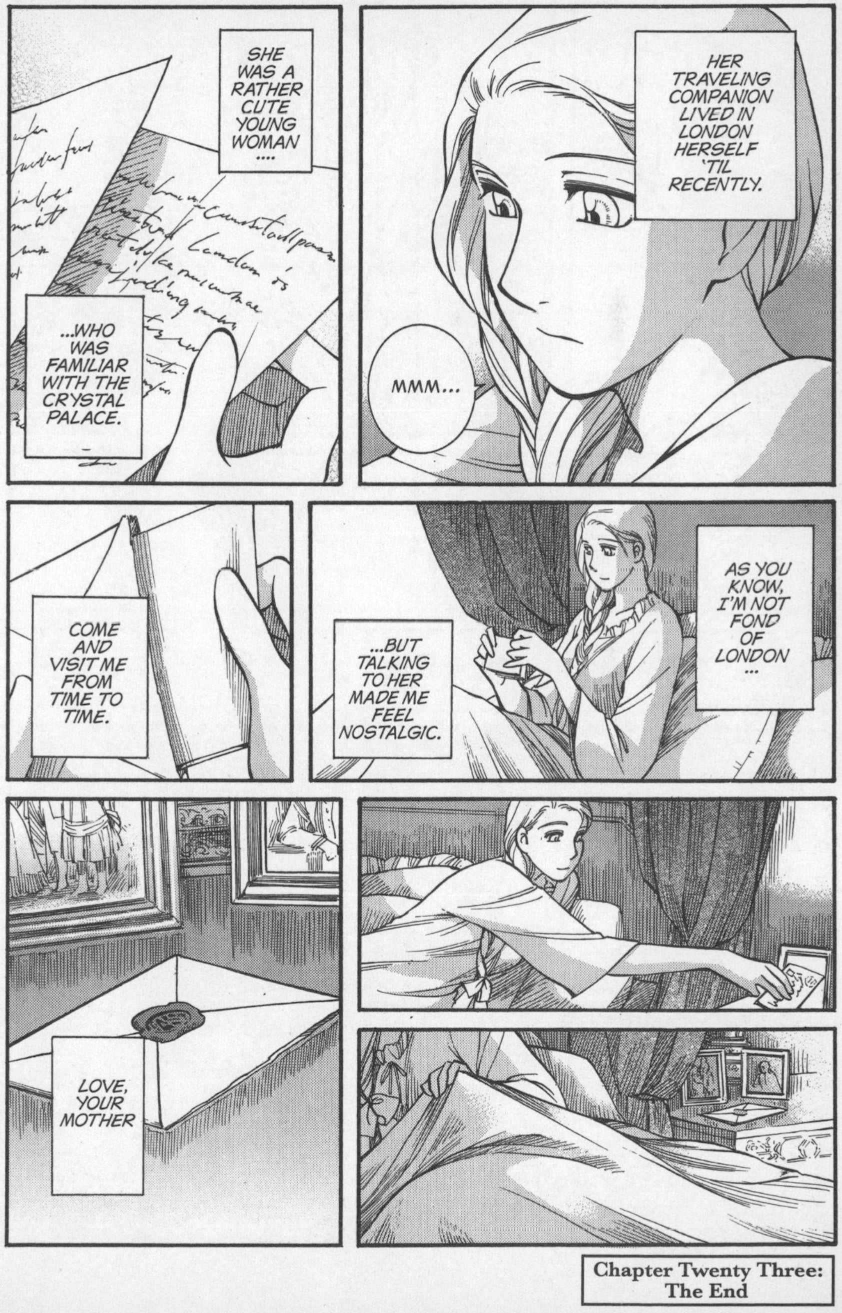
HER TRAVELING COMPANION LIVED IN LONDON HERSELF 'TIL RECENTLY.
MMM...
SHE WAS A RATHER CUTE YOUNG WOMAN ....
...WHO WAS FAMILIAR WITH THE CRYSTAL PALACE.
AS YOU KNOW, I'M NOT FOND OF LONDON ...
...BUT TALKING TO HER MADE ME FEEL NOSTALGIC.
COME AND VISIT ME FROM TIME TO TIME.
LOVE, YOUR MOTHER

Chapter Twenty Three: The End

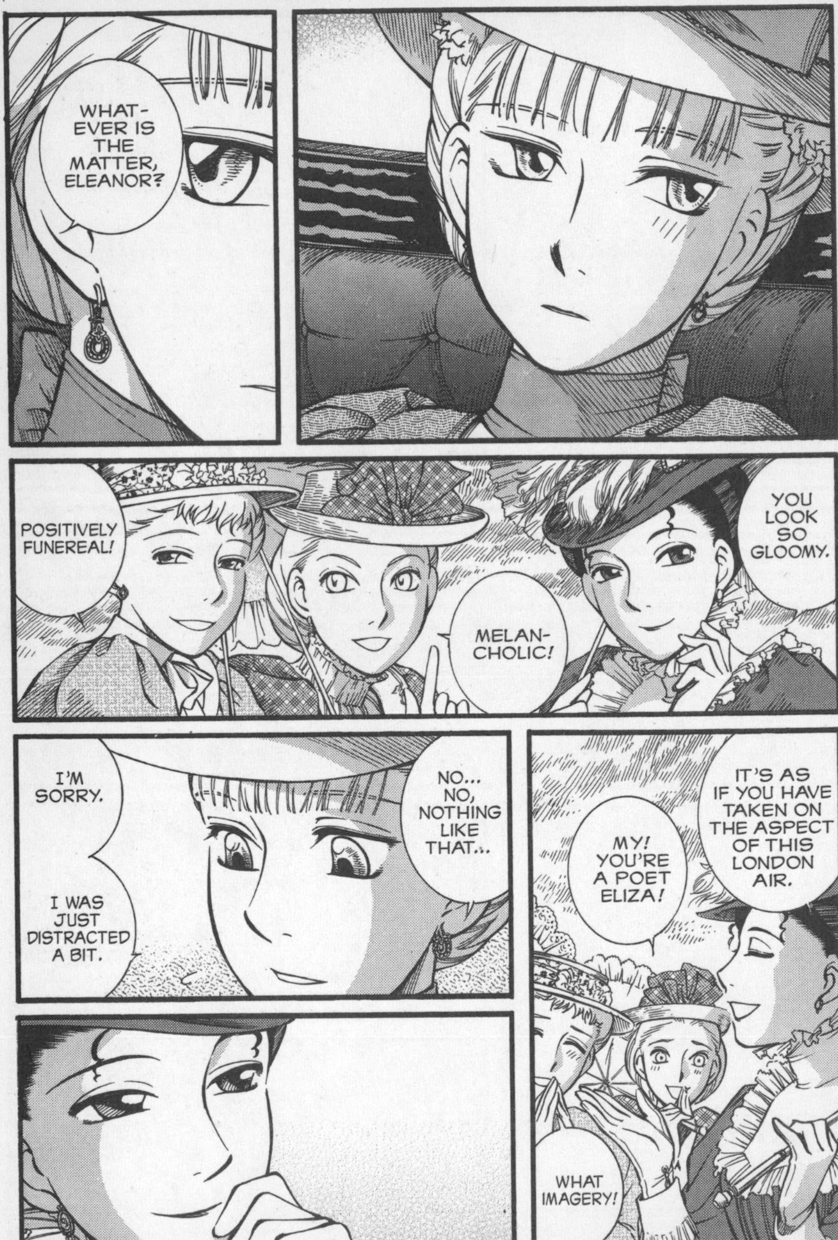
WHAT-EVER IS THE MATTER, ELEANOR?
YOU LOOK SO GLOOMY.
MELAN-CHOLIC!
POSITIVELY FUNEREAL!
IT'S AS IF YOU HAVE TAKEN ON THE ASPECT OF THIS LONDON AIR.
MY! YOU'RE A POET ELIZA!
WHAT IMAGERY!
NO... NO, NOTHING LIKE THAT...
I'M SORRY.
I WAS JUST DISTRACTED A BIT.

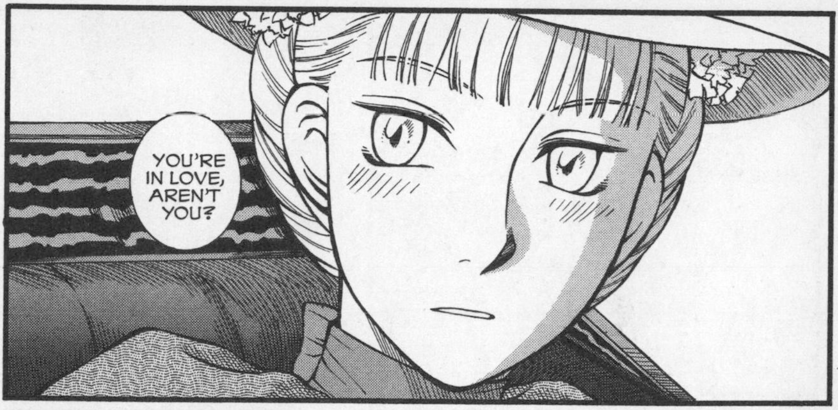
YOU'RE IN LOVE, AREN'T YOU?

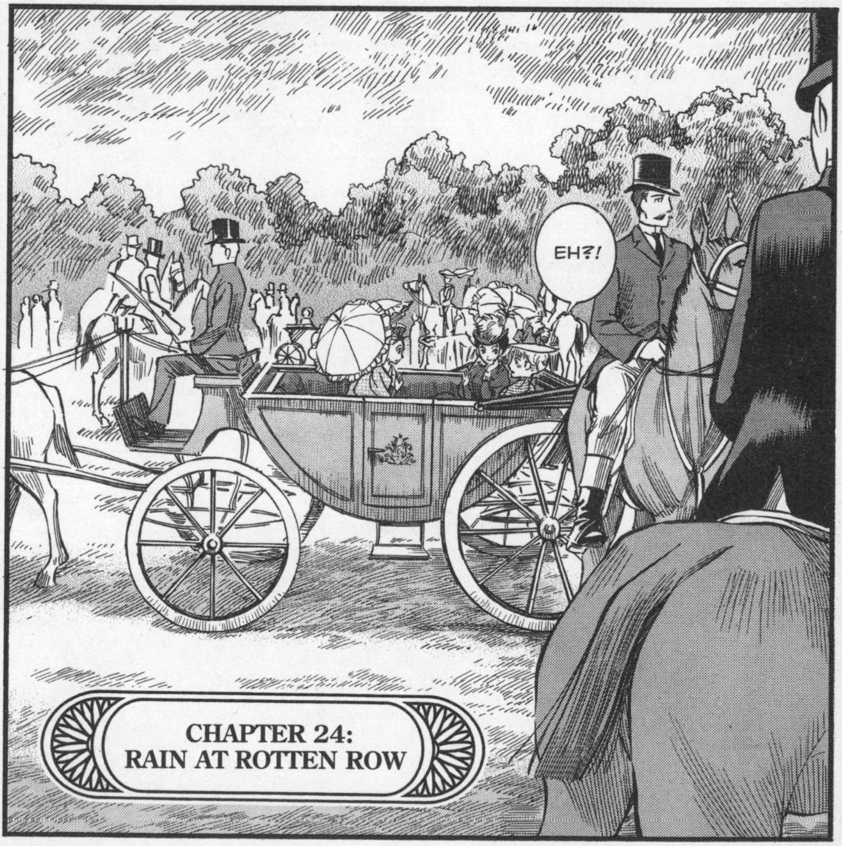
EH?!
CHAPTER 24:
RAIN AT ROTTEN ROW

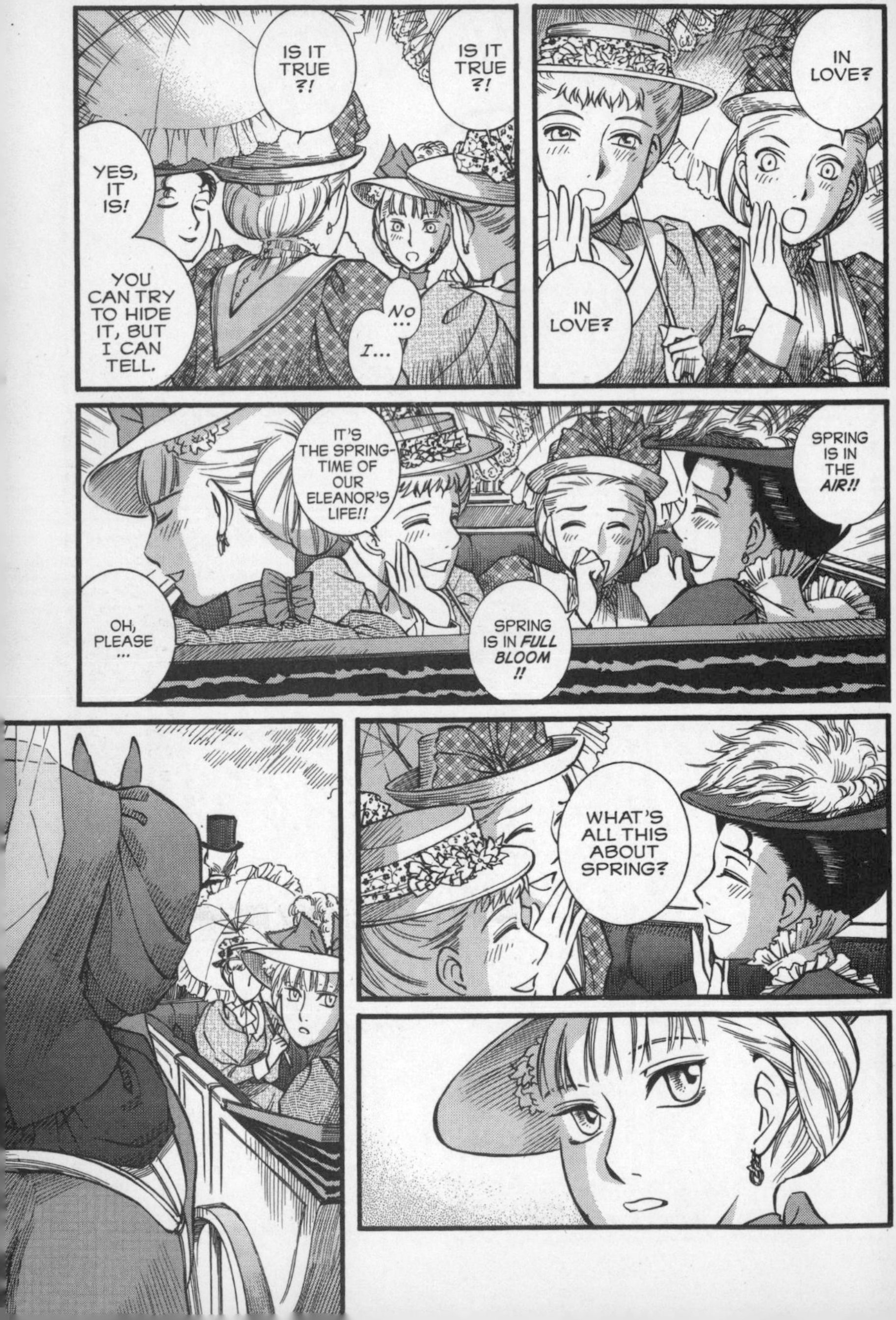
IN LOVE?
IN LOVE?
IS IT TRUE?!
IS IT TRUE?!
YES, IT IS!
YOU CAN TRY TO HIDE IT, BUT I CAN TELL.
No... I...
SPRING IS IN THE AIR!!
IT'S THE SPRING-TIME OF OUR ELEANOR'S LIFE!!
SPRING IS IN FULL BLOOM!!
OH, PLEASE...
WHAT'S ALL THIS ABOUT SPRING?

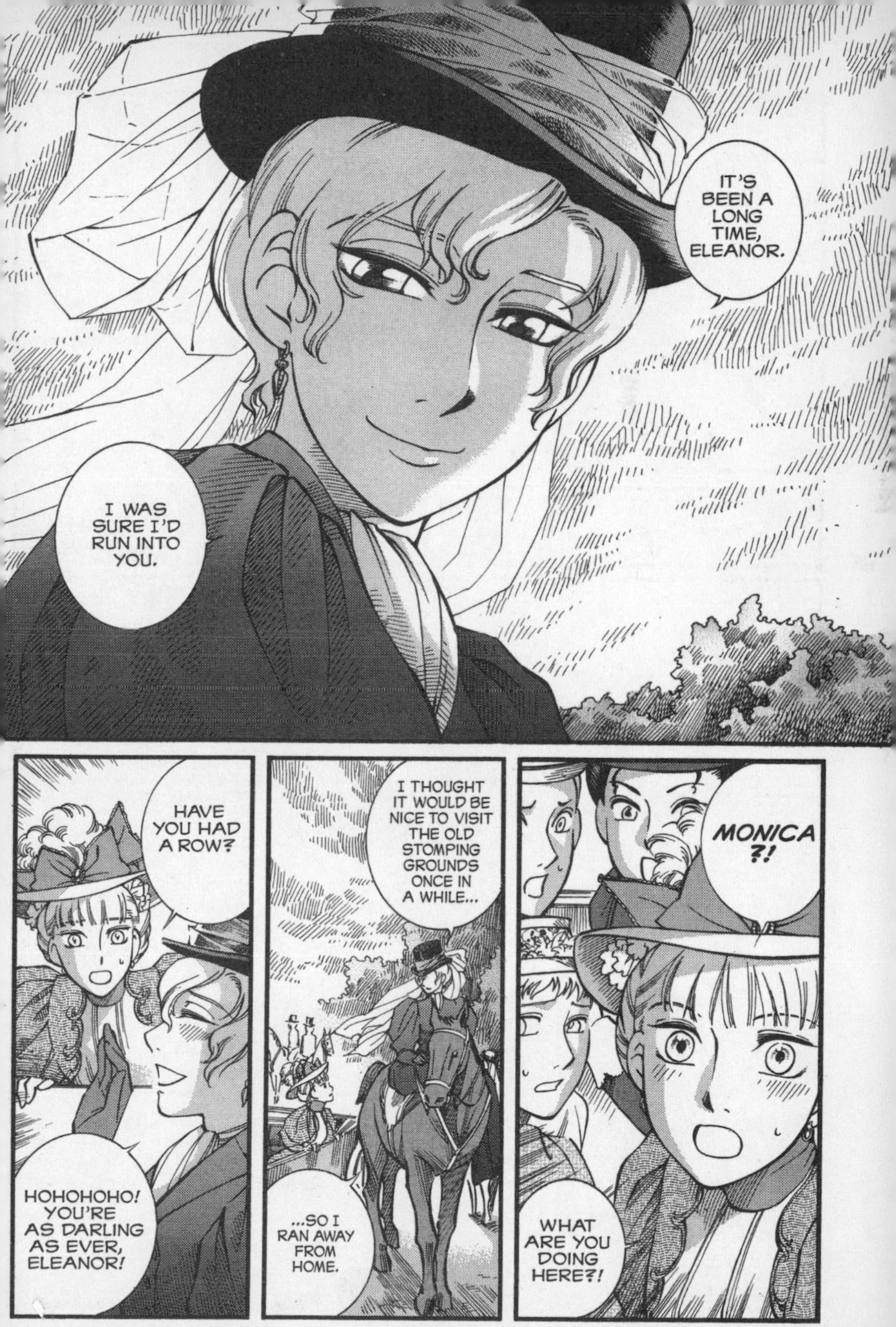
IT'S BEEN A LONG TIME, ELEANOR.
I WAS SURE I'D RUN INTO YOU.
MONICA?!
WHAT ARE YOU DOING HERE?!
I THOUGHT IT WOULD BE NICE TO VISIT THE OLD STOMPING GROUNDS ONCE IN A WHILE...
...SO I RAN AWAY FROM HOME.
HAVE YOU HAD A ROW?
HOHOHOHO! YOU'RE AS DARLING AS EVER, ELEANOR!

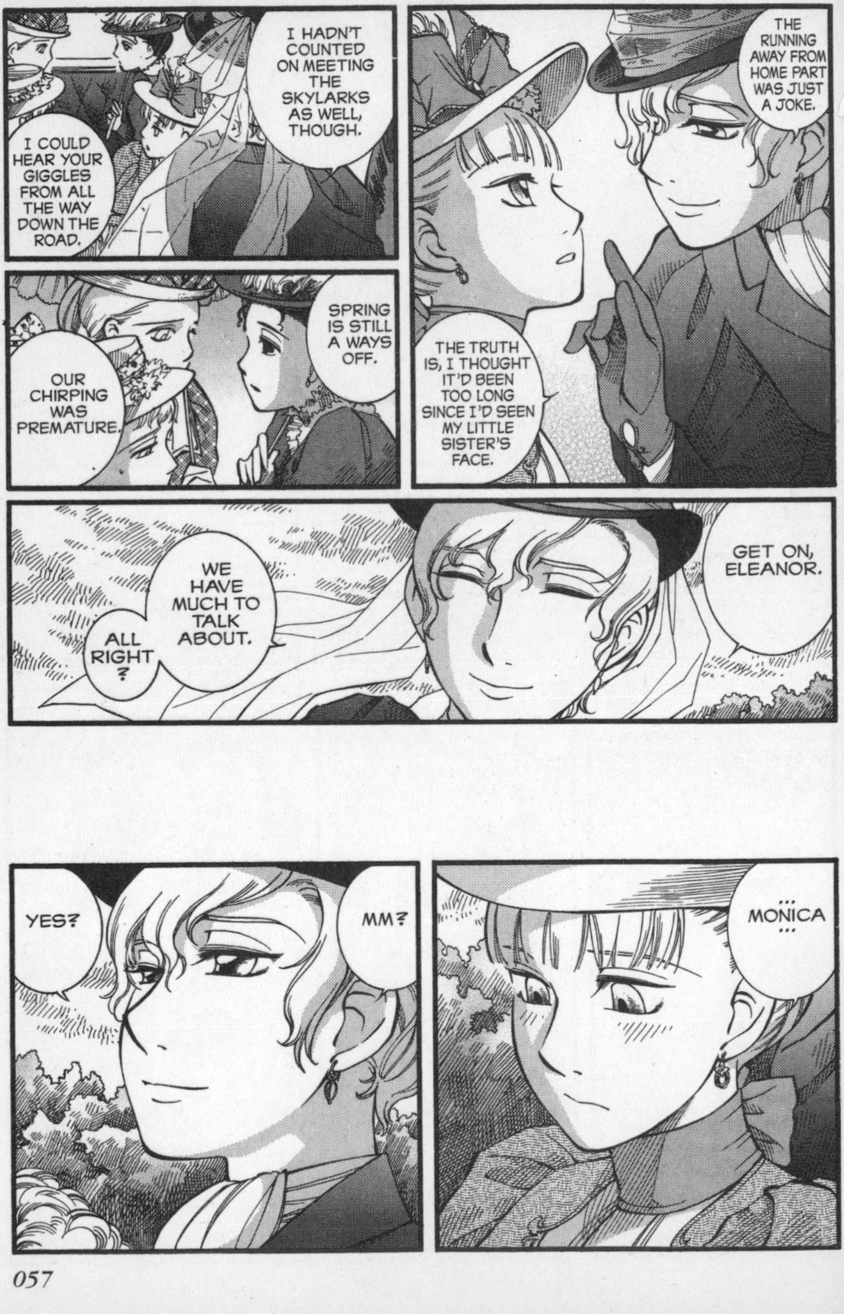
THE RUNNING AWAY FROM HOME PART WAS JUST A JOKE.
THE TRUTH IS, I THOUGHT IT'D BEEN TOO LONG SINCE I'D SEEN MY LITTLE SISTER'S FACE.
I HADN'T COUNTED ON MEETING THE SKYLARKS AS WELL, THOUGH.
I COULD HEAR YOUR GIGGLES FROM ALL THE WAY DOWN THE ROAD.
SPRING IS STILL A WAYS OFF.
OUR CHIRPING WAS PREMATURE.
GET ON, ELEANOR.
WE HAVE MUCH TO TALK ABOUT.
ALL RIGHT?
... MONICA ...
MM?
YES?

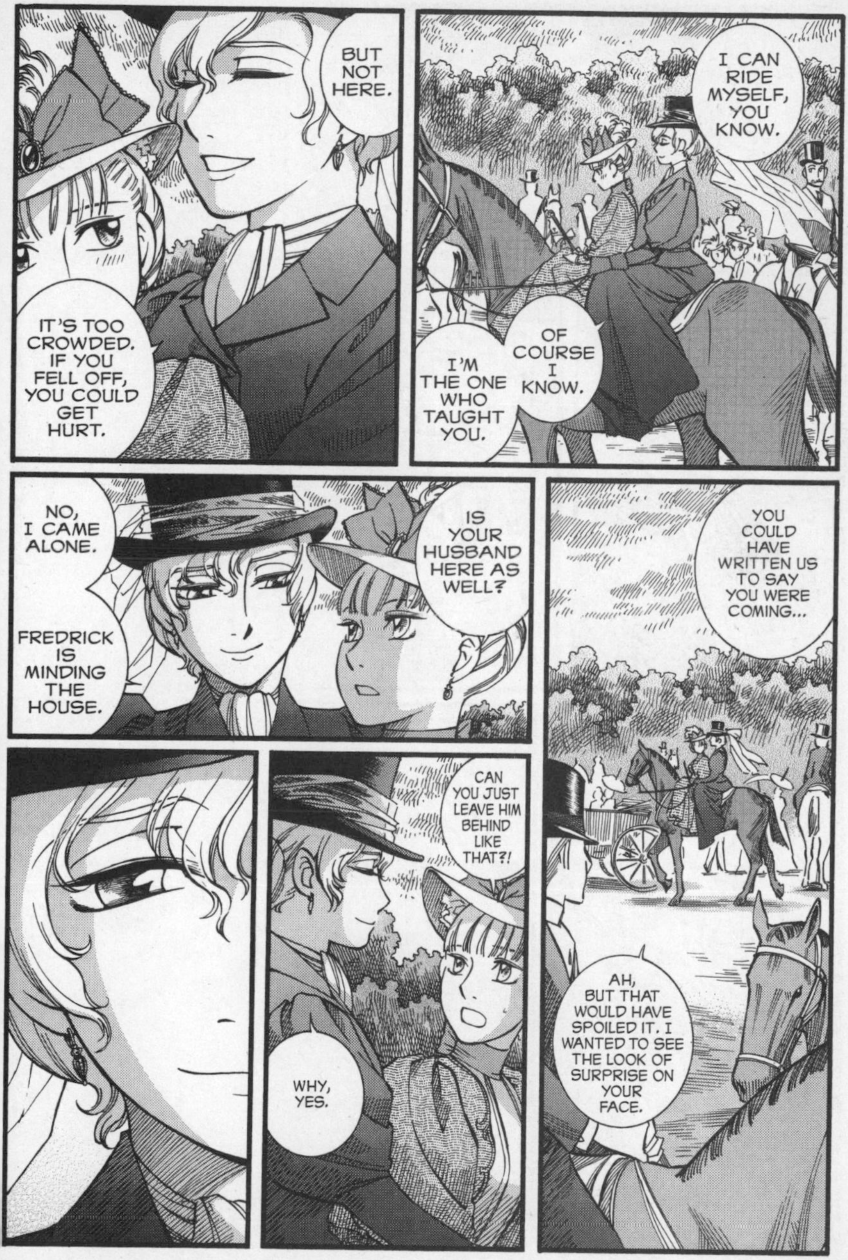
I CAN RIDE MYSELF, YOU KNOW.
OF COURSE I KNOW.
I'M THE ONE WHO TAUGHT YOU.
BUT NOT HERE.
IT'S TOO CROWDED. IF YOU FELL OFF, YOU COULD GET HURT.
YOU COULD HAVE WRITTEN US TO SAY YOU WERE COMING...
AH, BUT THAT WOULD HAVE SPOILED IT. I WANTED TO SEE THE LOOK OF SURPRISE ON YOUR FACE.
IS YOUR HUSBAND HERE AS WELL?
NO, I CAME ALONE.
FREDRICK IS MINDING THE HOUSE.
CAN YOU JUST LEAVE HIM BEHIND LIKE THAT?!
WHY, YES.

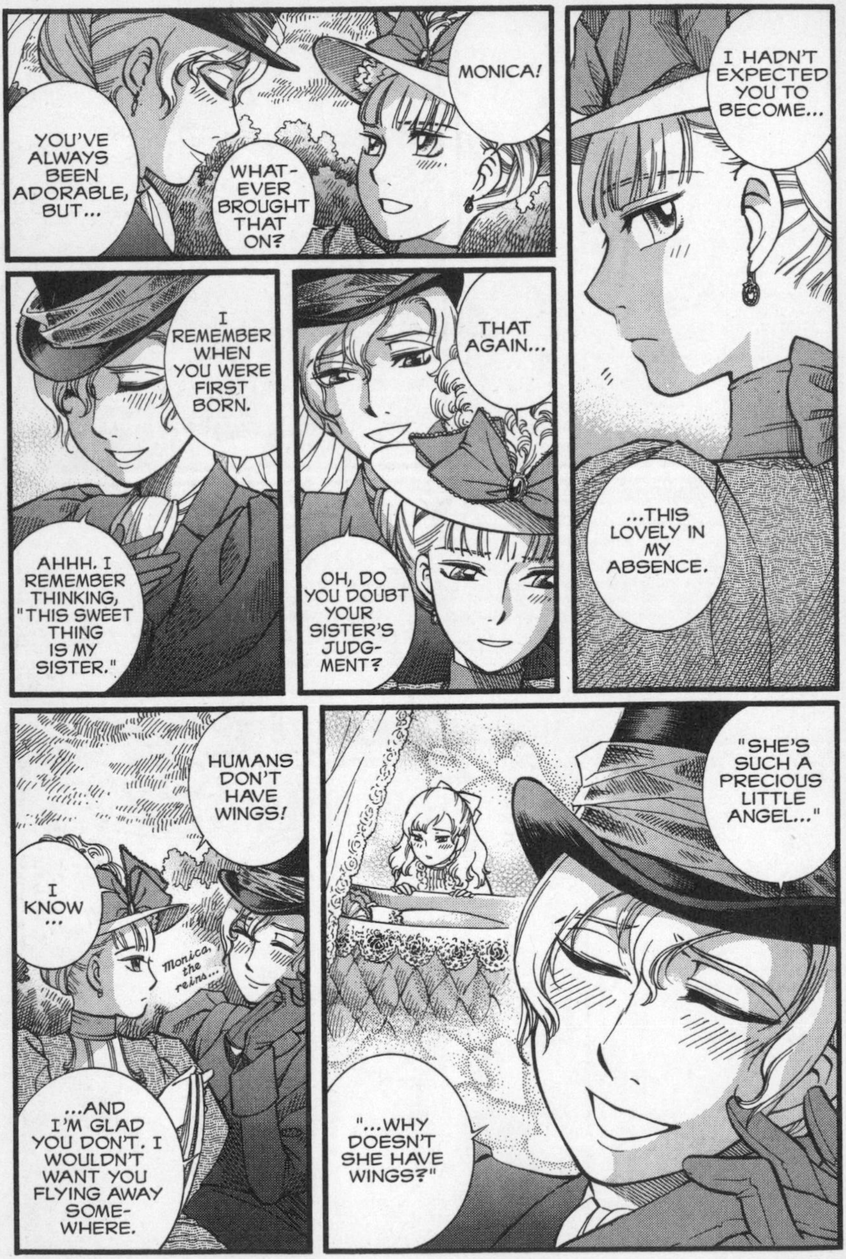
I HADN'T EXPECTED YOU TO BECOME...
...THIS LOVELY IN MY ABSENCE.
MONICA!
WHAT-EVER BROUGHT THAT ON?
YOU'VE ALWAYS BEEN ADORABLE, BUT...
THAT AGAIN...
OH, DO YOU DOUBT YOUR SISTER'S JUDG-MENT?
I REMEMBER WHEN YOU WERE FIRST BORN.
AHHH. I REMEMBER THINKING, "THIS SWEET THING IS MY SISTER."
"SHE'S SUCH A PRECIOUS LITTLE ANGEL..."
"...WHY DOESN'T SHE HAVE WINGS?"
HUMANS DON'T HAVE WINGS!
I KNOW...
Monica, the reins...
...AND I'M GLAD YOU DON'T. I WOULDN'T WANT YOU FLYING AWAY SOME-WHERE.

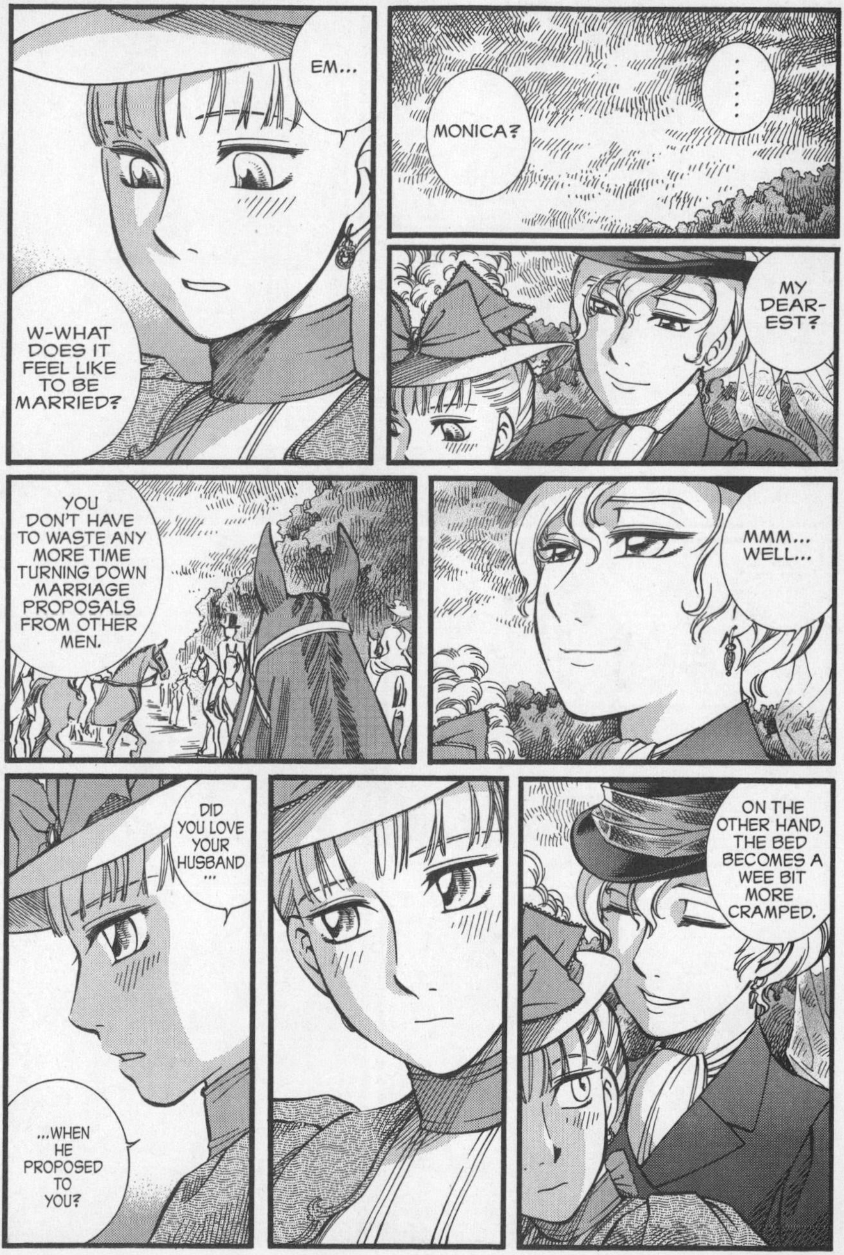
......
MONICA?
MY DEAREST?
EM...
W-WHAT DOES IT FEEL LIKE TO BE MARRIED?
MMM... WELL...
YOU DON'T HAVE TO WASTE ANY MORE TIME TURNING DOWN MARRIAGE PROPOSALS FROM OTHER MEN.
ON THE OTHER HAND, THE BED BECOMES A WEE BIT MORE CRAMPED.
DID YOU LOVE YOUR HUSBAND...
...WHEN HE PROPOSED TO YOU?

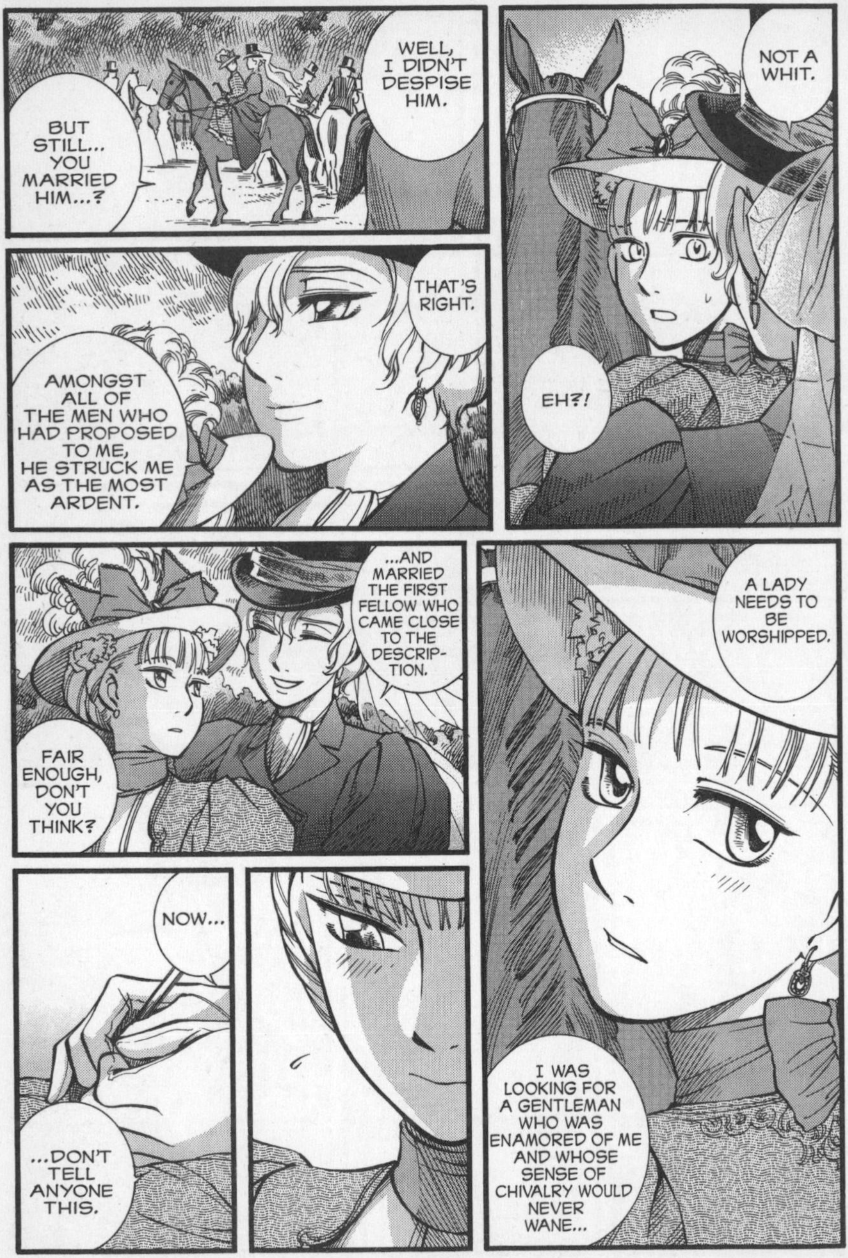
NOT A WHIT.
EH?!
BUT STILL... YOU MARRIED HIM...?
WELL, I DIDN'T DESPISE HIM.
THAT'S RIGHT.
AMONGST ALL OF THE MEN WHO HAD PROPOSED TO ME, HE STRUCK ME AS THE MOST ARDENT.
A LADY NEEDS TO BE WORSHIPPED.
I WAS LOOKING FOR A GENTLEMAN WHO WAS ENAMORED OF ME AND WHOSE SENSE OF CHIVALRY WOULD NEVER WANE...
...AND MARRIED THE FIRST FELLOW WHO CAME CLOSE TO THE DESCRIPTION.
FAIR ENOUGH, DON'T YOU THINK?
NOW...
...DON'T TELL ANYONE THIS.

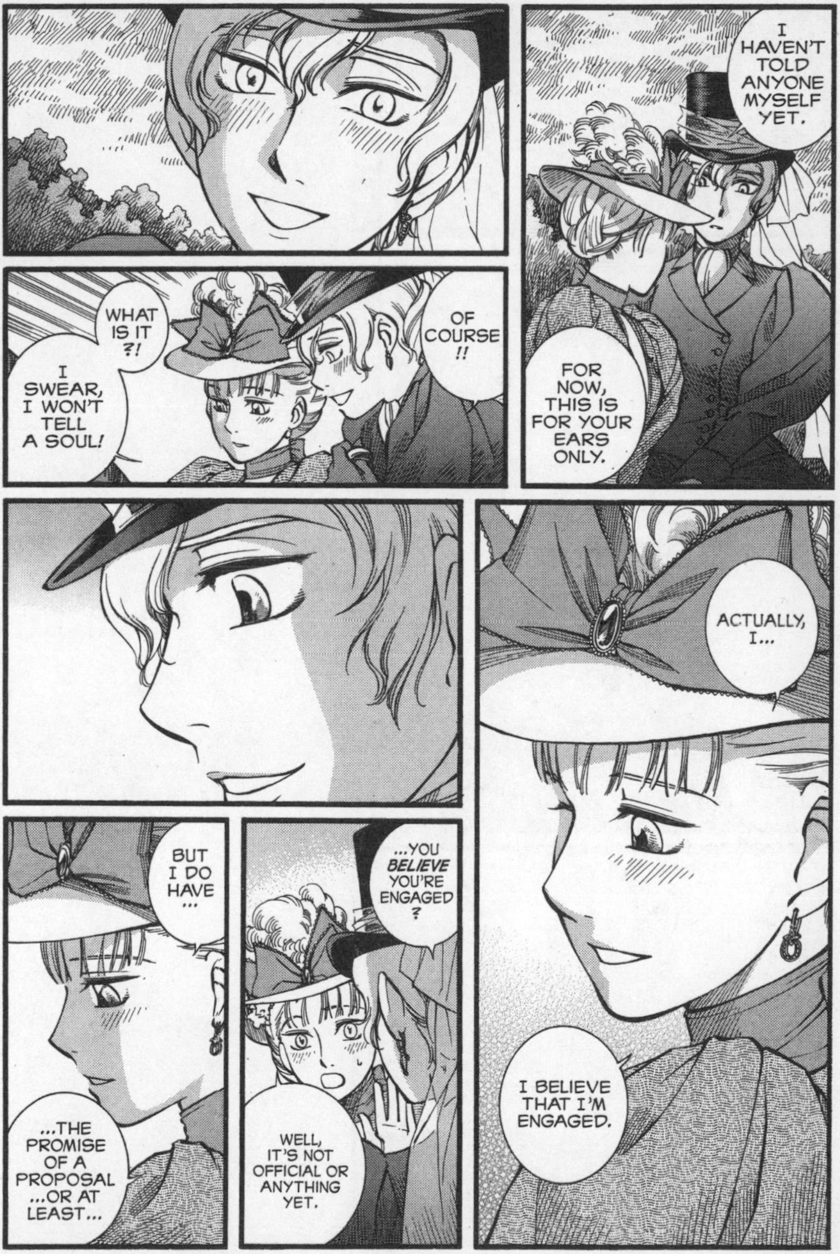
I HAVEN'T TOLD ANYONE MYSELF YET.
FOR NOW, THIS IS FOR YOUR EARS ONLY.
OF COURSE!!
WHAT IS IT?!
I SWEAR, I WON'T TELL A SOUL!
ACTUALLY, I...
I BELIEVE THAT I'M ENGAGED.
...YOU *BELIEVE* YOU'RE ENGAGED?
WELL, IT'S NOT OFFICIAL OR ANYTHING YET.
BUT I DO HAVE...
...THE PROMISE OF A PROPOSAL ...OR AT LEAST...

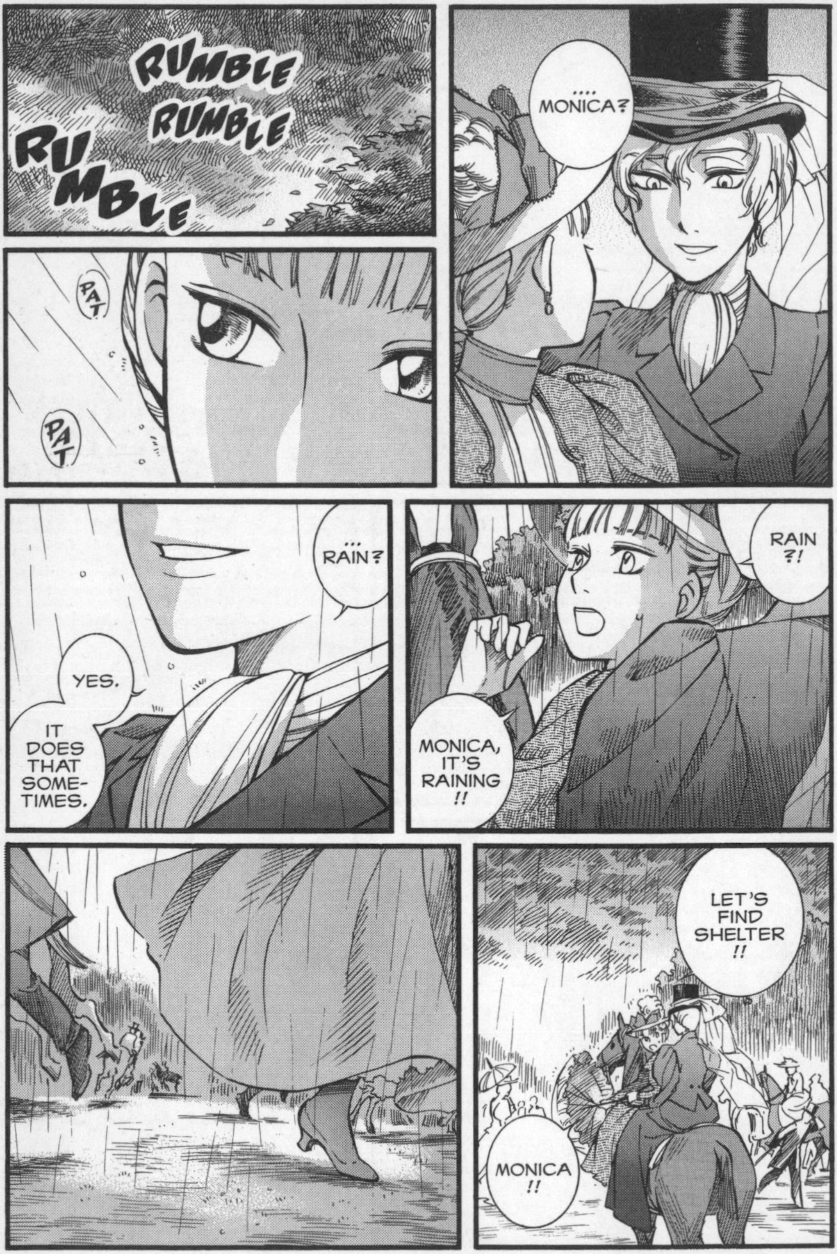
....MONICA?
RUMBLE
RUMBLE
RUMBLE
PAT
PAT
RAIN ?!
MONICA, IT'S RAINING !!
...RAIN?
YES.
IT DOES THAT SOME-TIMES.
LET'S FIND SHELTER !!
MONICA !!

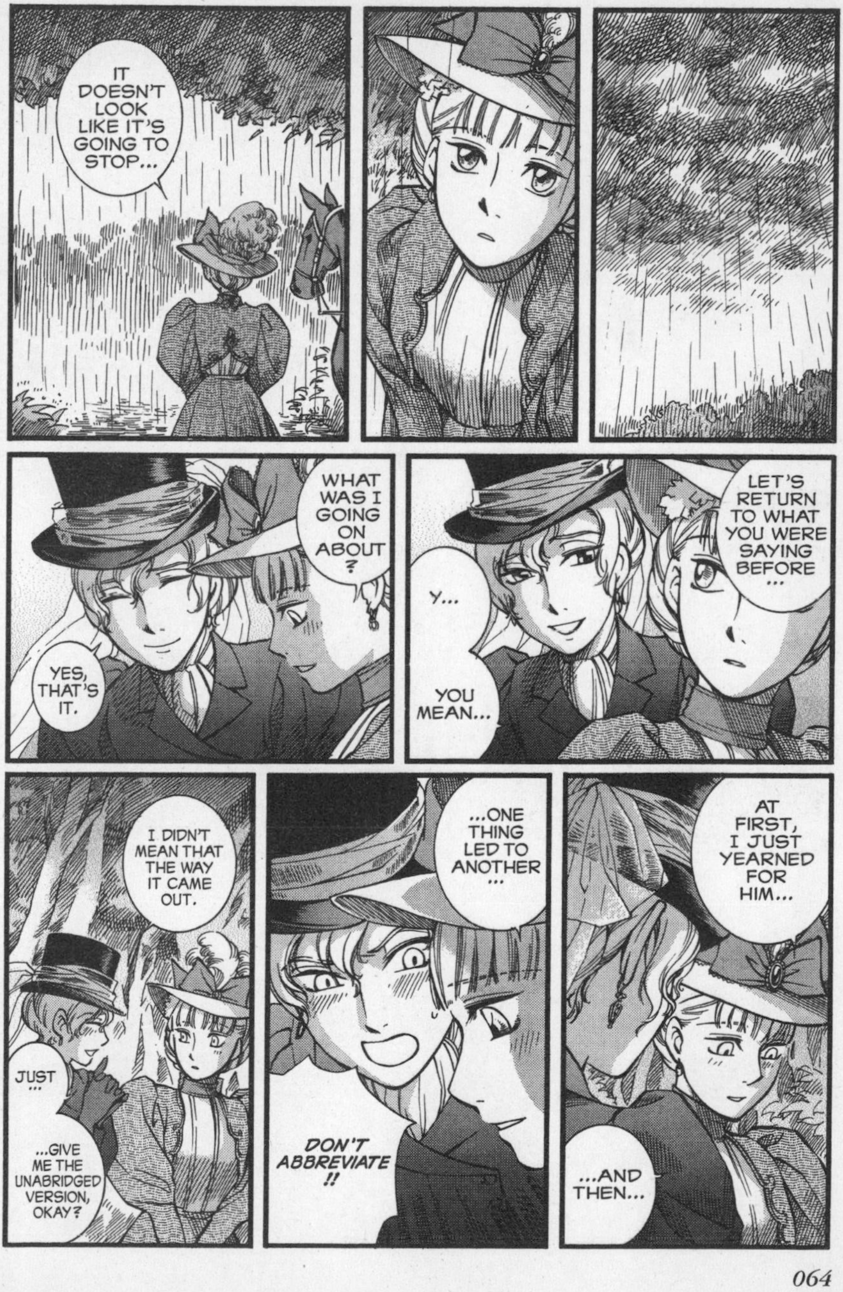
IT DOESN'T LOOK LIKE IT'S GOING TO STOP...
LET'S RETURN TO WHAT YOU WERE SAYING BEFORE ...
Y...
YOU MEAN...
WHAT WAS I GOING ON ABOUT ?
YES, THAT'S IT.
AT FIRST, I JUST YEARNED FOR HIM...
...AND THEN...
...ONE THING LED TO ANOTHER ...
DON'T ABBREVIATE !!
I DIDN'T MEAN THAT THE WAY IT CAME OUT.
JUST ...
...GIVE ME THE UNABRIDGED VERSION, OKAY?

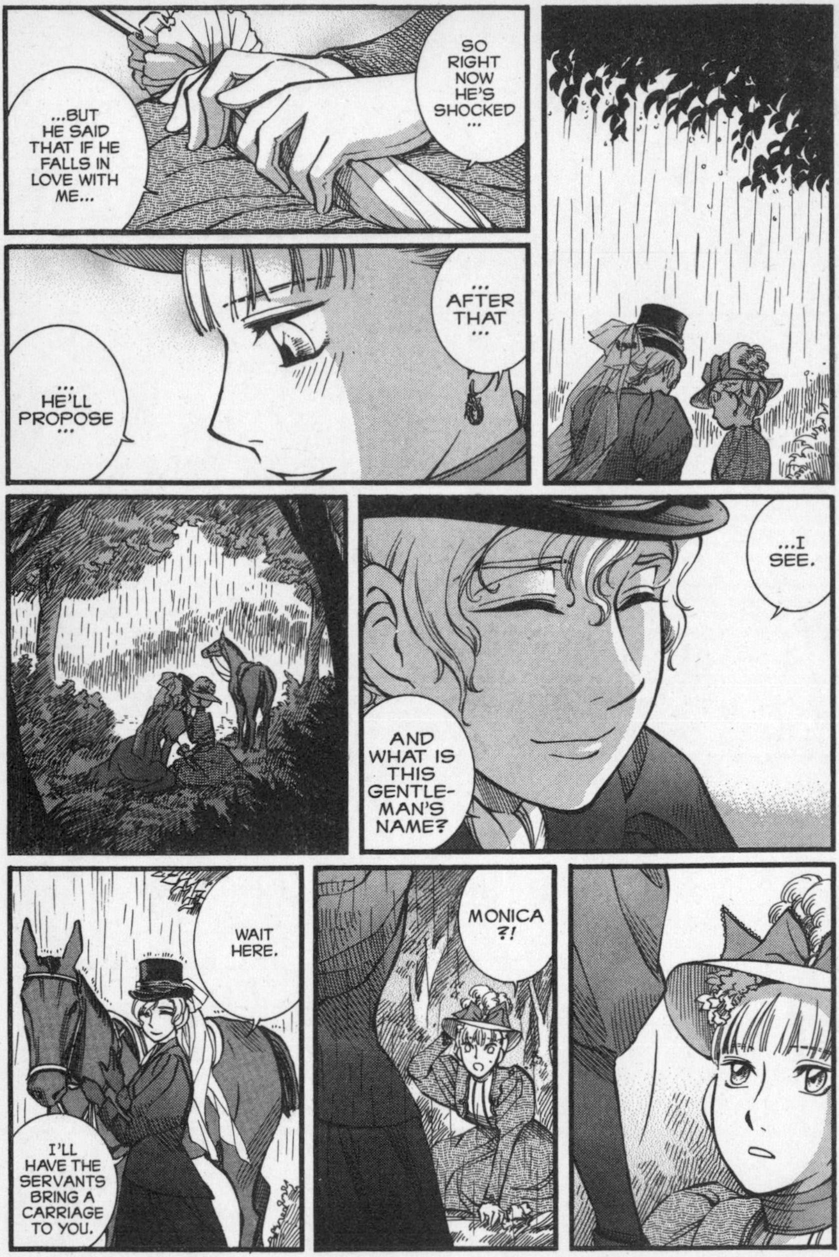
SO RIGHT NOW HE'S SHOCKED...
...BUT HE SAID THAT IF HE FALLS IN LOVE WITH ME...
...AFTER THAT...
...HE'LL PROPOSE...
...I SEE.
AND WHAT IS THIS GENTLEMAN'S NAME?
MONICA?!
WAIT HERE.
I'LL HAVE THE SERVANTS BRING A CARRIAGE TO YOU.

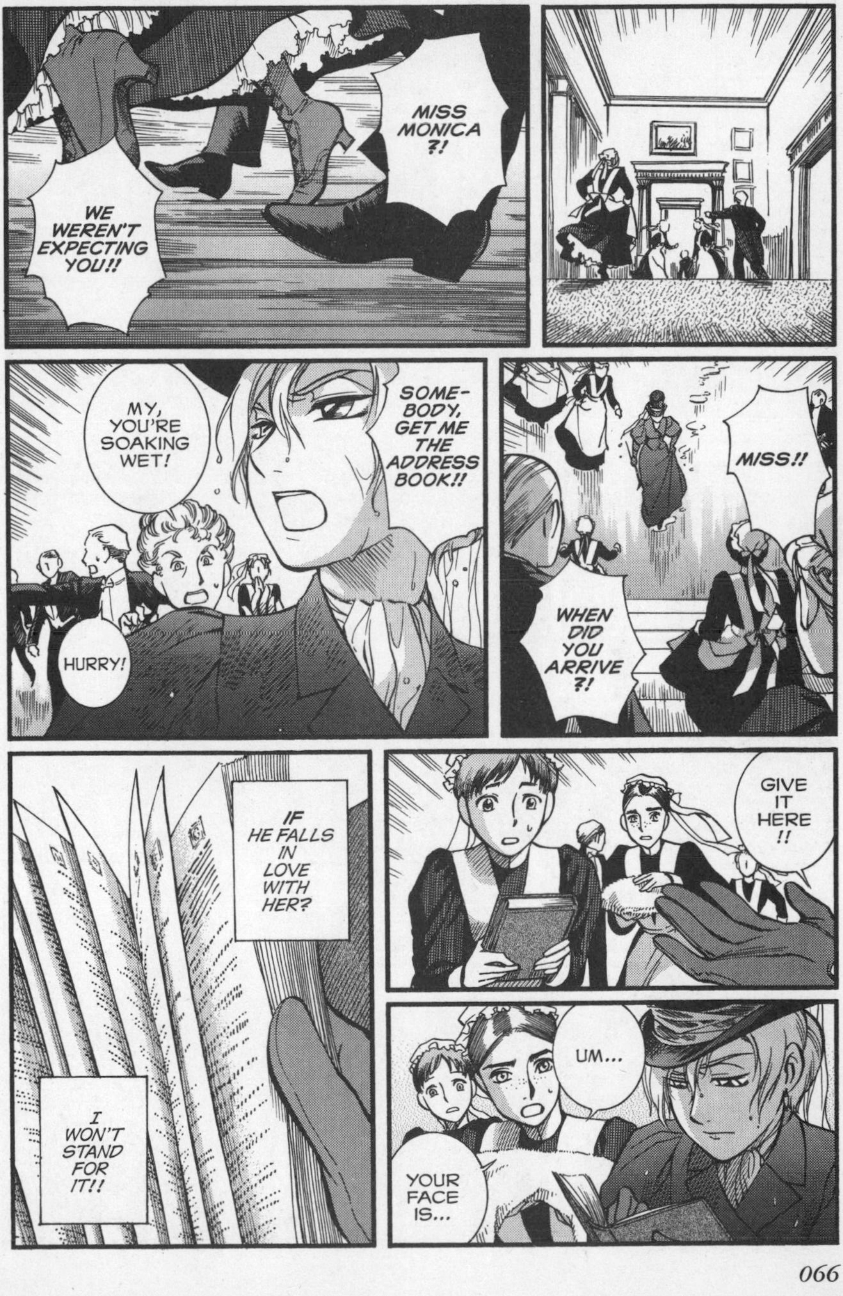
MISS MONICA ?!
WE WEREN'T EXPECTING YOU!!
MISS!!
WHEN DID YOU ARRIVE ?!
SOMEBODY, GET ME THE ADDRESS BOOK!!
MY, YOU'RE SOAKING WET!
HURRY!
GIVE IT HERE !!
UM...
YOUR FACE IS...
IF HE FALLS IN LOVE WITH HER?
I WON'T STAND FOR IT!!

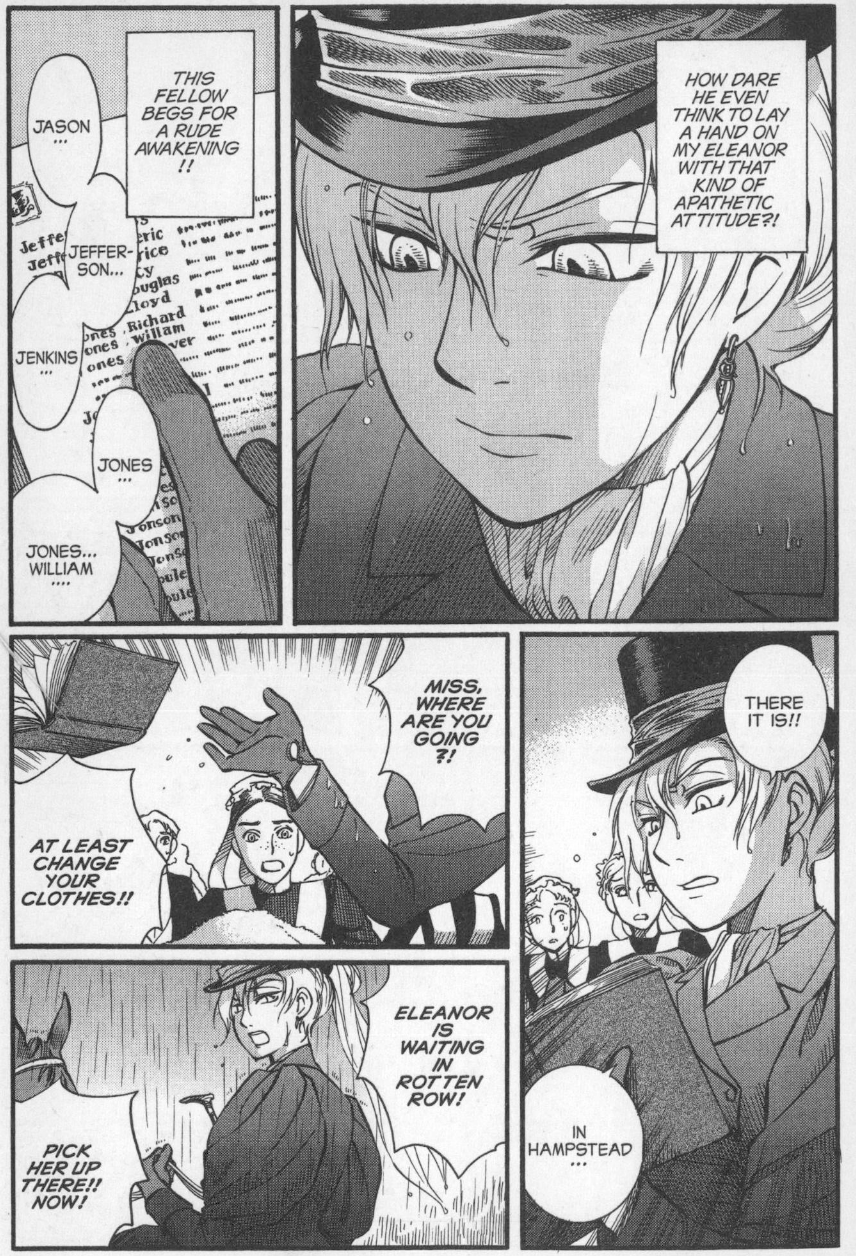
HOW DARE HE EVEN THINK TO LAY A HAND ON MY ELEANOR WITH THAT KIND OF APATHETIC ATTITUDE?!
THIS FELLOW BEGS FOR A RUDE AWAKENING !!
JASON ...
JEFFERSON...
JENKINS ...
JONES ...
JONES... WILLIAM ....
THERE IT IS!!
IN HAMPSTEAD ...
MISS, WHERE ARE YOU GOING ?!
AT LEAST CHANGE YOUR CLOTHES!!
ELEANOR IS WAITING IN ROTTEN ROW!
PICK HER UP THERE!! NOW!

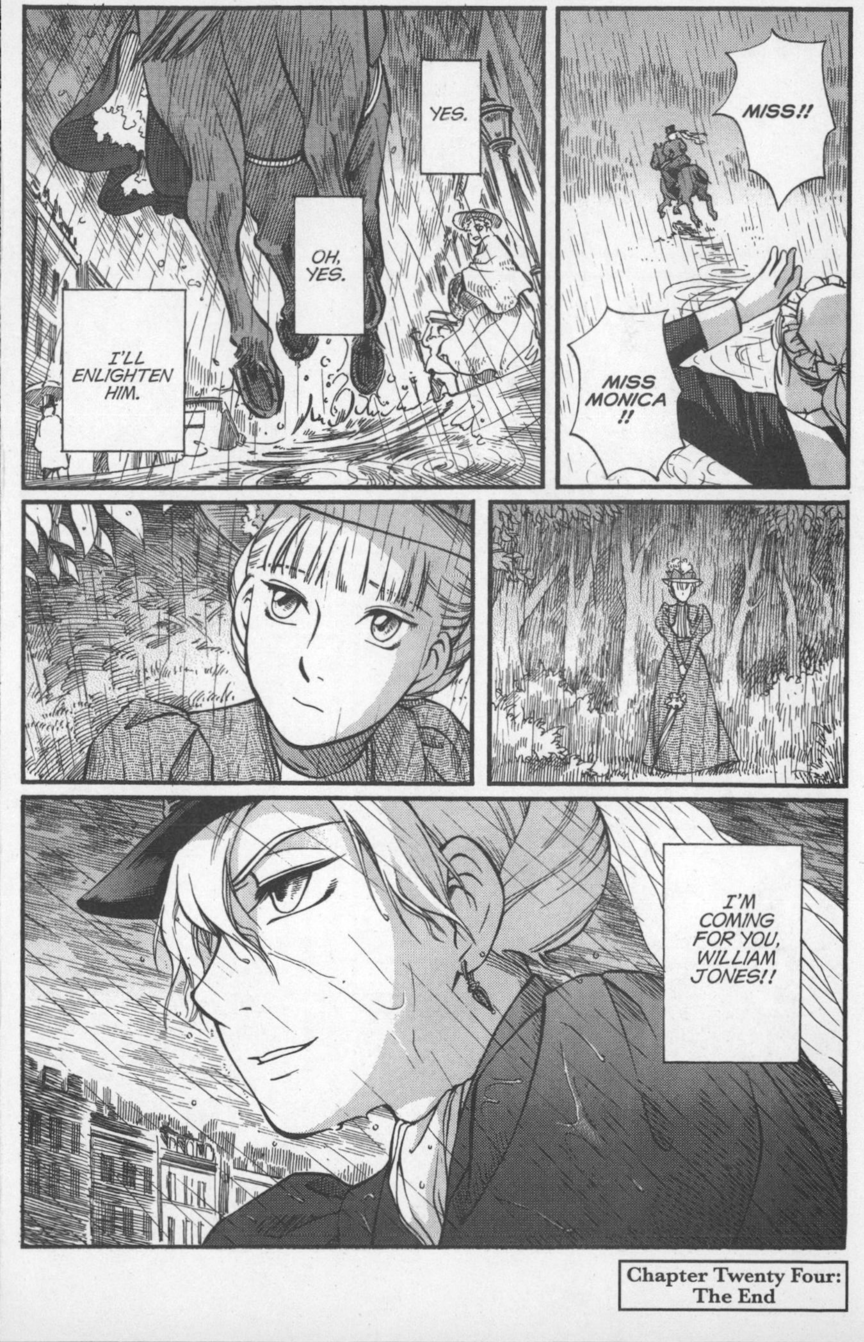
MISS!!
MISS MONICA!!
YES.
OH, YES.
I'LL ENLIGHTEN HIM.
I'M COMING FOR YOU, WILLIAM JONES!!

Chapter Twenty Four: The End

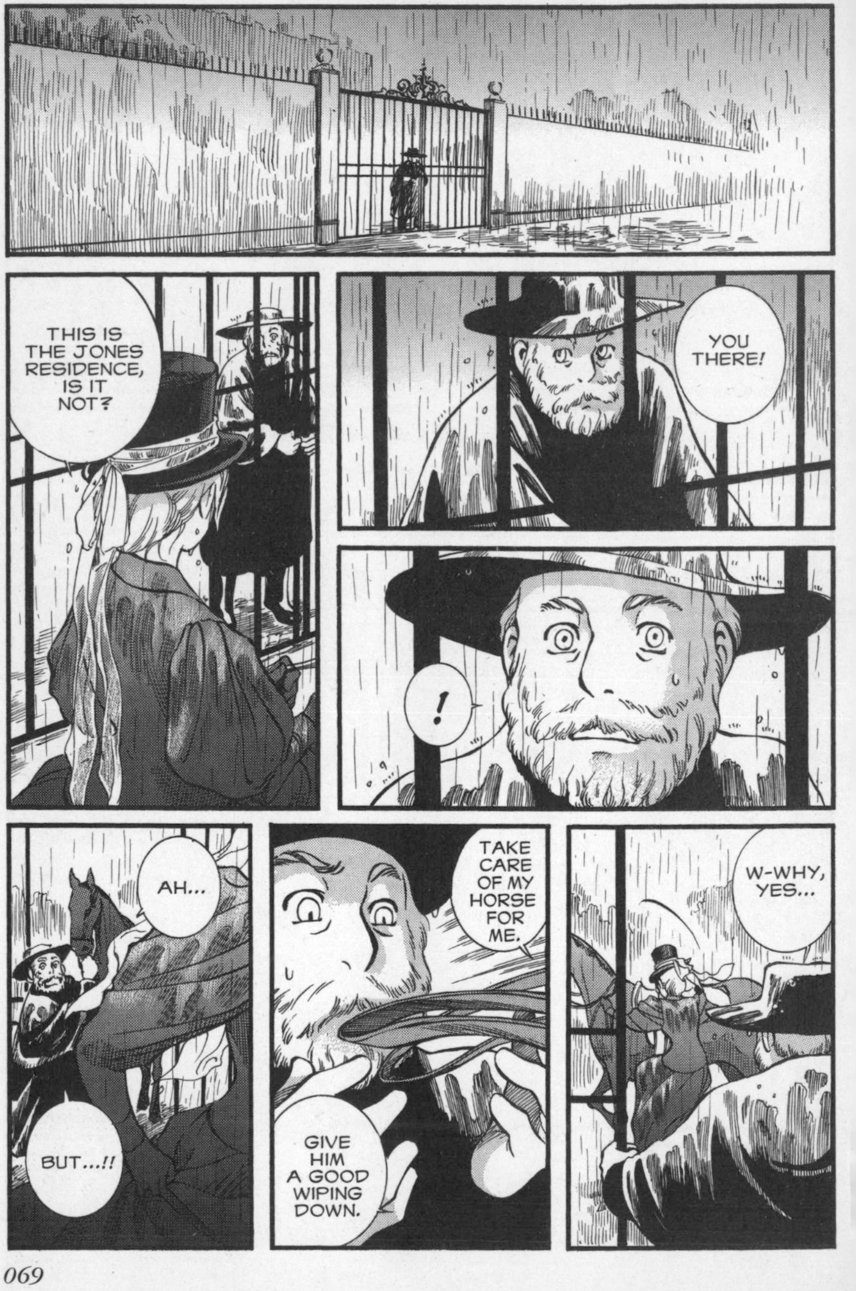
YOU THERE!
!
THIS IS THE JONES RESIDENCE, IS IT NOT?
W-WHY, YES...
TAKE CARE OF MY HORSE FOR ME.
GIVE HIM A GOOD WIPING DOWN.
AH...
BUT...!!

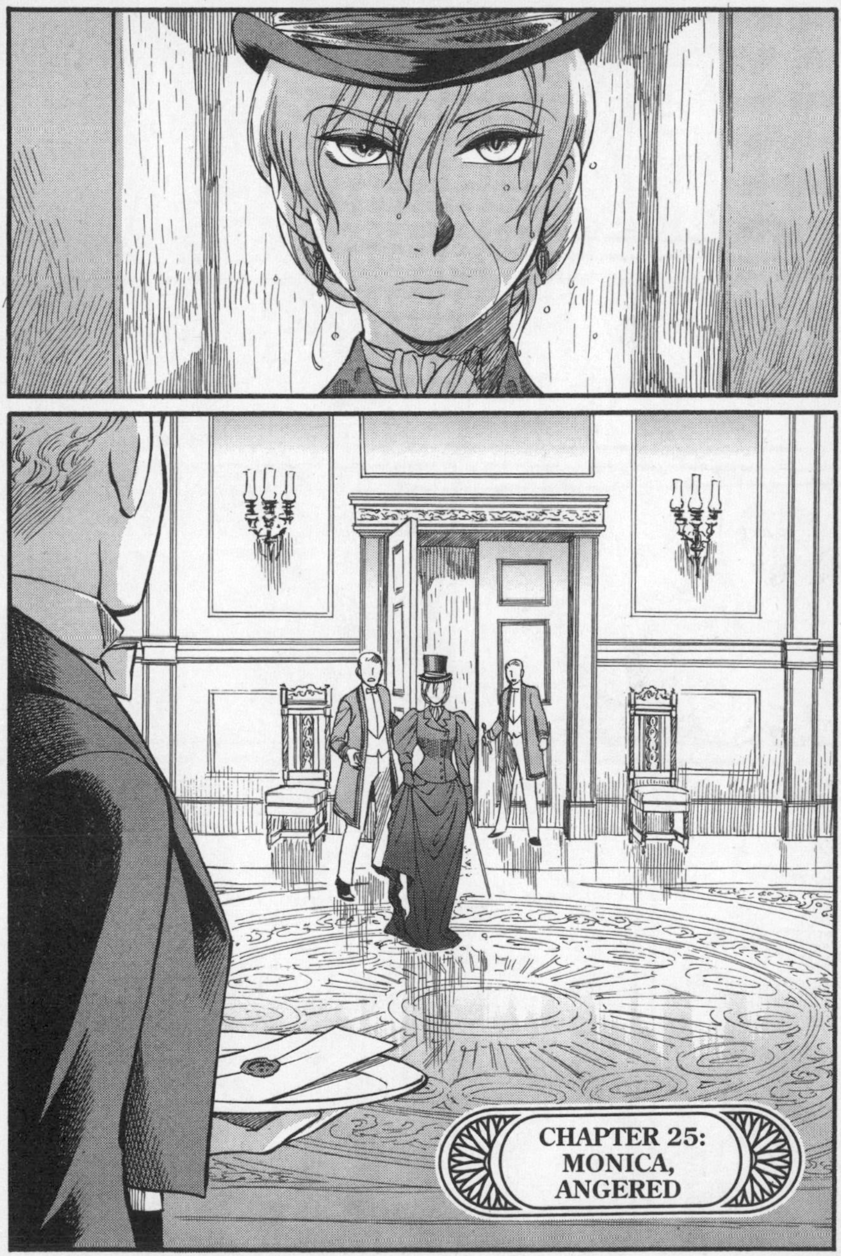
CHAPTER 25:
MONICA,
ANGERED

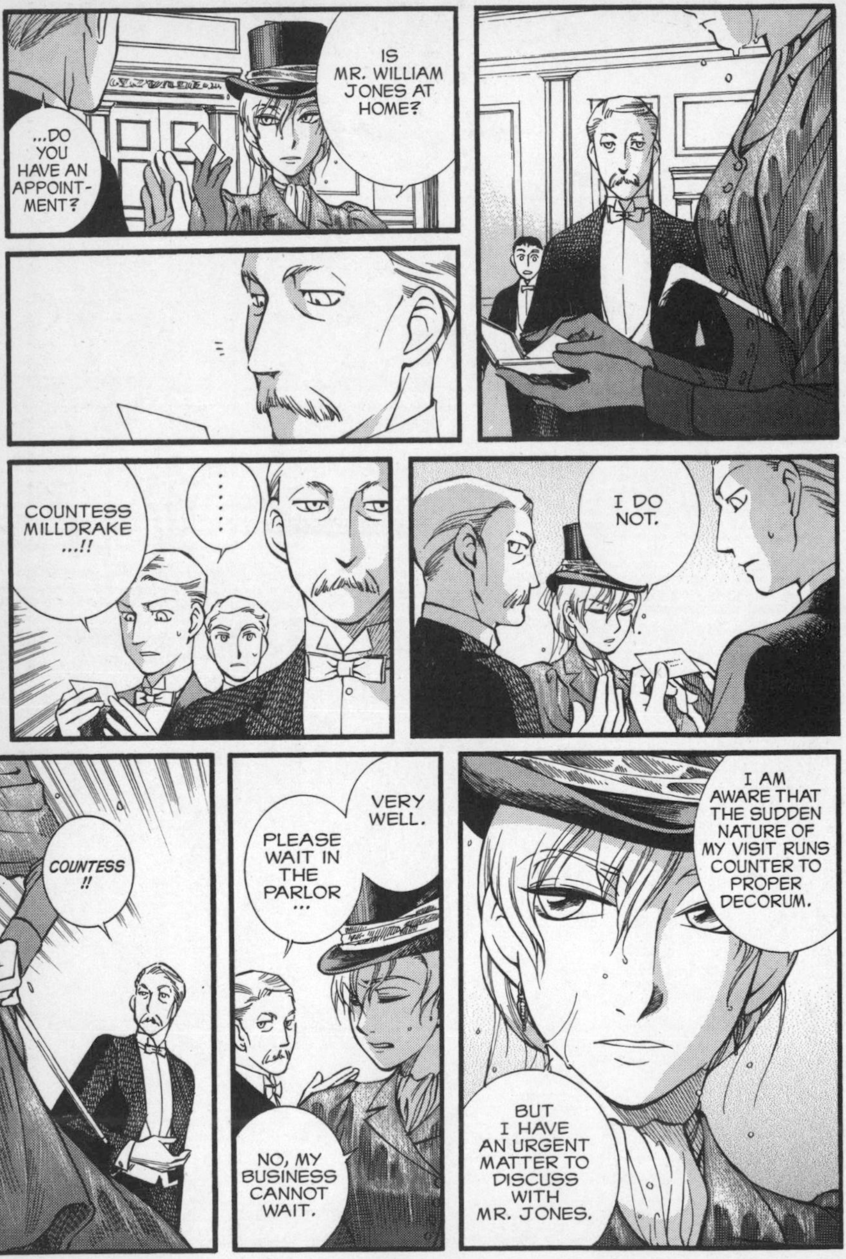
IS MR. WILLIAM JONES AT HOME?
...DO YOU HAVE AN APPOINT-MENT?
I DO NOT.
......
COUNTESS MILLDRAKE ...!!
I AM AWARE THAT THE SUDDEN NATURE OF MY VISIT RUNS COUNTER TO PROPER DECORUM.
BUT I HAVE AN URGENT MATTER TO DISCUSS WITH MR. JONES.
VERY WELL.
PLEASE WAIT IN THE PARLOR ...
NO, MY BUSINESS CANNOT WAIT.
COUNTESS !!

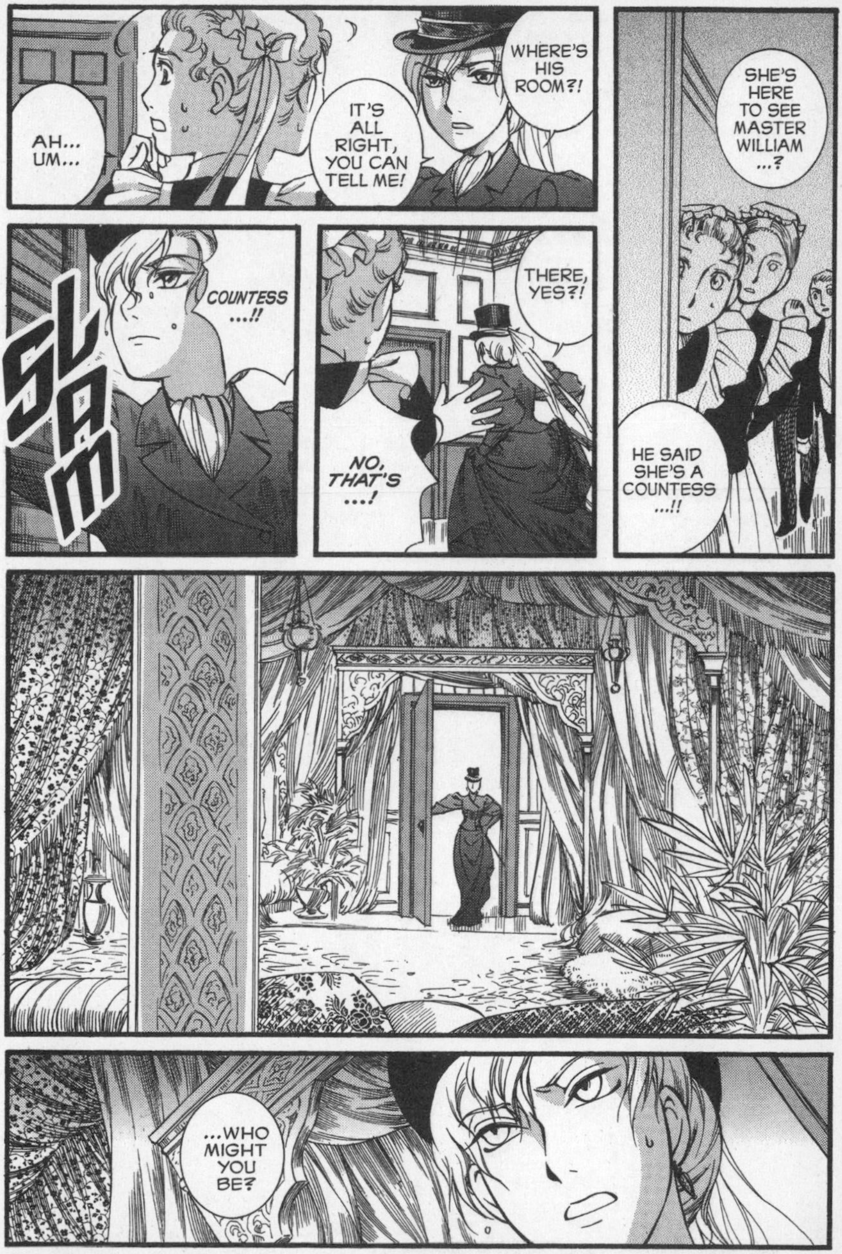
SHE'S HERE TO SEE MASTER WILLIAM ...?
HE SAID SHE'S A COUNTESS ...!!
WHERE'S HIS ROOM?!
IT'S ALL RIGHT, YOU CAN TELL ME!
AH... UM...
THERE, YES?!
NO, THAT'S ...!
COUNTESS ...!!
SLAM
...WHO MIGHT YOU BE?

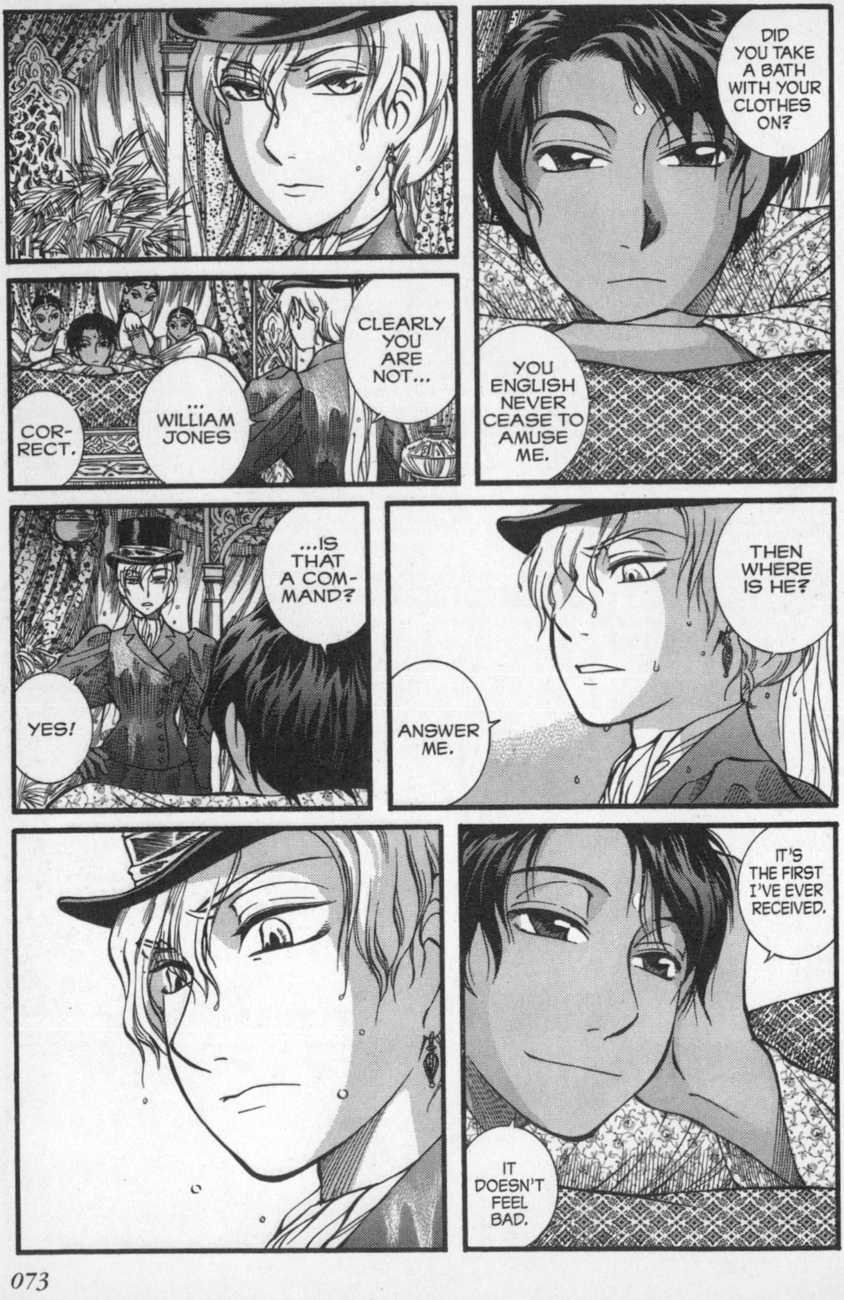
DID YOU TAKE A BATH WITH YOUR CLOTHES ON?
YOU ENGLISH NEVER CEASE TO AMUSE ME.
CLEARLY YOU ARE NOT...
... WILLIAM JONES
COR-RECT.
THEN WHERE IS HE?
ANSWER ME.
...IS THAT A COM-MAND?
YES!
IT'S THE FIRST I'VE EVER RECEIVED.
IT DOESN'T FEEL BAD.

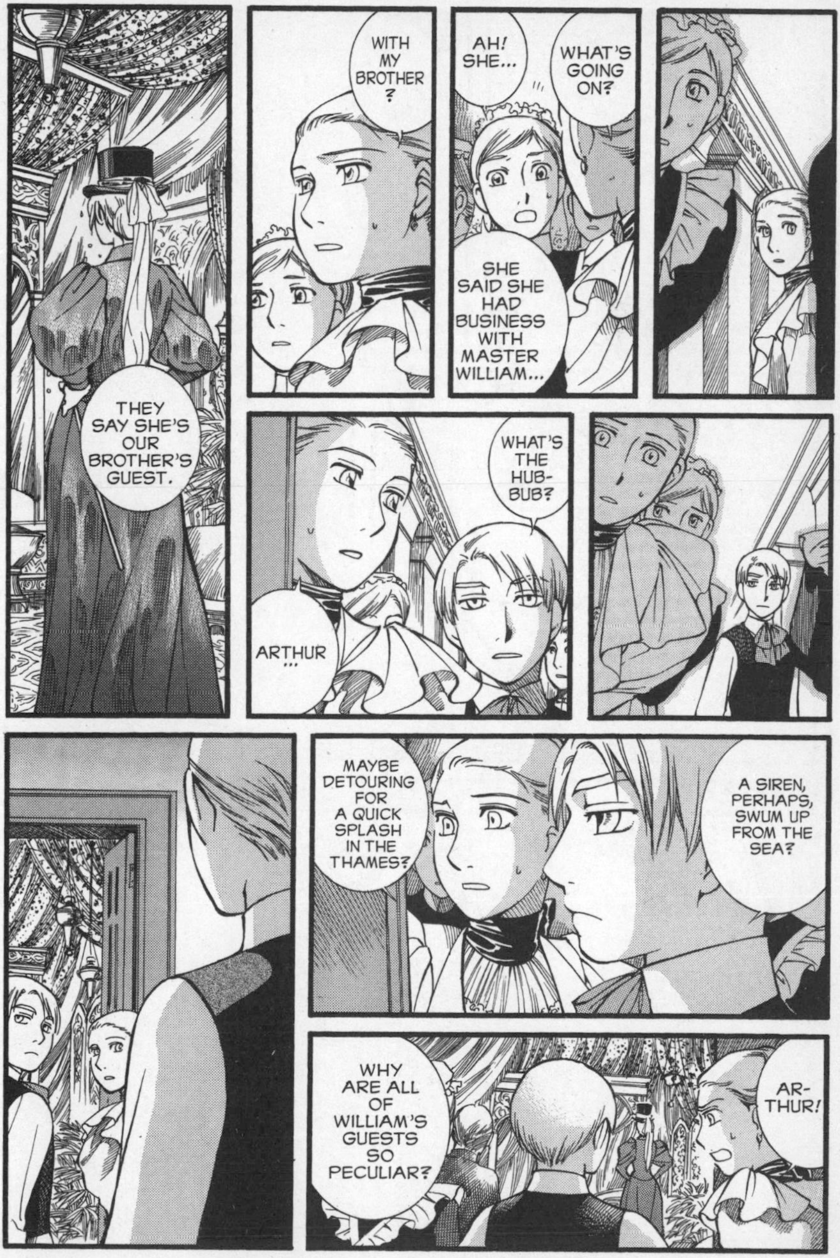
WHAT'S GOING ON?
AH! SHE...
SHE SAID SHE HAD BUSINESS WITH MASTER WILLIAM...
WITH MY BROTHER?
WHAT'S THE HUB-BUB?
ARTHUR...
THEY SAY SHE'S OUR BROTHER'S GUEST.
A SIREN, PERHAPS, SWUM UP FROM THE SEA?
MAYBE DETOURING FOR A QUICK SPLASH IN THE THAMES?
AR-THUR!
WHY ARE ALL OF WILLIAM'S GUESTS SO PECULIAR?

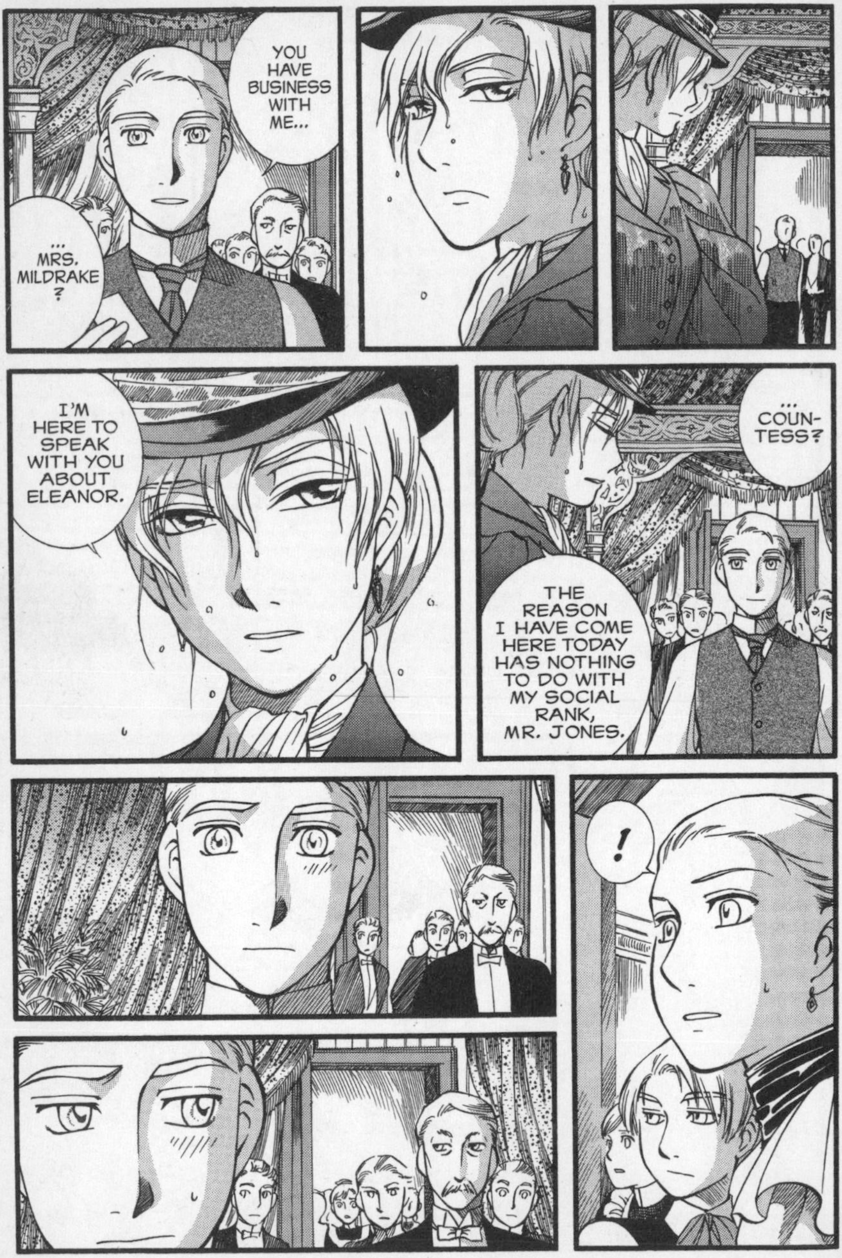
YOU HAVE BUSINESS WITH ME...
... MRS. MILDRAKE?
... COUNTESS?
THE REASON I HAVE COME HERE TODAY HAS NOTHING TO DO WITH MY SOCIAL RANK, MR. JONES.
I'M HERE TO SPEAK WITH YOU ABOUT ELEANOR.
!

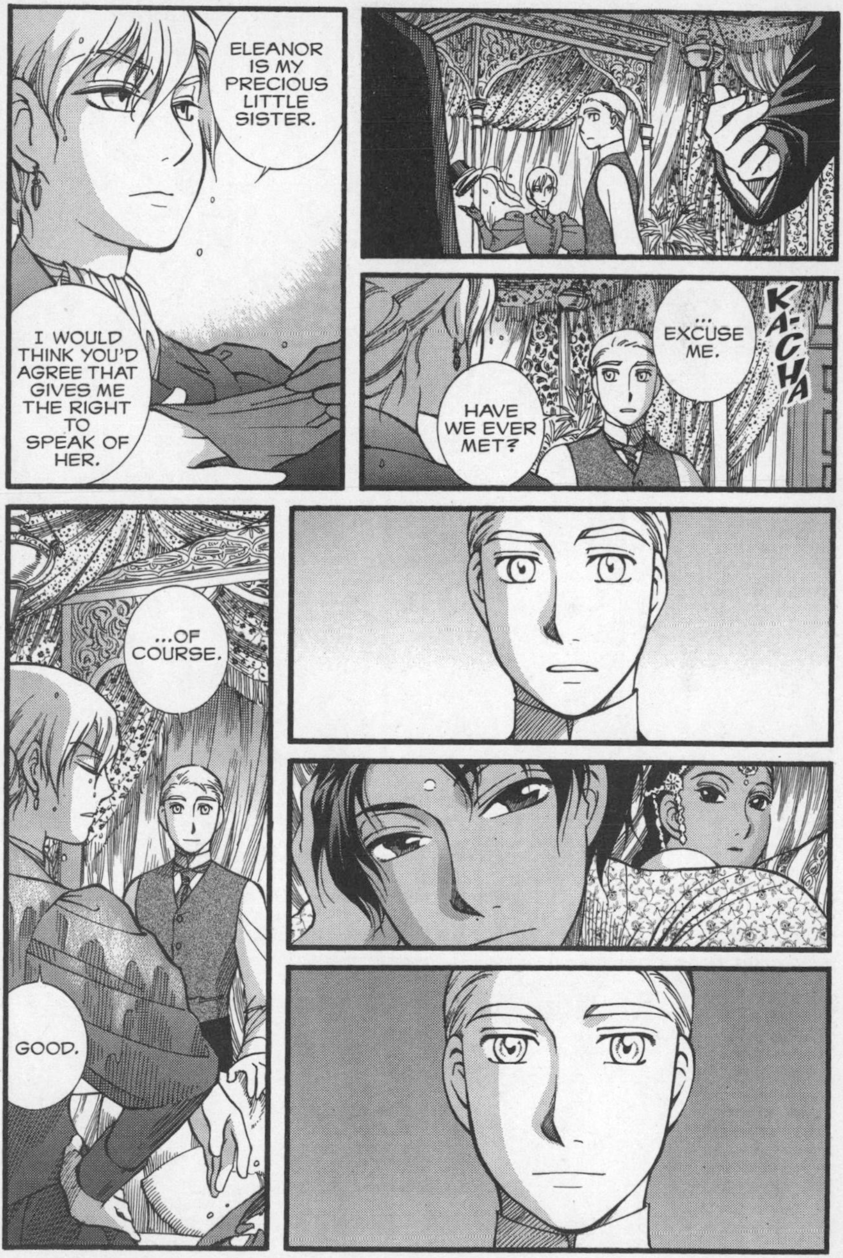
KA-CHA
...EXCUSE ME.
HAVE WE EVER MET?
ELEANOR IS MY PRECIOUS LITTLE SISTER.
I WOULD THINK YOU'D AGREE THAT GIVES ME THE RIGHT TO SPEAK OF HER.
...OF COURSE.
GOOD.

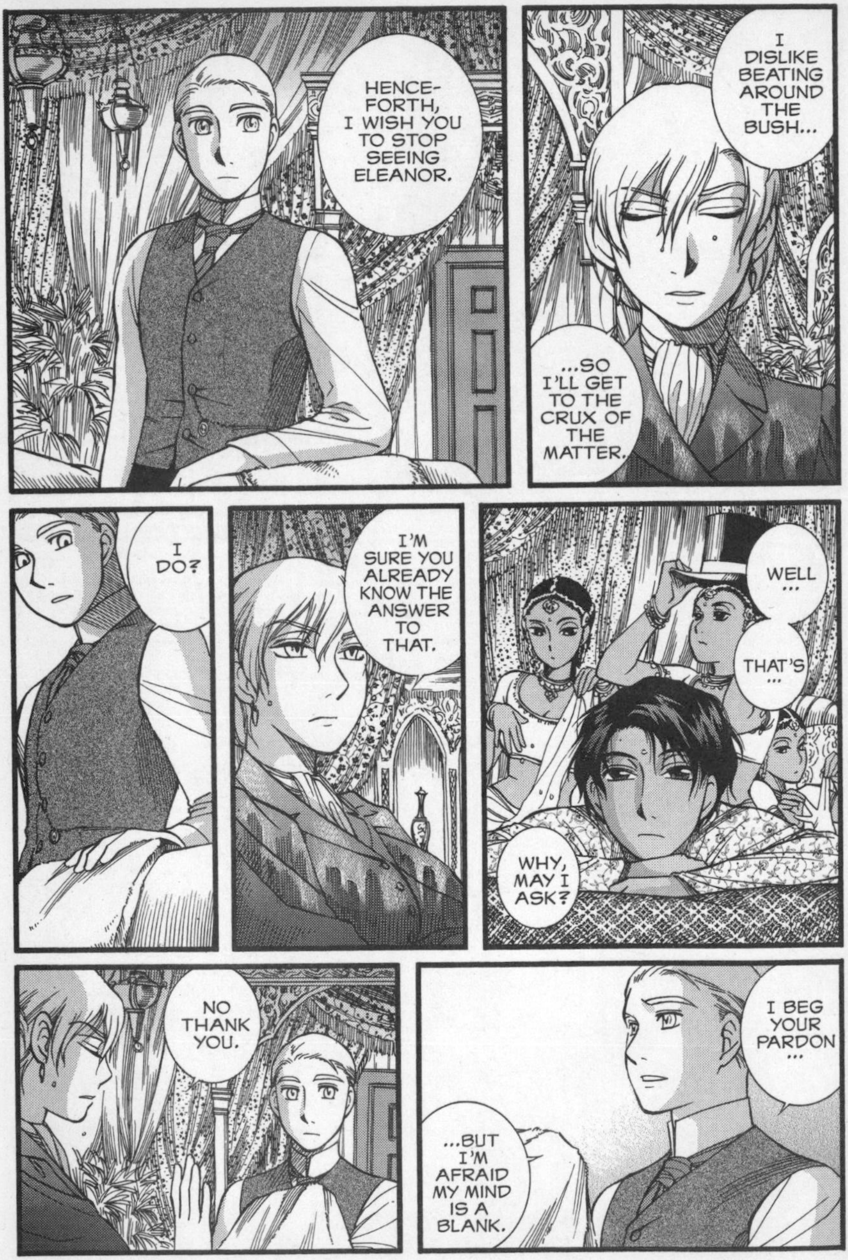
I DISLIKE BEATING AROUND THE BUSH...
...SO I'LL GET TO THE CRUX OF THE MATTER.
HENCE-FORTH, I WISH YOU TO STOP SEEING ELEANOR.
WELL ...
THAT'S ...
WHY, MAY I ASK?
I'M SURE YOU ALREADY KNOW THE ANSWER TO THAT.
I DO?
I BEG YOUR PARDON ...
...BUT I'M AFRAID MY MIND IS A BLANK.
NO THANK YOU.

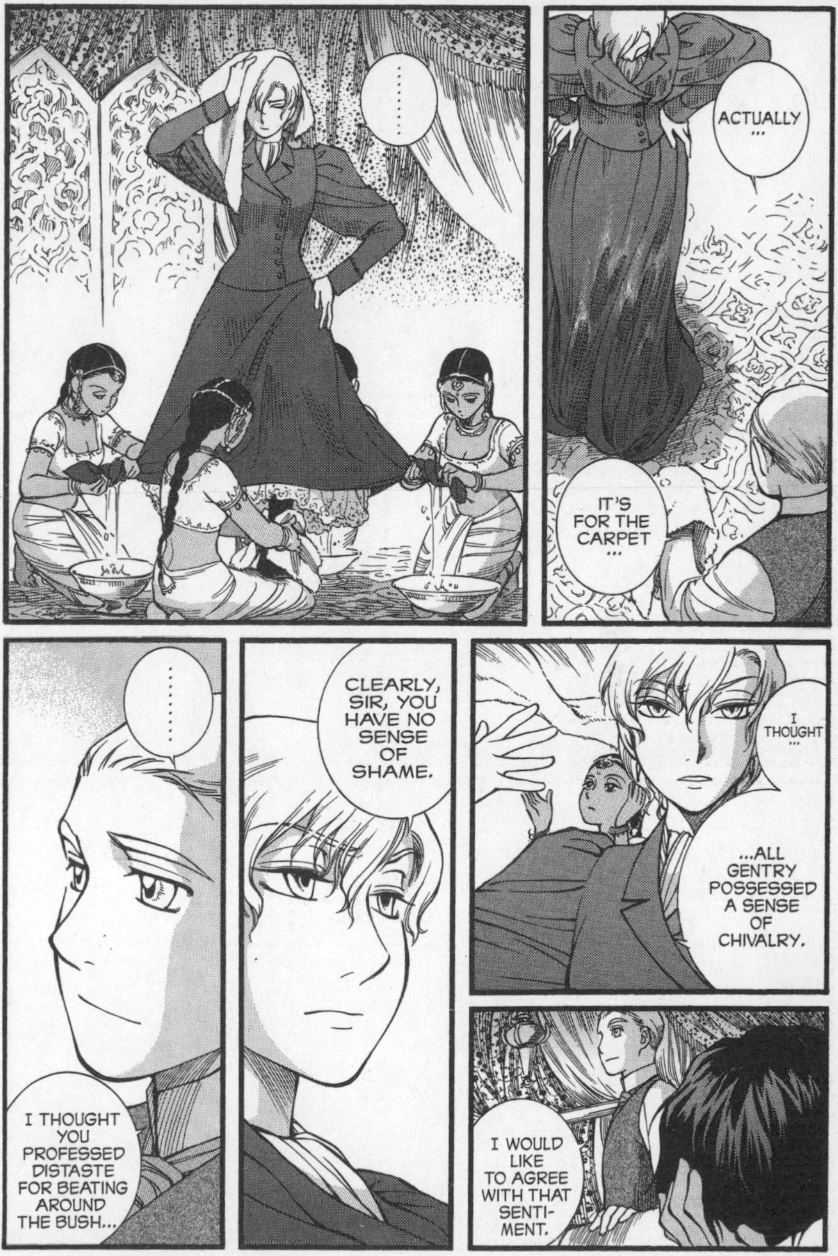
ACTUALLY ...
IT'S FOR THE CARPET ...
......
I THOUGHT ...
...ALL GENTRY POSSESSED A SENSE OF CHIVALRY.
I WOULD LIKE TO AGREE WITH THAT SENTI-MENT.
CLEARLY, SIR, YOU HAVE NO SENSE OF SHAME.
......
I THOUGHT YOU PROFESSED DISTASTE FOR BEATING AROUND THE BUSH...

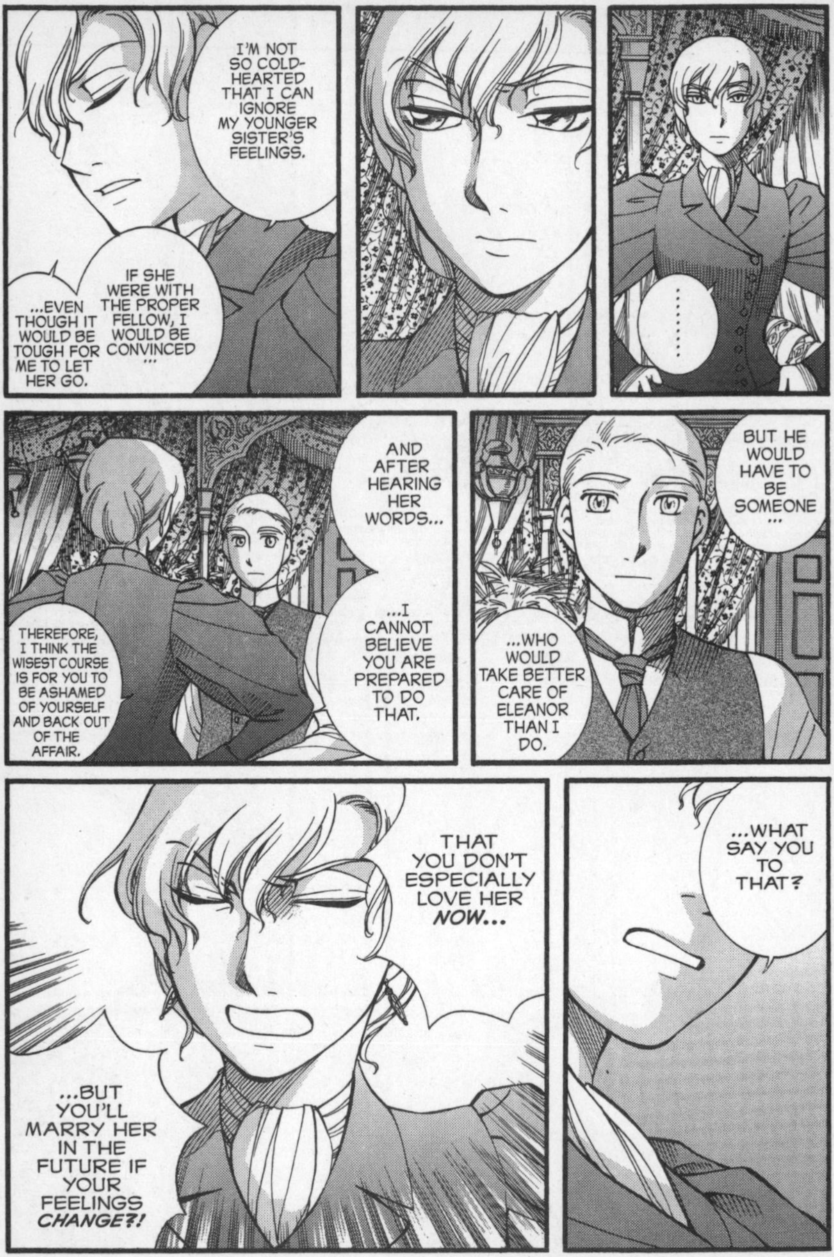
......
I'M NOT SO COLD-HEARTED THAT I CAN IGNORE MY YOUNGER SISTER'S FEELINGS.
IF SHE WERE WITH THE PROPER FELLOW, I WOULD BE CONVINCED...
...EVEN THOUGH IT WOULD BE TOUGH FOR ME TO LET HER GO.
BUT HE WOULD HAVE TO BE SOMEONE...
...WHO WOULD TAKE BETTER CARE OF ELEANOR THAN I DO.
AND AFTER HEARING HER WORDS...
...I CANNOT BELIEVE YOU ARE PREPARED TO DO THAT.
THEREFORE, I THINK THE WISEST COURSE IS FOR YOU TO BE ASHAMED OF YOURSELF AND BACK OUT OF THE AFFAIR.
...WHAT SAY YOU TO THAT?
THAT YOU DON'T ESPECIALLY LOVE HER NOW...
...BUT YOU'LL MARRY HER IN THE FUTURE IF YOUR FEELINGS CHANGE?!

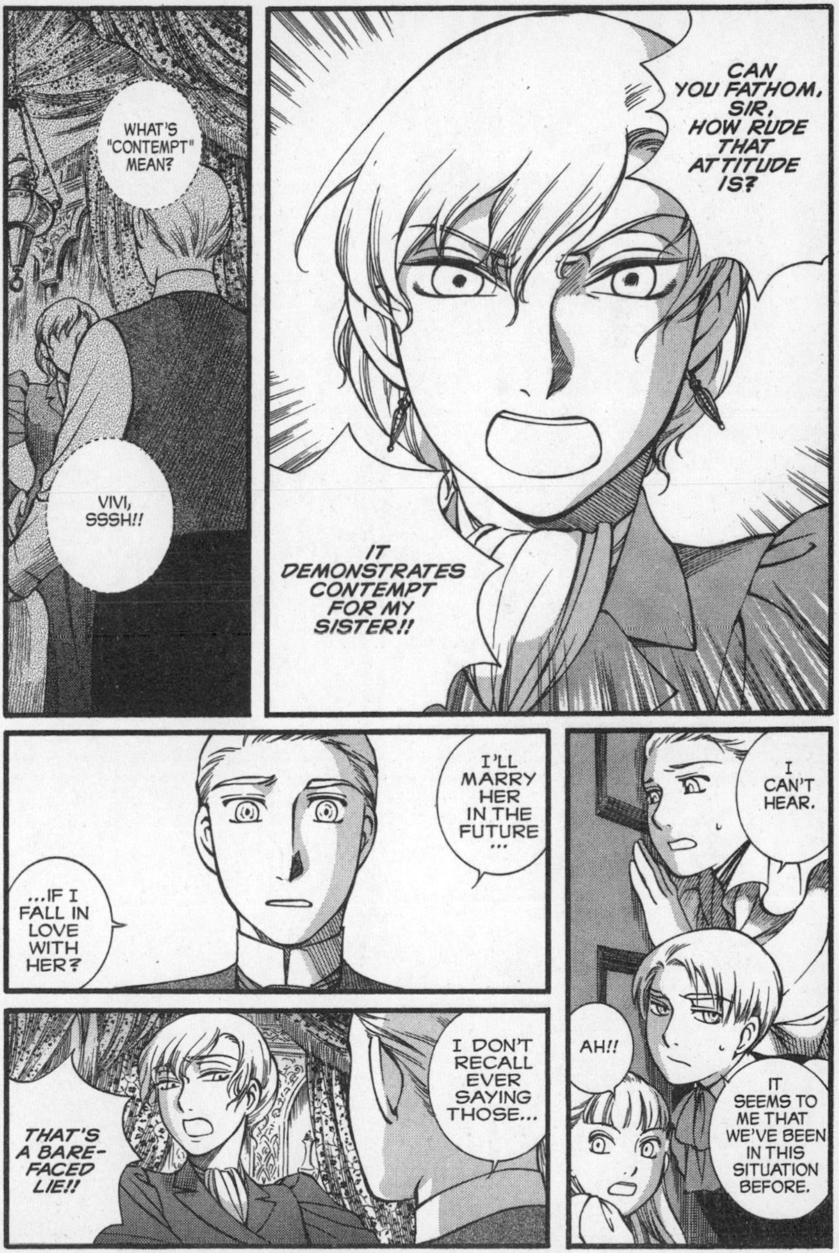
CAN YOU FATHOM, SIR, HOW RUDE THAT ATTITUDE IS?
IT DEMONSTRATES CONTEMPT FOR MY SISTER!!
WHAT'S "CONTEMPT" MEAN?
VIVI, SSSH!!
I CAN'T HEAR.
AH!!
IT SEEMS TO ME THAT WE'VE BEEN IN THIS SITUATION BEFORE.
I'LL MARRY HER IN THE FUTURE...
...IF I FALL IN LOVE WITH HER?
I DON'T RECALL EVER SAYING THOSE...
THAT'S A BARE-FACED LIE!!

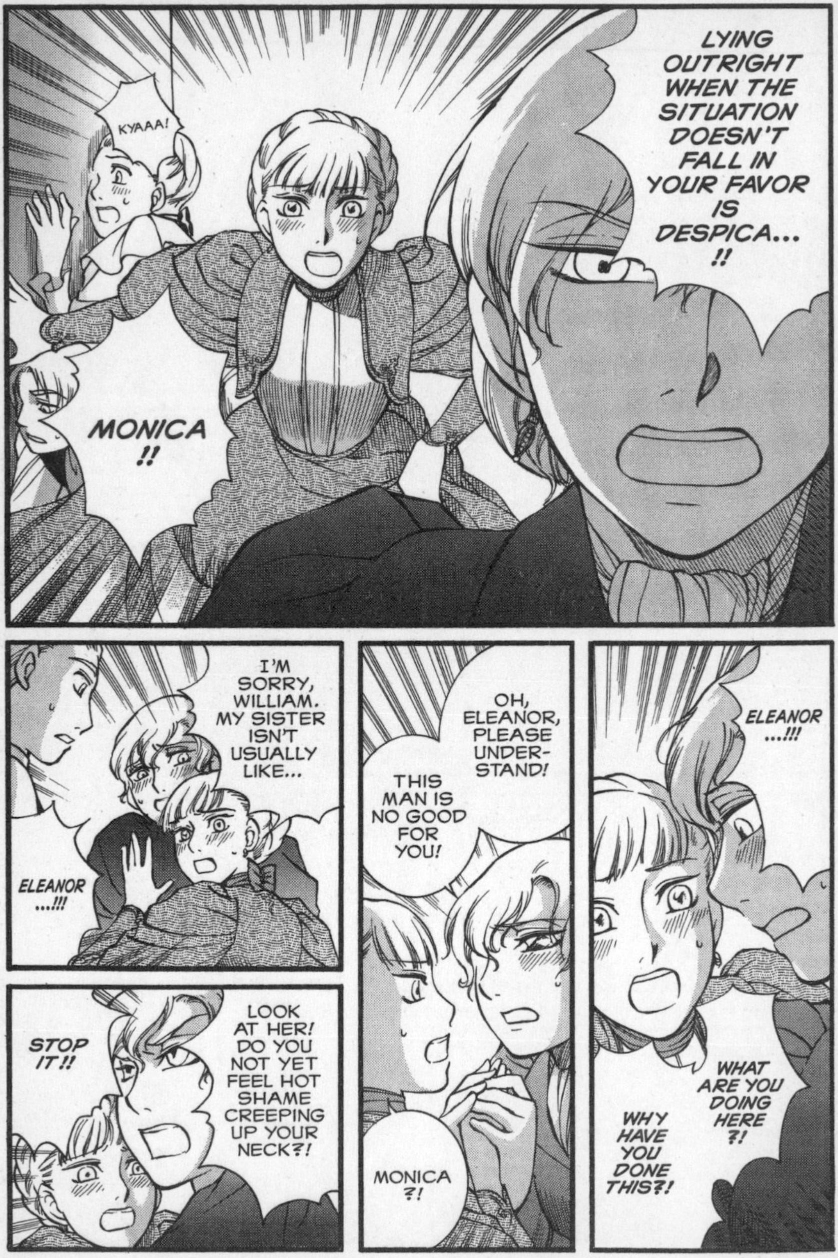

LYING OUTRIGHT WHEN THE SITUATION DOESN'T FALL IN YOUR FAVOR IS DESPICA...!!
KYAAA!
MONICA!!
ELEANOR...!!!
WHAT ARE YOU DOING HERE?!
WHY HAVE YOU DONE THIS?!
OH, ELEANOR, PLEASE UNDER-STAND!
THIS MAN IS NO GOOD FOR YOU!
MONICA?!
I'M SORRY, WILLIAM. MY SISTER ISN'T USUALLY LIKE...
ELEANOR...!!!
LOOK AT HER! DO YOU NOT YET FEEL HOT SHAME CREEPING UP YOUR NECK?!
STOP IT!!

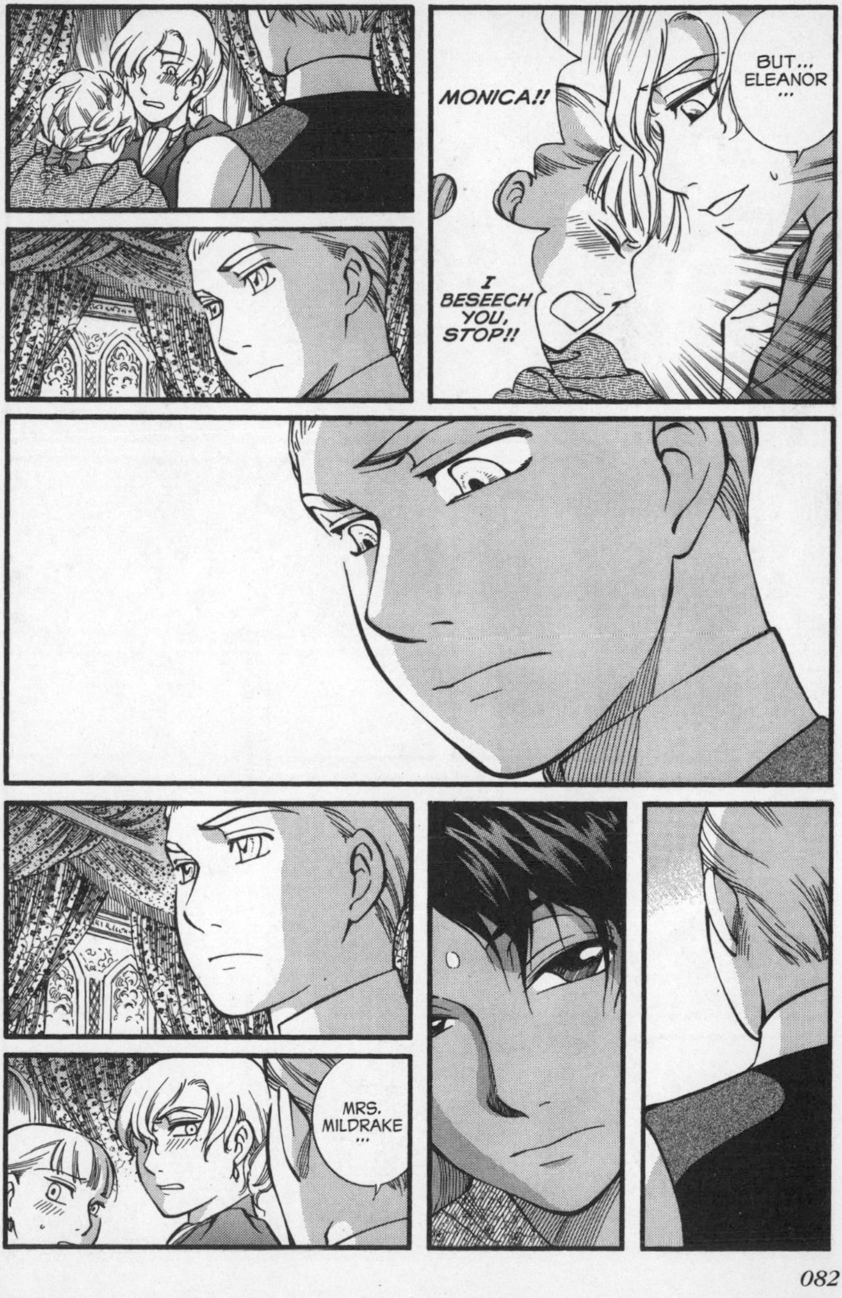
BUT... ELEANOR ...
MONICA!!
I BESEECH YOU, STOP!!
MRS. MILDRAKE ...

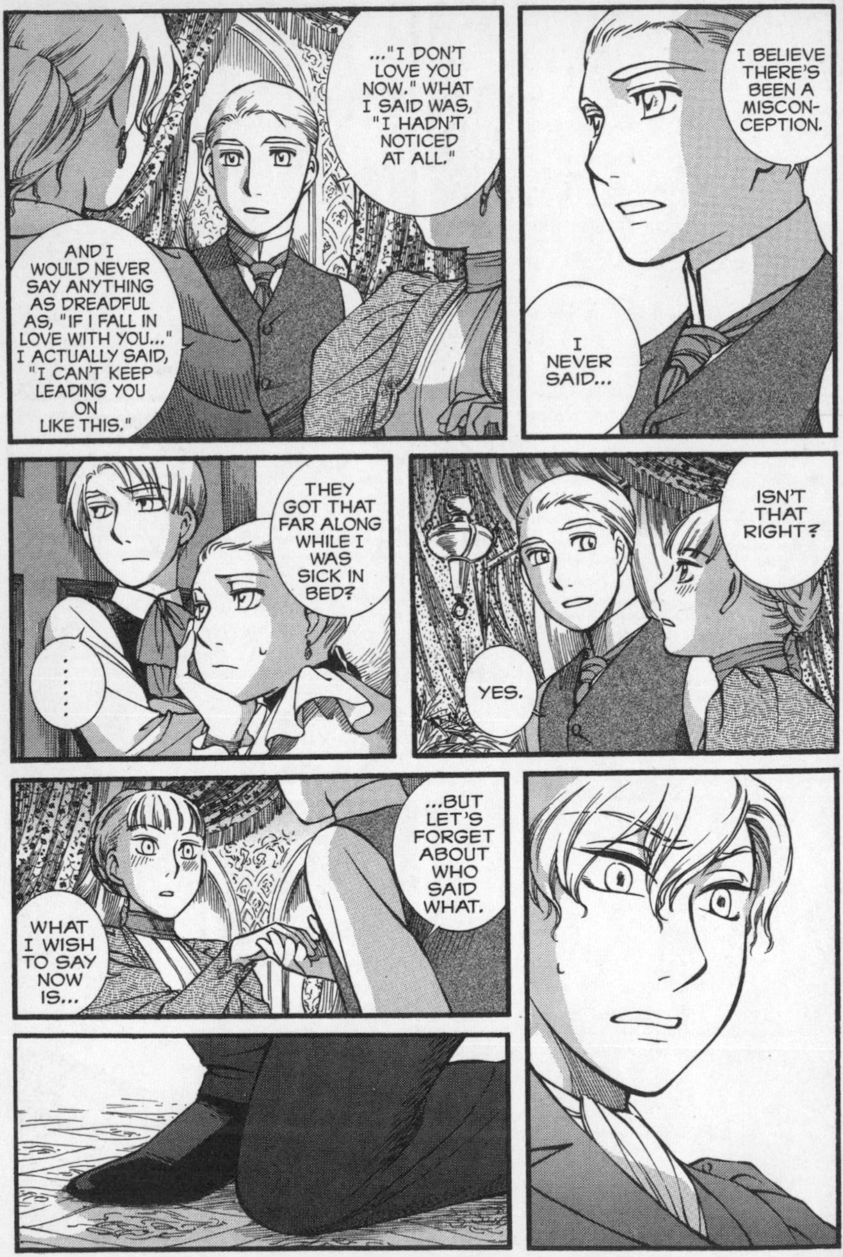
I BELIEVE THERE'S BEEN A MISCONCEPTION.
I NEVER SAID...
..."I DON'T LOVE YOU NOW." WHAT I SAID WAS, "I HADN'T NOTICED AT ALL."
AND I WOULD NEVER SAY ANYTHING AS DREADFUL AS, "IF I FALL IN LOVE WITH YOU..." I ACTUALLY SAID, "I CAN'T KEEP LEADING YOU ON LIKE THIS."
ISN'T THAT RIGHT?
YES.
THEY GOT THAT FAR ALONG WHILE I WAS SICK IN BED?
......
...BUT LET'S FORGET ABOUT WHO SAID WHAT.
WHAT I WISH TO SAY NOW IS...

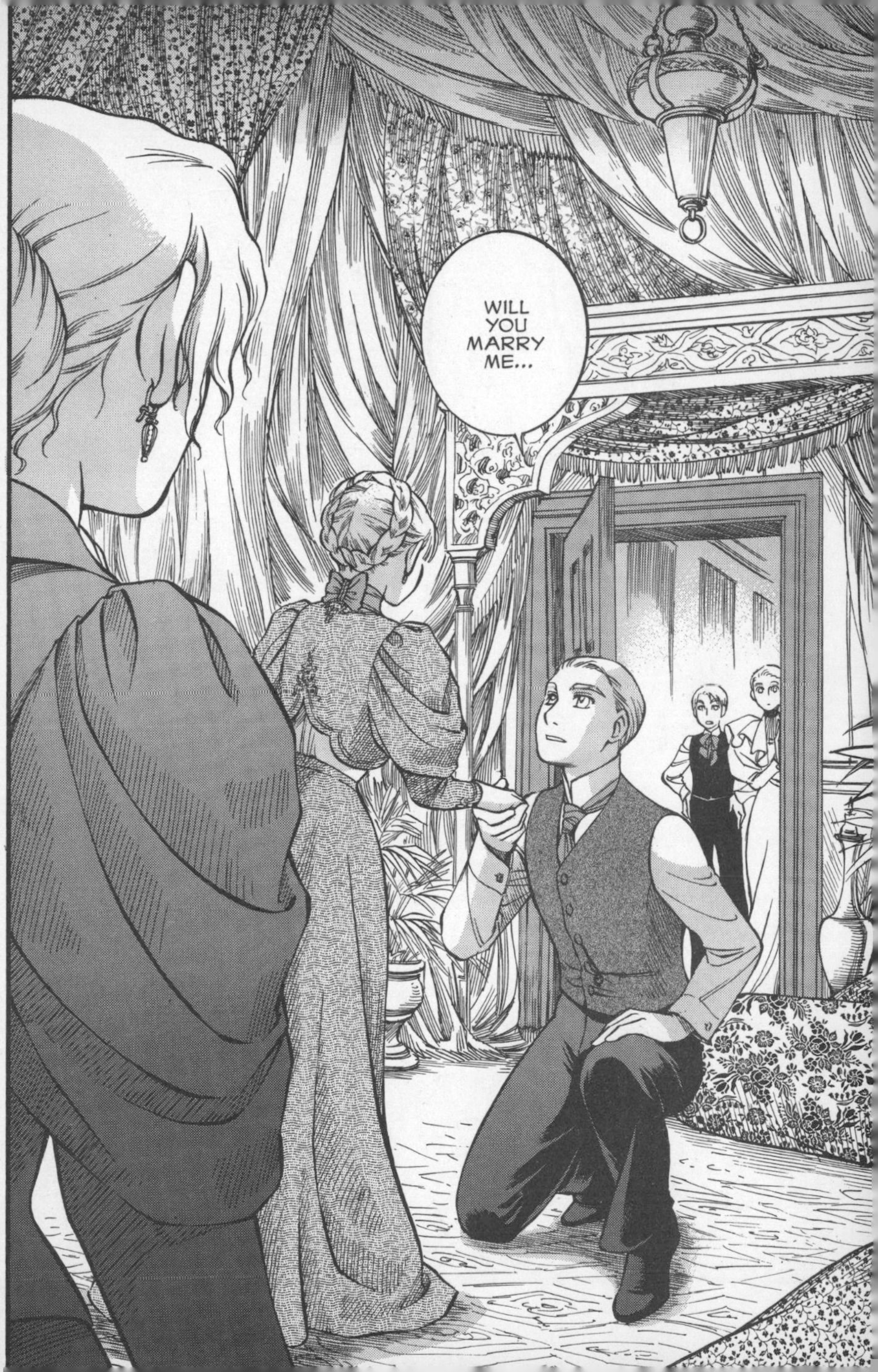
WILL YOU MARRY ME...

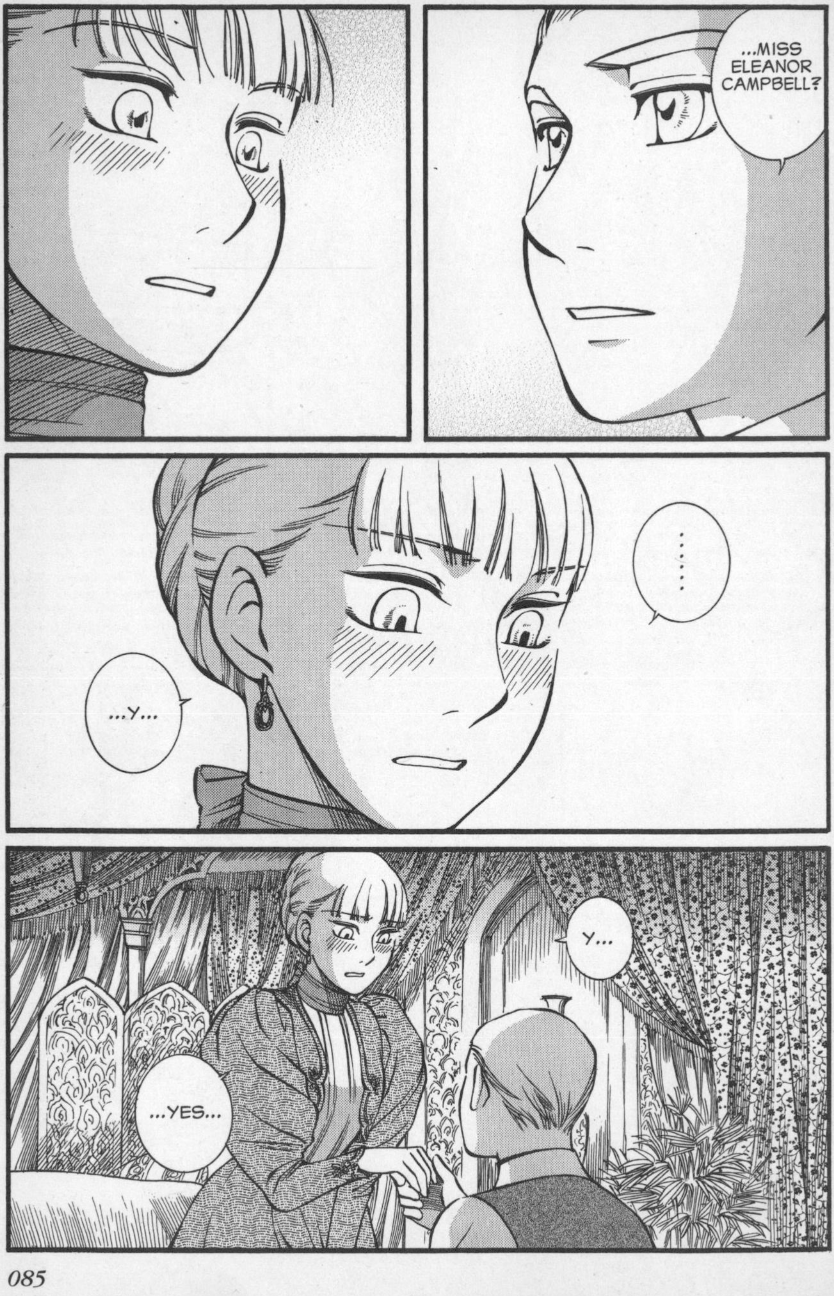
...MISS ELEANOR CAMPBELL?
......
...Y...
Y...
...YES...

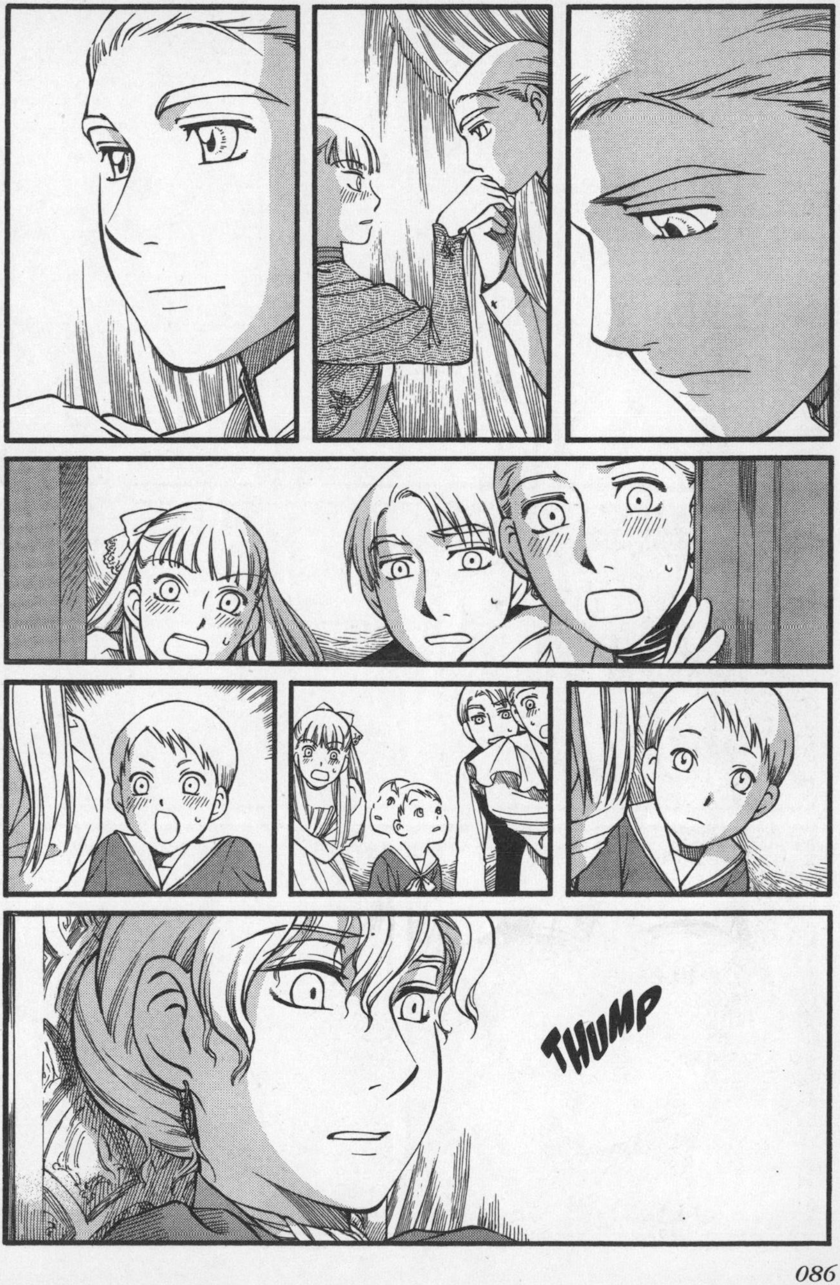
THUMP

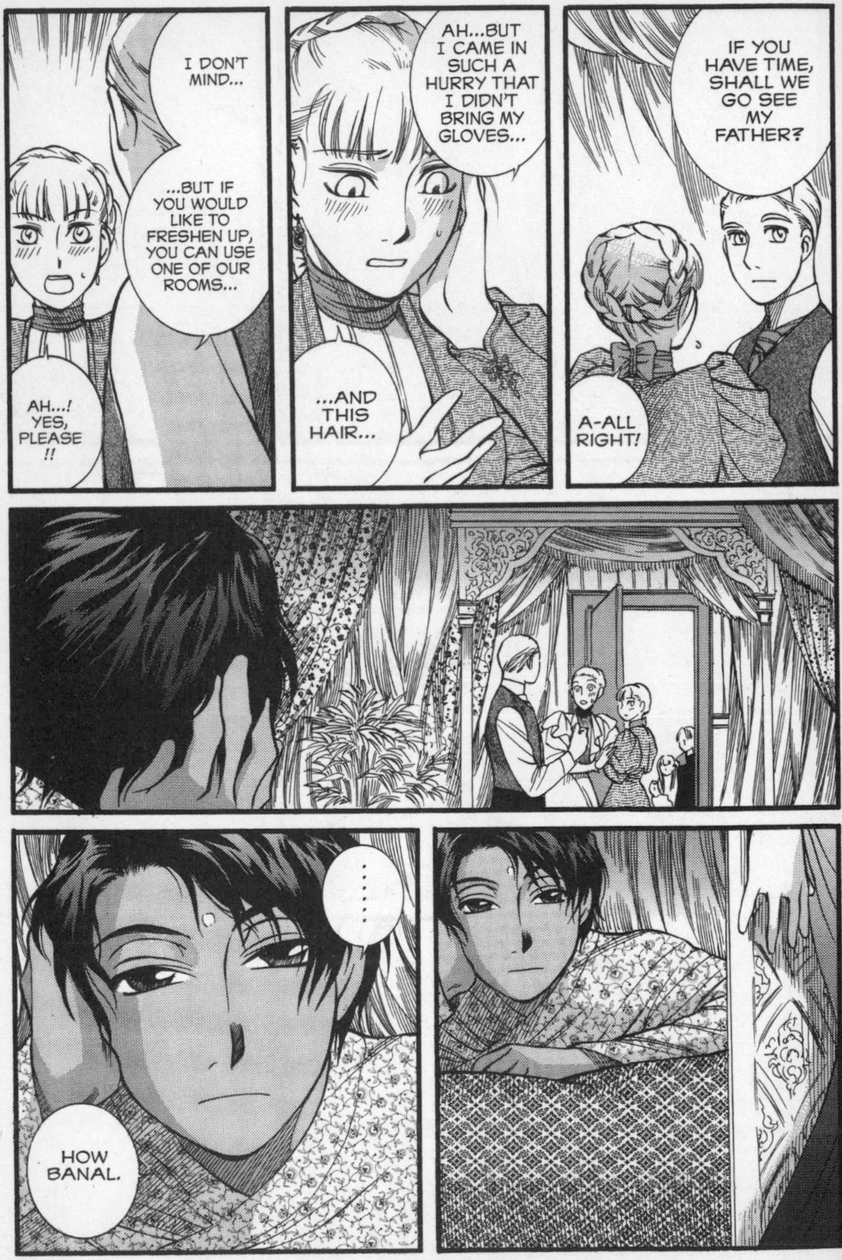
IF YOU HAVE TIME, SHALL WE GO SEE MY FATHER?
A-ALL RIGHT!
AH...BUT I CAME IN SUCH A HURRY THAT I DIDN'T BRING MY GLOVES...
...AND THIS HAIR...
I DON'T MIND...
...BUT IF YOU WOULD LIKE TO FRESHEN UP, YOU CAN USE ONE OF OUR ROOMS...
AH...! YES, PLEASE !!
......
HOW BANAL.

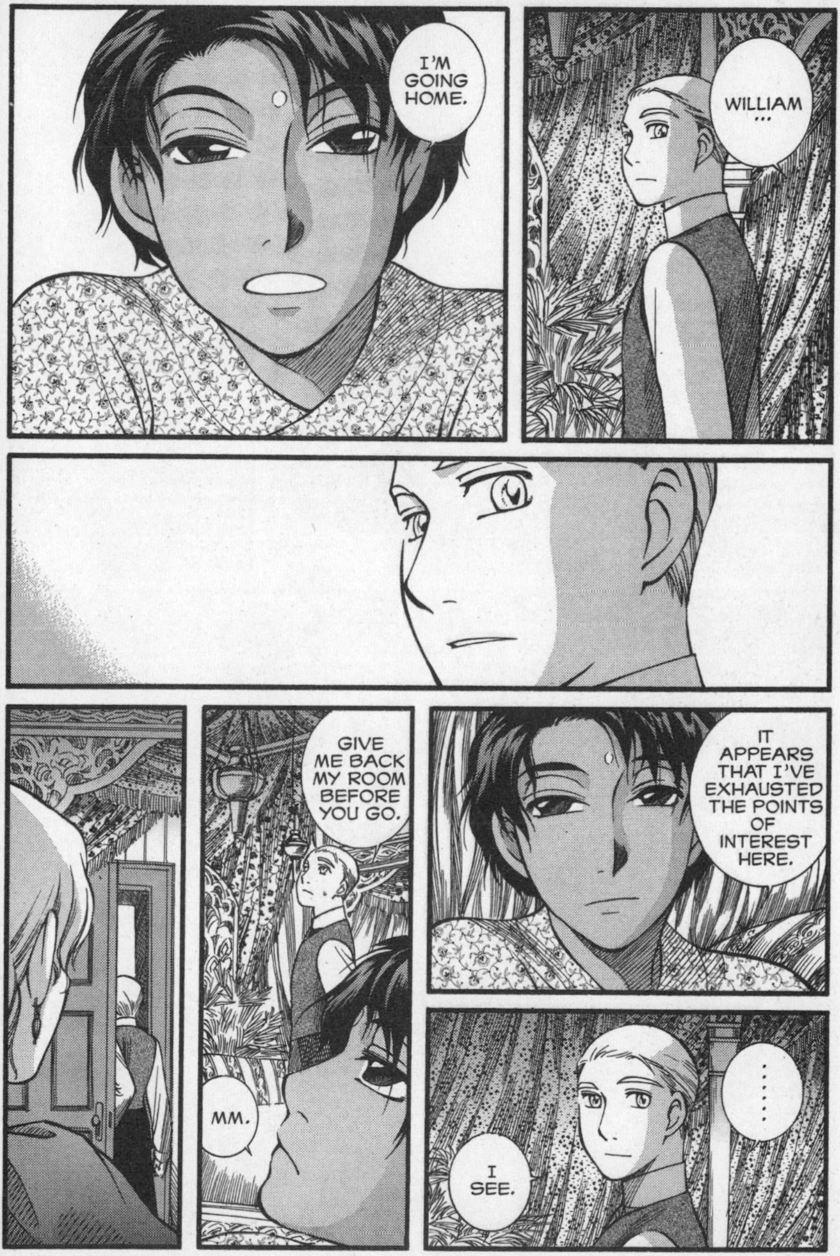
WILLIAM ...
I'M GOING HOME.
IT APPEARS THAT I'VE EXHAUSTED THE POINTS OF INTEREST HERE.
......
I SEE.
GIVE ME BACK MY ROOM BEFORE YOU GO.
MM.

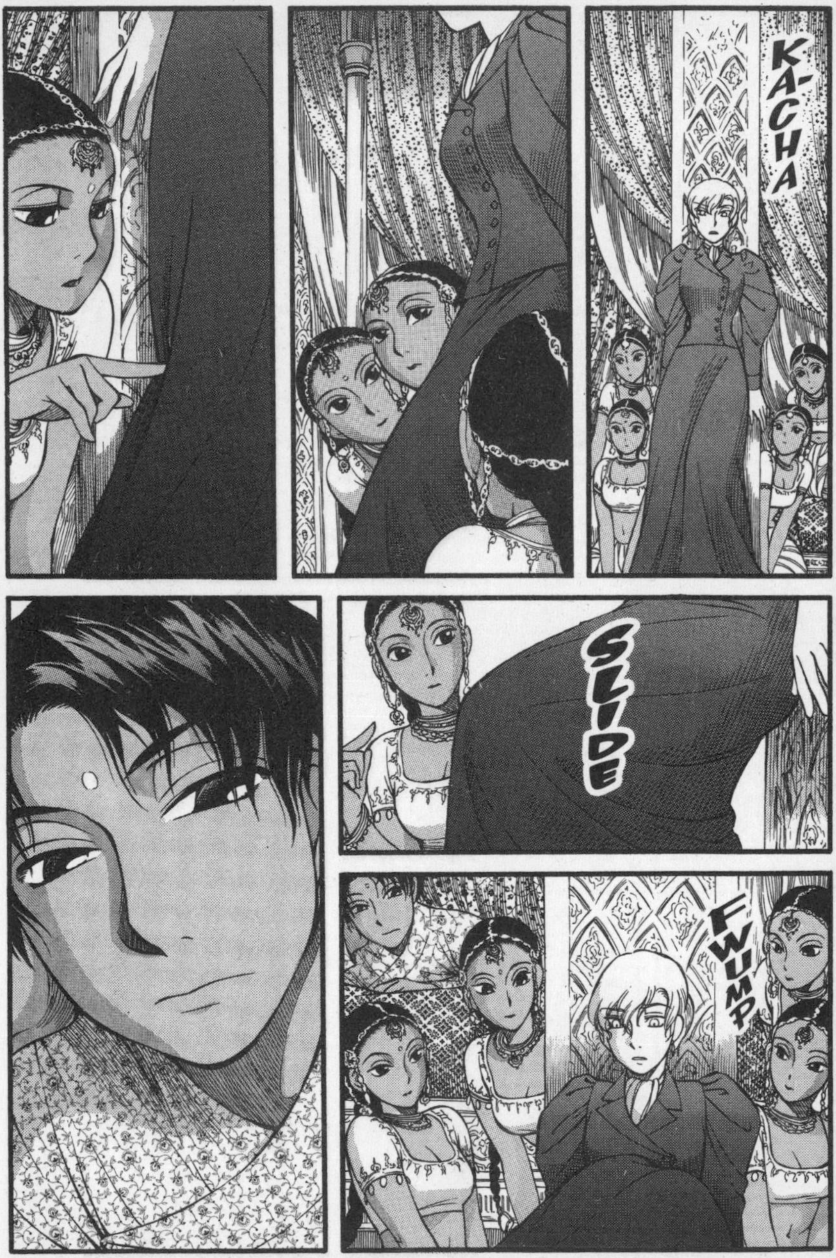
KA-CHA
SLIDE
FWUMP

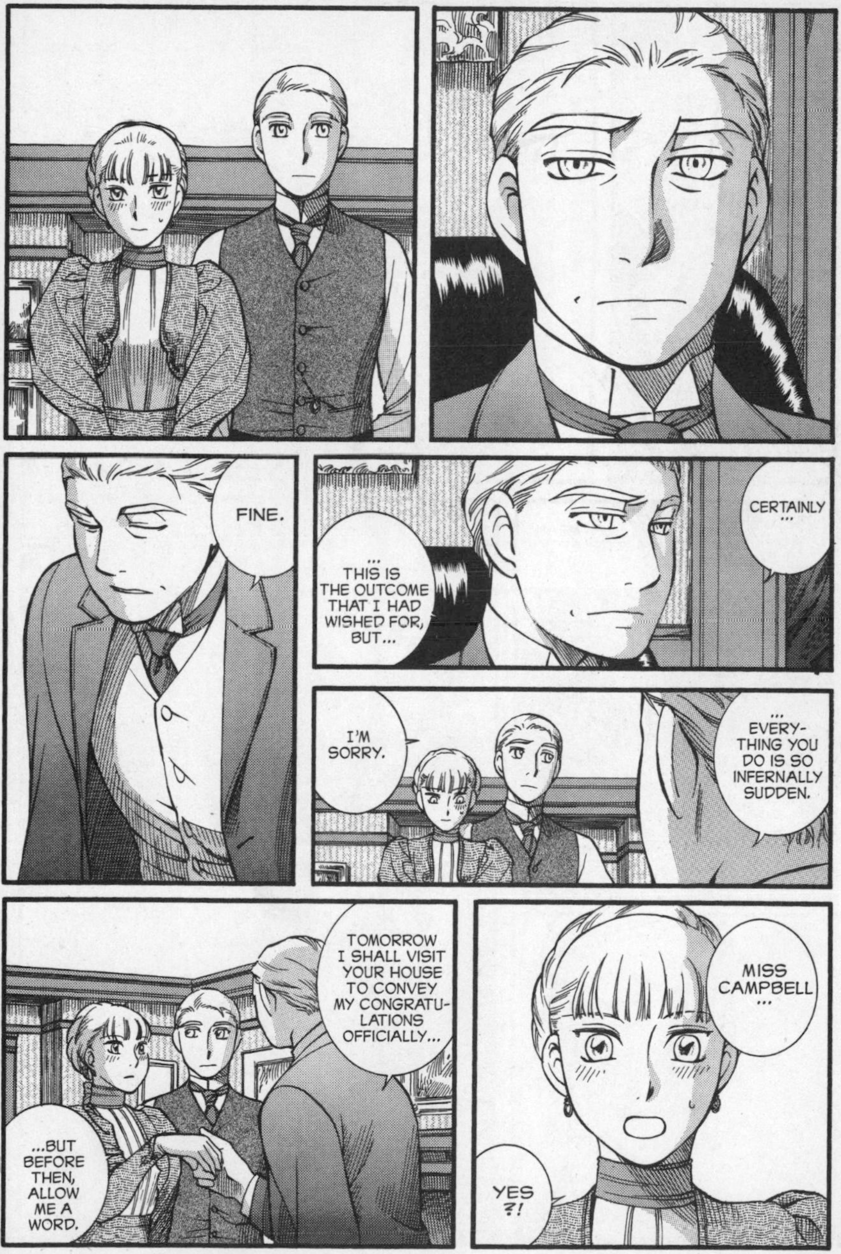
CERTAINLY...
...THIS IS THE OUTCOME THAT I HAD WISHED FOR, BUT...
...EVERYTHING YOU DO IS SO INFERNALLY SUDDEN.
I'M SORRY.
FINE.
MISS CAMPBELL...
YES?!
TOMORROW I SHALL VISIT YOUR HOUSE TO CONVEY MY CONGRATULATIONS OFFICIALLY...
...BUT BEFORE THEN, ALLOW ME A WORD.

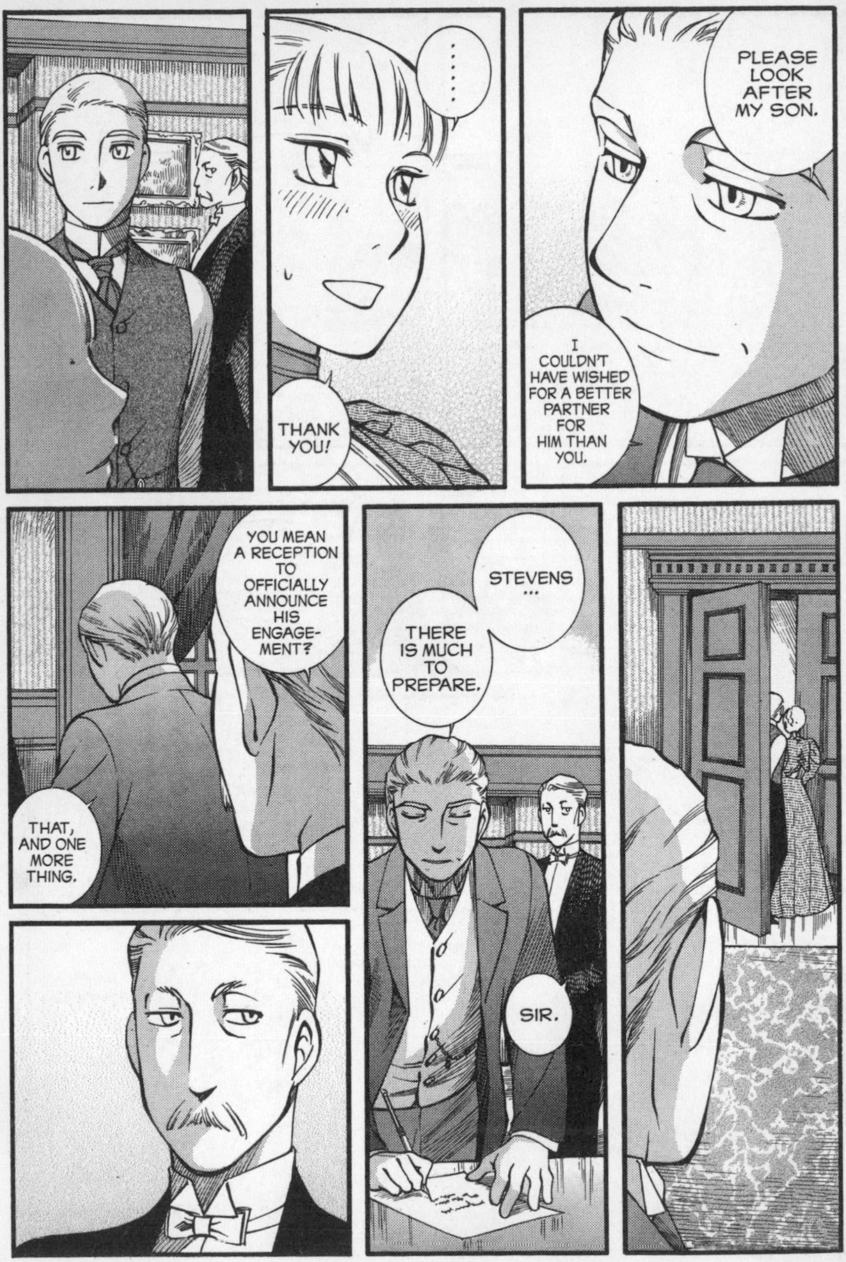
PLEASE LOOK AFTER MY SON.
I COULDN'T HAVE WISHED FOR A BETTER PARTNER FOR HIM THAN YOU.
......
THANK YOU!
STEVENS ...
THERE IS MUCH TO PREPARE.
SIR.
YOU MEAN A RECEPTION TO OFFICIALLY ANNOUNCE HIS ENGAGEMENT?
THAT, AND ONE MORE THING.

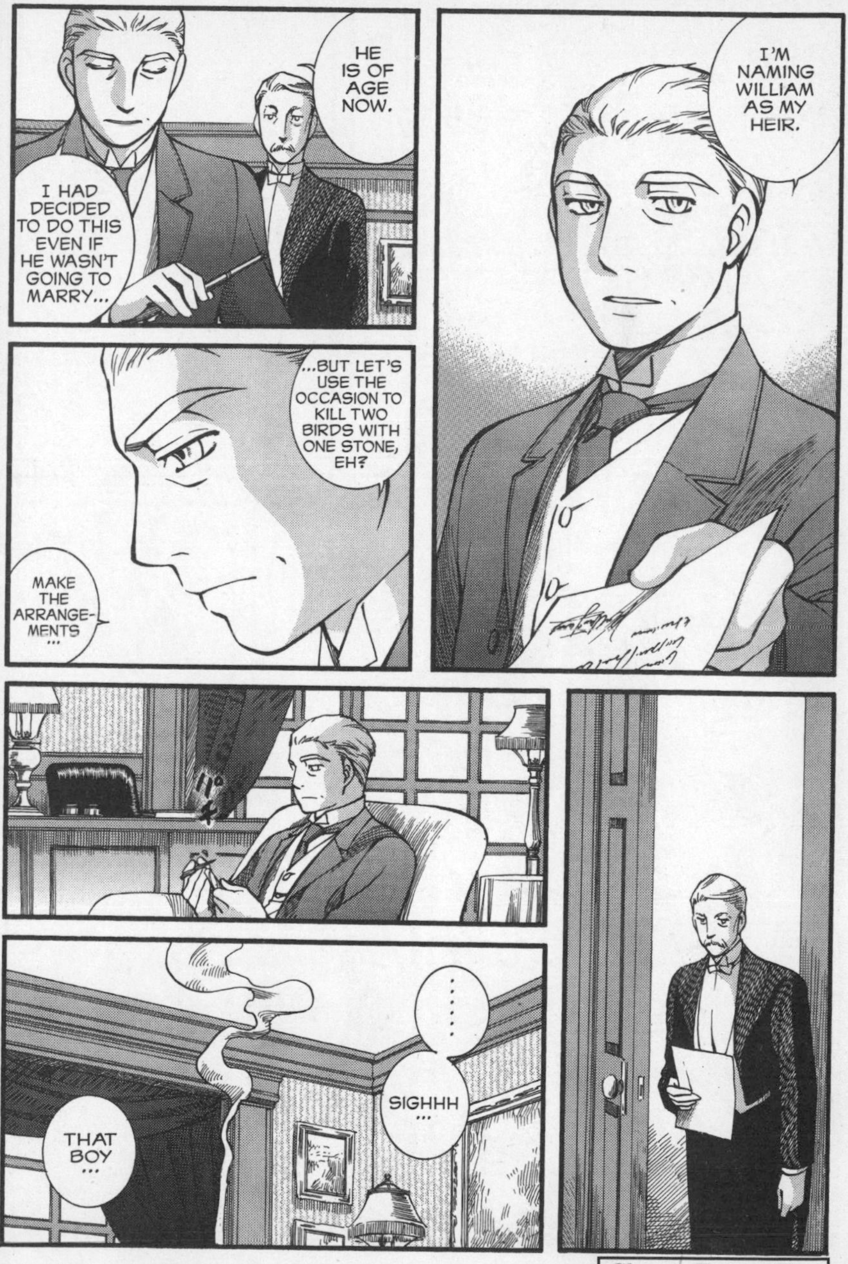
I'M NAMING WILLIAM AS MY HEIR.
HE IS OF AGE NOW.
I HAD DECIDED TO DO THIS EVEN IF HE WASN'T GOING TO MARRY...
...BUT LET'S USE THE OCCASION TO KILL TWO BIRDS WITH ONE STONE, EH?
MAKE THE ARRANGE-MENTS...
......
SIGHHH...
THAT BOY...

Chapter Twenty Five:
The End

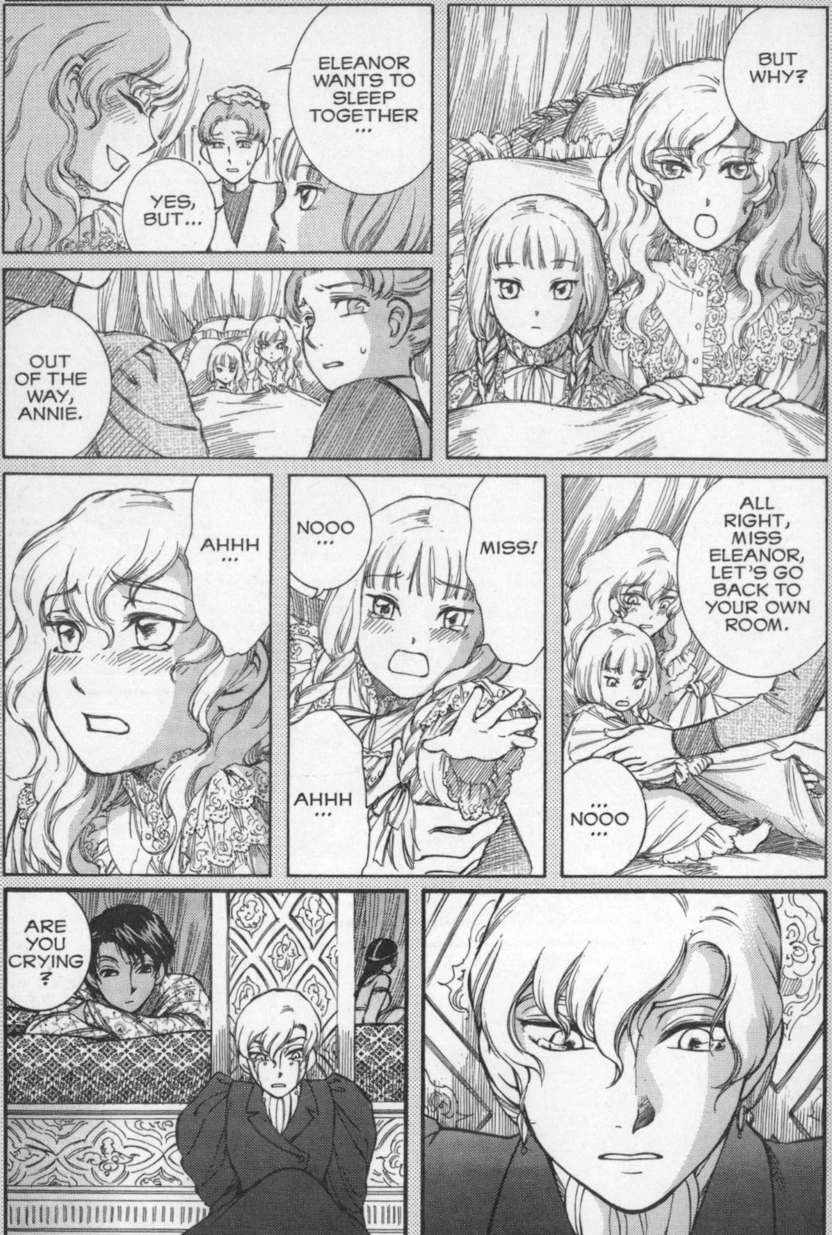
BUT WHY?
ELEANOR WANTS TO SLEEP TOGETHER...
YES, BUT...
OUT OF THE WAY, ANNIE.
ALL RIGHT, MISS ELEANOR, LET'S GO BACK TO YOUR OWN ROOM.
...NOOO...
MISS!
NOOO...
AHHH...
AHHH...
ARE YOU CRYING?

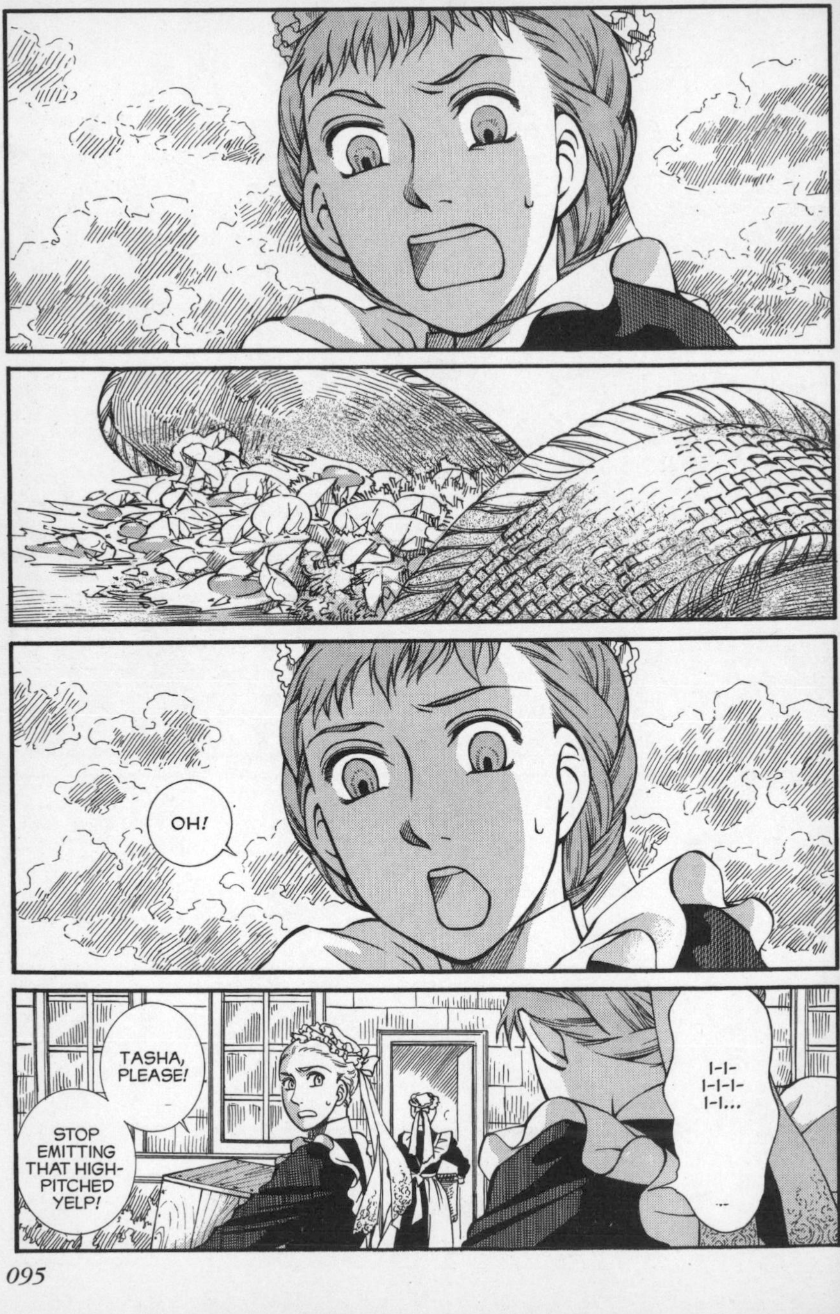
OH!
I-I- I-I-I- I-I...
TASHA, PLEASE!
STOP EMITTING THAT HIGH-PITCHED YELP!

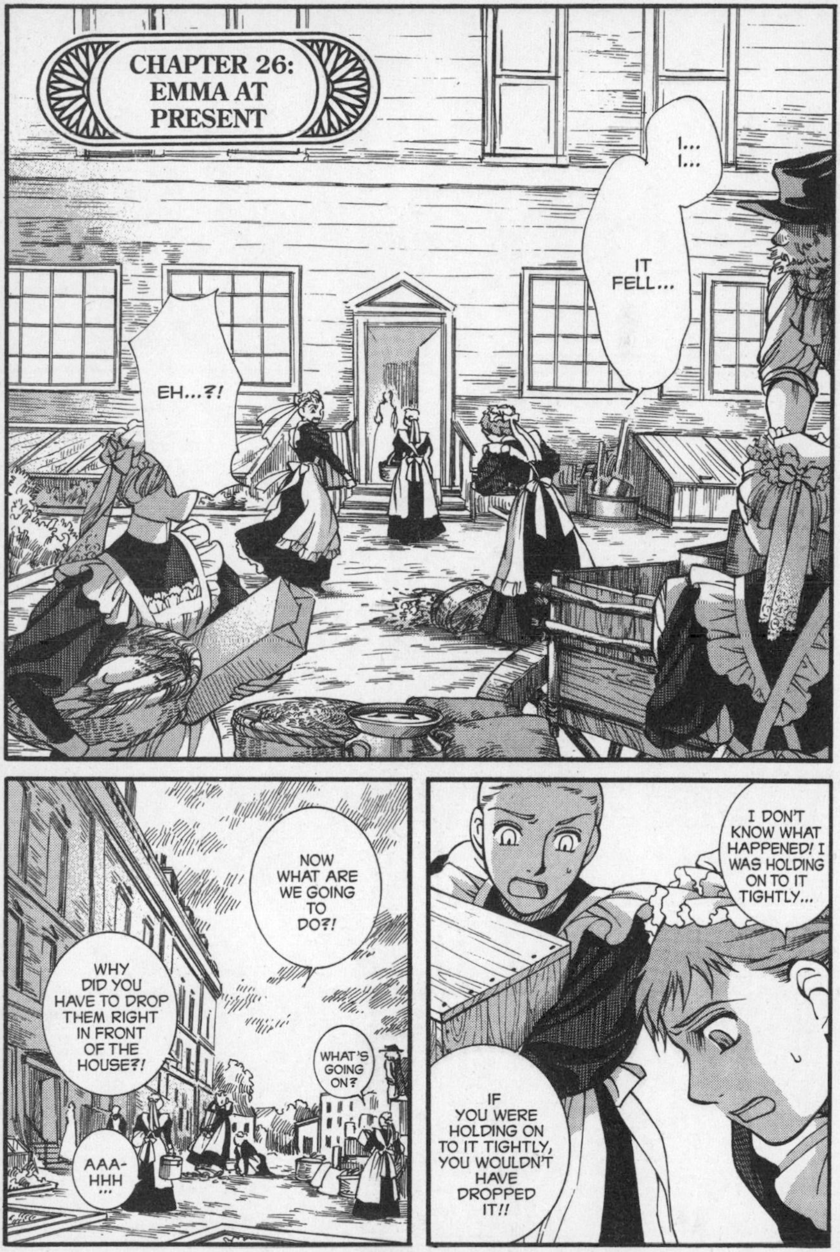
CHAPTER 26: EMMA AT PRESENT
I... I... IT FELL...
EH...?!
I DON'T KNOW WHAT HAPPENED! I WAS HOLDING ON TO IT TIGHTLY...
IF YOU WERE HOLDING ON TO IT TIGHTLY, YOU WOULDN'T HAVE DROPPED IT!!
NOW WHAT ARE WE GOING TO DO?!
WHY DID YOU HAVE TO DROP THEM RIGHT IN FRONT OF THE HOUSE?!
WHAT'S GOING ON?
AAA-HHH...

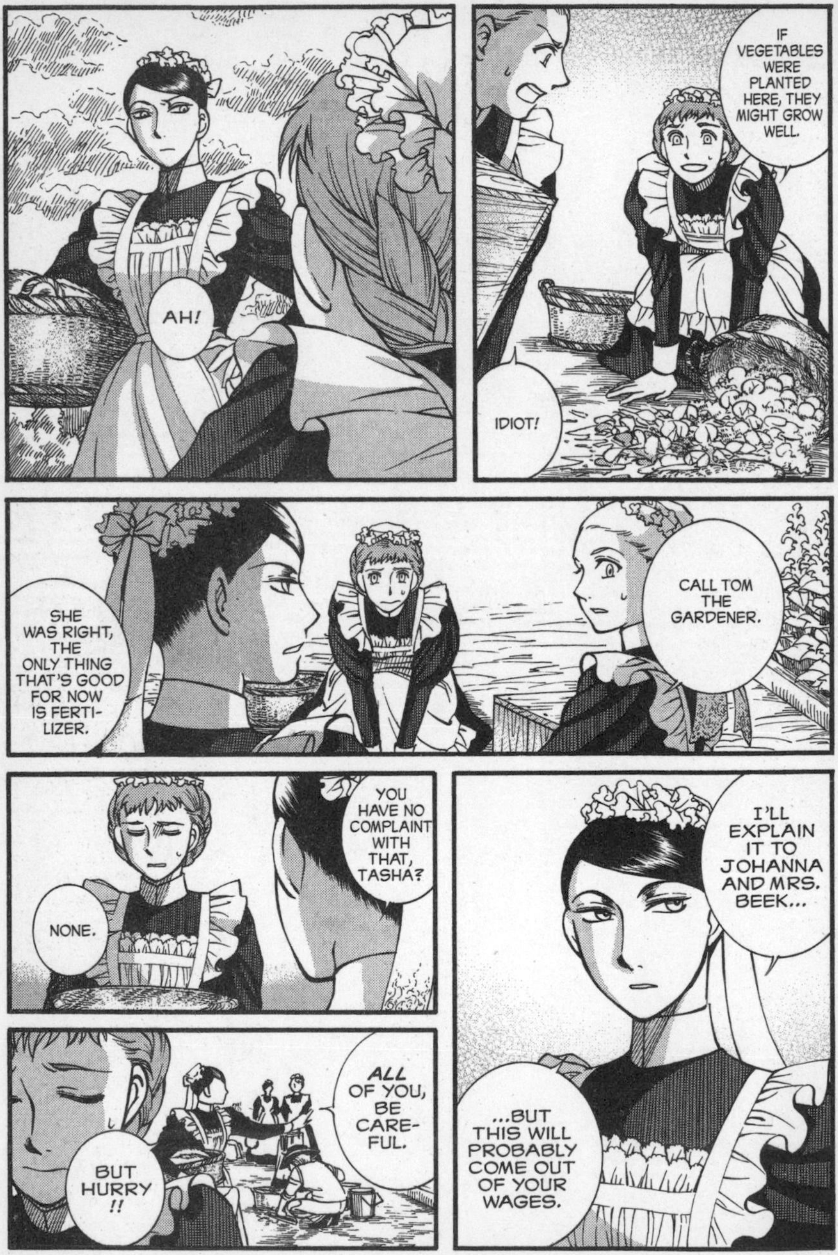
IF VEGETABLES WERE PLANTED HERE, THEY MIGHT GROW WELL.
IDIOT!
AH!
CALL TOM THE GARDENER.
SHE WAS RIGHT, THE ONLY THING THAT'S GOOD FOR NOW IS FERTILIZER.
I'LL EXPLAIN IT TO JOHANNA AND MRS. BEEK...
...BUT THIS WILL PROBABLY COME OUT OF YOUR WAGES.
YOU HAVE NO COMPLAINT WITH THAT, TASHA?
NONE.
ALL OF YOU, BE CAREFUL.
BUT HURRY !!

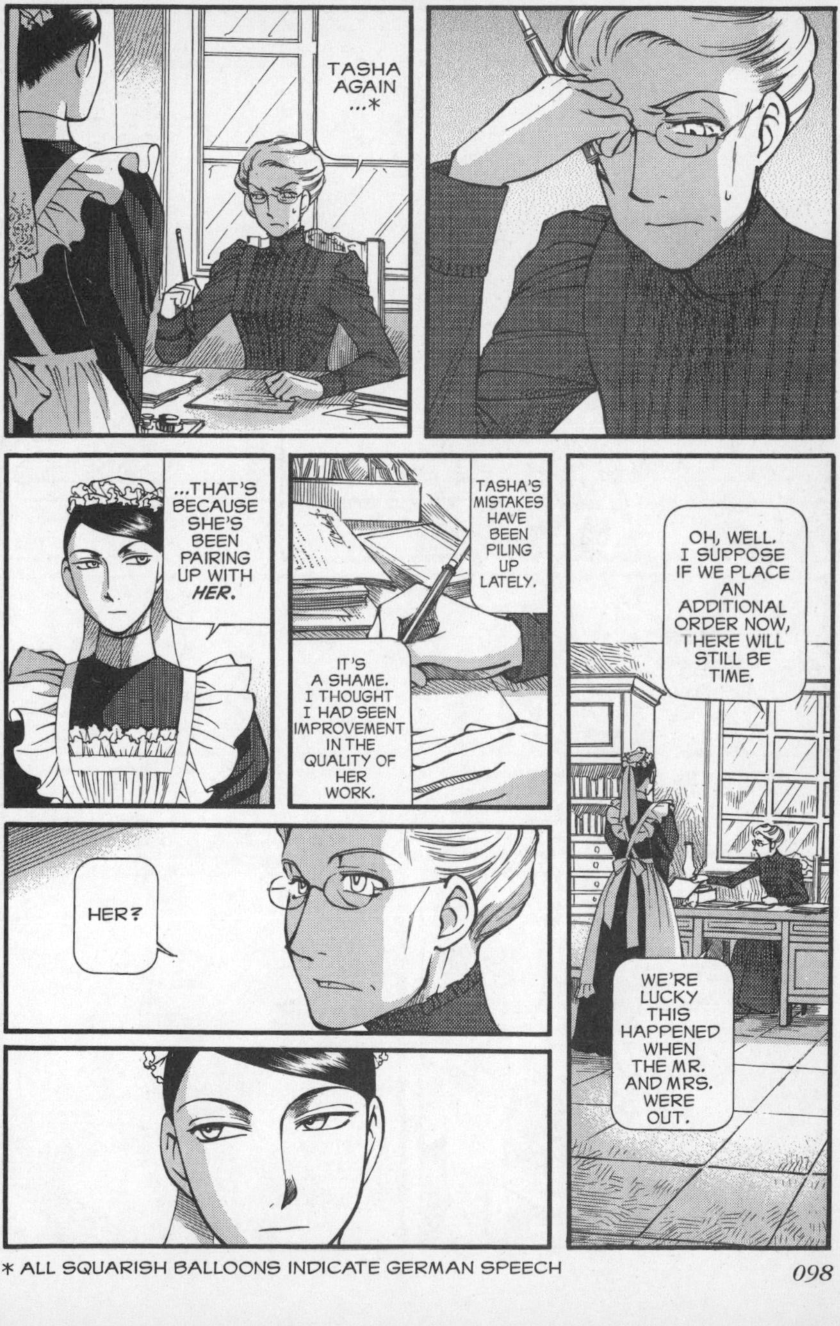
TASHA AGAIN ...*
OH, WELL. I SUPPOSE IF WE PLACE AN ADDITIONAL ORDER NOW, THERE WILL STILL BE TIME.
WE'RE LUCKY THIS HAPPENED WHEN THE MR. AND MRS. WERE OUT.
TASHA'S MISTAKES HAVE BEEN PILING UP LATELY.
IT'S A SHAME. I THOUGHT I HAD SEEN IMPROVEMENT IN THE QUALITY OF HER WORK.
...THAT'S BECAUSE SHE'S BEEN PAIRING UP WITH ***HER***.
HER?

* ALL SQUARISH BALLOONS INDICATE GERMAN SPEECH

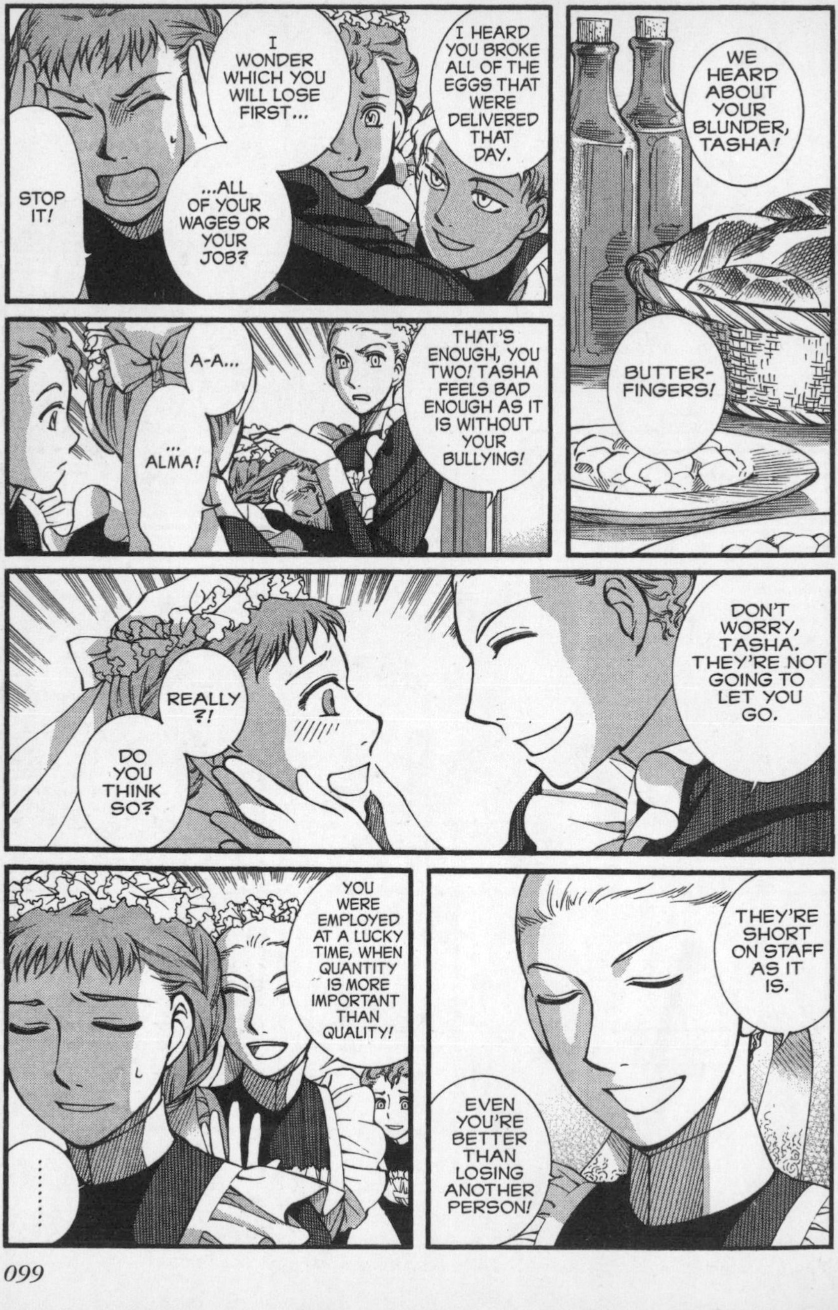
WE HEARD ABOUT YOUR BLUNDER, TASHA!
BUTTER-FINGERS!
I HEARD YOU BROKE ALL OF THE EGGS THAT WERE DELIVERED THAT DAY.
I WONDER WHICH YOU WILL LOSE FIRST...
...ALL OF YOUR WAGES OR YOUR JOB?
STOP IT!
THAT'S ENOUGH, YOU TWO! TASHA FEELS BAD ENOUGH AS IT IS WITHOUT YOUR BULLYING!
A-A...
...ALMA!
DON'T WORRY, TASHA. THEY'RE NOT GOING TO LET YOU GO.
REALLY?!
DO YOU THINK SO?
THEY'RE SHORT ON STAFF AS IT IS.
EVEN YOU'RE BETTER THAN LOSING ANOTHER PERSON!
YOU WERE EMPLOYED AT A LUCKY TIME, WHEN QUANTITY IS MORE IMPORTANT THAN QUALITY!
......

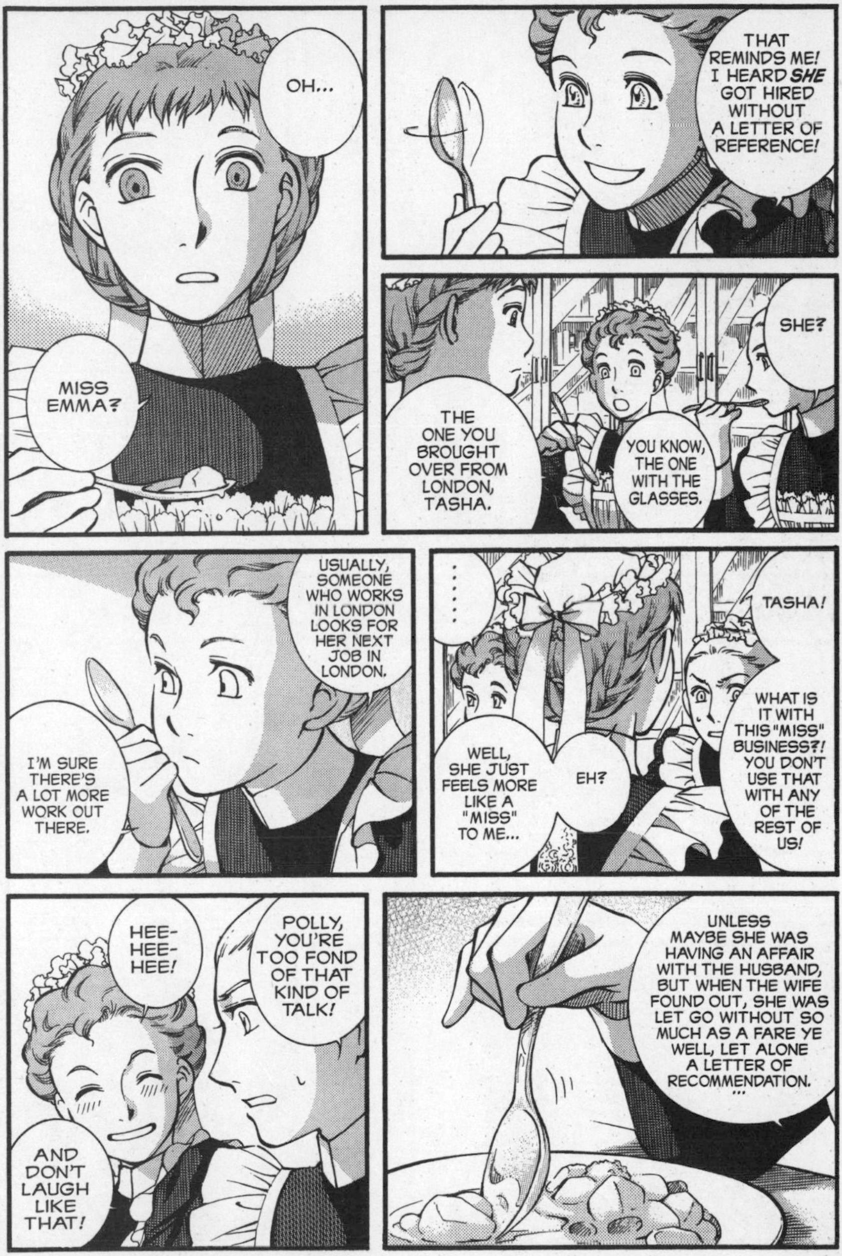
THAT REMINDS ME! I HEARD *SHE* GOT HIRED WITHOUT A LETTER OF REFERENCE!
SHE?
THE ONE YOU BROUGHT OVER FROM LONDON, TASHA.
YOU KNOW, THE ONE WITH THE GLASSES.
OH...
MISS EMMA?
TASHA!
WHAT IS IT WITH THIS "MISS" BUSINESS?! YOU DON'T USE THAT WITH ANY OF THE REST OF US!
EH?
WELL, SHE JUST FEELS MORE LIKE A "MISS" TO ME...
......
USUALLY, SOMEONE WHO WORKS IN LONDON LOOKS FOR HER NEXT JOB IN LONDON.
I'M SURE THERE'S A LOT MORE WORK OUT THERE.
UNLESS MAYBE SHE WAS HAVING AN AFFAIR WITH THE HUSBAND, BUT WHEN THE WIFE FOUND OUT, SHE WAS LET GO WITHOUT SO MUCH AS A FARE YE WELL, LET ALONE A LETTER OF RECOMMENDATION...
POLLY, YOU'RE TOO FOND OF THAT KIND OF TALK!
HEE-HEE-HEE!
AND DON'T LAUGH LIKE THAT!

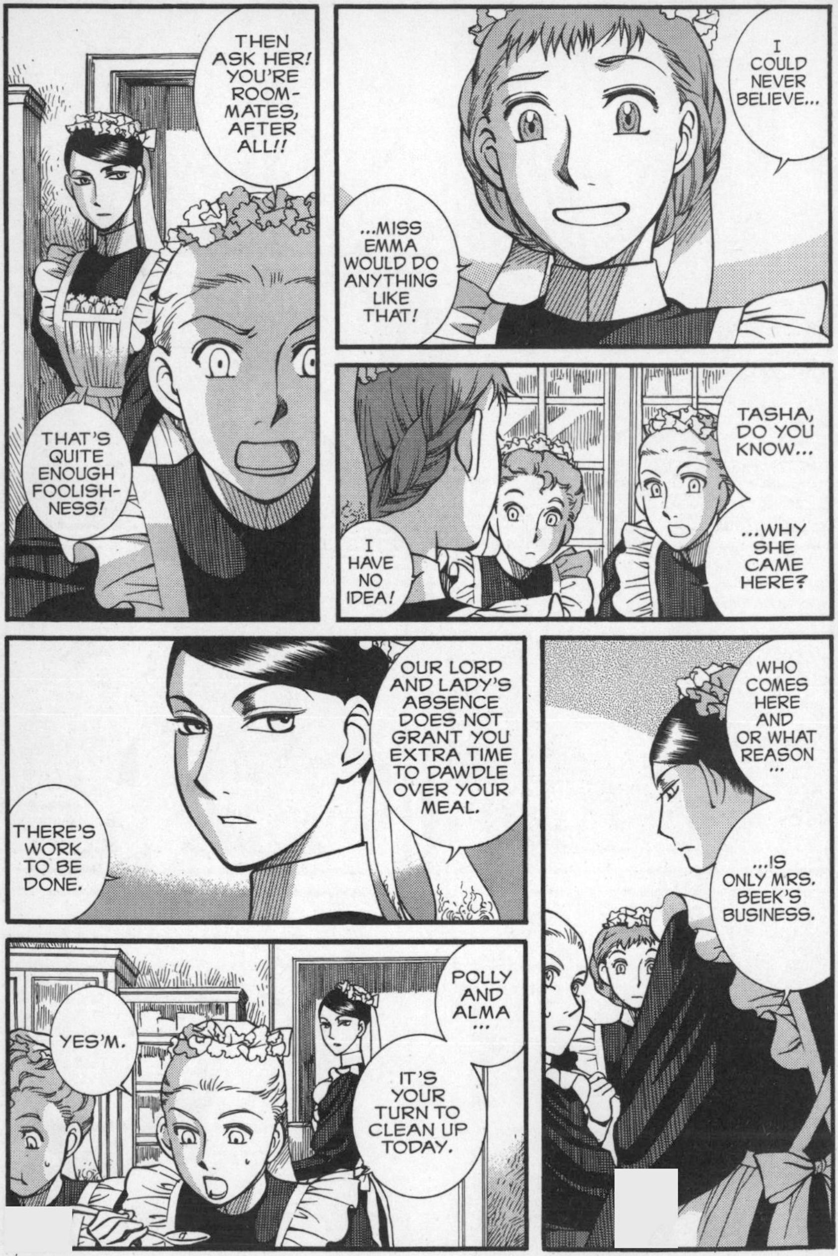
I COULD NEVER BELIEVE...
...MISS EMMA WOULD DO ANYTHING LIKE THAT!
TASHA, DO YOU KNOW...
...WHY SHE CAME HERE?
I HAVE NO IDEA!
THEN ASK HER! YOU'RE ROOM-MATES, AFTER ALL!!
THAT'S QUITE ENOUGH FOOLISH-NESS!
WHO COMES HERE AND OR WHAT REASON ...
...IS ONLY MRS. BEEK'S BUSINESS.
OUR LORD AND LADY'S ABSENCE DOES NOT GRANT YOU EXTRA TIME TO DAWDLE OVER YOUR MEAL.
THERE'S WORK TO BE DONE.
POLLY AND ALMA ...
IT'S YOUR TURN TO CLEAN UP TODAY.
YES'M.

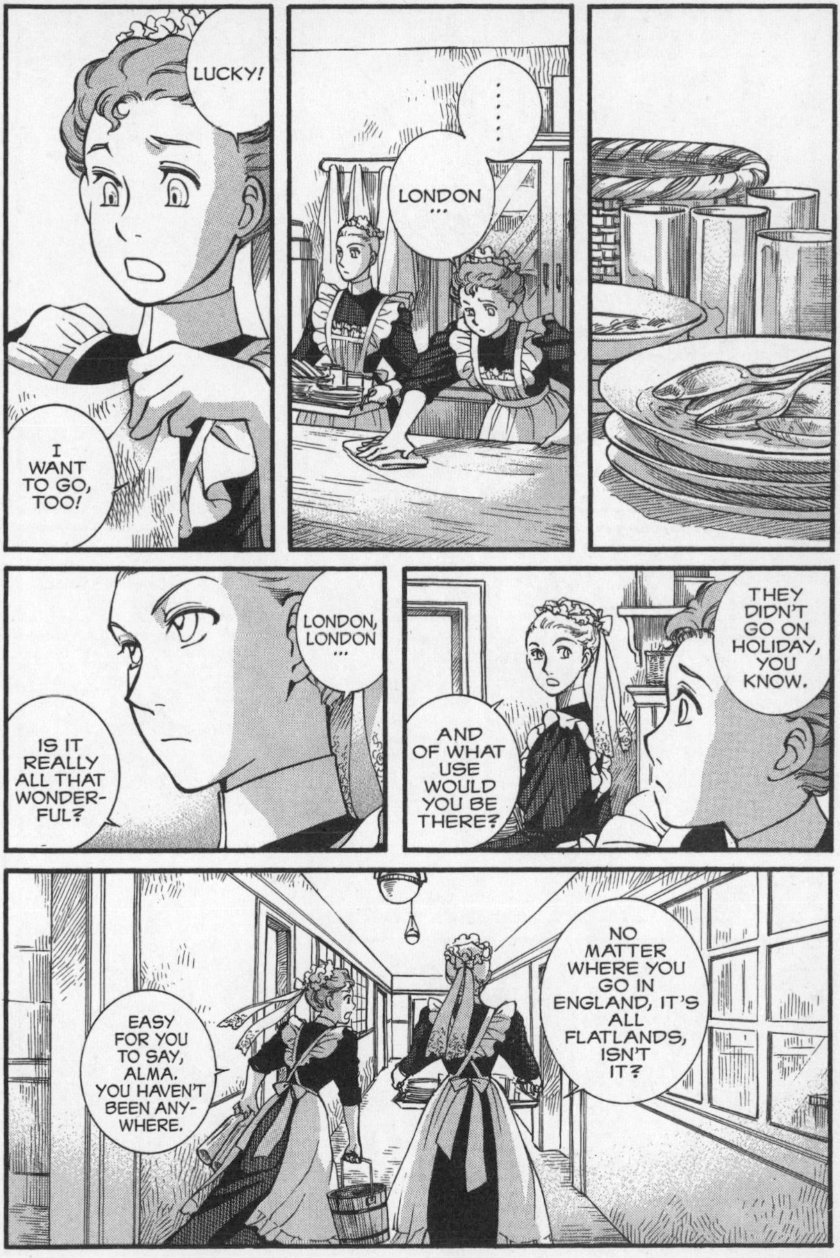
......
LONDON...
LUCKY!
I WANT TO GO, TOO!
THEY DIDN'T GO ON HOLIDAY, YOU KNOW.
AND OF WHAT USE WOULD YOU BE THERE?
LONDON, LONDON...
IS IT REALLY ALL THAT WONDERFUL?
NO MATTER WHERE YOU GO IN ENGLAND, IT'S ALL FLATLANDS, ISN'T IT?
EASY FOR YOU TO SAY, ALMA. YOU HAVEN'T BEEN ANYWHERE.

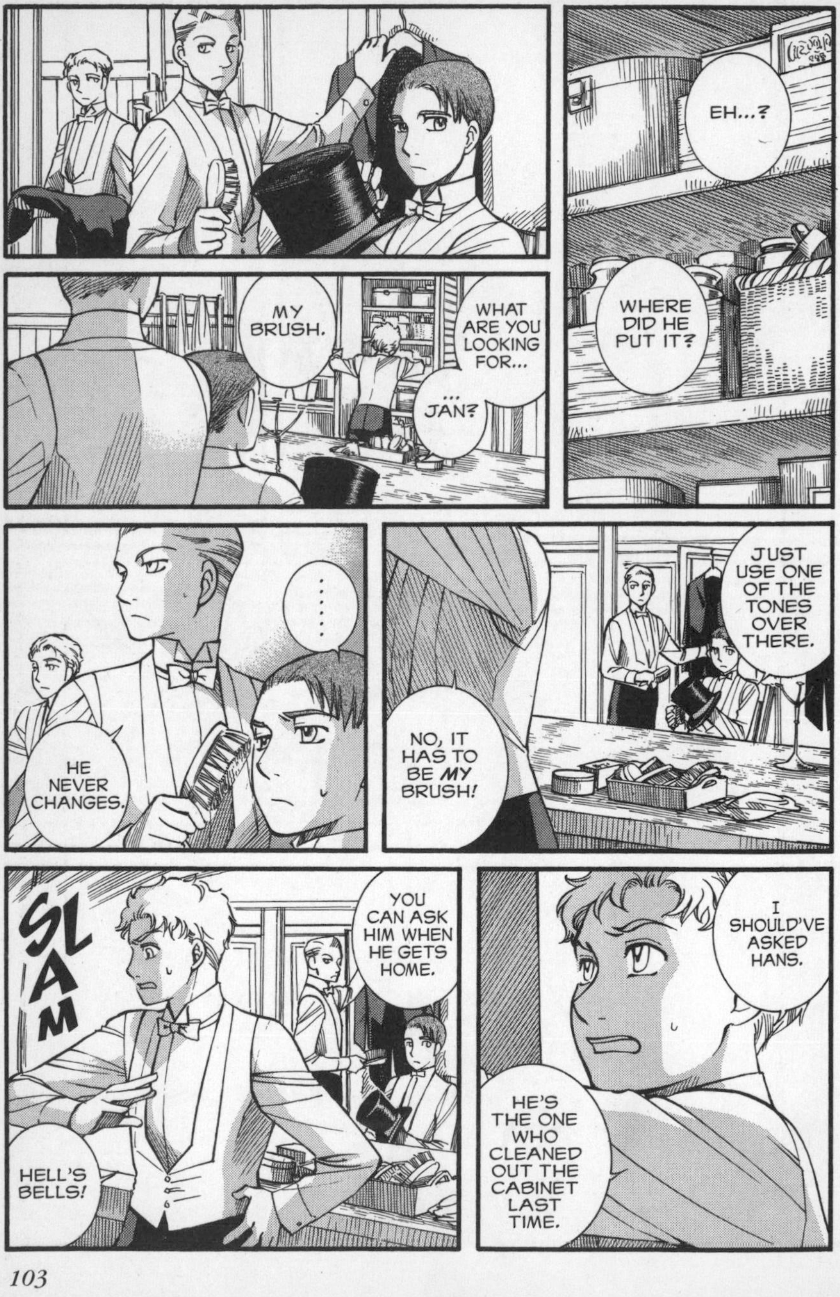
EH...?
WHERE DID HE PUT IT?
WHAT ARE YOU LOOKING FOR...
... JÄN?
MY BRUSH.
JUST USE ONE OF THE TONES OVER THERE.
NO, IT HAS TO BE *MY* BRUSH!
......
HE NEVER CHANGES.
I SHOULD'VE ASKED HANS.
HE'S THE ONE WHO CLEANED OUT THE CABINET LAST TIME.
YOU CAN ASK HIM WHEN HE GETS HOME.
SLAM
HELL'S BELLS!

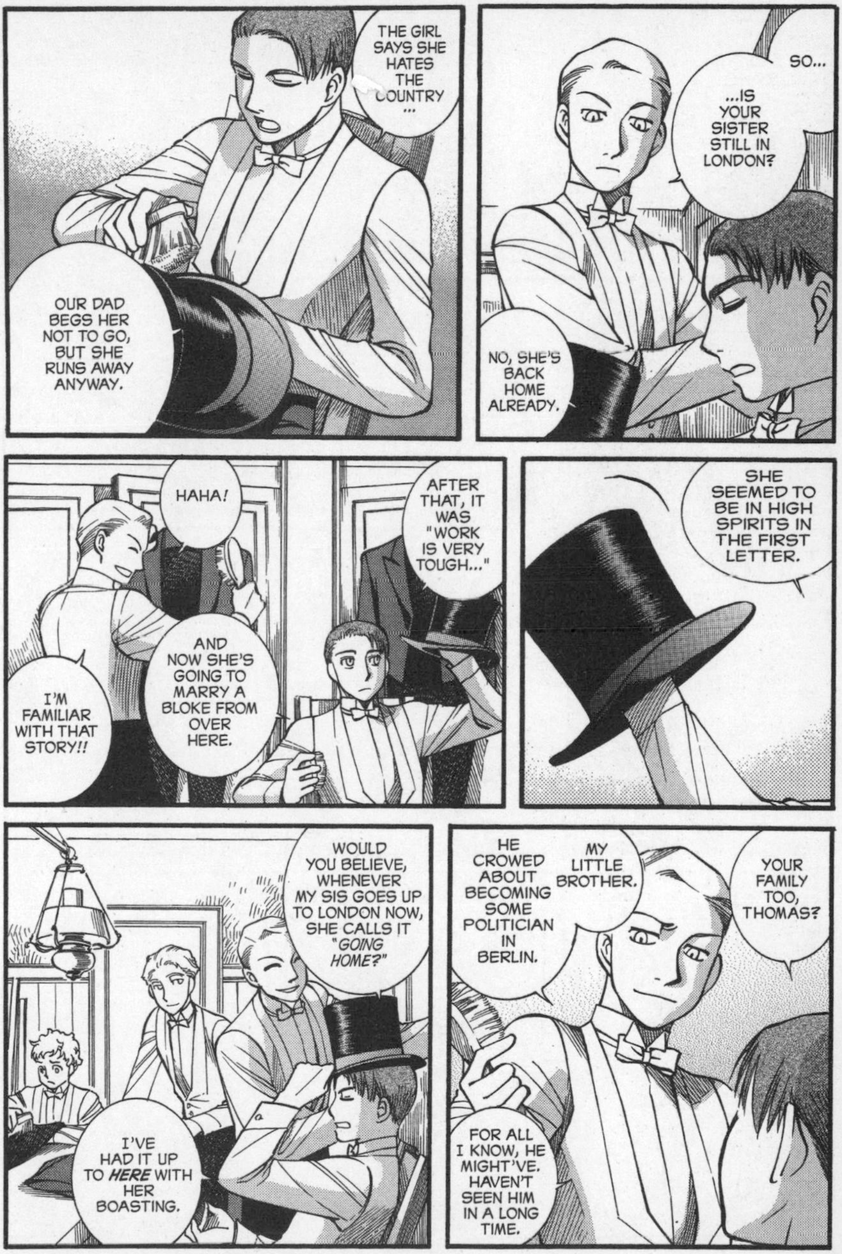
SO...
...IS YOUR SISTER STILL IN LONDON?
NO, SHE'S BACK HOME ALREADY.
THE GIRL SAYS SHE HATES THE COUNTRY...
OUR DAD BEGS HER NOT TO GO, BUT SHE RUNS AWAY ANYWAY.
SHE SEEMED TO BE IN HIGH SPIRITS IN THE FIRST LETTER.
AFTER THAT, IT WAS "WORK IS VERY TOUGH..."
HAHA!
AND NOW SHE'S GOING TO MARRY A BLOKE FROM OVER HERE.
I'M FAMILIAR WITH THAT STORY!!
YOUR FAMILY TOO, THOMAS?
MY LITTLE BROTHER.
HE CROWED ABOUT BECOMING SOME POLITICIAN IN BERLIN.
FOR ALL I KNOW, HE MIGHT'VE. HAVEN'T SEEN HIM IN A LONG TIME.
WOULD YOU BELIEVE, WHENEVER MY SIS GOES UP TO LONDON NOW, SHE CALLS IT *"GOING HOME?"*
I'VE HAD IT UP TO ***HERE*** WITH HER BOASTING.

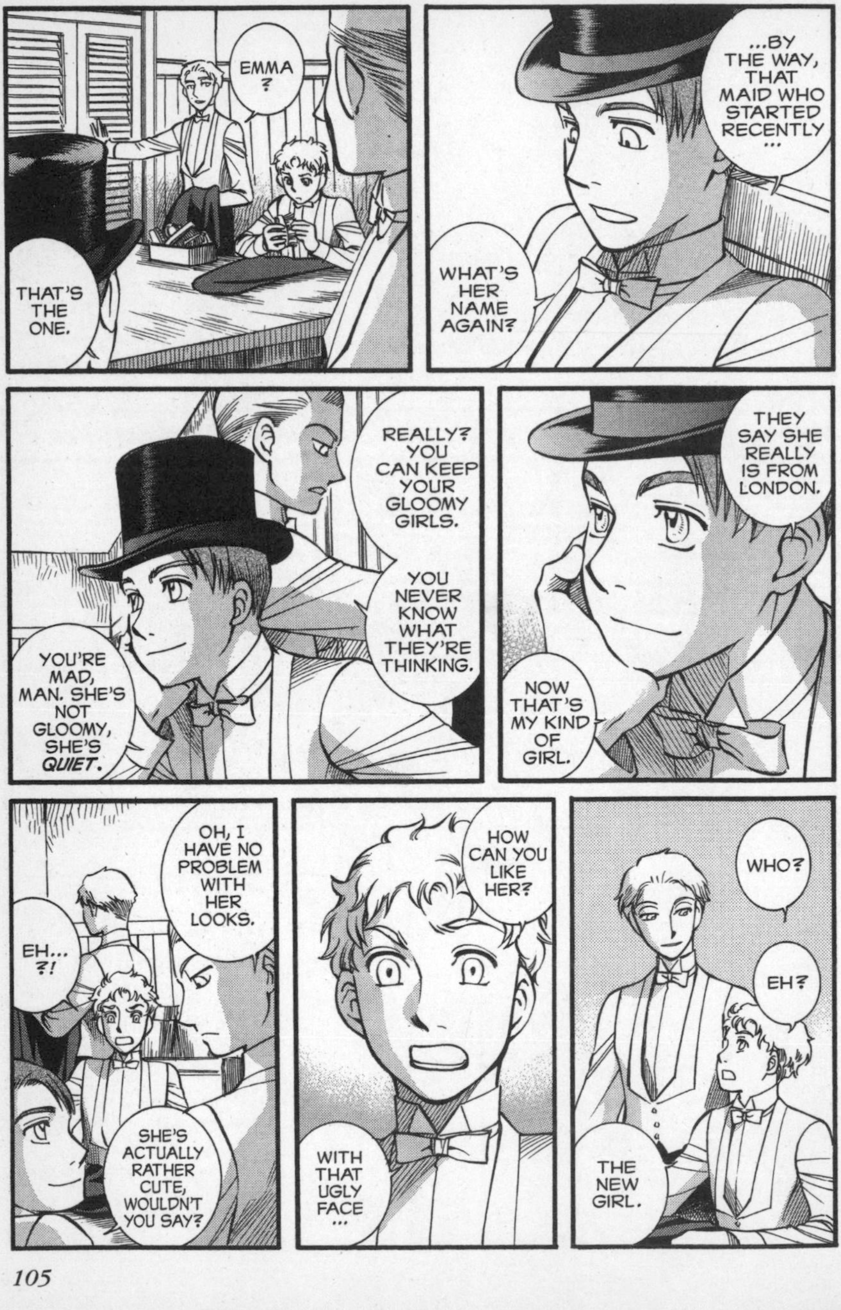
...BY THE WAY, THAT MAID WHO STARTED RECENTLY ...
WHAT'S HER NAME AGAIN?
EMMA?
THAT'S THE ONE.
THEY SAY SHE REALLY IS FROM LONDON.
NOW THAT'S MY KIND OF GIRL.
REALLY? YOU CAN KEEP YOUR GLOOMY GIRLS.
YOU NEVER KNOW WHAT THEY'RE THINKING.
YOU'RE MAD, MAN. SHE'S NOT GLOOMY, SHE'S *QUIET*.
WHO?
EH?
THE NEW GIRL.
HOW CAN YOU LIKE HER?
WITH THAT UGLY FACE ...
OH, I HAVE NO PROBLEM WITH HER LOOKS.
EH... ?!
SHE'S ACTUALLY RATHER CUTE, WOULDN'T YOU SAY?

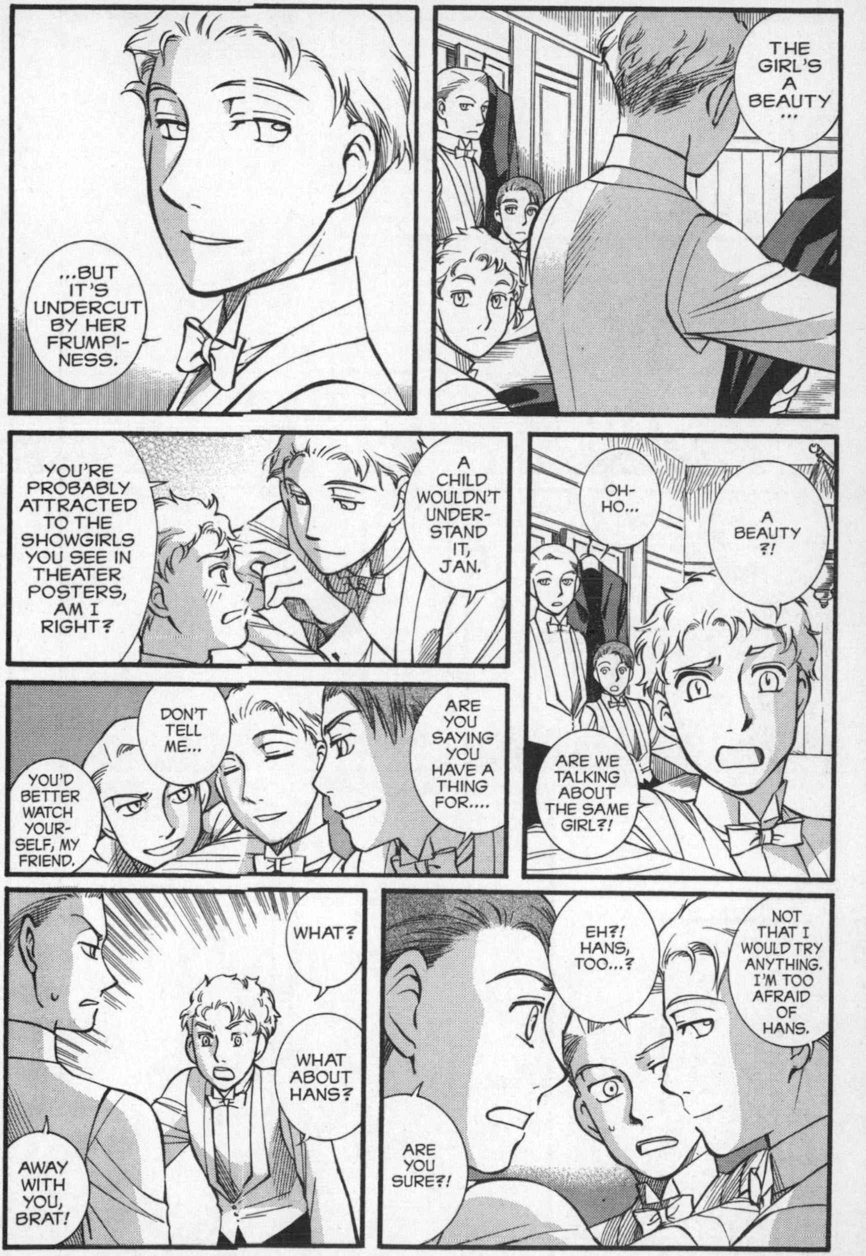

THE GIRL'S A BEAUTY...
...BUT IT'S UNDERCUT BY HER FRUMPI-NESS.
A BEAUTY?!
OH-HO...
ARE WE TALKING ABOUT THE SAME GIRL?!
A CHILD WOULDN'T UNDER-STAND IT, JAN.
YOU'RE PROBABLY ATTRACTED TO THE SHOWGIRLS YOU SEE IN THEATER POSTERS, AM I RIGHT?
ARE YOU SAYING YOU HAVE A THING FOR....
DON'T TELL ME...
YOU'D BETTER WATCH YOUR-SELF, MY FRIEND.
NOT THAT I WOULD TRY ANYTHING. I'M TOO AFRAID OF HANS.
EH?! HANS, TOO...?
ARE YOU SURE?!
WHAT?
WHAT ABOUT HANS?
AWAY WITH YOU, BRAT!

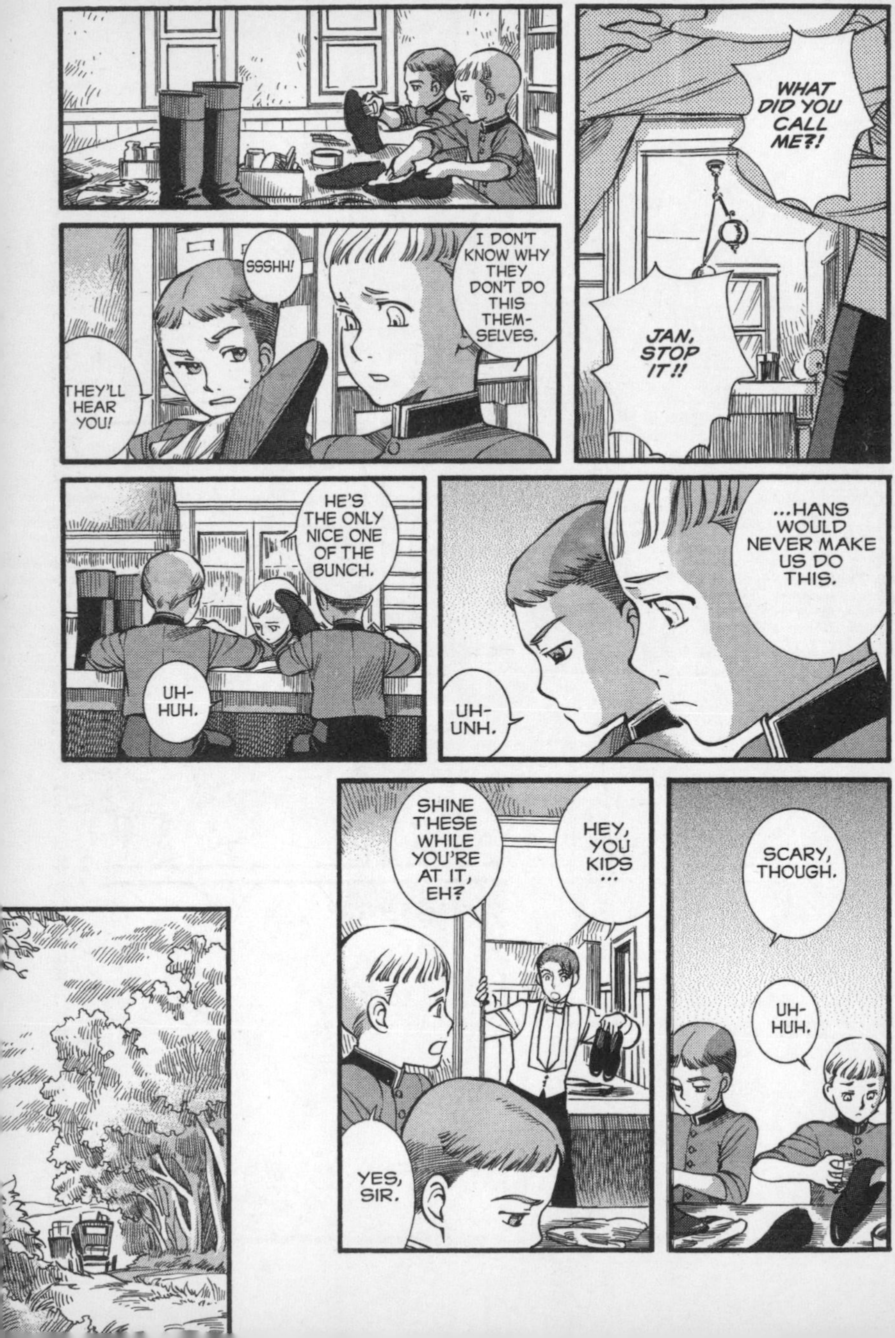
WHAT DID YOU CALL ME?!
JAN, STOP IT!!
I DON'T KNOW WHY THEY DON'T DO THIS THEM-SELVES.
SSSHH!
THEY'LL HEAR YOU!
...HANS WOULD NEVER MAKE US DO THIS.
UH-UNH.
HE'S THE ONLY NICE ONE OF THE BUNCH.
UH-HUH.
SCARY, THOUGH.
UH-HUH.
HEY, YOU KIDS...
SHINE THESE WHILE YOU'RE AT IT, EH?
YES, SIR.

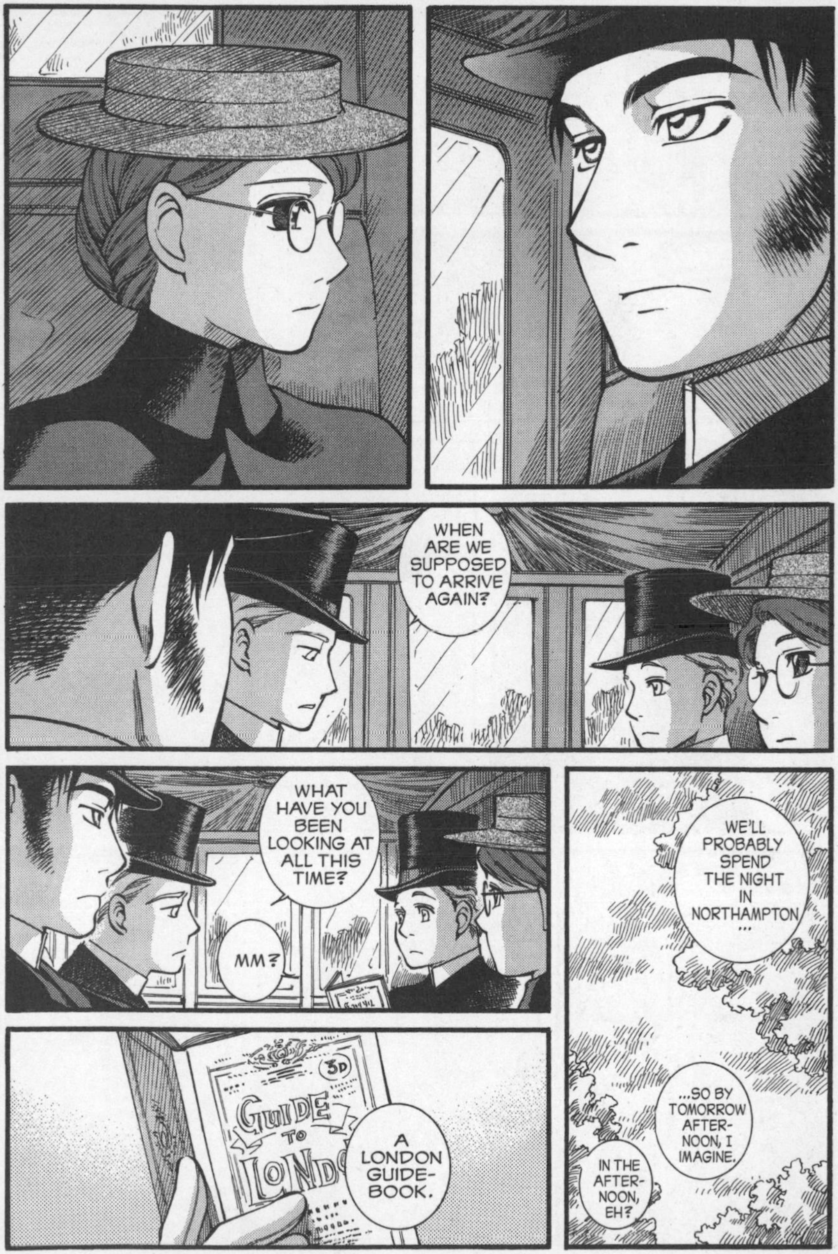
WHEN ARE WE SUPPOSED TO ARRIVE AGAIN?
WE'LL PROBABLY SPEND THE NIGHT IN NORTHAMPTON ...
...SO BY TOMORROW AFTER-NOON, I IMAGINE.
IN THE AFTER-NOON, EH?
WHAT HAVE YOU BEEN LOOKING AT ALL THIS TIME?
MM?
3D
GUIDE TO
A LONDON GUIDE-BOOK.

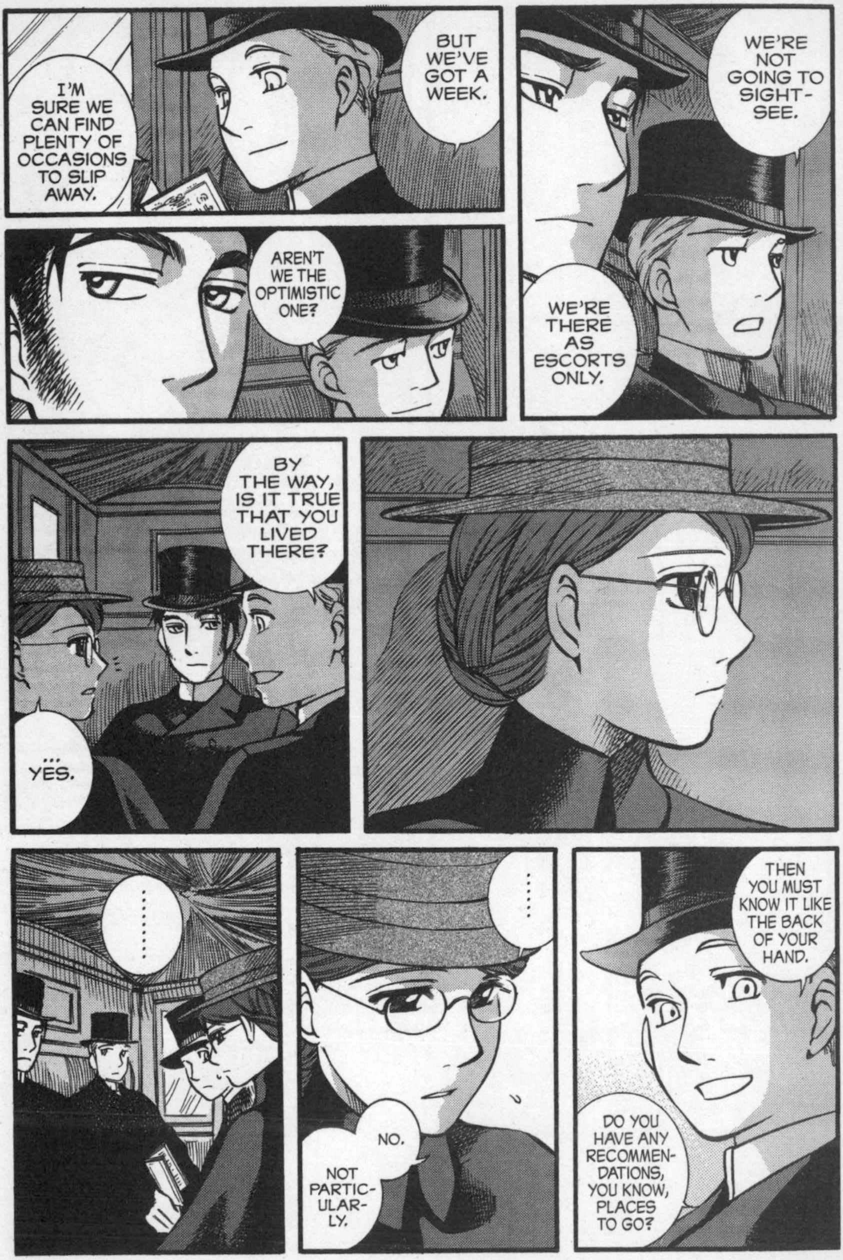
WE'RE NOT GOING TO SIGHT-SEE.
WE'RE THERE AS ESCORTS ONLY.
BUT WE'VE GOT A WEEK.
I'M SURE WE CAN FIND PLENTY OF OCCASIONS TO SLIP AWAY.
AREN'T WE THE OPTIMISTIC ONE?
BY THE WAY, IS IT TRUE THAT YOU LIVED THERE?
... YES.
THEN YOU MUST KNOW IT LIKE THE BACK OF YOUR HAND.
DO YOU HAVE ANY RECOMMEN-DATIONS, YOU KNOW, PLACES TO GO?
......
NO.
NOT PARTIC-ULAR-LY.
......

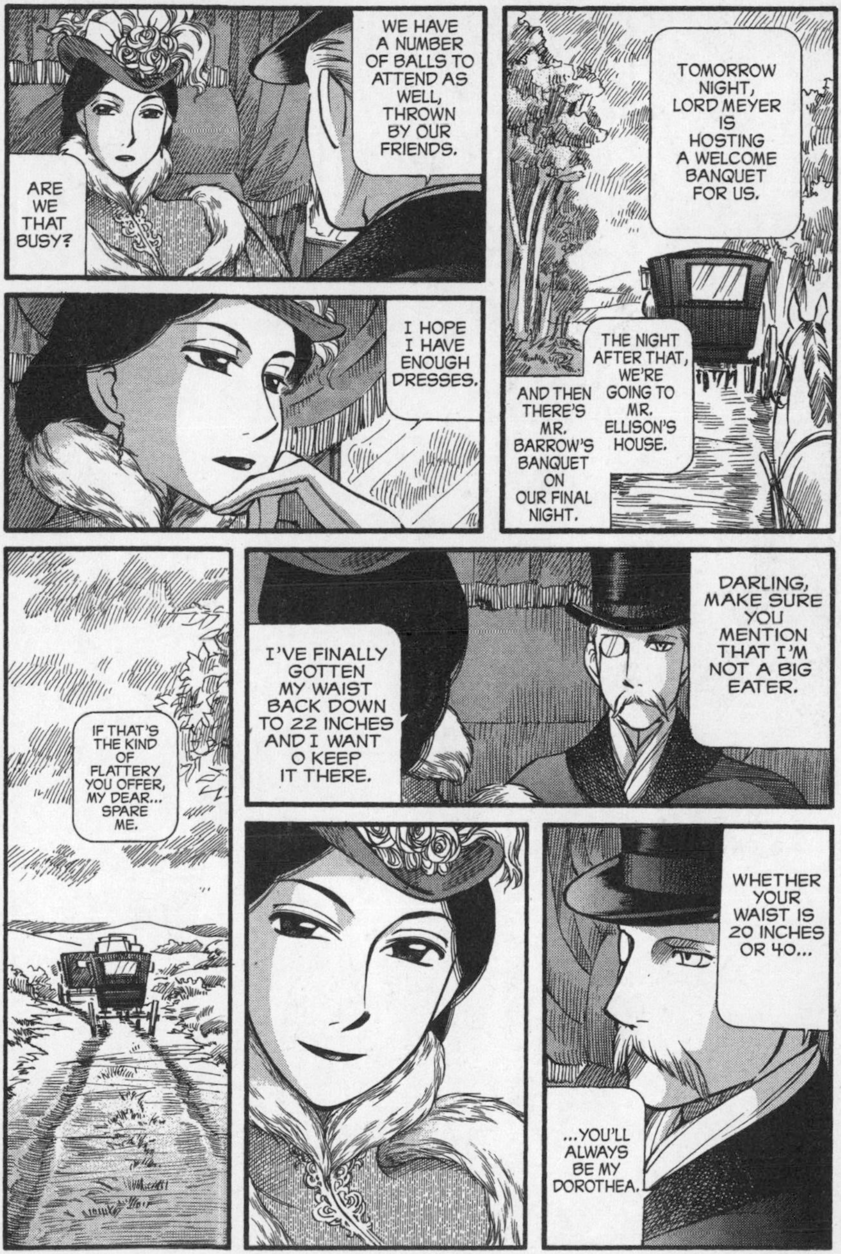
TOMORROW NIGHT, LORD MEYER IS HOSTING A WELCOME BANQUET FOR US.
THE NIGHT AFTER THAT, WE'RE GOING TO MR. ELLISON'S HOUSE.
AND THEN THERE'S MR. BARROW'S BANQUET ON OUR FINAL NIGHT.
WE HAVE A NUMBER OF BALLS TO ATTEND AS WELL, THROWN BY OUR FRIENDS.
ARE WE THAT BUSY?
I HOPE I HAVE ENOUGH DRESSES.
DARLING, MAKE SURE YOU MENTION THAT I'M NOT A BIG EATER.
I'VE FINALLY GOTTEN MY WAIST BACK DOWN TO 22 INCHES AND I WANT O KEEP IT THERE.
WHETHER YOUR WAIST IS 20 INCHES OR 40...
...YOU'LL ALWAYS BE MY DOROTHEA.
IF THAT'S THE KIND OF FLATTERY YOU OFFER, MY DEAR... SPARE ME.

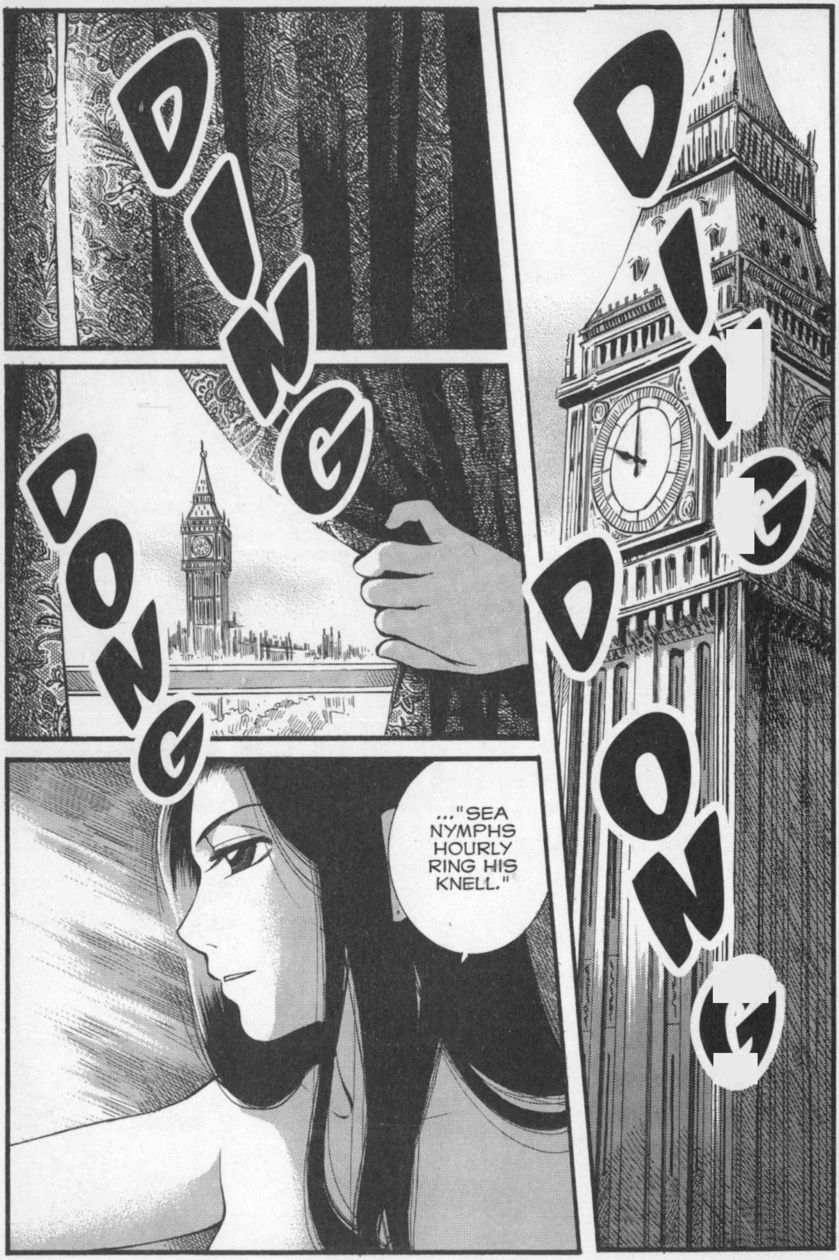
DING
DONG
..."SEA NYMPHS HOURLY RING HIS KNELL."

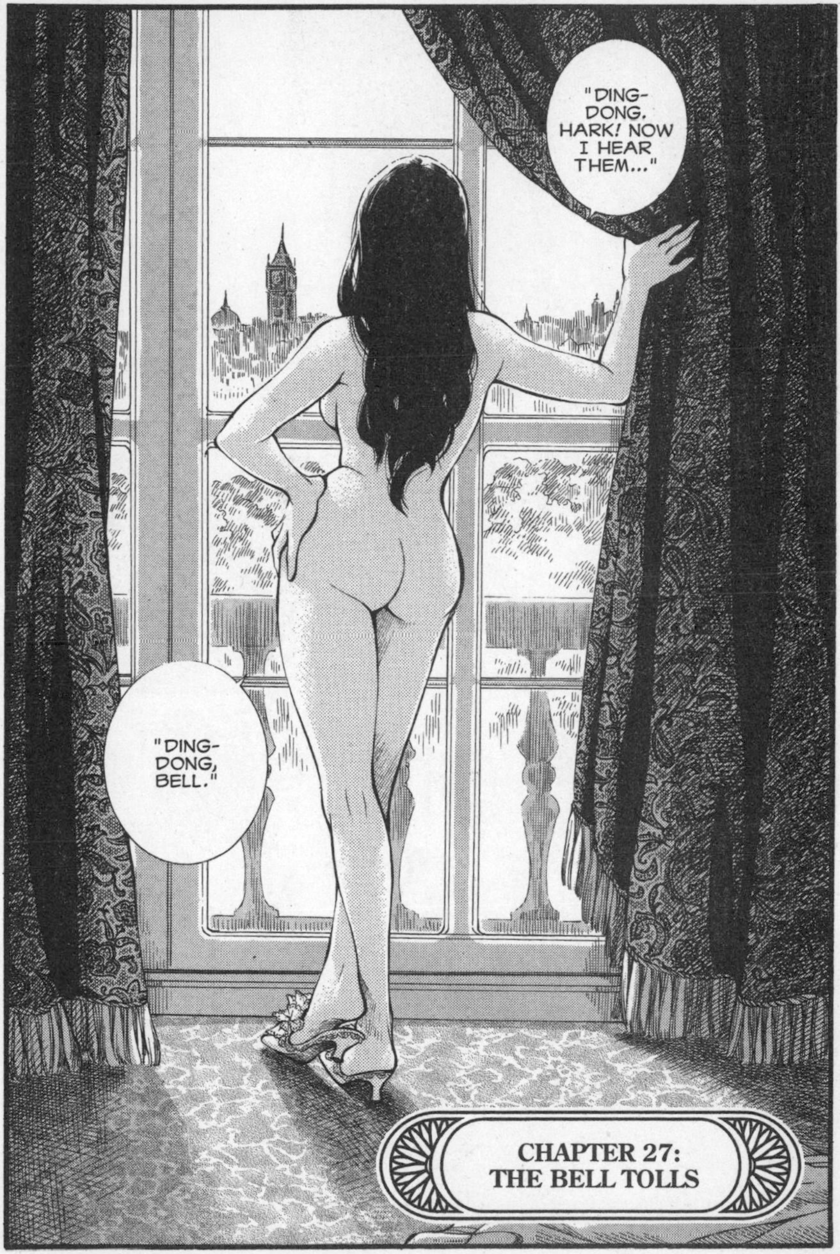
"DING-DONG. HARK! NOW I HEAR THEM..."
"DING-DONG, BELL."
CHAPTER 27: THE BELL TOLLS

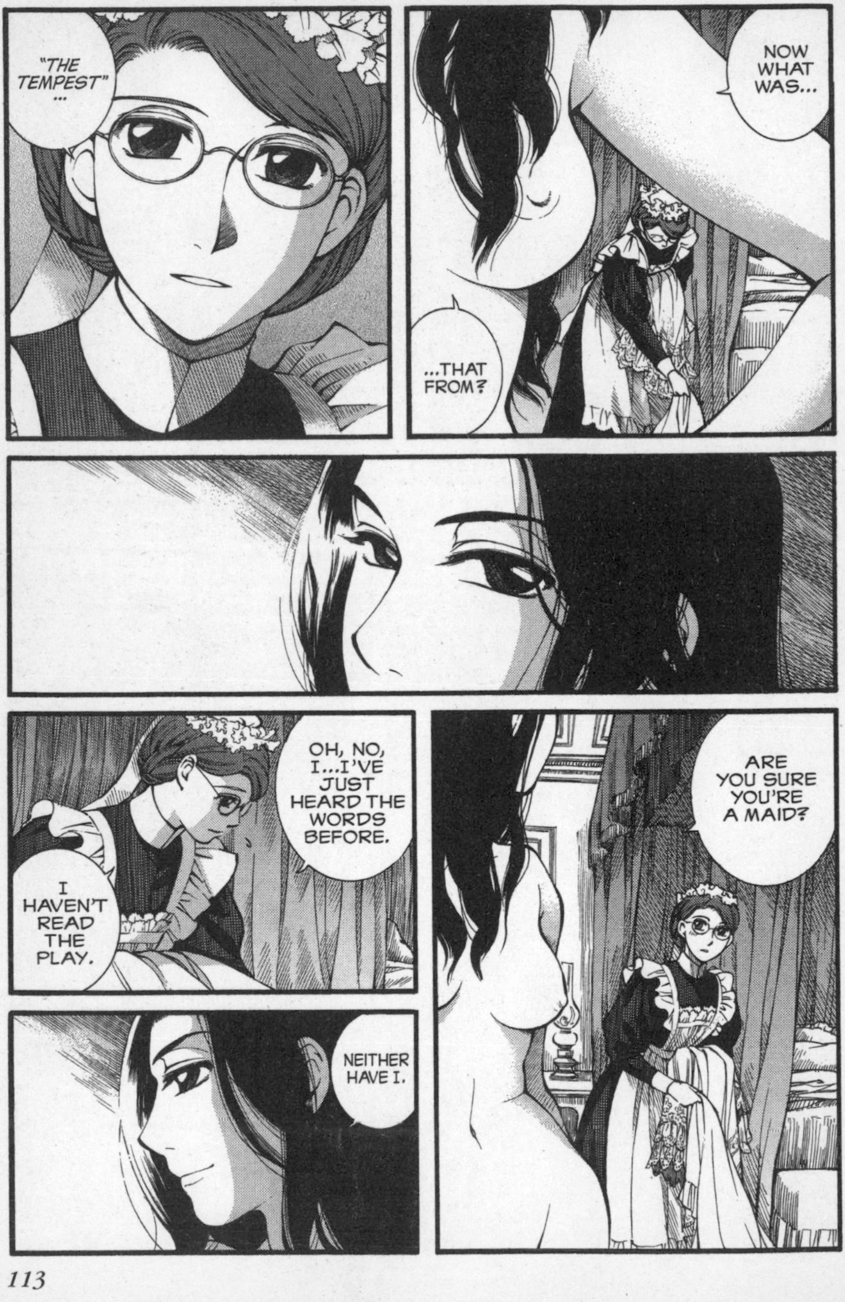
NOW WHAT WAS...
...THAT FROM?
"THE TEMPEST" ...
ARE YOU SURE YOU'RE A MAID?
OH, NO, I...I'VE JUST HEARD THE WORDS BEFORE.
I HAVEN'T READ THE PLAY.
NEITHER HAVE I.

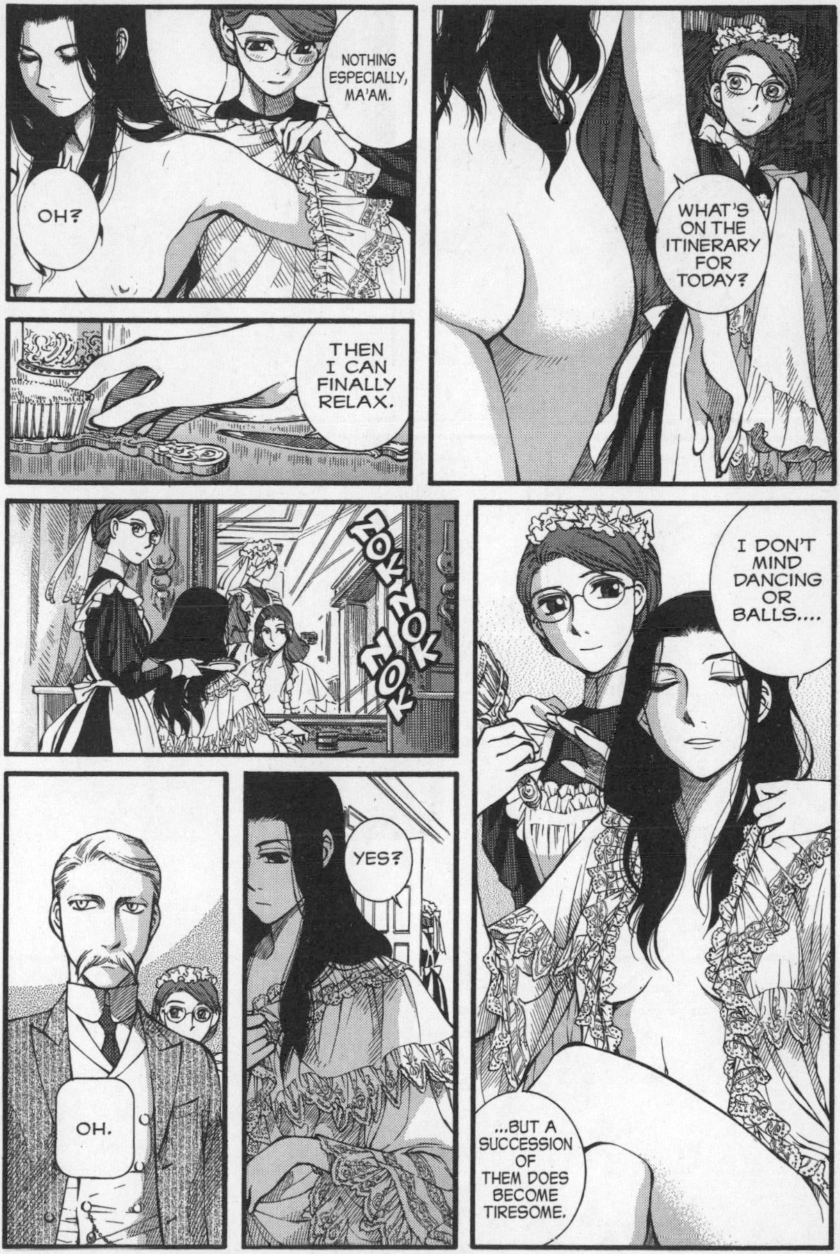
WHAT'S ON THE ITINERARY FOR TODAY?
NOTHING ESPECIALLY, MA'AM.
OH?
THEN I CAN FINALLY RELAX.
I DON'T MIND DANCING OR BALLS....
...BUT A SUCCESSION OF THEM DOES BECOME TIRESOME.
KNOK KNOK
YES?
OH.

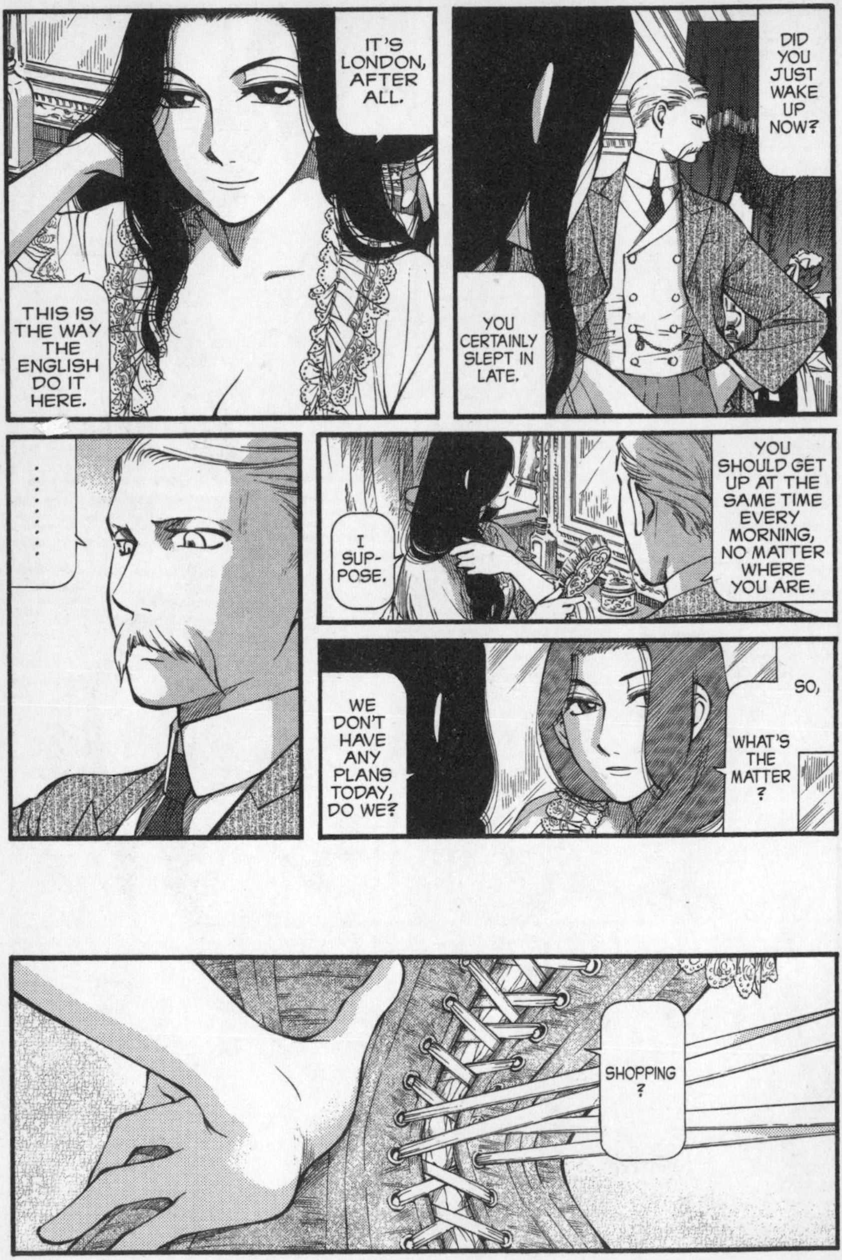
DID YOU JUST WAKE UP NOW?
YOU CERTAINLY SLEPT IN LATE.
IT'S LONDON, AFTER ALL.
THIS IS THE WAY THE ENGLISH DO IT HERE.
YOU SHOULD GET UP AT THE SAME TIME EVERY MORNING, NO MATTER WHERE YOU ARE.
I SUP-POSE.
SO,
WHAT'S THE MATTER?
WE DON'T HAVE ANY PLANS TODAY, DO WE?
......
SHOPPING?

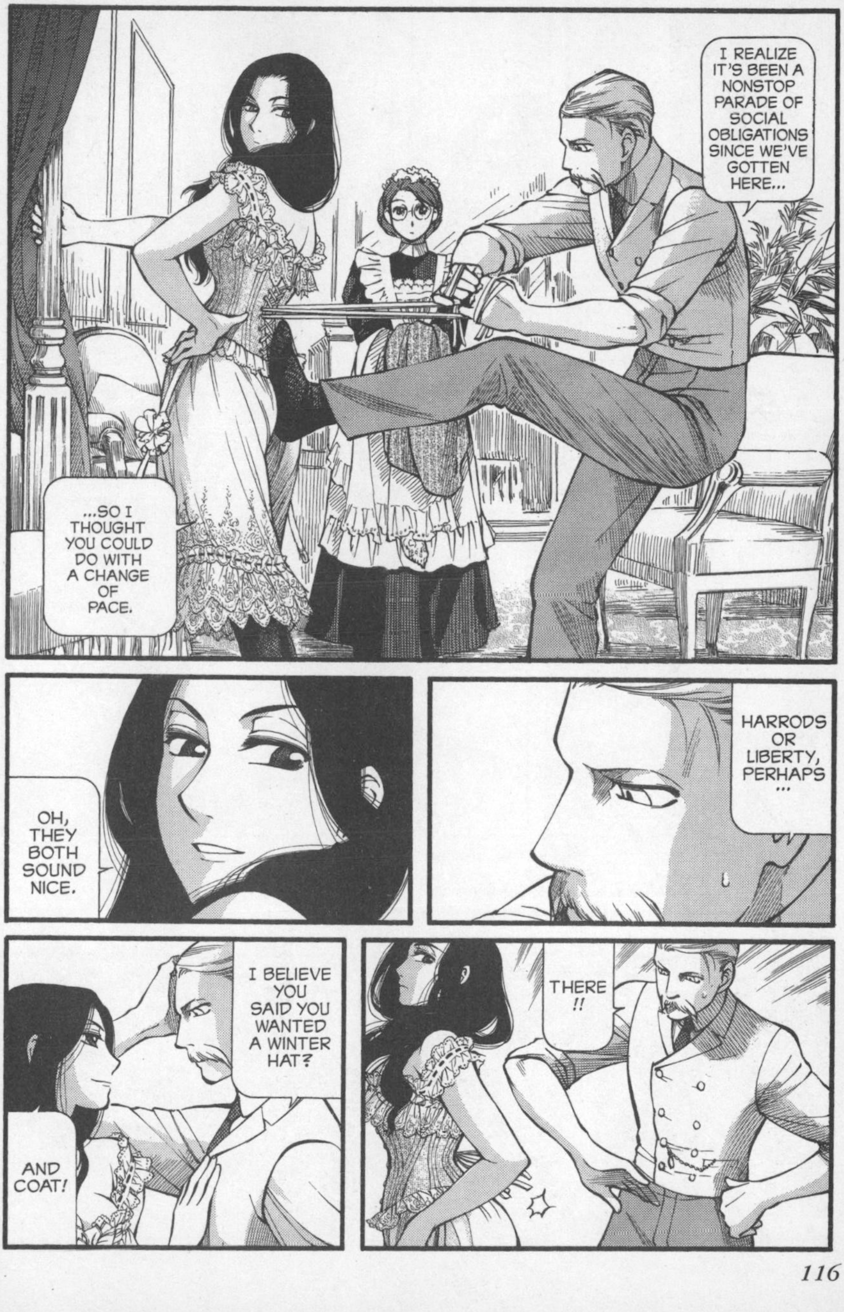
I REALIZE IT'S BEEN A NONSTOP PARADE OF SOCIAL OBLIGATIONS SINCE WE'VE GOTTEN HERE...
...SO I THOUGHT YOU COULD DO WITH A CHANGE OF PACE.
HARRODS OR LIBERTY, PERHAPS...
OH, THEY BOTH SOUND NICE.
THERE!!
I BELIEVE YOU SAID YOU WANTED A WINTER HAT?
AND COAT!

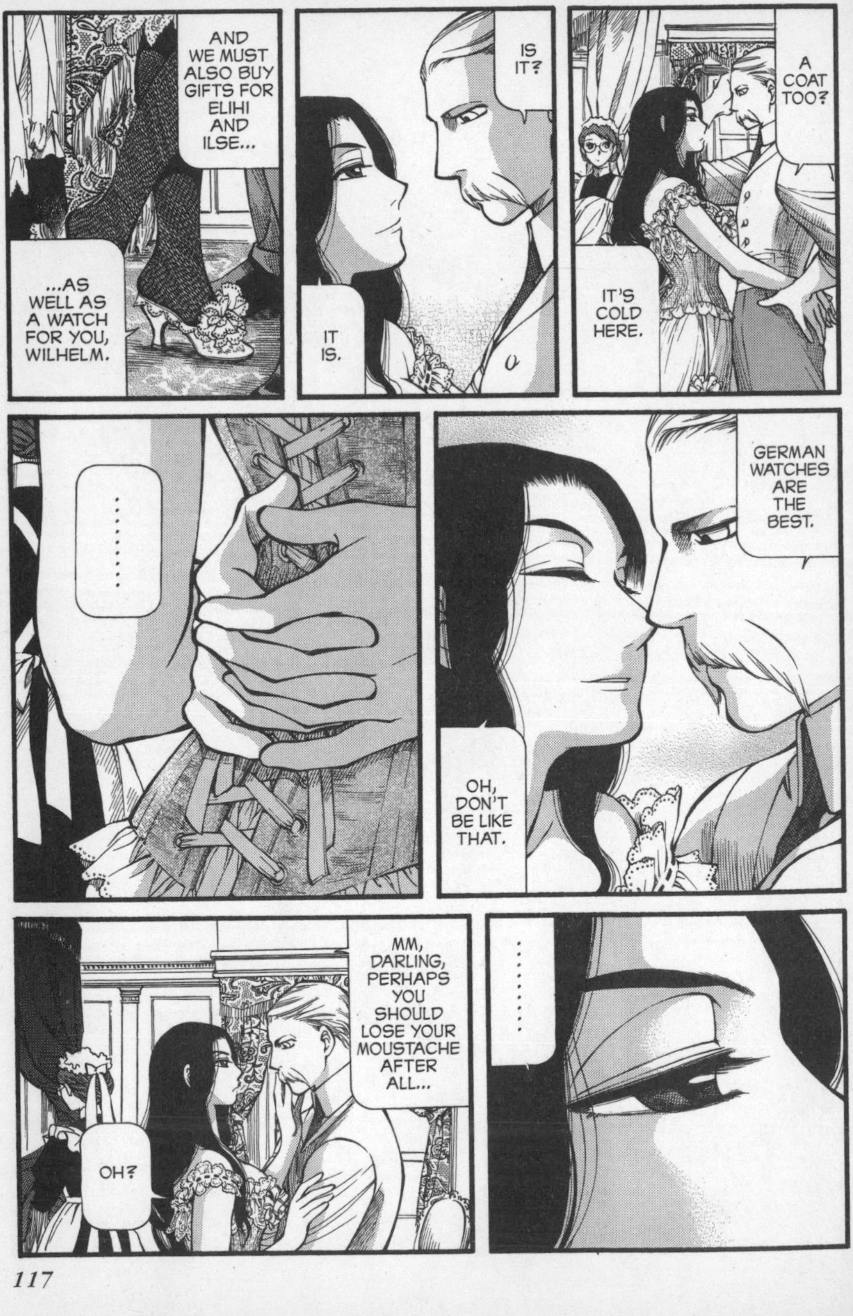
A COAT TOO?
IT'S COLD HERE.
IS IT?
IT IS.
AND WE MUST ALSO BUY GIFTS FOR ELIHI AND ILSE...
...AS WELL AS A WATCH FOR YOU, WILHELM.
GERMAN WATCHES ARE THE BEST.
OH, DON'T BE LIKE THAT.
......
......
MM, DARLING, PERHAPS YOU SHOULD LOSE YOUR MOUSTACHE AFTER ALL...
OH?

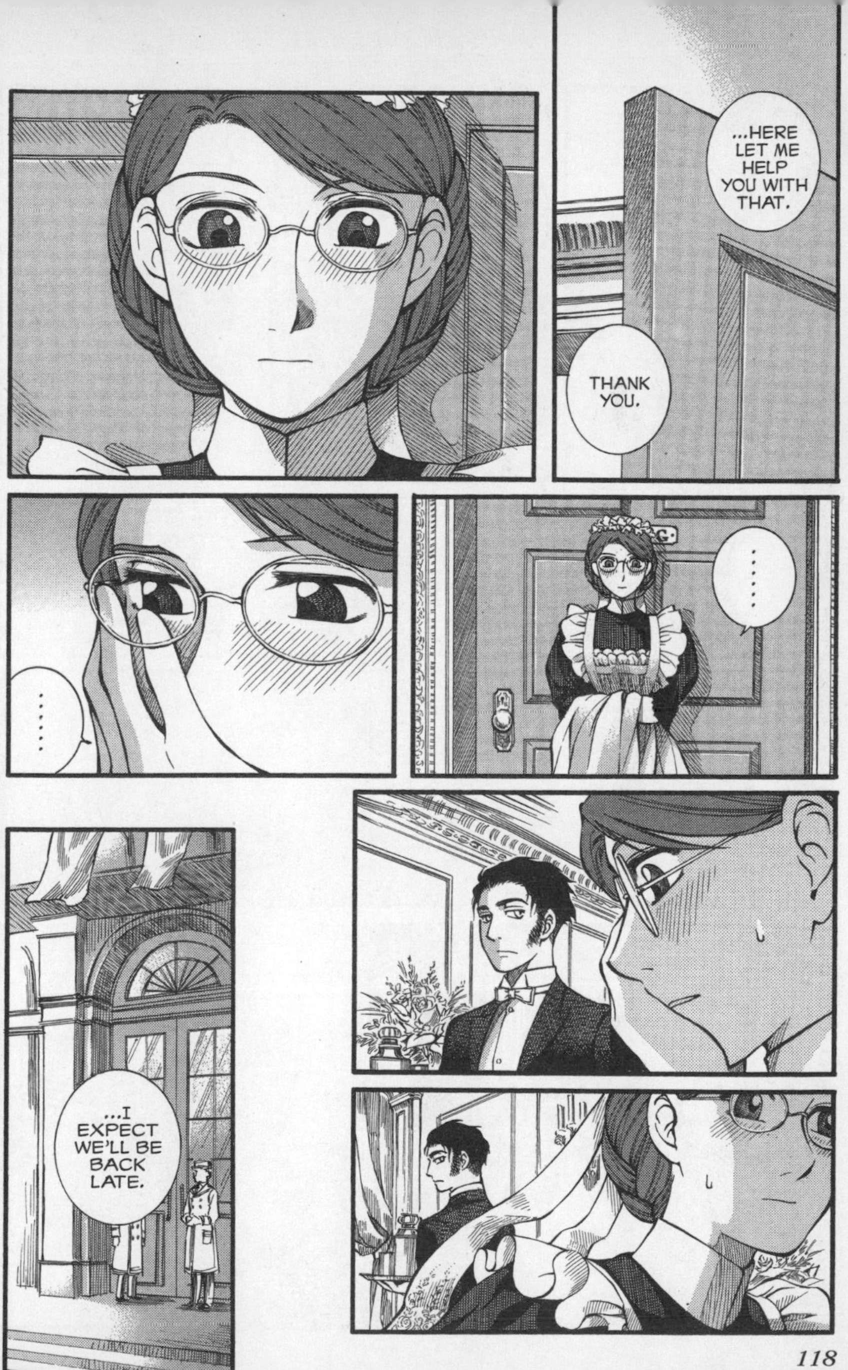
...HERE LET ME HELP YOU WITH THAT.
THANK YOU.
......
......
...I EXPECT WE'LL BE BACK LATE.

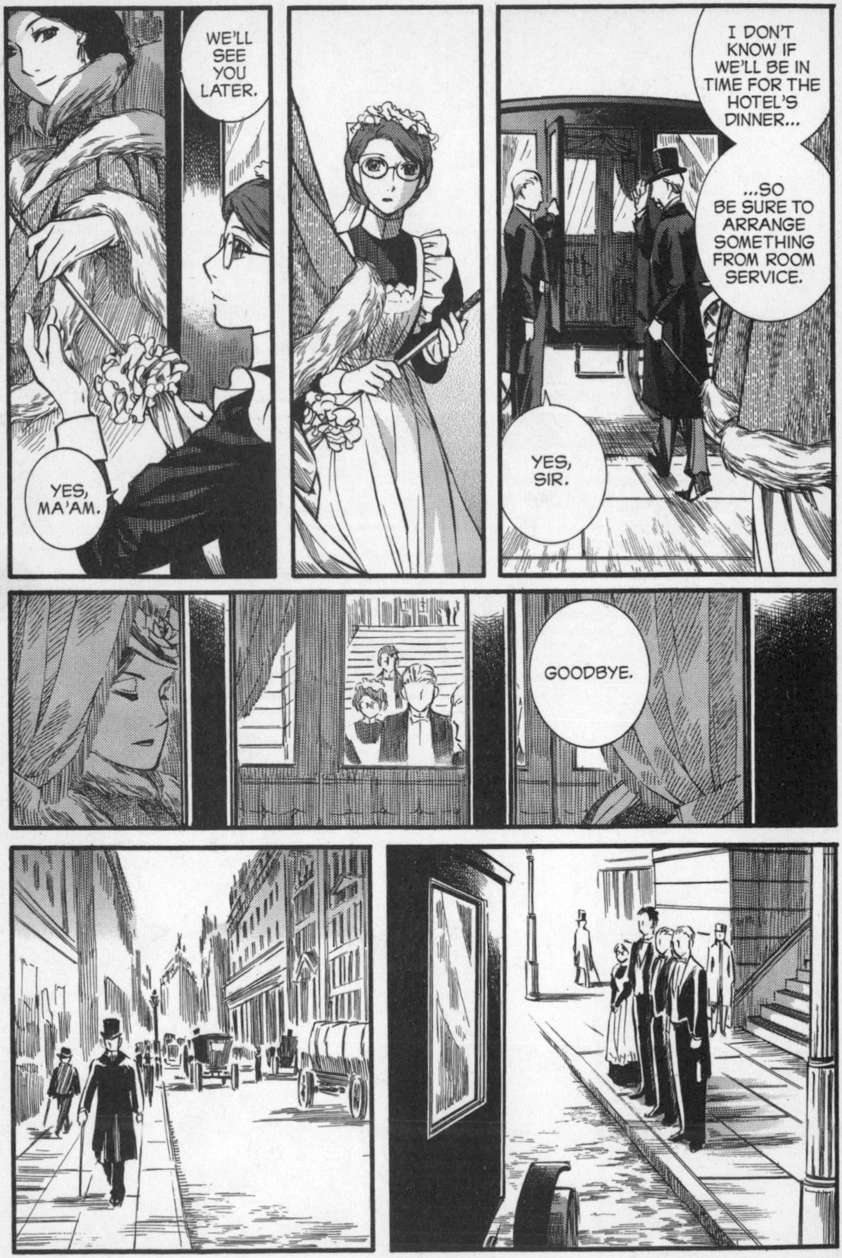
I DON'T KNOW IF WE'LL BE IN TIME FOR THE HOTEL'S DINNER...
...SO BE SURE TO ARRANGE SOMETHING FROM ROOM SERVICE.
YES, SIR.
WE'LL SEE YOU LATER.
YES, MA'AM.
GOODBYE.

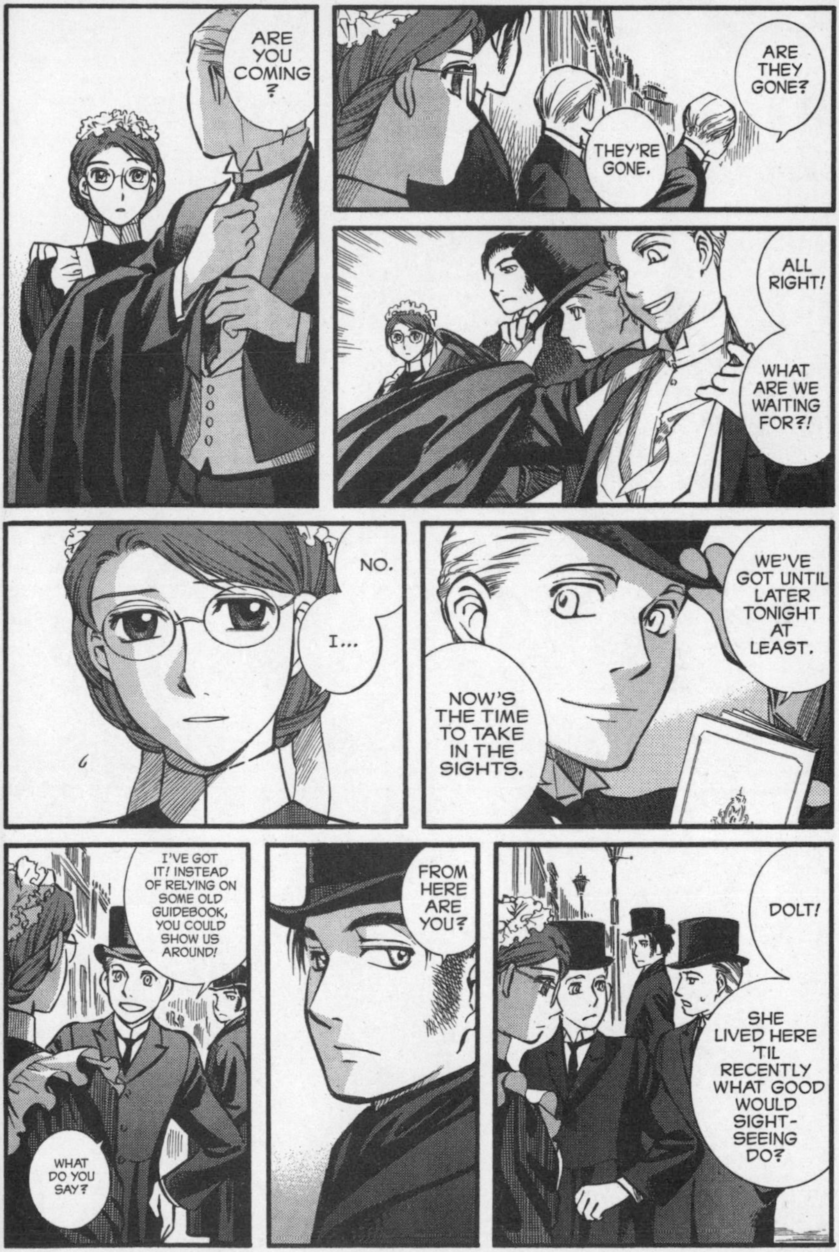
ARE YOU COMING?
ARE THEY GONE?
THEY'RE GONE.
ALL RIGHT!
WHAT ARE WE WAITING FOR?!
NO.
I...
WE'VE GOT UNTIL LATER TONIGHT AT LEAST.
NOW'S THE TIME TO TAKE IN THE SIGHTS.
I'VE GOT IT! INSTEAD OF RELYING ON SOME OLD GUIDEBOOK, YOU COULD SHOW US AROUND!
WHAT DO YOU SAY?
FROM HERE ARE YOU?
DOLT!
SHE LIVED HERE 'TIL RECENTLY WHAT GOOD WOULD SIGHT-SEEING DO?

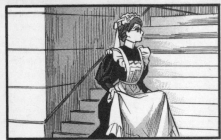

I SEE.

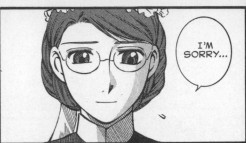

I'M SORRY...

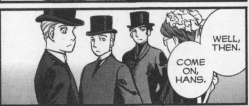

WELL, THEN.

COME ON, HANS.

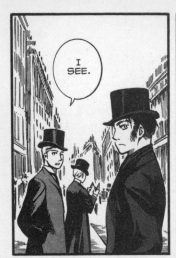

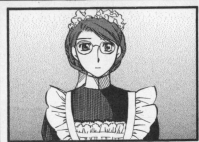

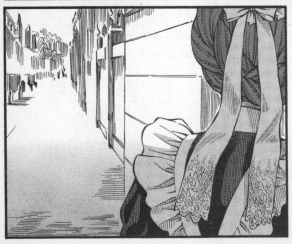

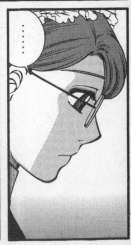

121

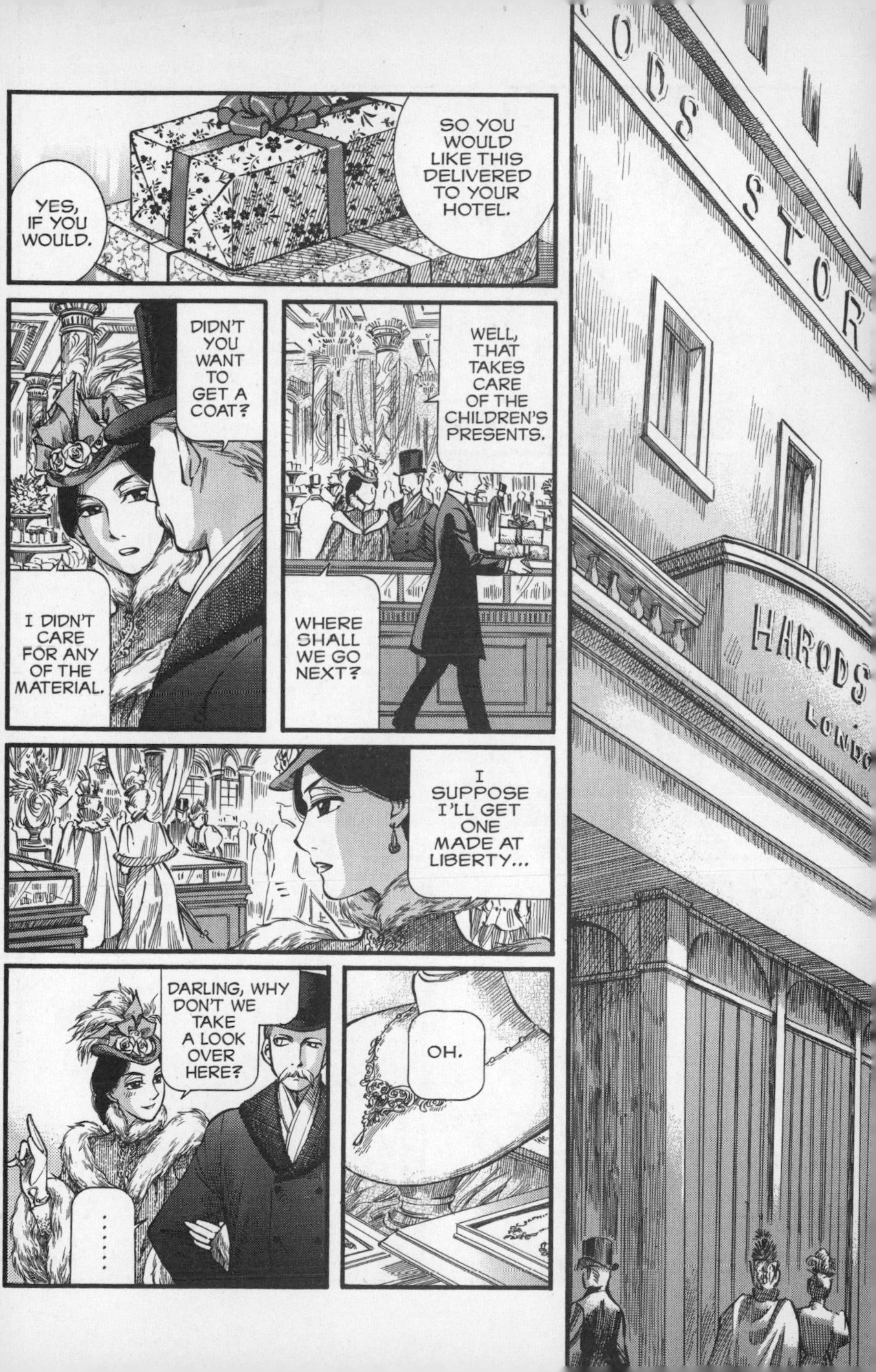
HARODS
SO YOU WOULD LIKE THIS DELIVERED TO YOUR HOTEL.
YES, IF YOU WOULD.
WELL, THAT TAKES CARE OF THE CHILDREN'S PRESENTS.
WHERE SHALL WE GO NEXT?
DIDN'T YOU WANT TO GET A COAT?
I DIDN'T CARE FOR ANY OF THE MATERIAL.
I SUPPOSE I'LL GET ONE MADE AT LIBERTY...
OH.
DARLING, WHY DON'T WE TAKE A LOOK OVER HERE?
......

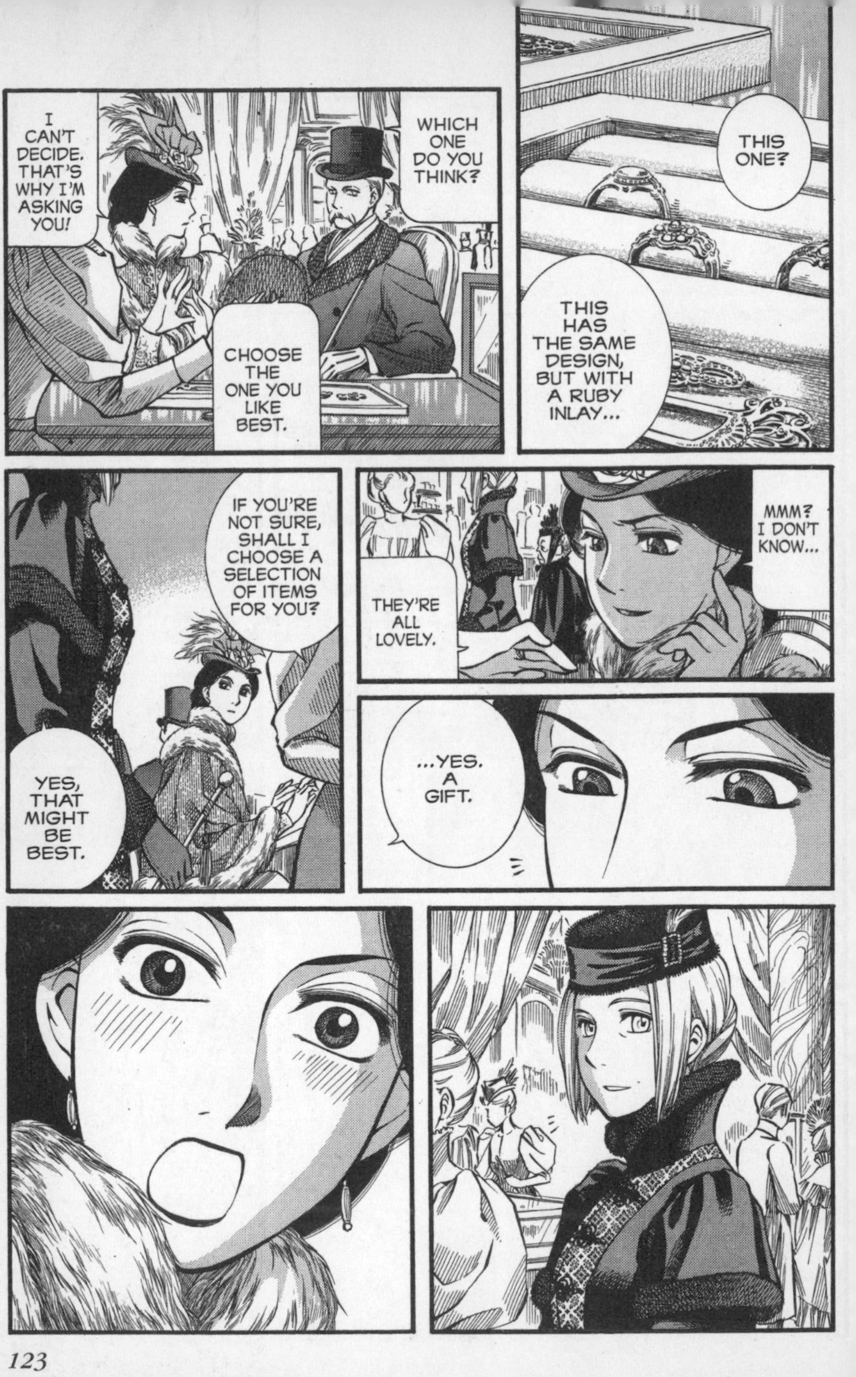
THIS ONE?
THIS HAS THE SAME DESIGN, BUT WITH A RUBY INLAY...
WHICH ONE DO YOU THINK?
I CAN'T DECIDE. THAT'S WHY I'M ASKING YOU!
CHOOSE THE ONE YOU LIKE BEST.
MMM? I DON'T KNOW...
THEY'RE ALL LOVELY.
...YES. A GIFT.
IF YOU'RE NOT SURE, SHALL I CHOOSE A SELECTION OF ITEMS FOR YOU?
YES, THAT MIGHT BE BEST.

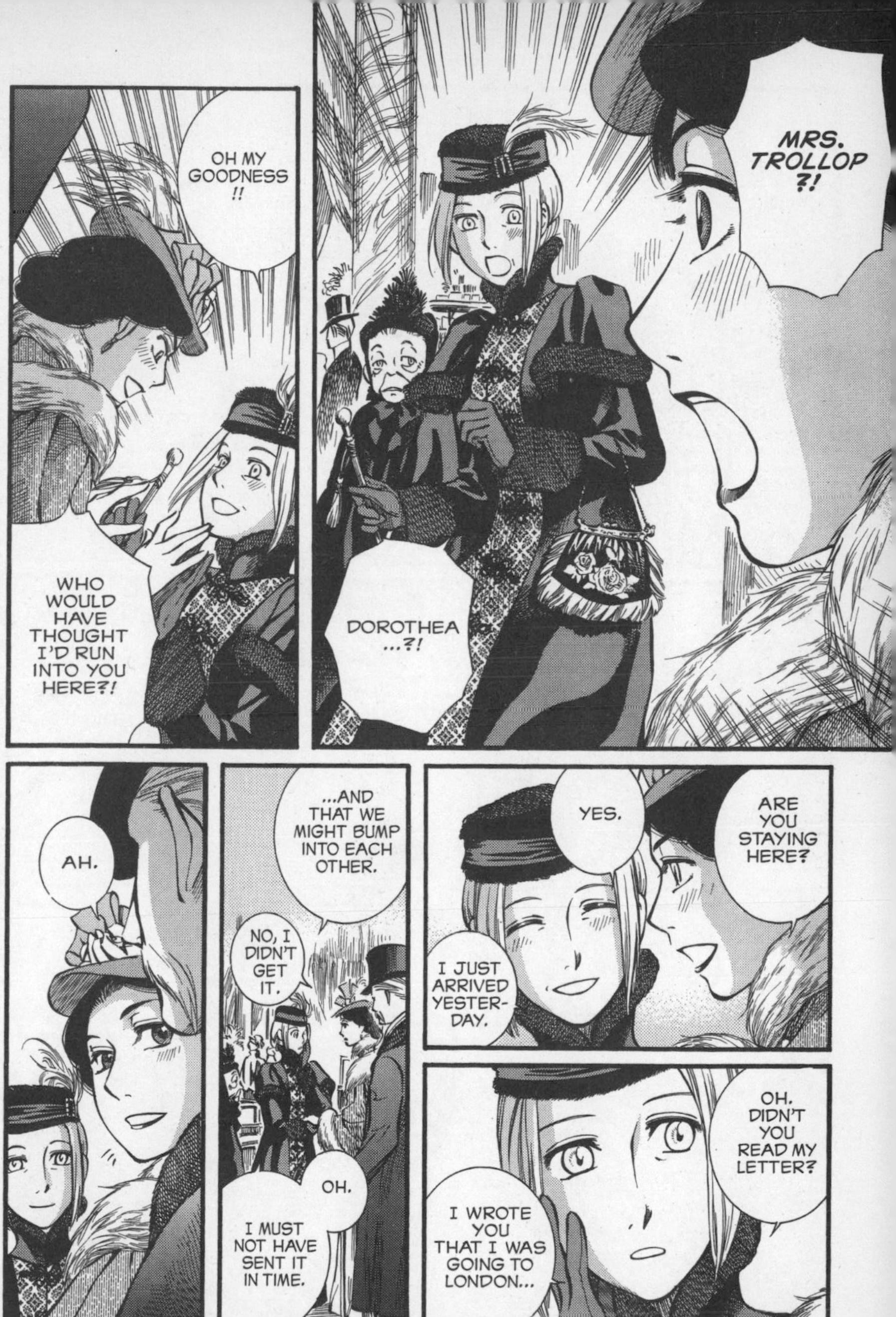
MRS. TROLLOP ?!
DOROTHEA ...?!
OH MY GOODNESS !!
WHO WOULD HAVE THOUGHT I'D RUN INTO YOU HERE?!
ARE YOU STAYING HERE?
YES.
I JUST ARRIVED YESTER-DAY.
OH. DIDN'T YOU READ MY LETTER?
I WROTE YOU THAT I WAS GOING TO LONDON...
...AND THAT WE MIGHT BUMP INTO EACH OTHER.
NO, I DIDN'T GET IT.
OH.
I MUST NOT HAVE SENT IT IN TIME.
AH.

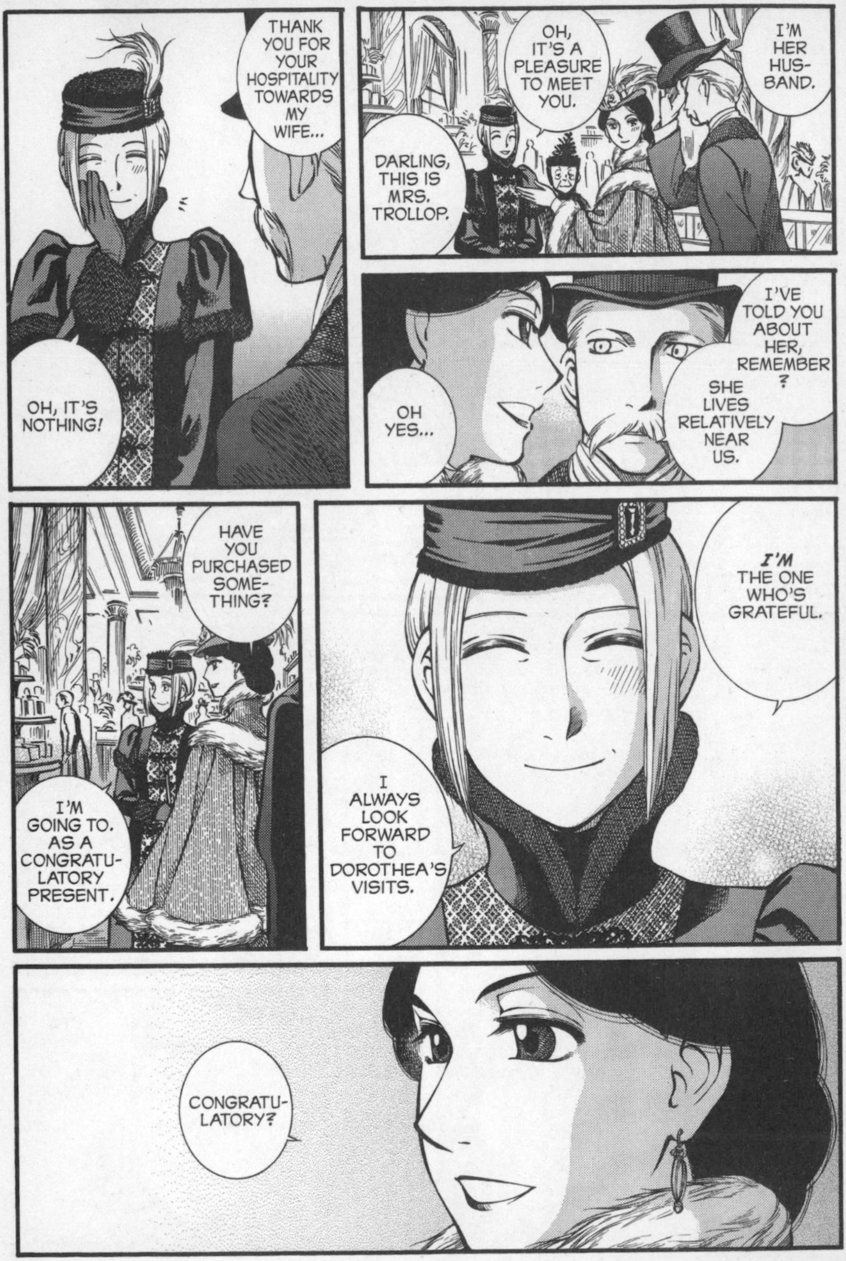
I'M HER HUSBAND.
OH, IT'S A PLEASURE TO MEET YOU.
DARLING, THIS IS MRS. TROLLOP.
I'VE TOLD YOU ABOUT HER, REMEMBER?
SHE LIVES RELATIVELY NEAR US.
OH YES...
THANK YOU FOR YOUR HOSPITALITY TOWARDS MY WIFE...
OH, IT'S NOTHING!
I'M THE ONE WHO'S GRATEFUL.
I ALWAYS LOOK FORWARD TO DOROTHEA'S VISITS.
HAVE YOU PURCHASED SOMETHING?
I'M GOING TO. AS A CONGRATULATORY PRESENT.
CONGRATULATORY?

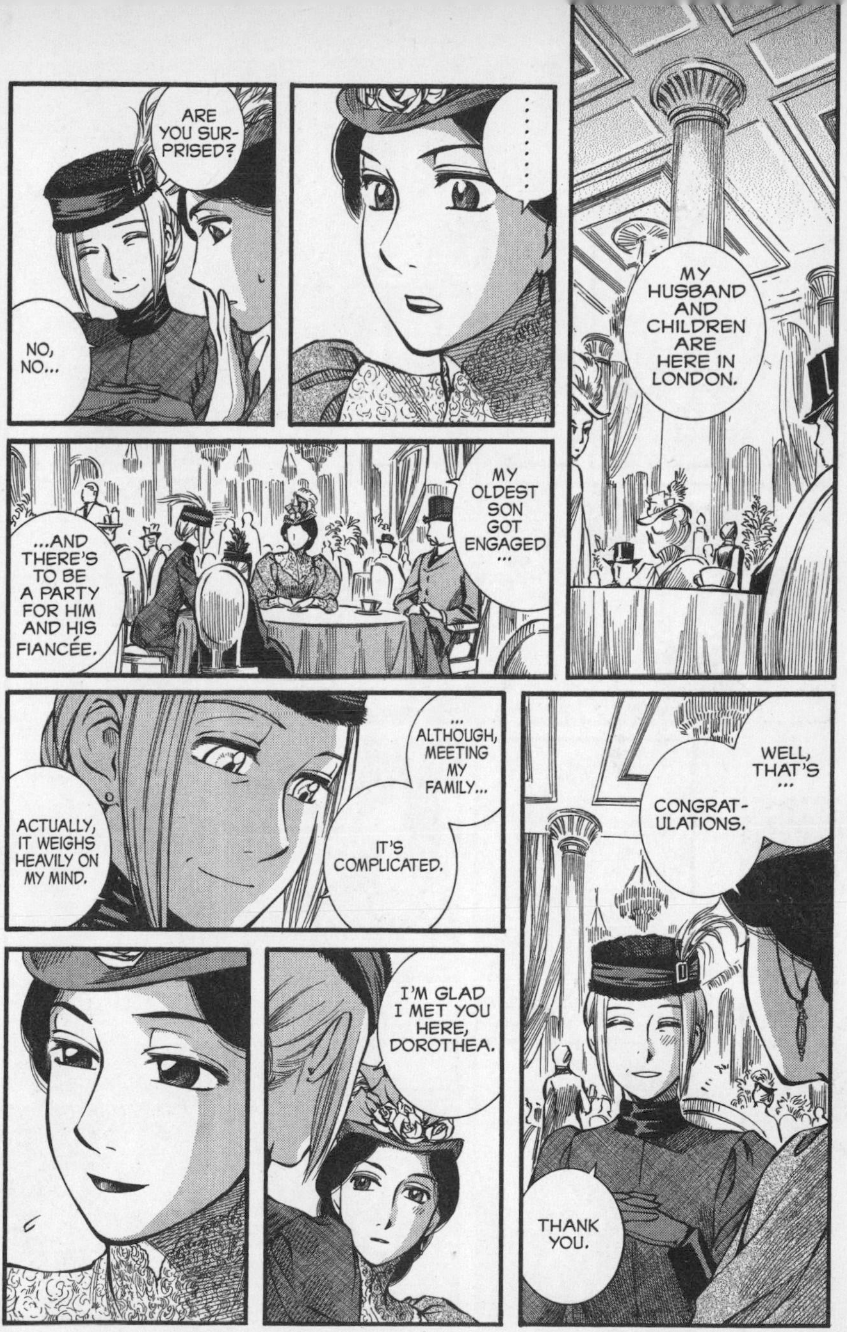
MY HUSBAND AND CHILDREN ARE HERE IN LONDON.
......
ARE YOU SURPRISED?
NO, NO...
MY OLDEST SON GOT ENGAGED...
...AND THERE'S TO BE A PARTY FOR HIM AND HIS FIANCÉE.
WELL, THAT'S... CONGRATULATIONS.
THANK YOU.
...ALTHOUGH, MEETING MY FAMILY...
IT'S COMPLICATED.
ACTUALLY, IT WEIGHS HEAVILY ON MY MIND.
I'M GLAD I MET YOU HERE, DOROTHEA.

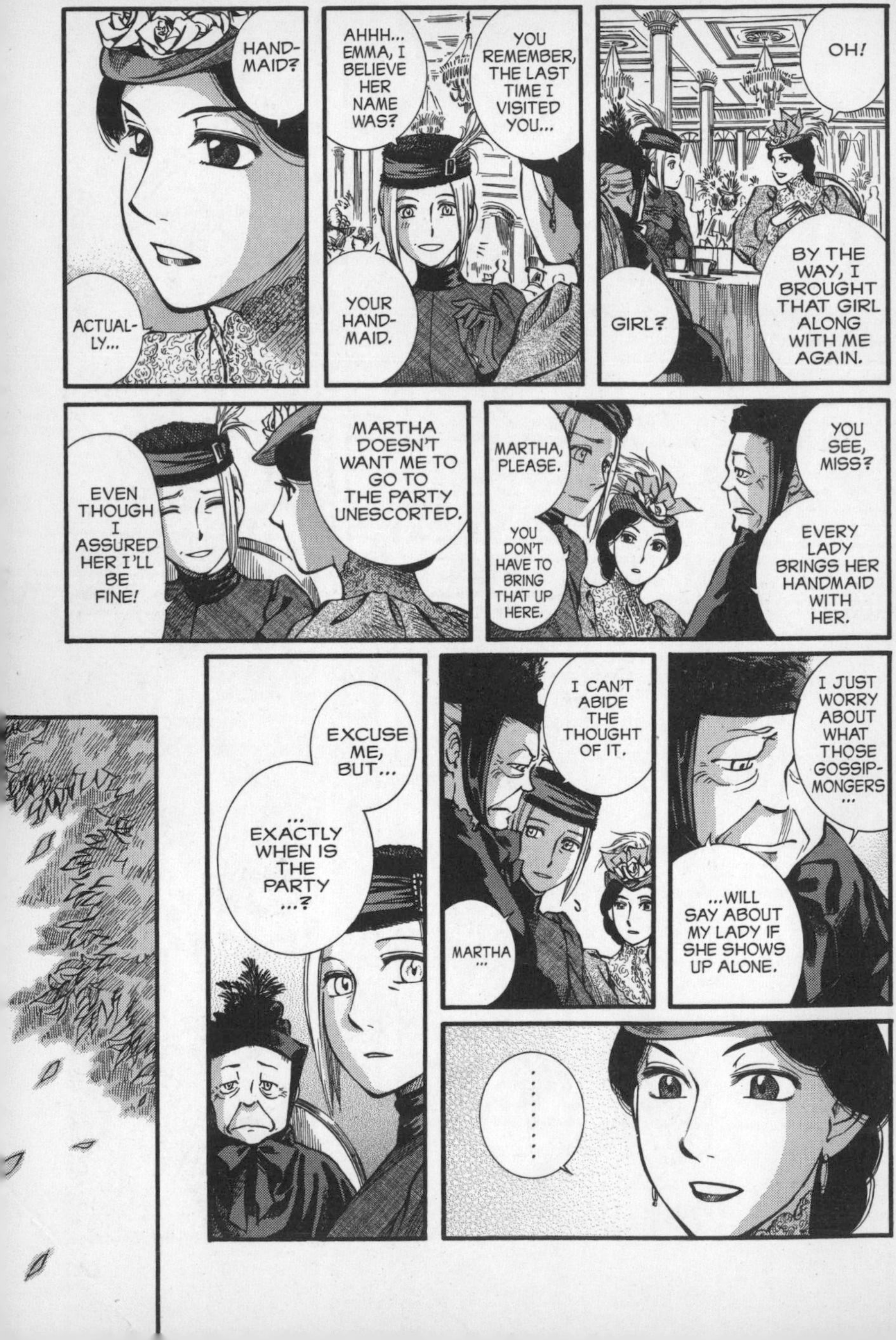
OH!
BY THE WAY, I BROUGHT THAT GIRL ALONG WITH ME AGAIN.
GIRL?
YOU REMEMBER, THE LAST TIME I VISITED YOU...
AHHH... EMMA, I BELIEVE HER NAME WAS?
YOUR HANDMAID.
HANDMAID?
ACTUALLY...
YOU SEE, MISS?
EVERY LADY BRINGS HER HANDMAID WITH HER.
MARTHA, PLEASE.
YOU DON'T HAVE TO BRING THAT UP HERE.
MARTHA DOESN'T WANT ME TO GO TO THE PARTY UNESCORTED.
EVEN THOUGH I ASSURED HER I'LL BE FINE!
I JUST WORRY ABOUT WHAT THOSE GOSSIPMONGERS...
...WILL SAY ABOUT MY LADY IF SHE SHOWS UP ALONE.
I CAN'T ABIDE THE THOUGHT OF IT.
MARTHA...
......
EXCUSE ME, BUT...
...EXACTLY WHEN IS THE PARTY...?

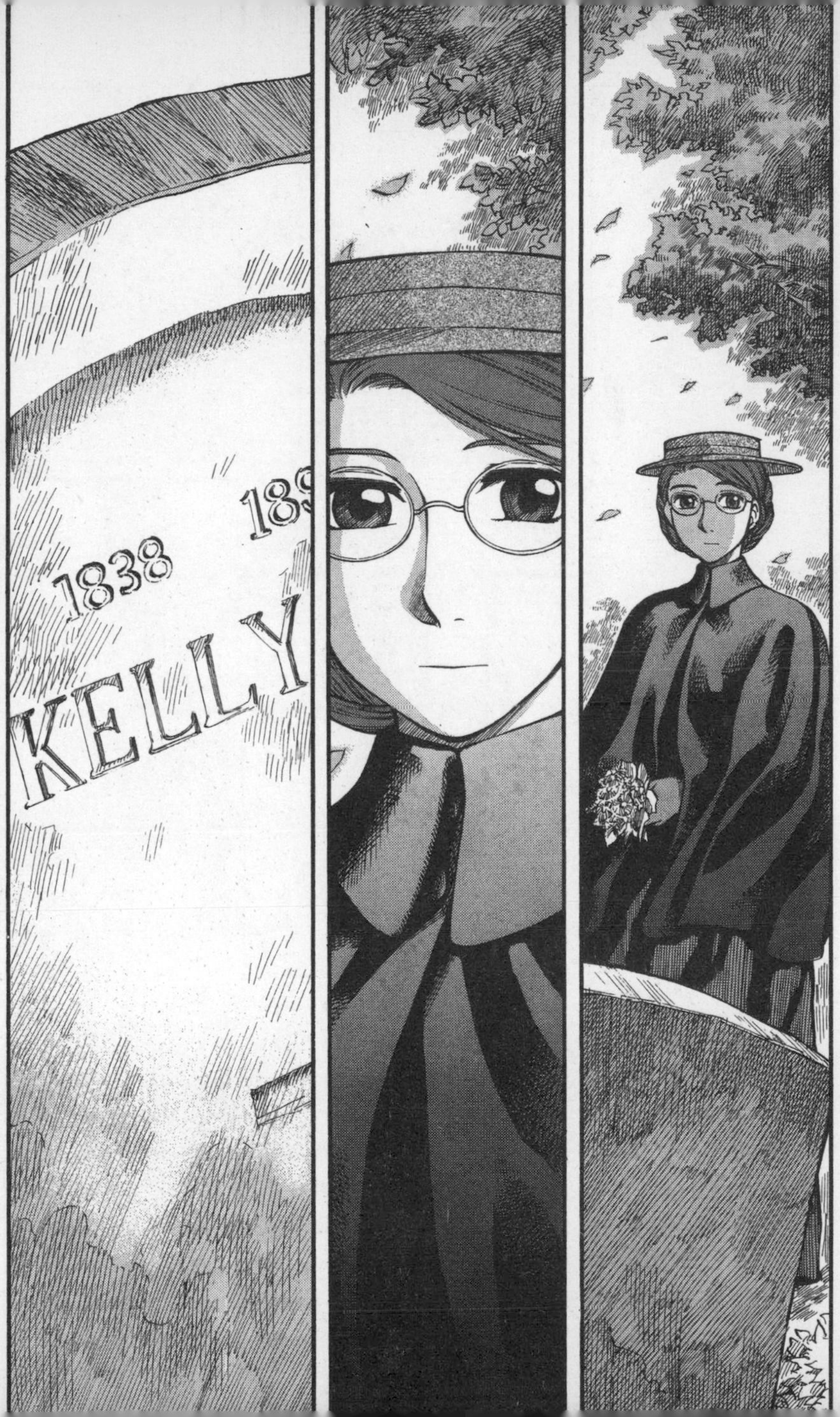
1838
KELLY

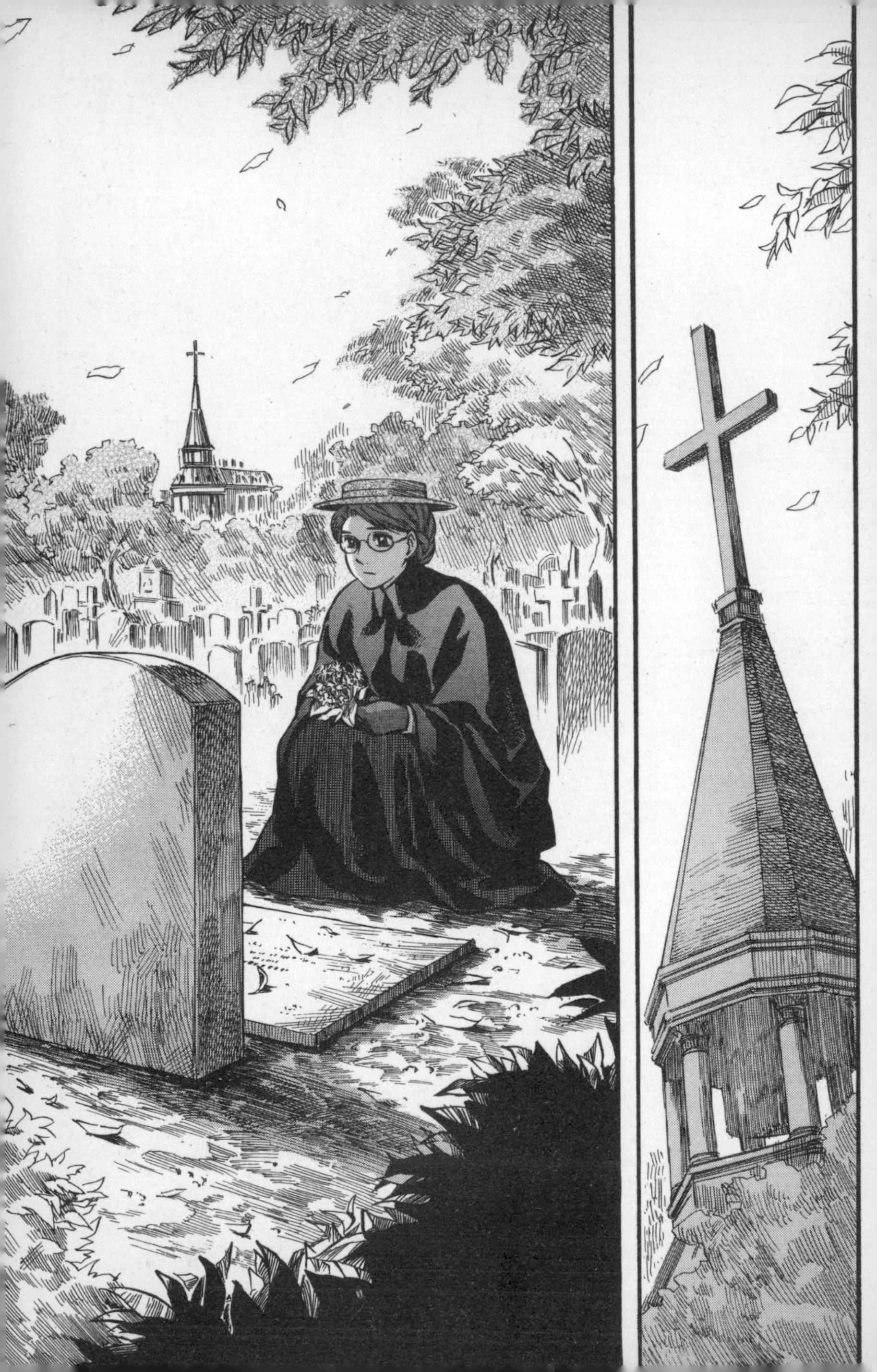

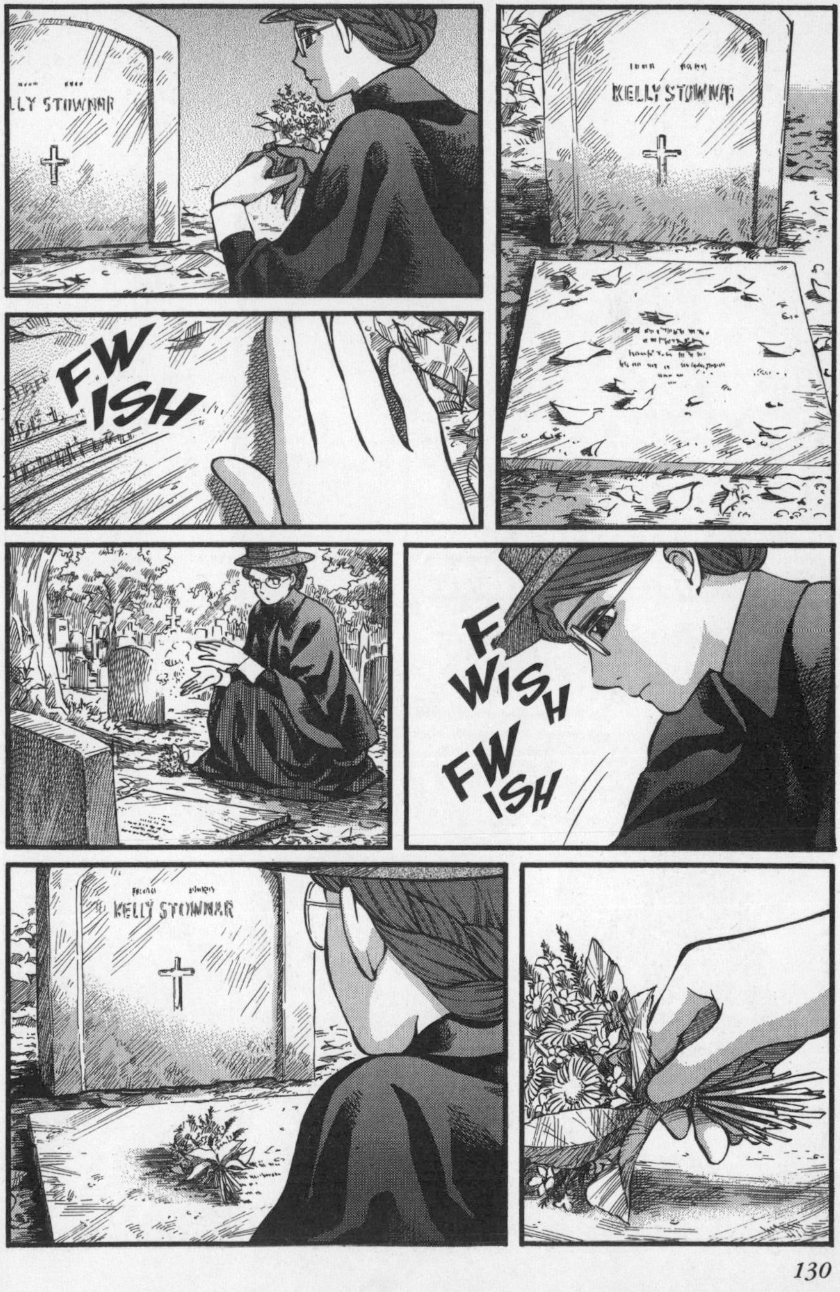

KELLY STOWNAR
LLY STOWNAR
FWISH
FWISH
FWISH
KELLY STOWNAR

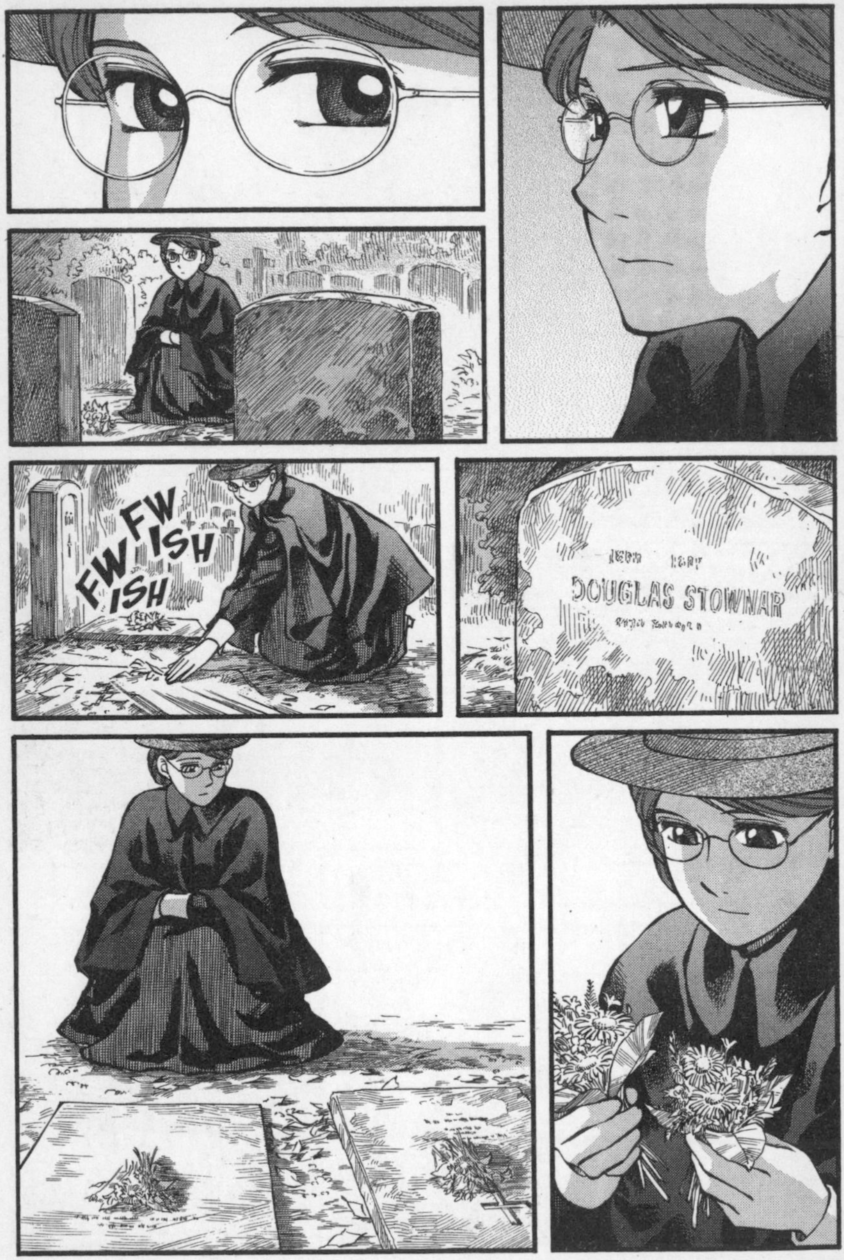
DOUGLAS STOWNAR
FWISH
FWISH

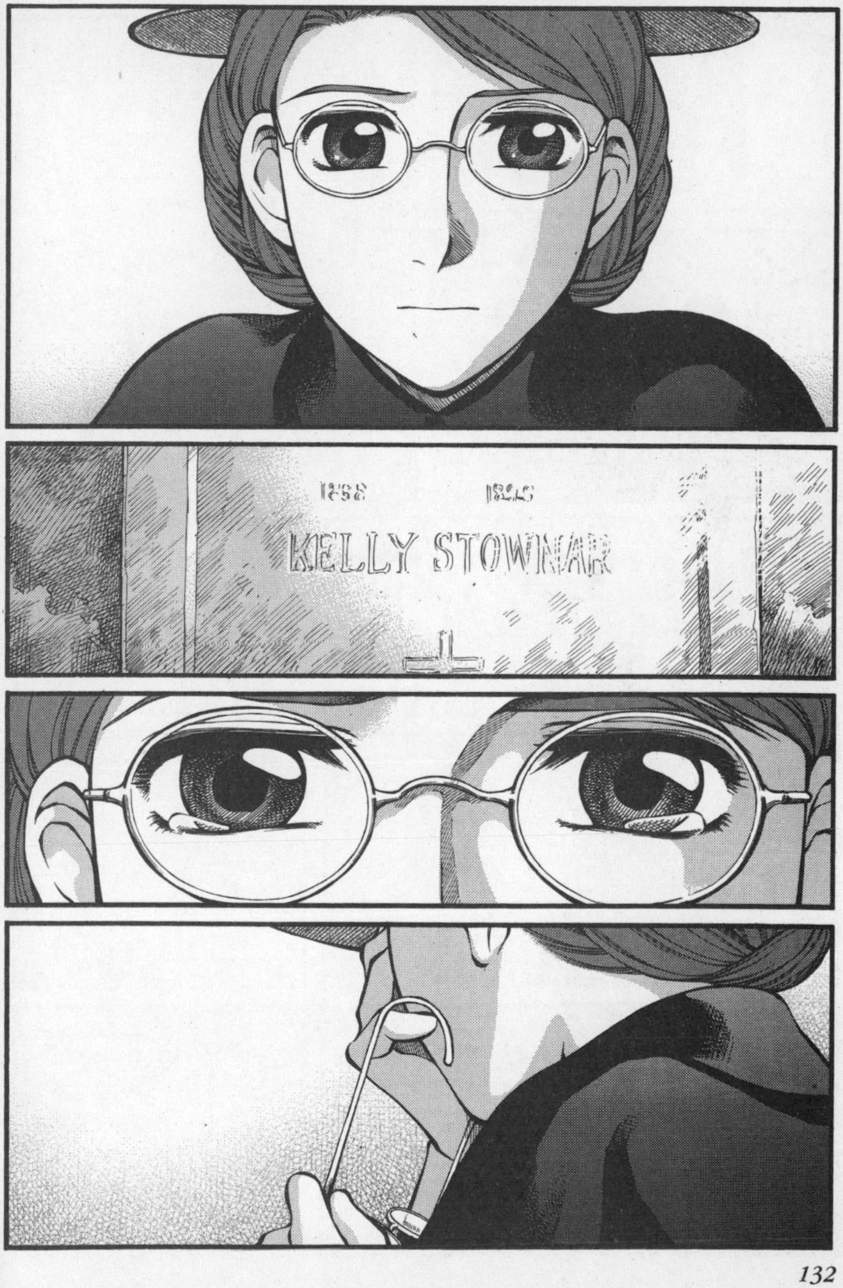
KELLY STOWNAR

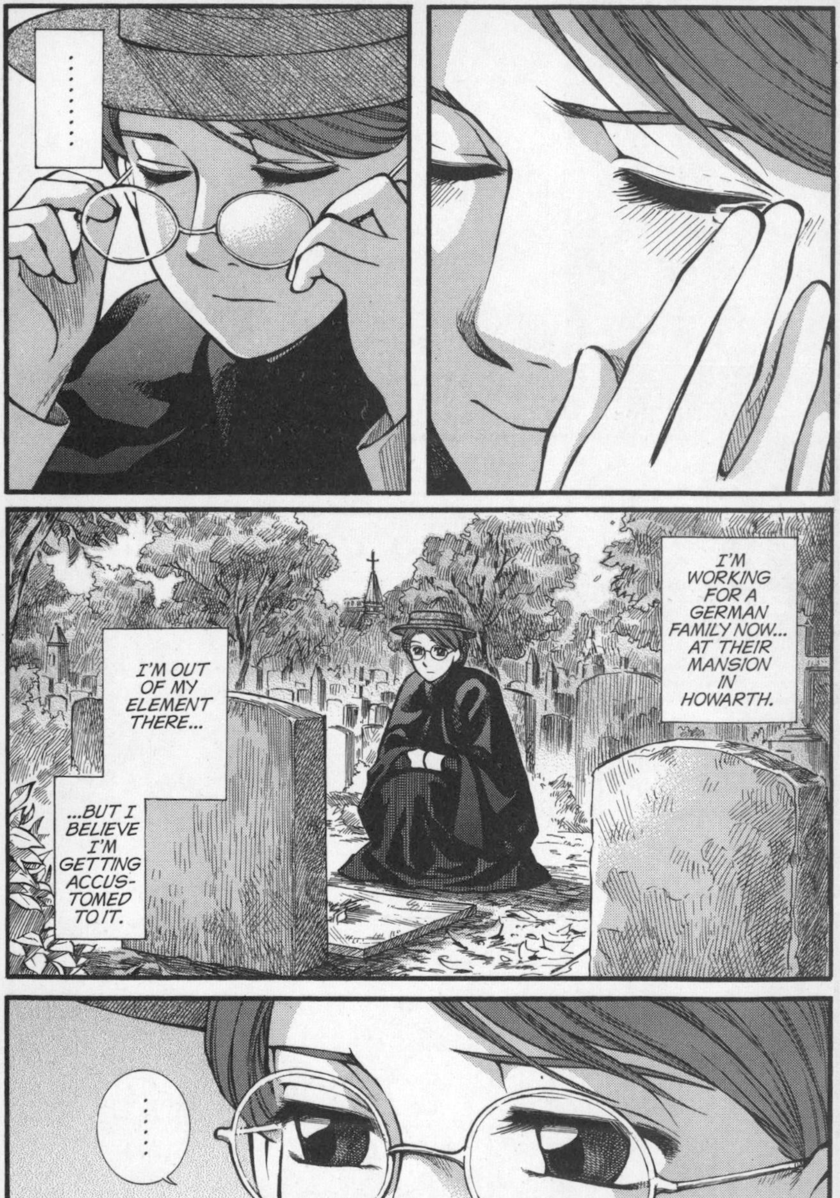
......
I'M WORKING FOR A GERMAN FAMILY NOW... AT THEIR MANSION IN HOWARTH.
I'M OUT OF MY ELEMENT THERE...
...BUT I BELIEVE I'M GETTING ACCUS-TOMED TO IT.
......

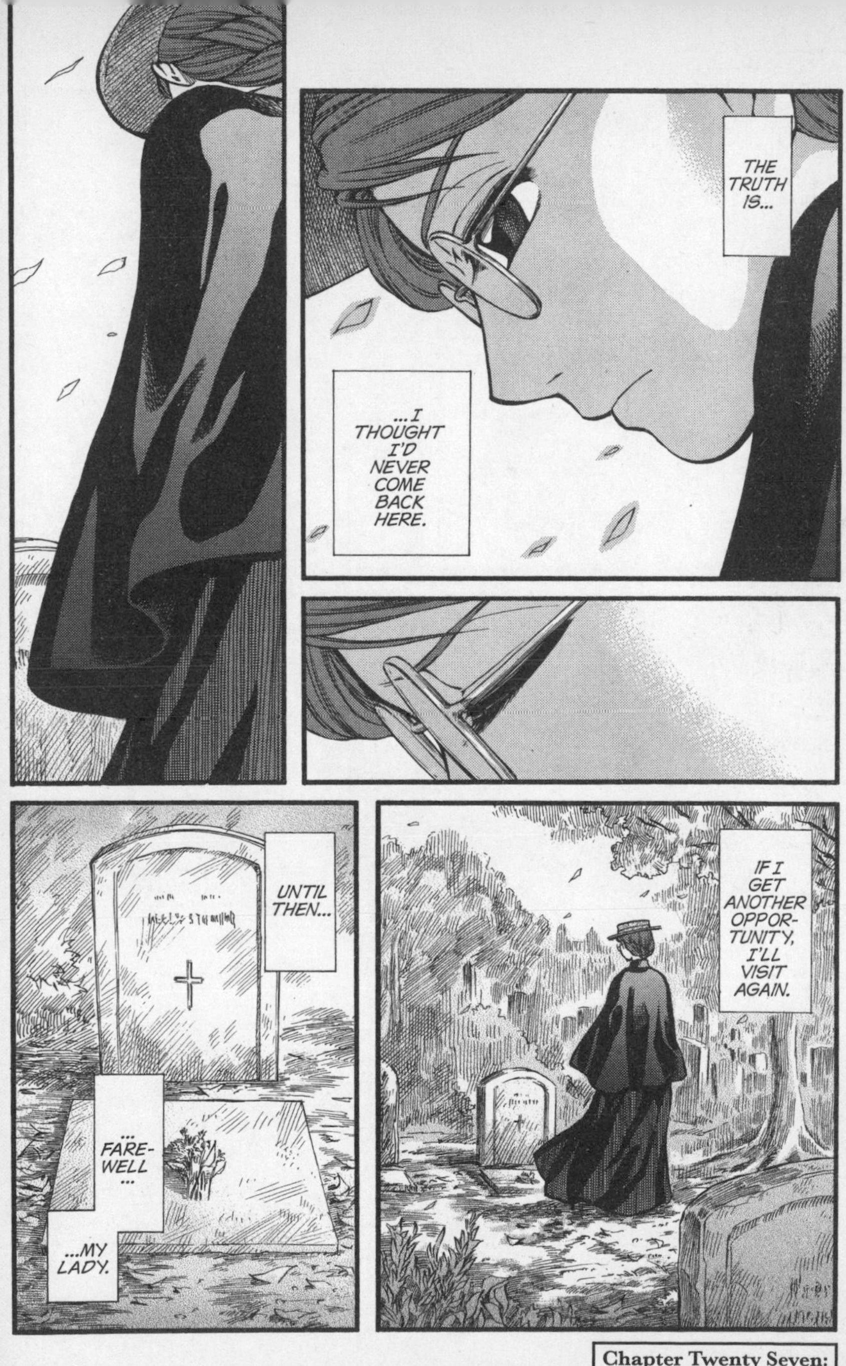
THE TRUTH IS...
...I THOUGHT I'D NEVER COME BACK HERE.
IF I GET ANOTHER OPPOR-TUNITY, I'LL VISIT AGAIN.
UNTIL THEN...
...FARE-WELL...
...MY LADY.

Chapter Twenty Seven:
The End

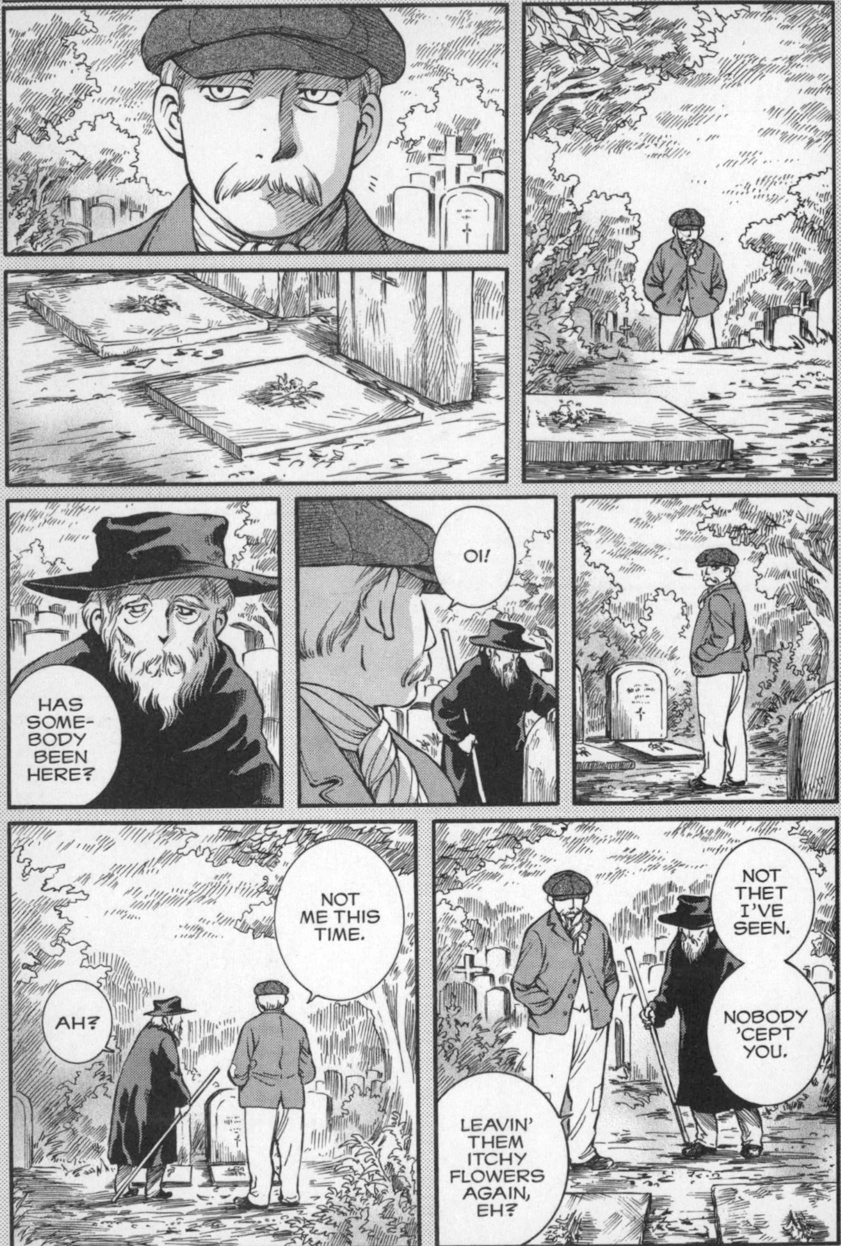
OI!
HAS SOMEBODY BEEN HERE?
NOT THET I'VE SEEN.
NOBODY 'CEPT YOU.
LEAVIN' THEM ITCHY FLOWERS AGAIN, EH?
NOT ME THIS TIME.
AH?

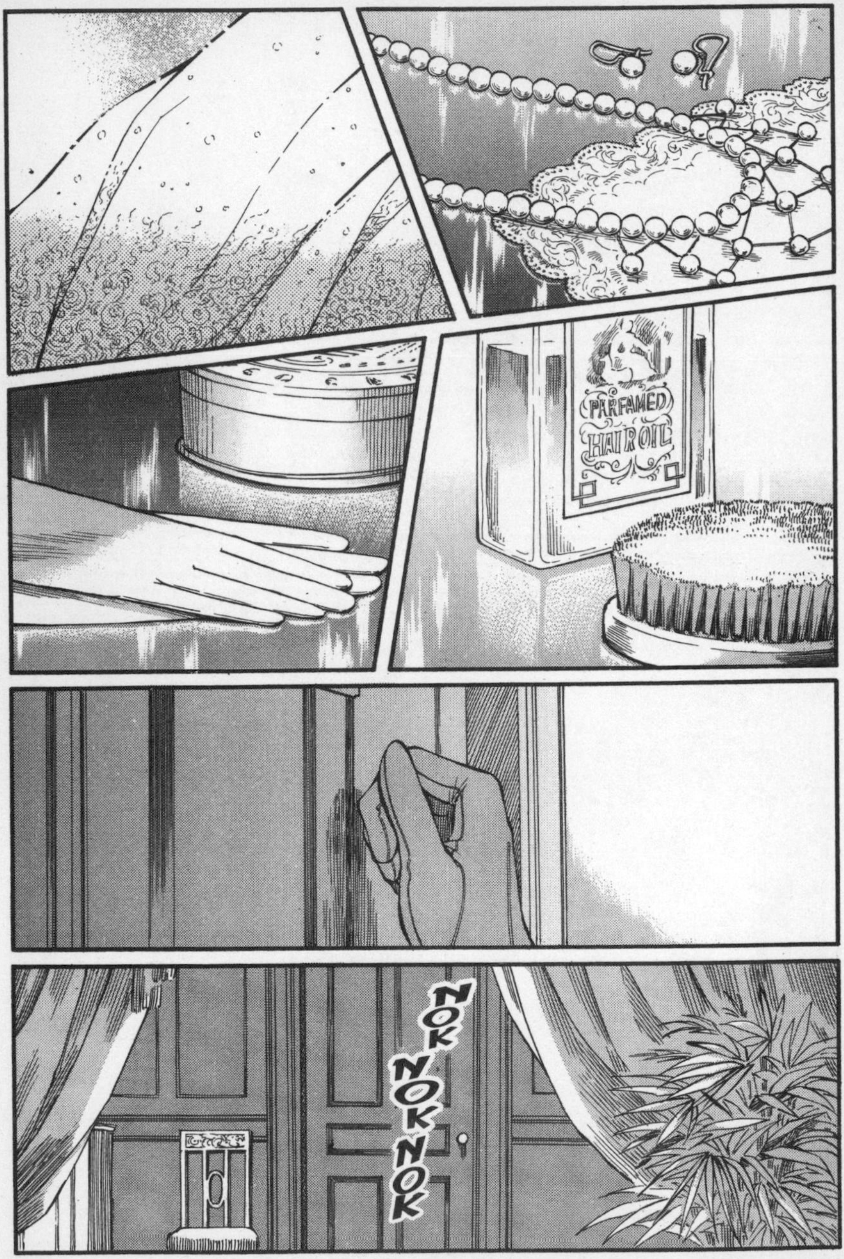
PARFAMED
HAIR OIL
NOK NOK NOK

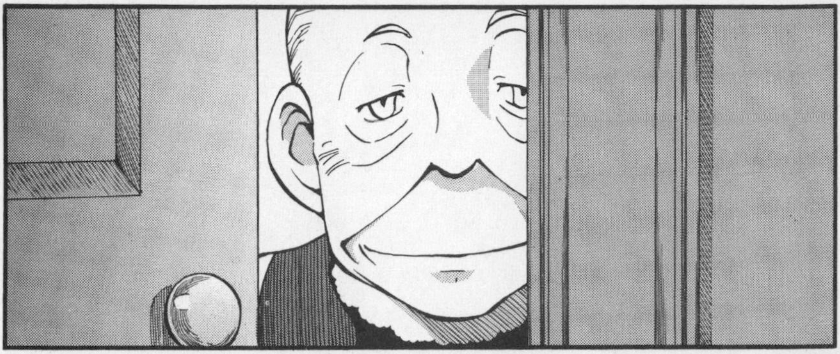

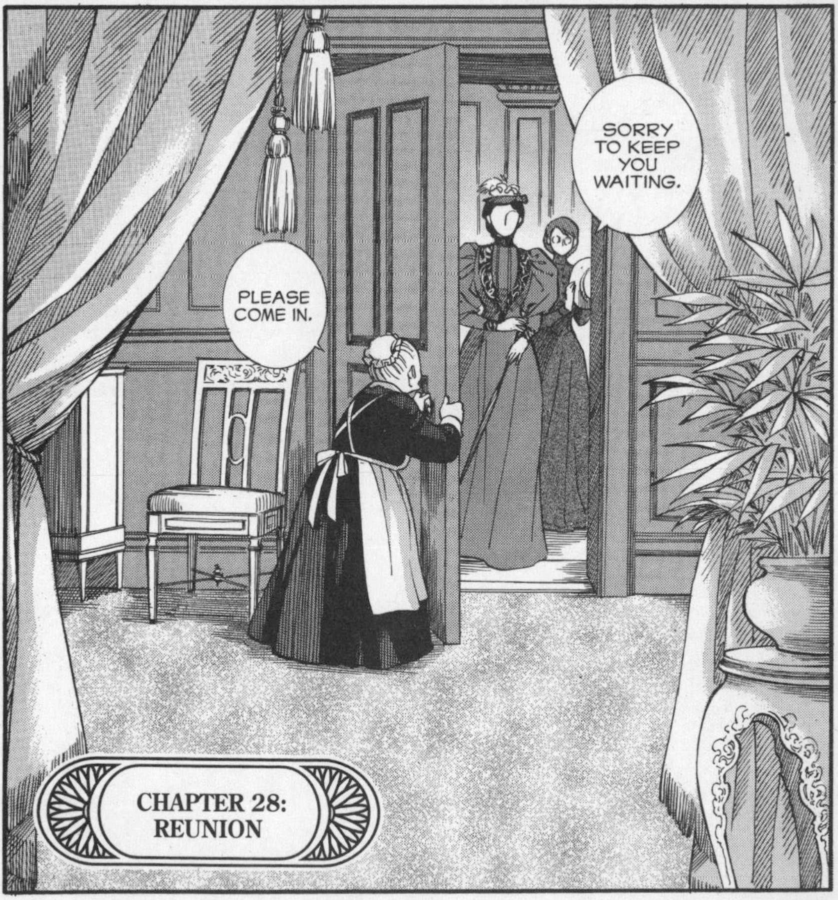
SORRY TO KEEP YOU WAITING.
PLEASE COME IN.
CHAPTER 28: REUNION

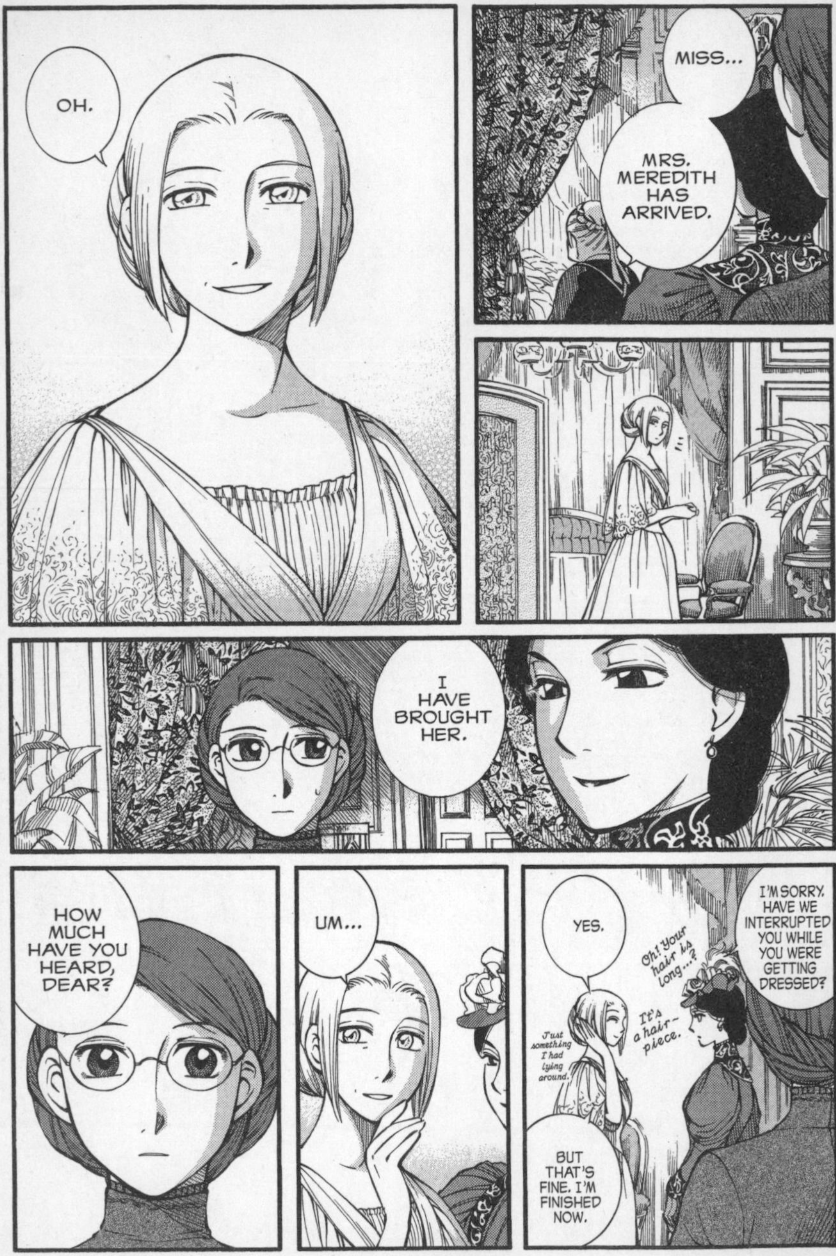
MISS...
MRS. MEREDITH HAS ARRIVED.
OH.
I HAVE BROUGHT HER.
I'M SORRY. HAVE WE INTERRUPTED YOU WHILE YOU WERE GETTING DRESSED?
YES.
Oh! Your hair is long...?
It's a hair-piece.
Just something I had lying around.
BUT THAT'S FINE. I'M FINISHED NOW.
UM...
HOW MUCH HAVE YOU HEARD, DEAR?

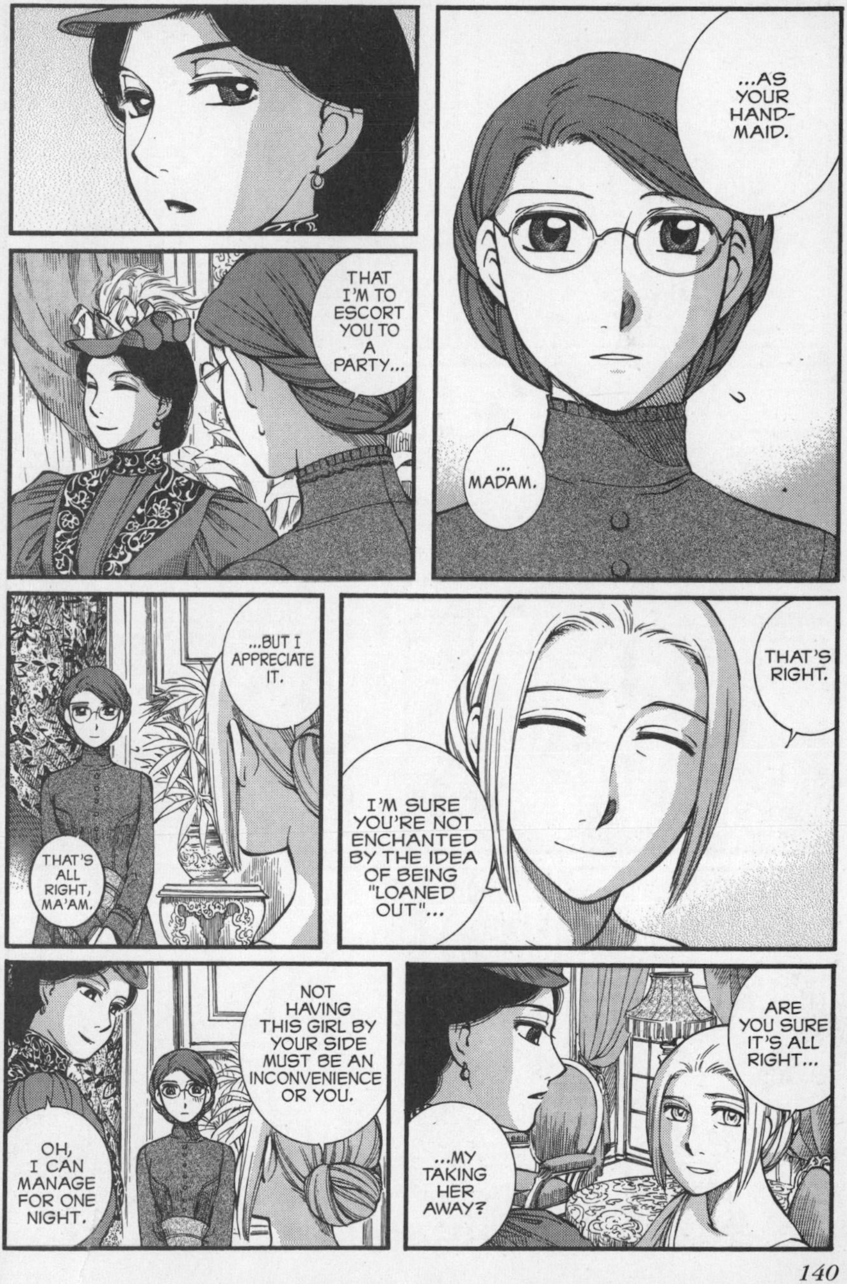
...AS YOUR HAND-MAID.
...MADAM.
THAT I'M TO ESCORT YOU TO A PARTY...
THAT'S SURE RIGHT.
I'M SURE YOU'RE NOT ENCHANTED BY THE IDEA OF BEING "LOANED OUT"...
...BUT I APPRECIATE IT.
THAT'S ALL RIGHT, MA'AM.
ARE YOU SURE IT'S ALL RIGHT...
...MY TAKING HER AWAY?
NOT HAVING THIS GIRL BY YOUR SIDE MUST BE AN INCONVENIENCE OR YOU.
OH, I CAN MANAGE FOR ONE NIGHT.

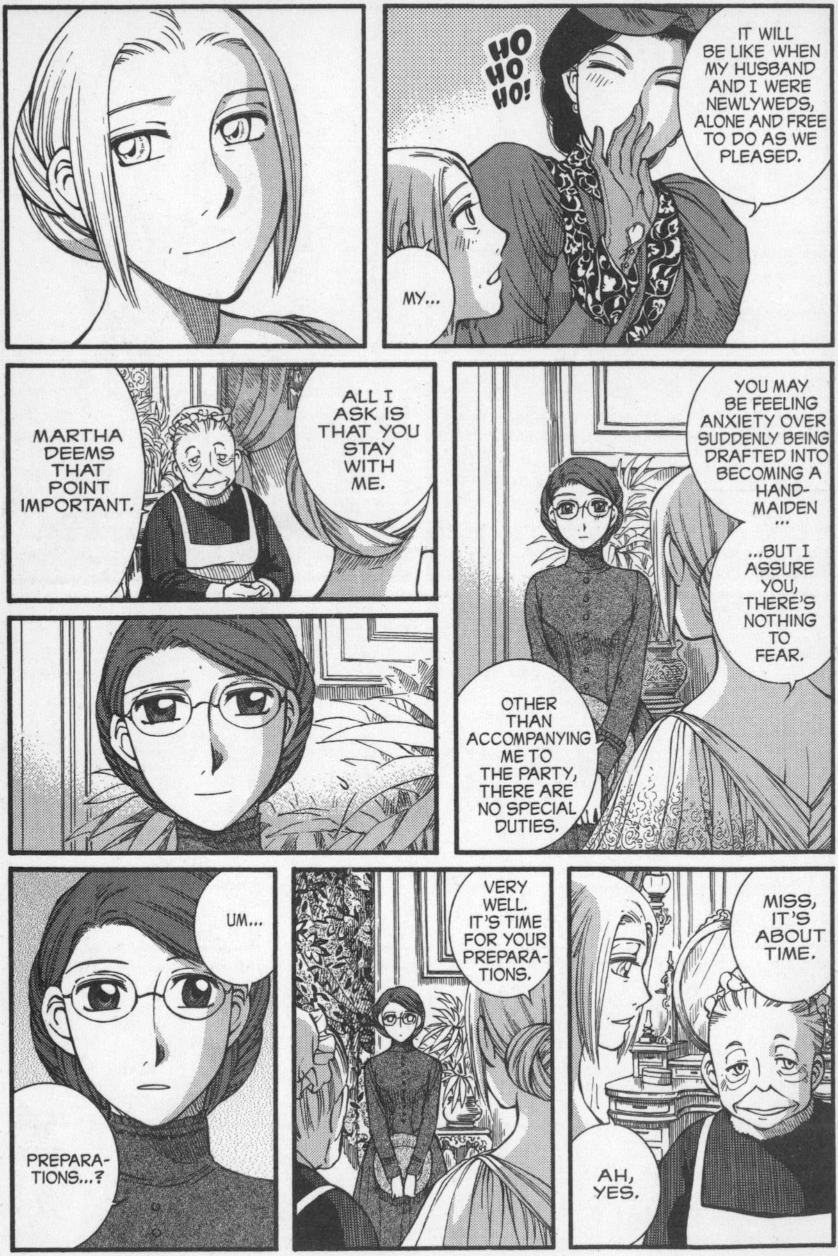
HO HO HO!
IT WILL BE LIKE WHEN MY HUSBAND AND I WERE NEWLYWEDS, ALONE AND FREE TO DO AS WE PLEASED.
MY...
YOU MAY BE FEELING ANXIETY OVER SUDDENLY BEING DRAFTED INTO BECOMING A HAND-MAIDEN...
...BUT I ASSURE YOU, THERE'S NOTHING TO FEAR.
OTHER THAN ACCOMPANYING ME TO THE PARTY, THERE ARE NO SPECIAL DUTIES.
ALL I ASK IS THAT YOU STAY WITH ME.
MARTHA DEEMS THAT POINT IMPORTANT.
MISS, IT'S ABOUT TIME.
AH, YES.
VERY WELL. IT'S TIME FOR YOUR PREPARA-TIONS.
UM...
PREPARA-TIONS...?

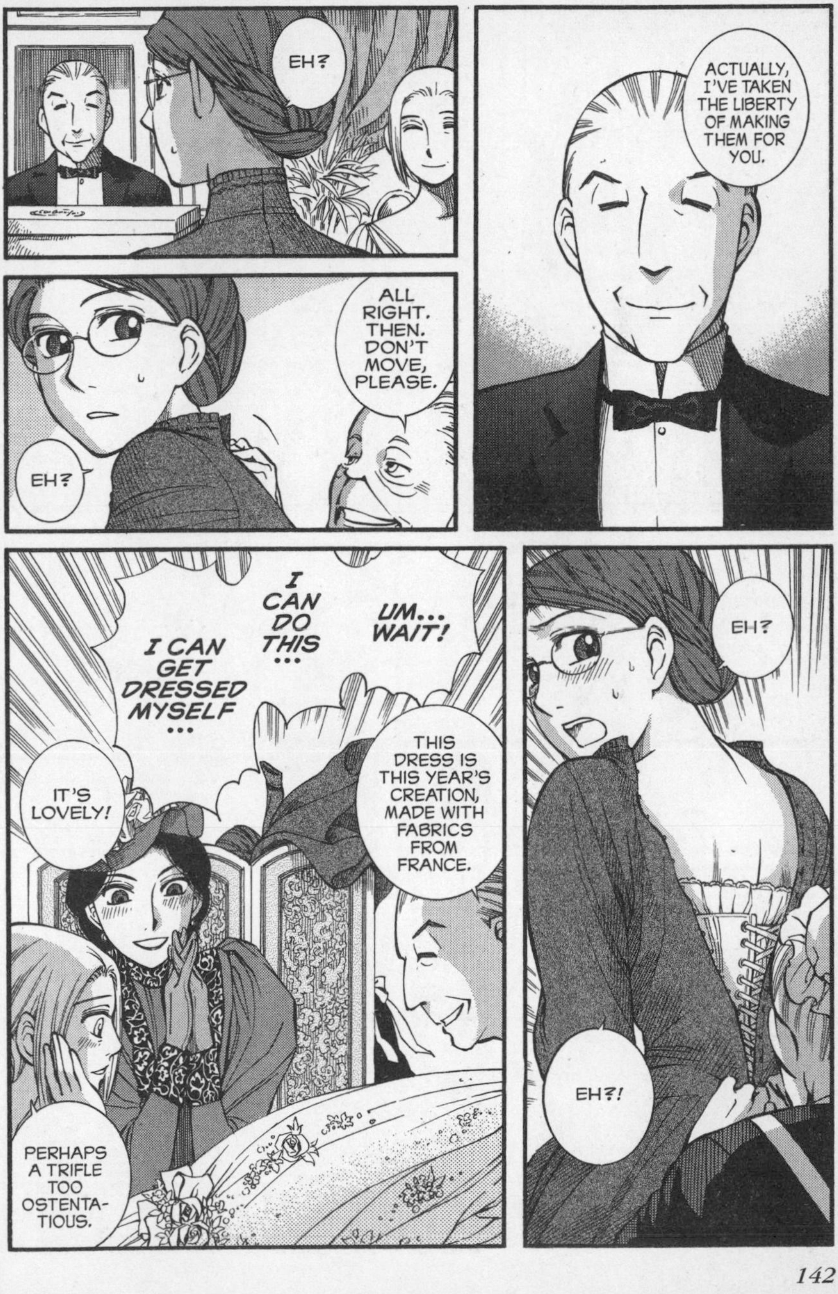
ACTUALLY, I'VE TAKEN THE LIBERTY OF MAKING THEM FOR YOU.
EH?
ALL RIGHT. THEN. DON'T MOVE, PLEASE.
EH?
EH?
EH?!
UM... WAIT!
I CAN DO THIS...
I CAN GET DRESSED MYSELF...
THIS DRESS IS THIS YEAR'S CREATION, MADE WITH FABRICS FROM FRANCE.
IT'S LOVELY!
PERHAPS A TRIFLE TOO OSTENTATIOUS.

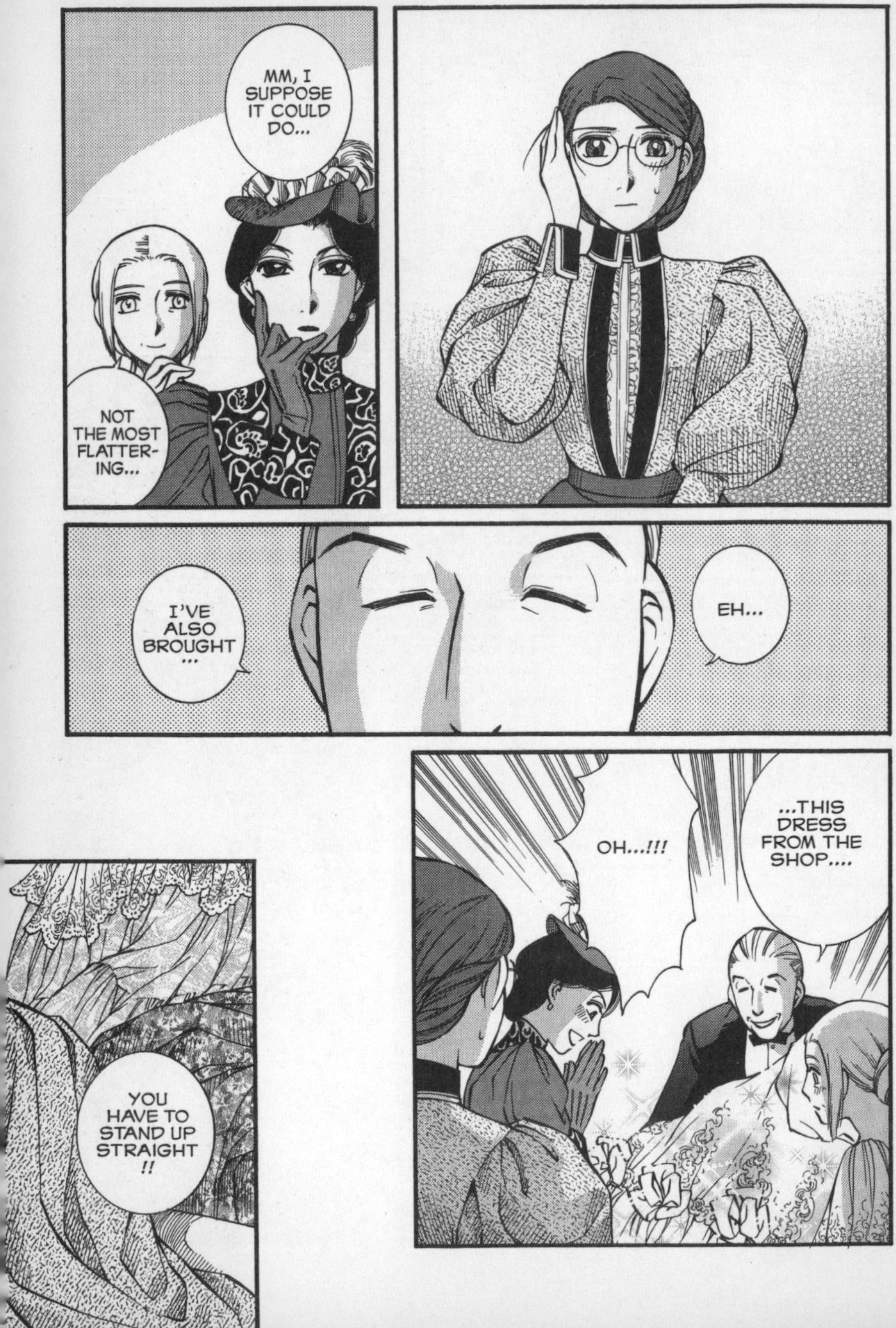
MM, I SUPPOSE IT COULD DO...
NOT THE MOST FLATTER-ING...
EH...
I'VE ALSO BROUGHT...
...THIS DRESS FROM THE SHOP....
OH...!!!
YOU HAVE TO STAND UP STRAIGHT!!

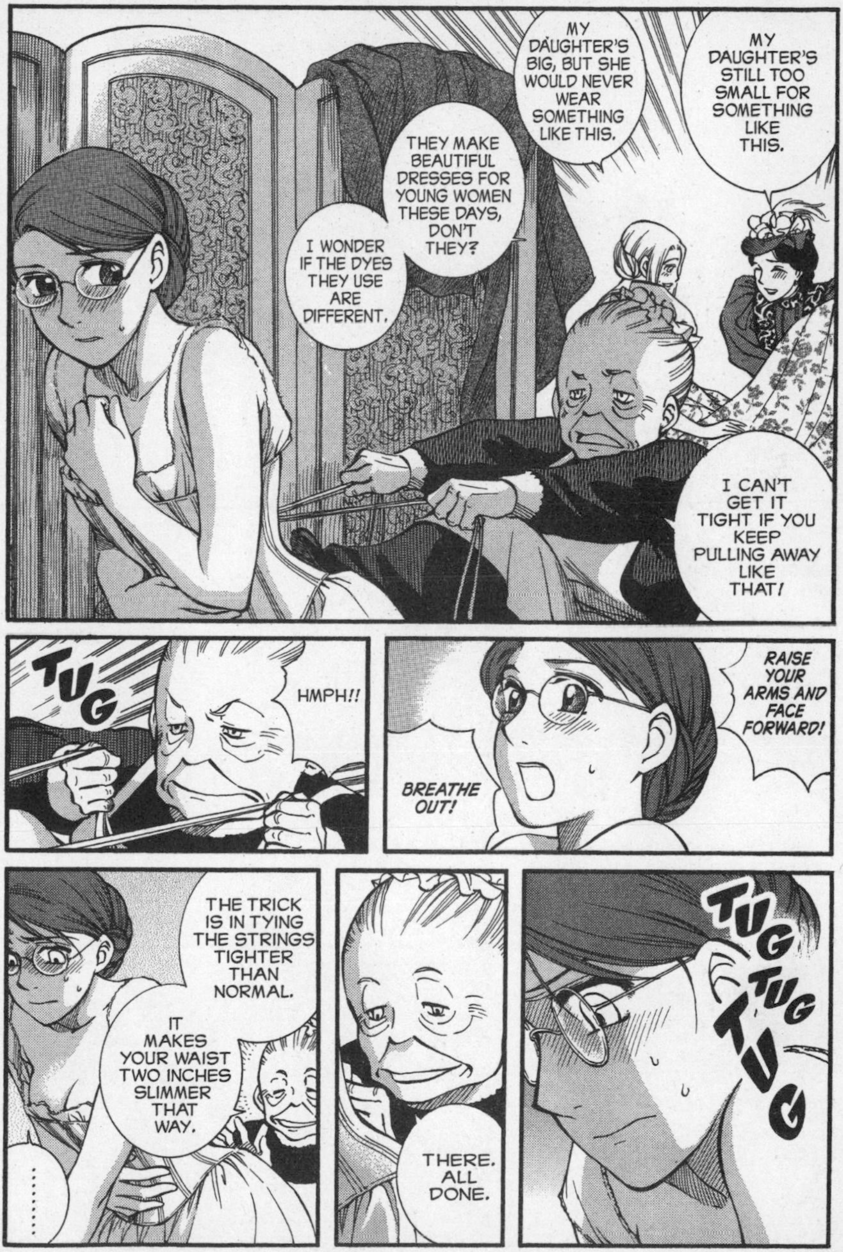
MY DAUGHTER'S STILL TOO SMALL FOR SOMETHING LIKE THIS.
MY DAUGHTER'S BIG, BUT SHE WOULD NEVER WEAR SOMETHING LIKE THIS.
THEY MAKE BEAUTIFUL DRESSES FOR YOUNG WOMEN THESE DAYS, DON'T THEY?
I WONDER IF THE DYES THEY USE ARE DIFFERENT.
I CAN'T GET IT TIGHT IF YOU KEEP PULLING AWAY LIKE THAT!
RAISE YOUR ARMS AND FACE FORWARD!
BREATHE OUT!
TUG
HMPH!!
TUG TUG TUG TUG
THERE. ALL DONE.
THE TRICK IS IN TYING THE STRINGS TIGHTER THAN NORMAL.
IT MAKES YOUR WAIST TWO INCHES SLIMMER THAT WAY.
......

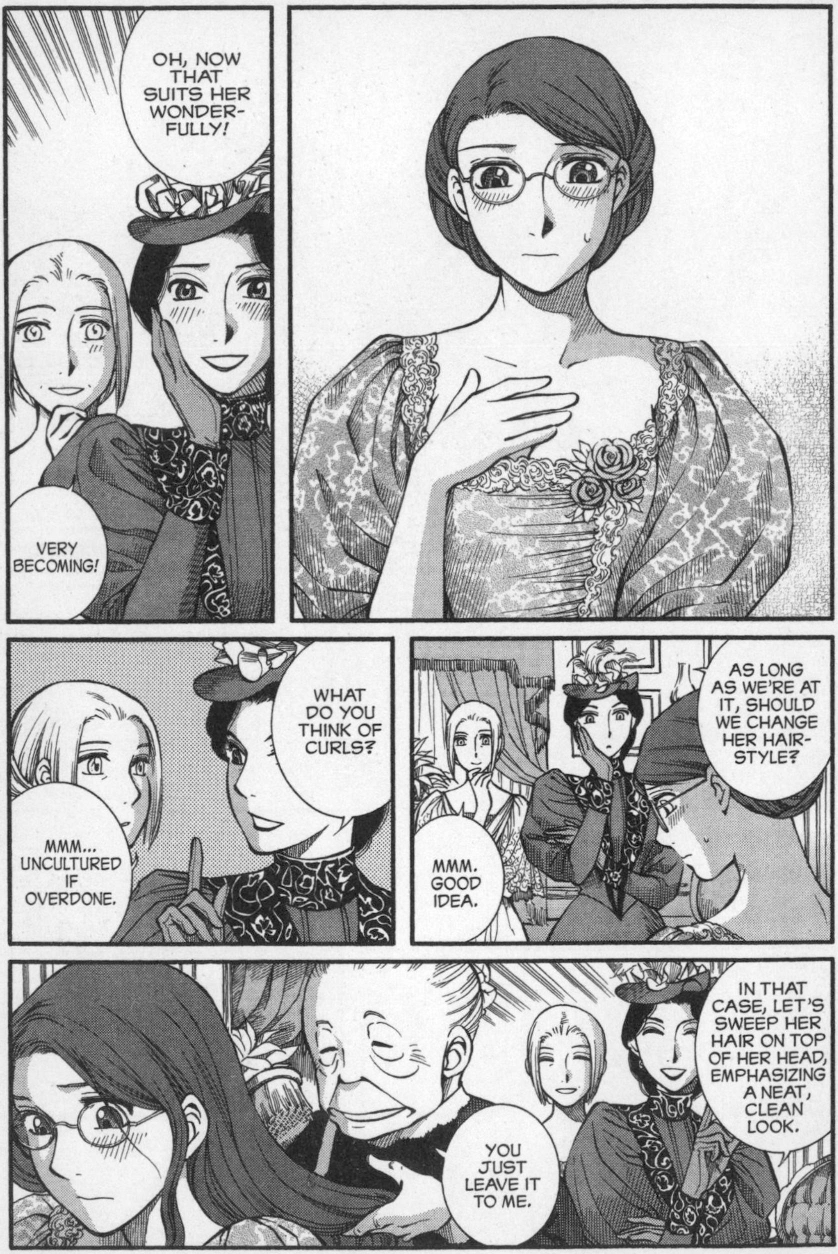
OH, NOW THAT SUITS HER WONDERFULLY!
VERY BECOMING!
AS LONG AS WE'RE AT IT, SHOULD WE CHANGE HER HAIRSTYLE?
MMM. GOOD IDEA.
WHAT DO YOU THINK OF CURLS?
MMM... UNCULTURED IF OVERDONE.
IN THAT CASE, LET'S SWEEP HER HAIR ON TOP OF HER HEAD, EMPHASIZING A NEAT, CLEAN LOOK.
YOU JUST LEAVE IT TO ME.

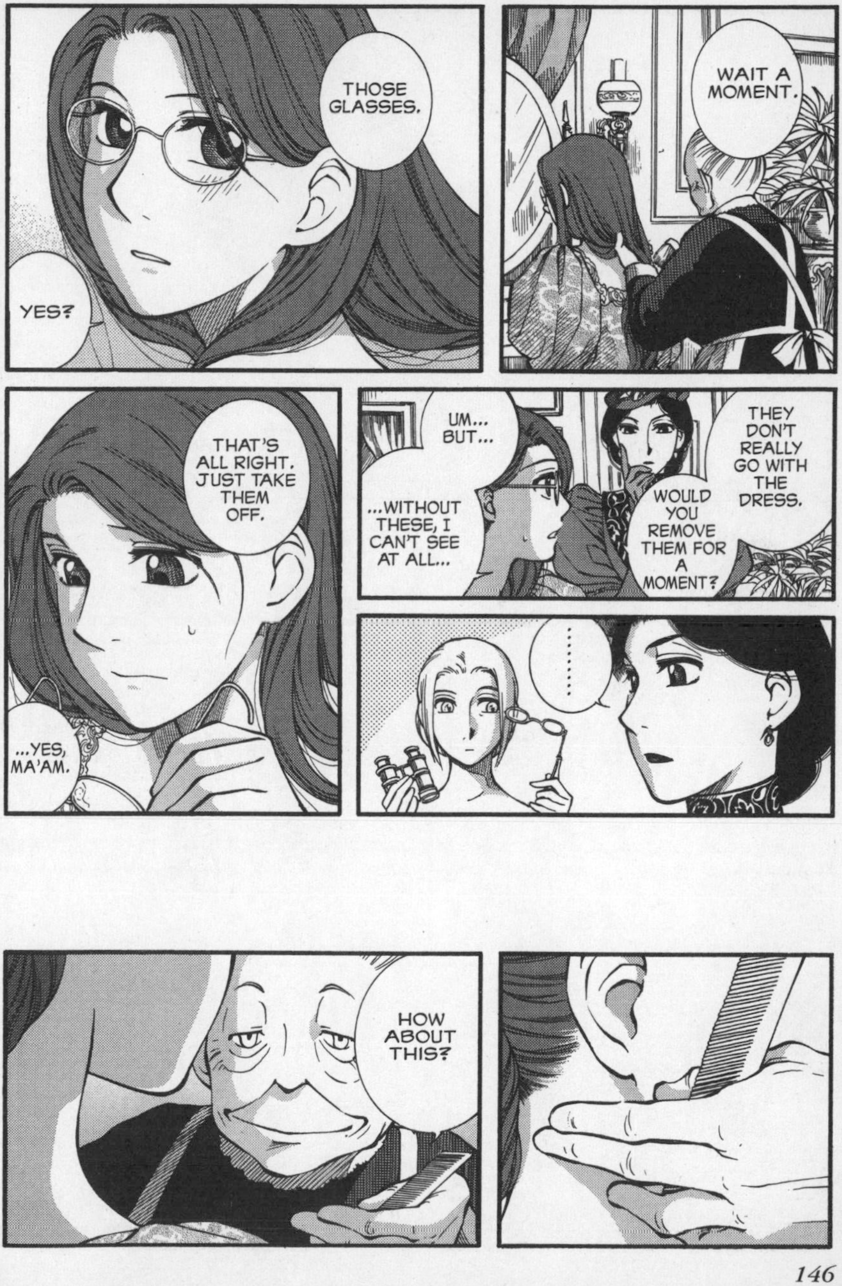
WAIT A MOMENT.
THOSE GLASSES.
YES?
THEY DON'T REALLY GO WITH THE DRESS.
WOULD YOU REMOVE THEM FOR A MOMENT?
UM... BUT...
...WITHOUT THESE, I CAN'T SEE AT ALL...
......
THAT'S ALL RIGHT. JUST TAKE THEM OFF.
...YES, MA'AM.
HOW ABOUT THIS?

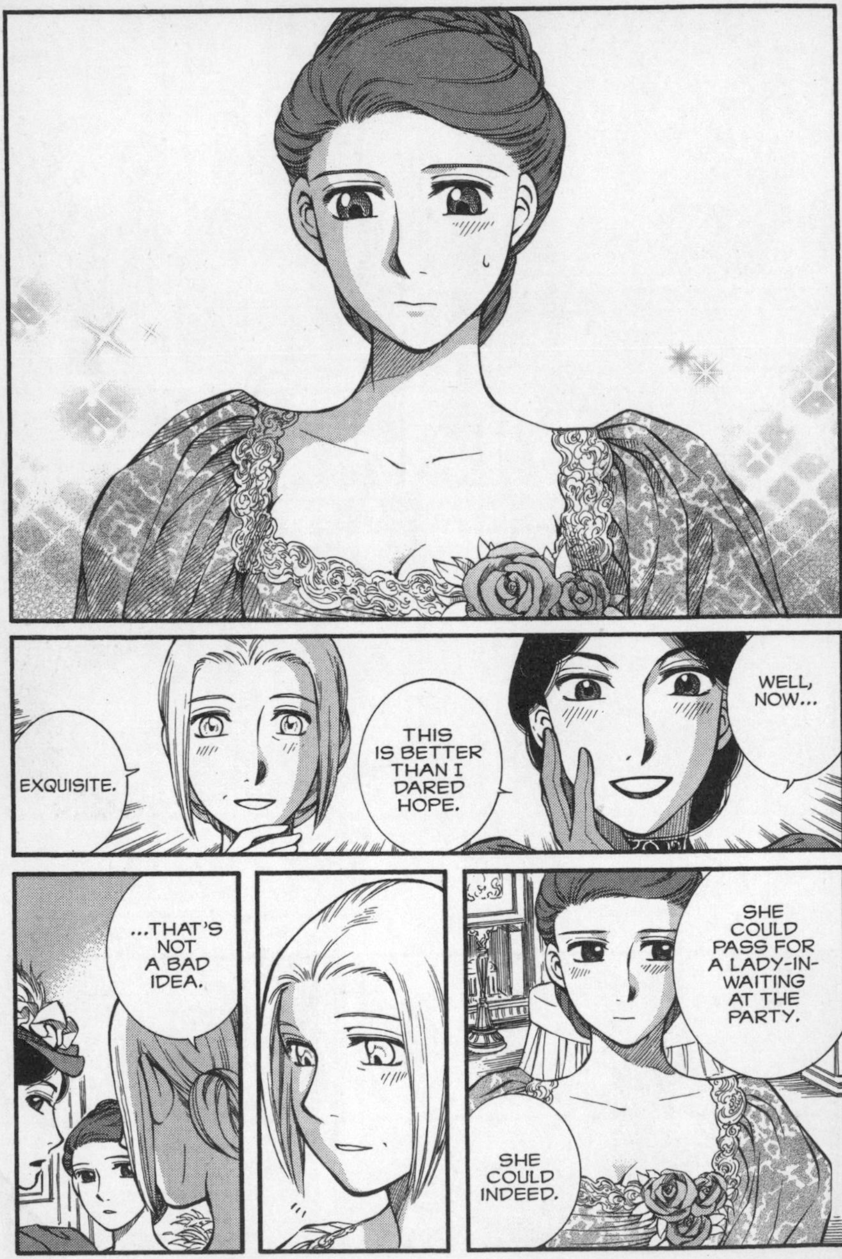
WELL, NOW...
THIS IS BETTER THAN I DARED HOPE.
EXQUISITE.
SHE COULD PASS FOR A LADY-IN-WAITING AT THE PARTY.
SHE COULD INDEED.
...THAT'S NOT A BAD IDEA.

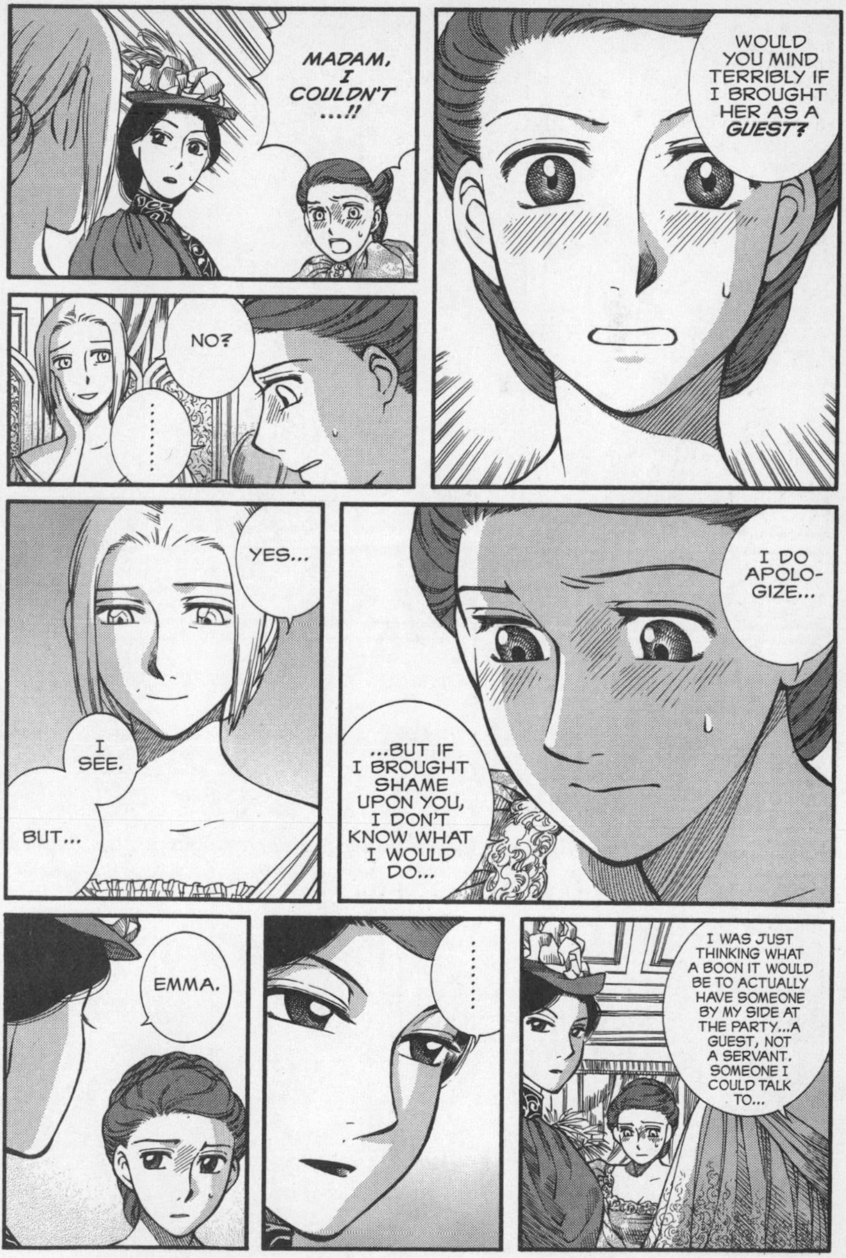
WOULD YOU MIND TERRIBLY IF I BROUGHT HER AS A *GUEST?*
MADAM, I COULDN'T ...!!
NO?
......
I DO APOLOGIZE...
...BUT IF I BROUGHT SHAME UPON YOU, I DON'T KNOW WHAT I WOULD DO...
YES...
I SEE.
BUT...
I WAS JUST THINKING WHAT A BOON IT WOULD BE TO ACTUALLY HAVE SOMEONE BY MY SIDE AT THE PARTY...A GUEST, NOT A SERVANT. SOMEONE I COULD TALK TO...
......
EMMA.

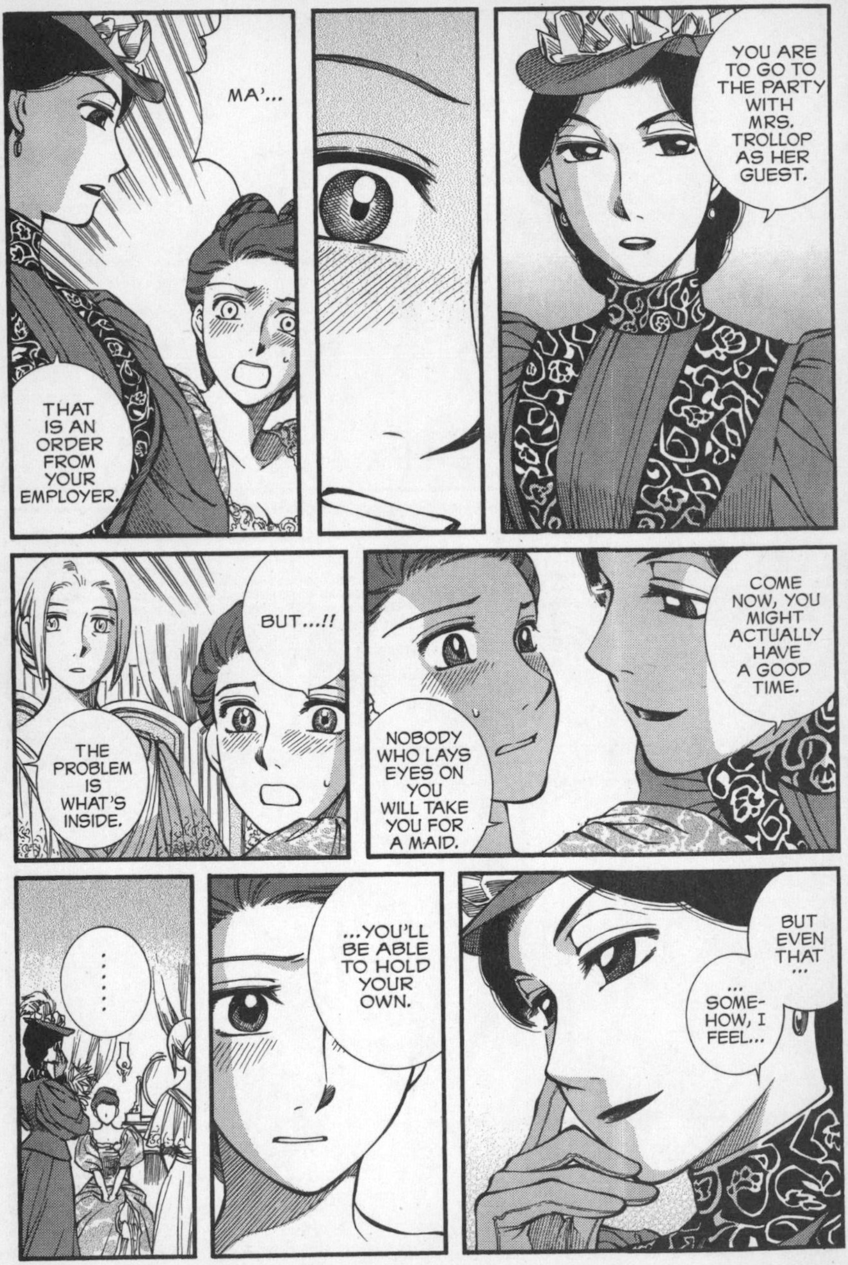
YOU ARE TO GO TO THE PARTY WITH MRS. TROLLOP AS HER GUEST.
MA'...
THAT IS AN ORDER FROM YOUR EMPLOYER.
COME NOW, YOU MIGHT ACTUALLY HAVE A GOOD TIME.
NOBODY WHO LAYS EYES ON YOU WILL TAKE YOU FOR A MAID.
BUT...!!
THE PROBLEM IS WHAT'S INSIDE.
BUT EVEN THAT...
...SOMEHOW, I FEEL...
...YOU'LL BE ABLE TO HOLD YOUR OWN.
......

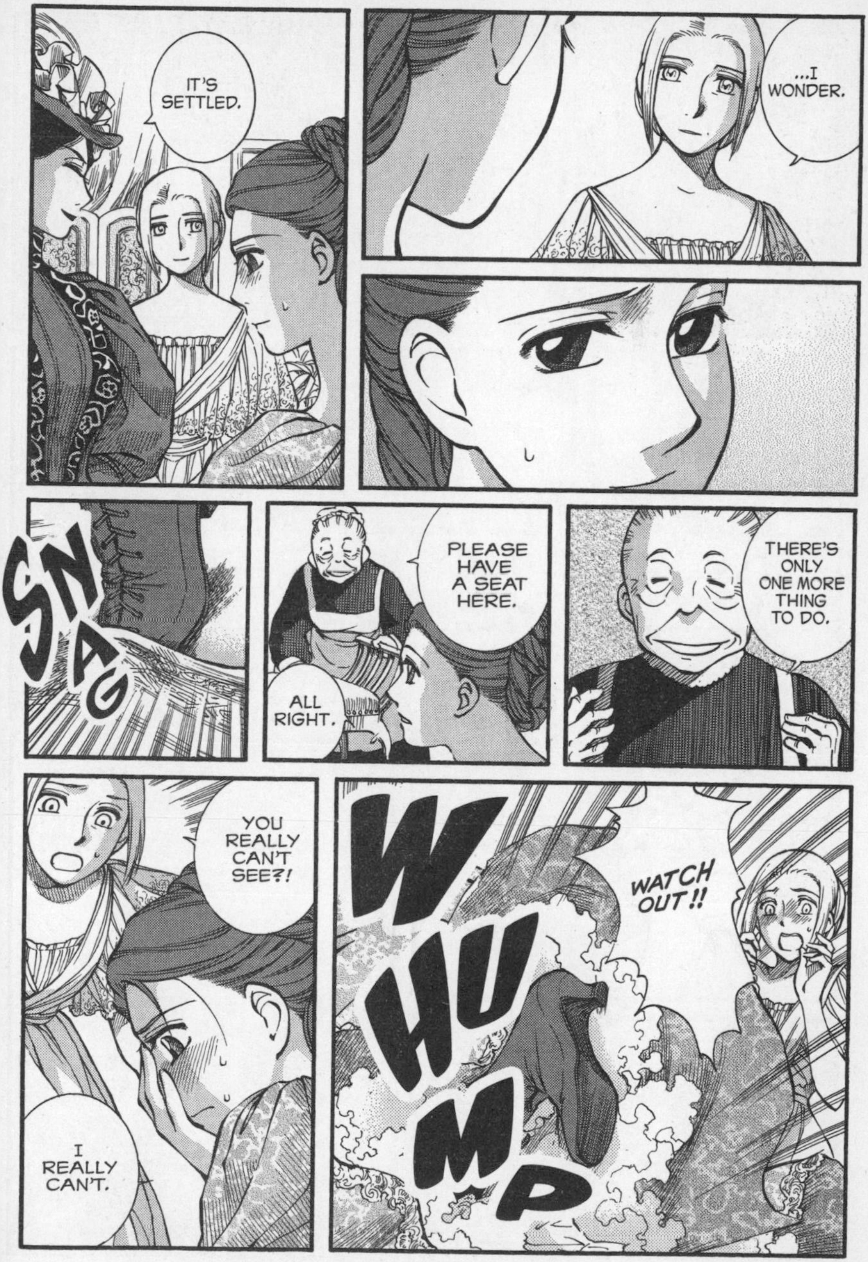
...I WONDER.
IT'S SETTLED.
THERE'S ONLY ONE MORE THING TO DO.
PLEASE HAVE A SEAT HERE.
ALL RIGHT.
SNAG
WATCH OUT!!
WHUMP
YOU REALLY CAN'T SEE?!
I REALLY CAN'T.

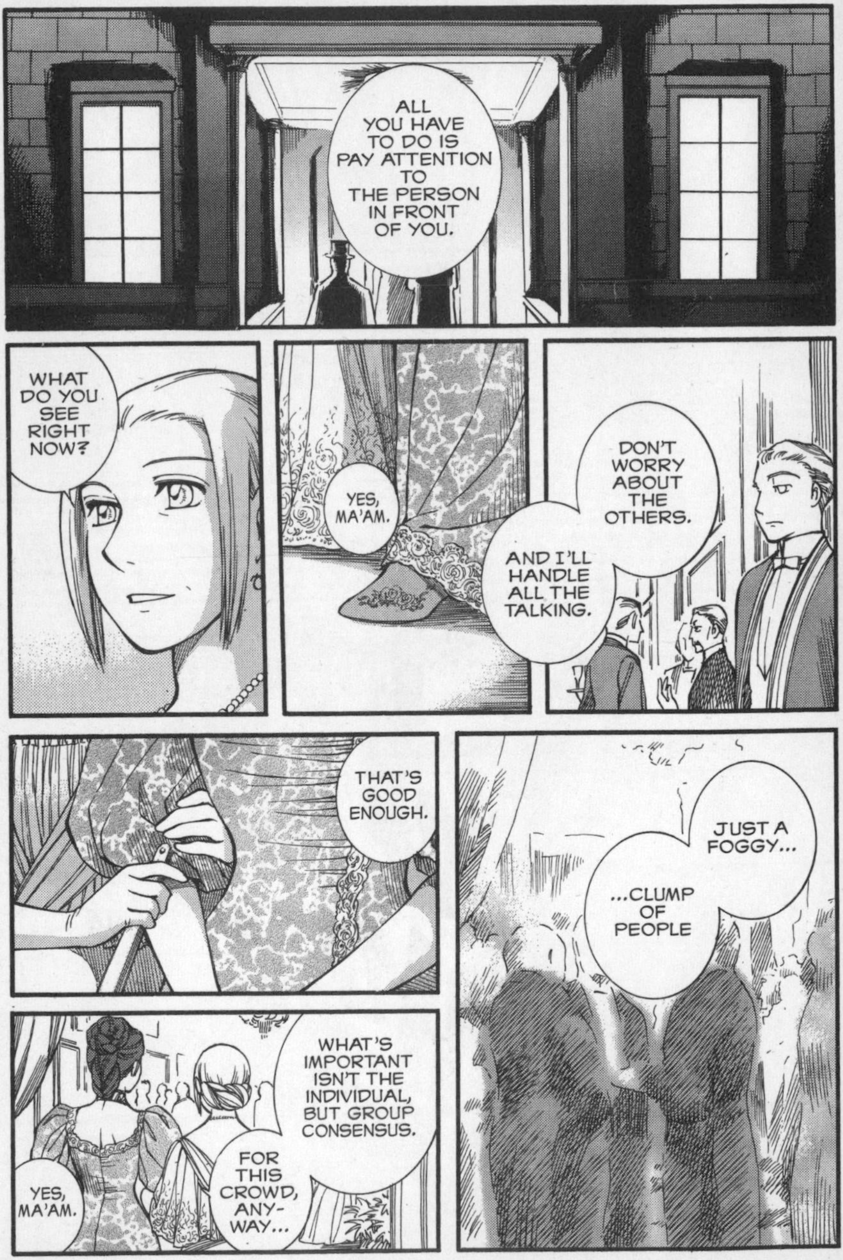
ALL YOU HAVE TO DO IS PAY ATTENTION TO THE PERSON IN FRONT OF YOU.
DON'T WORRY ABOUT THE OTHERS.
AND I'LL HANDLE ALL THE TALKING.
YES, MA'AM.
WHAT DO YOU SEE RIGHT NOW?
JUST A FOGGY...
...CLUMP OF PEOPLE
THAT'S GOOD ENOUGH.
WHAT'S IMPORTANT ISN'T THE INDIVIDUAL, BUT GROUP CONSENSUS.
FOR THIS CROWD, ANY-WAY...
YES, MA'AM.

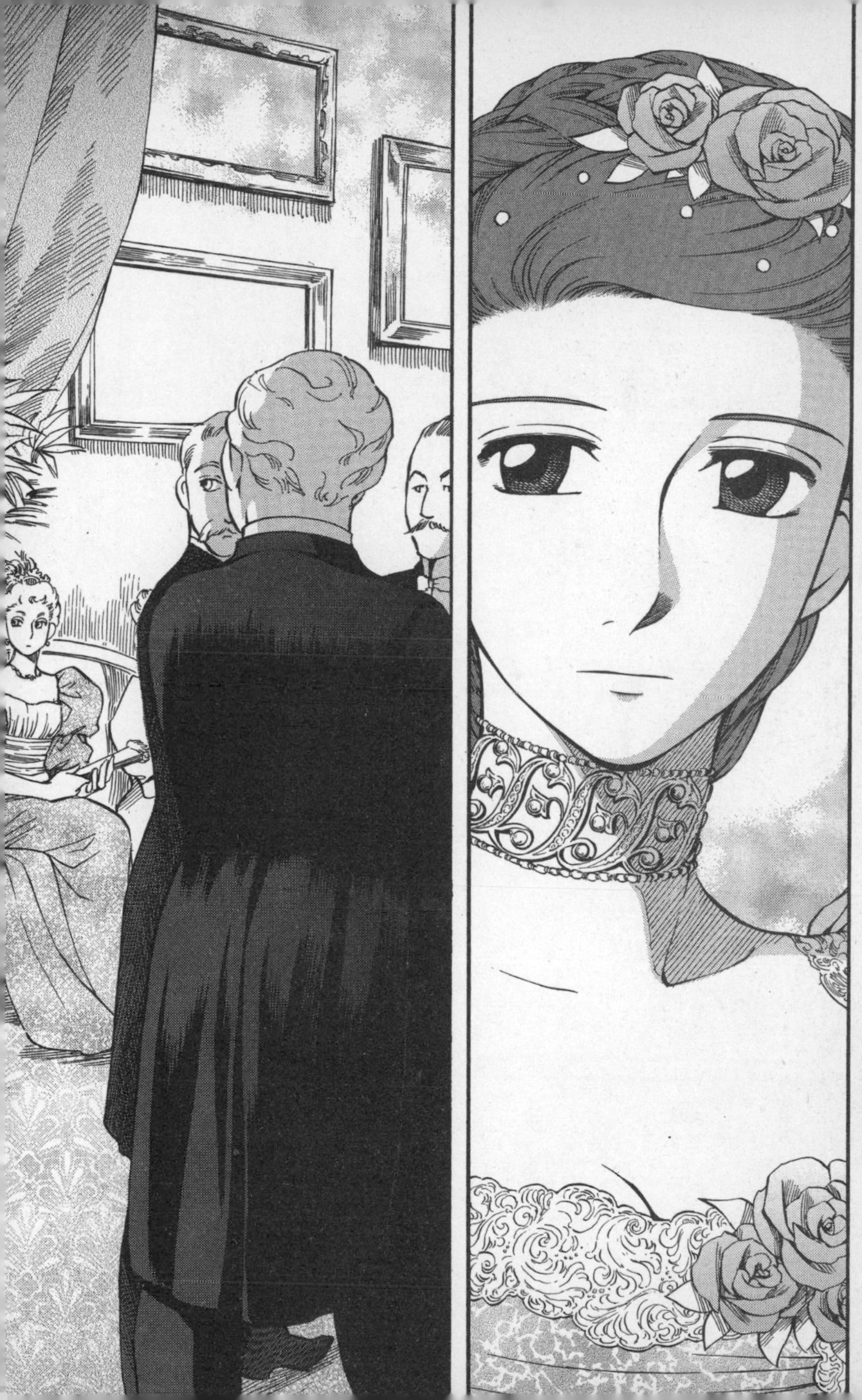

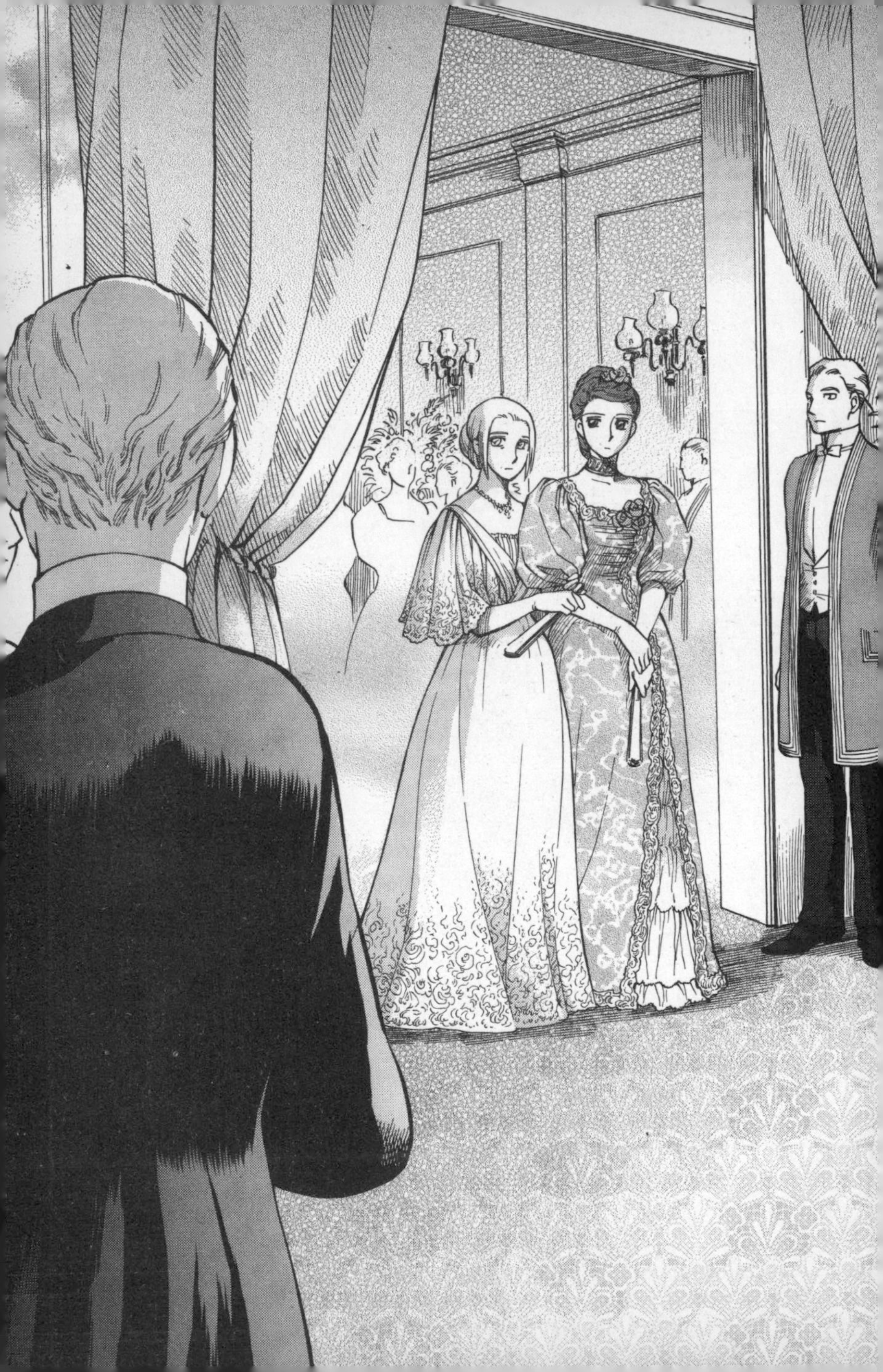

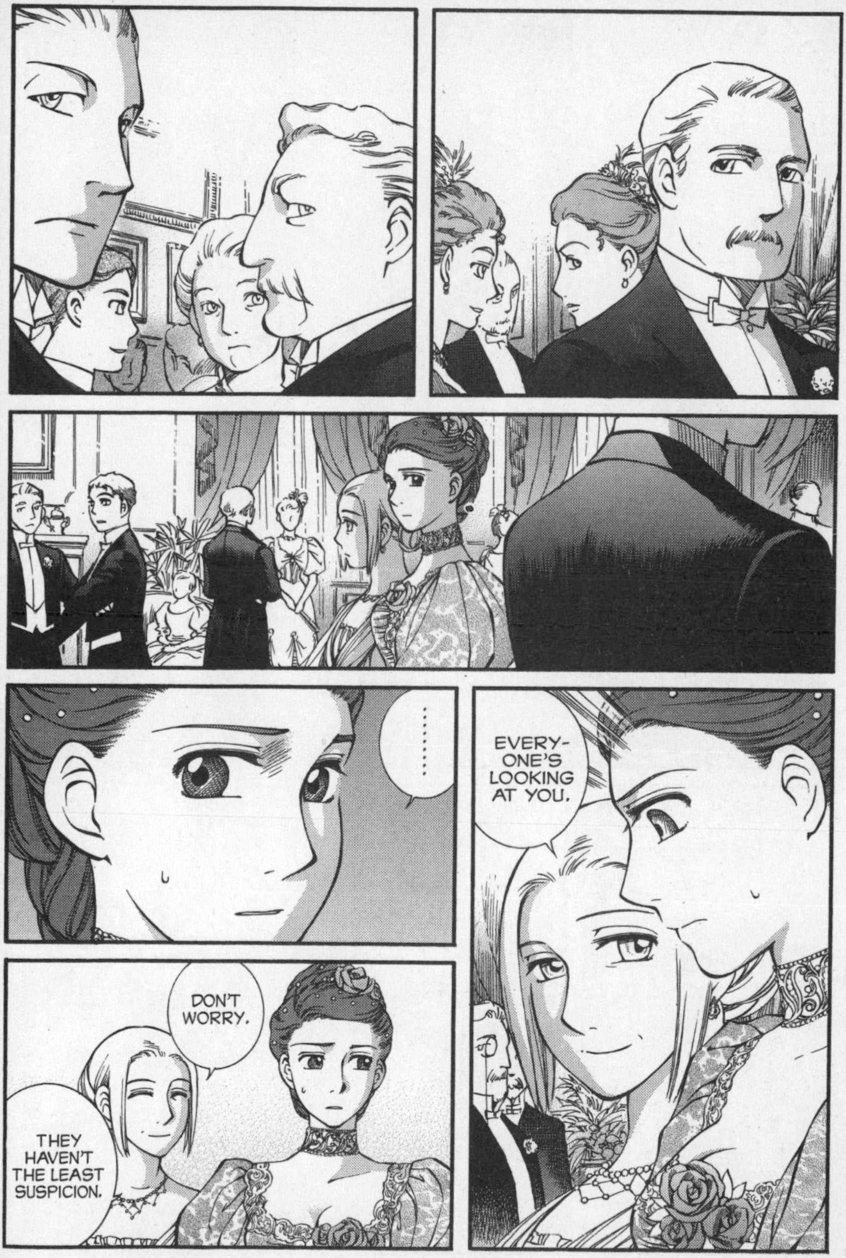
EVERY-ONE'S LOOKING AT YOU.
......
DON'T WORRY.
THEY HAVEN'T THE LEAST SUSPICION.

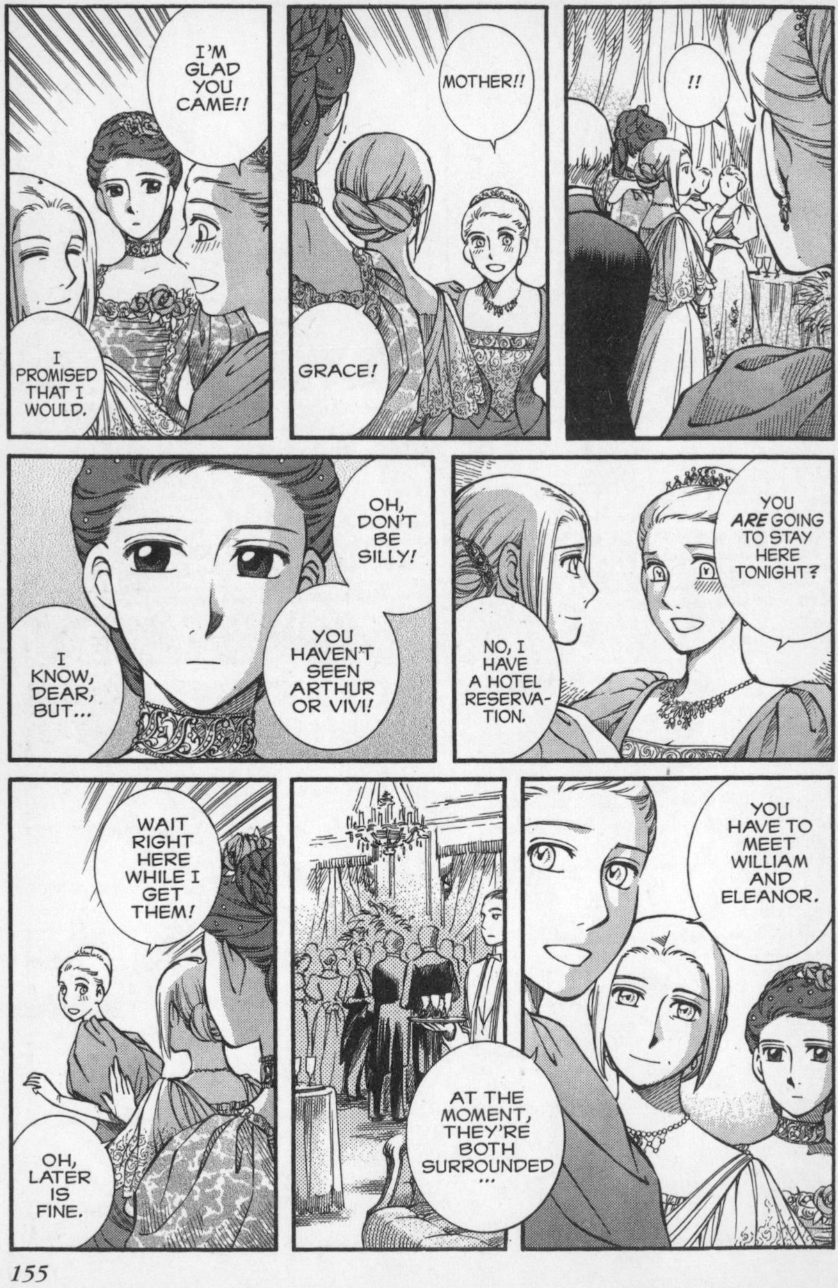
!!
MOTHER!!
GRACE!
I'M GLAD YOU CAME!!
I PROMISED THAT I WOULD.
YOU *ARE* GOING TO STAY HERE TONIGHT?
NO, I HAVE A HOTEL RESERVATION.
OH, DON'T BE SILLY!
YOU HAVEN'T SEEN ARTHUR OR VIVI!
I KNOW, DEAR, BUT...
YOU HAVE TO MEET WILLIAM AND ELEANOR.
AT THE MOMENT, THEY'RE BOTH SURROUNDED...
WAIT RIGHT HERE WHILE I GET THEM!
OH, LATER IS FINE.

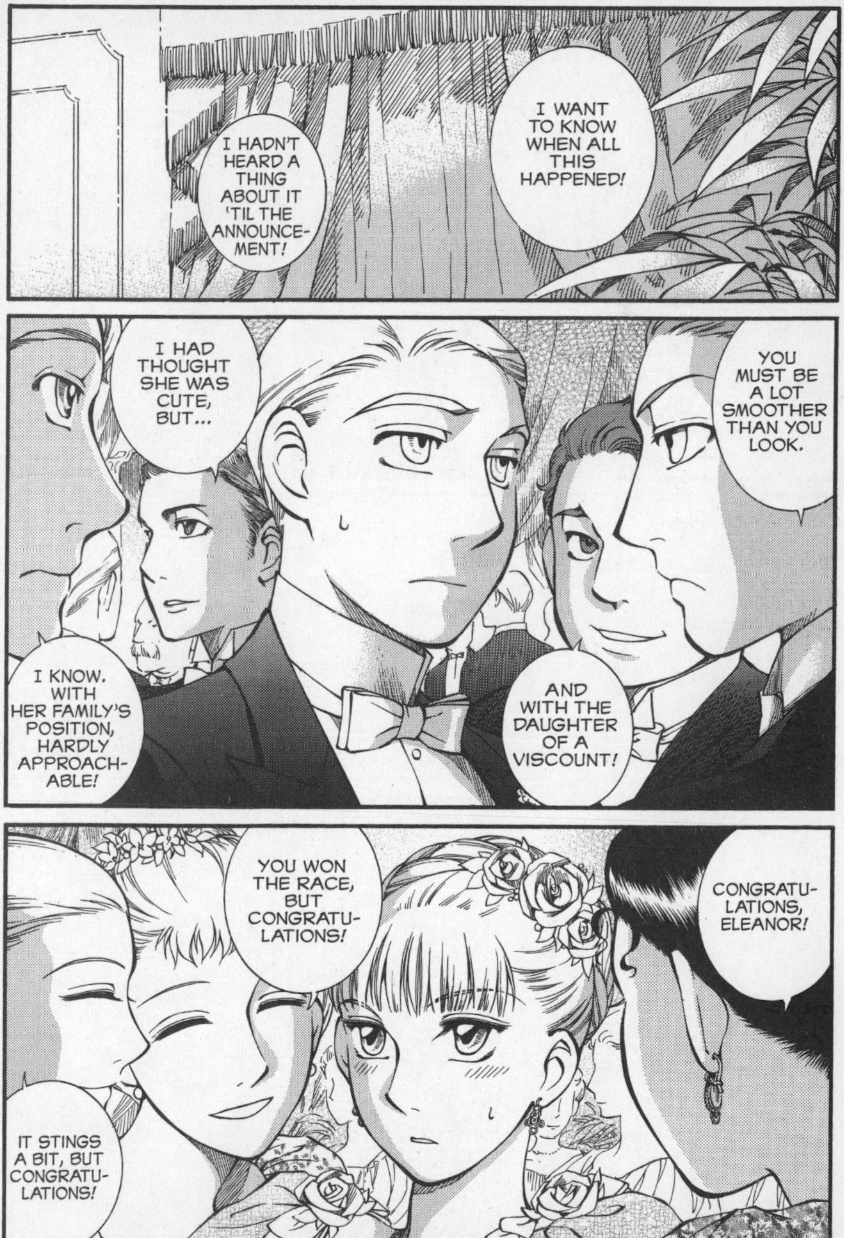
I WANT TO KNOW WHEN ALL THIS HAPPENED!
I HADN'T HEARD A THING ABOUT IT 'TIL THE ANNOUNCE-MENT!
YOU MUST BE A LOT SMOOTHER THAN YOU LOOK.
AND WITH THE DAUGHTER OF A VISCOUNT!
I HAD THOUGHT SHE WAS CUTE, BUT...
I KNOW. WITH HER FAMILY'S POSITION, HARDLY APPROACH-ABLE!
CONGRATU-LATIONS, ELEANOR!
YOU WON THE RACE, BUT CONGRATU-LATIONS!
IT STINGS A BIT, BUT CONGRATU-LATIONS!

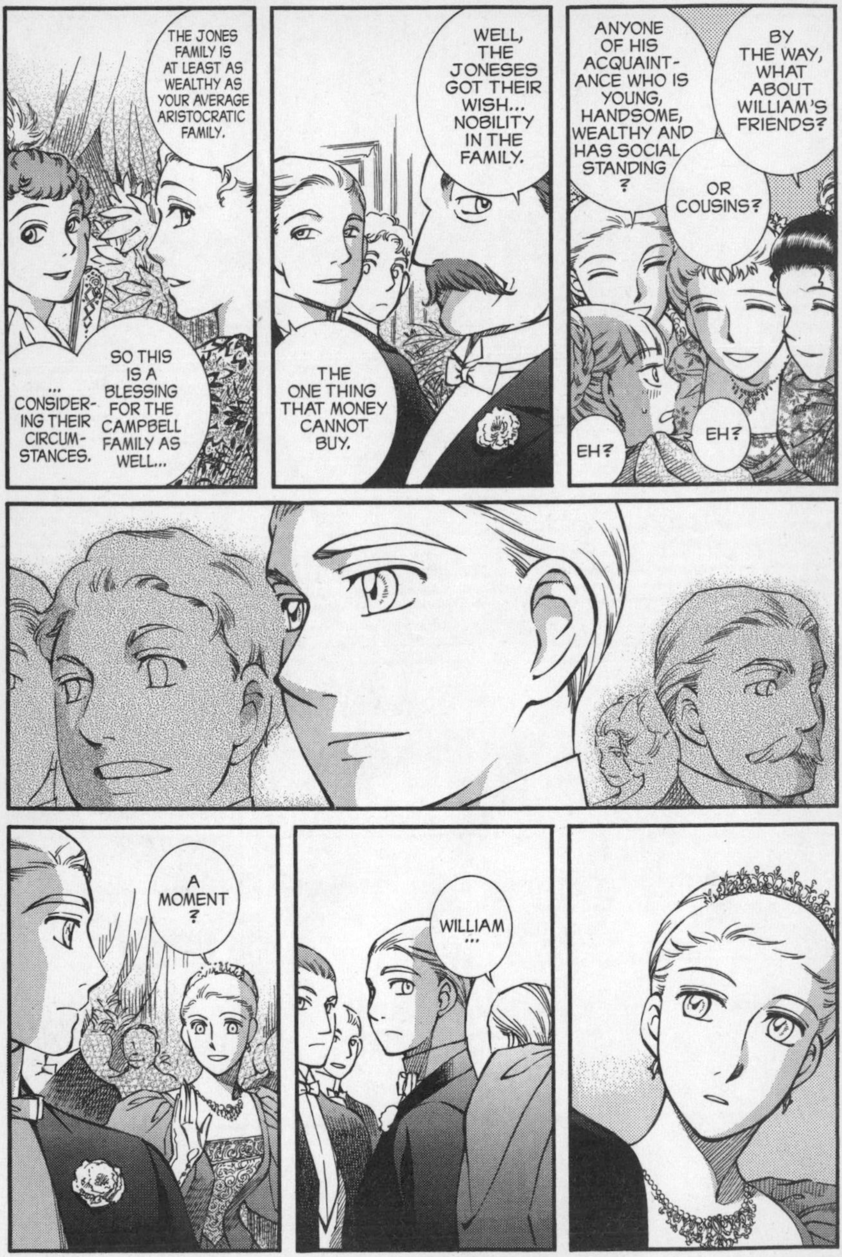
BY THE WAY, WHAT ABOUT WILLIAM'S FRIENDS?
ANYONE OF HIS ACQUAINTANCE WHO IS YOUNG, HANDSOME, WEALTHY AND HAS SOCIAL STANDING?
OR COUSINS?
EH?
EH?
WELL, THE JONESES GOT THEIR WISH... NOBILITY IN THE FAMILY.
THE ONE THING THAT MONEY CANNOT BUY.
THE JONES FAMILY IS AT LEAST AS WEALTHY AS YOUR AVERAGE ARISTOCRATIC FAMILY.
SO THIS IS A BLESSING FOR THE CAMPBELL FAMILY AS WELL...
...CONSIDERING THEIR CIRCUMSTANCES.
WILLIAM...
A MOMENT?

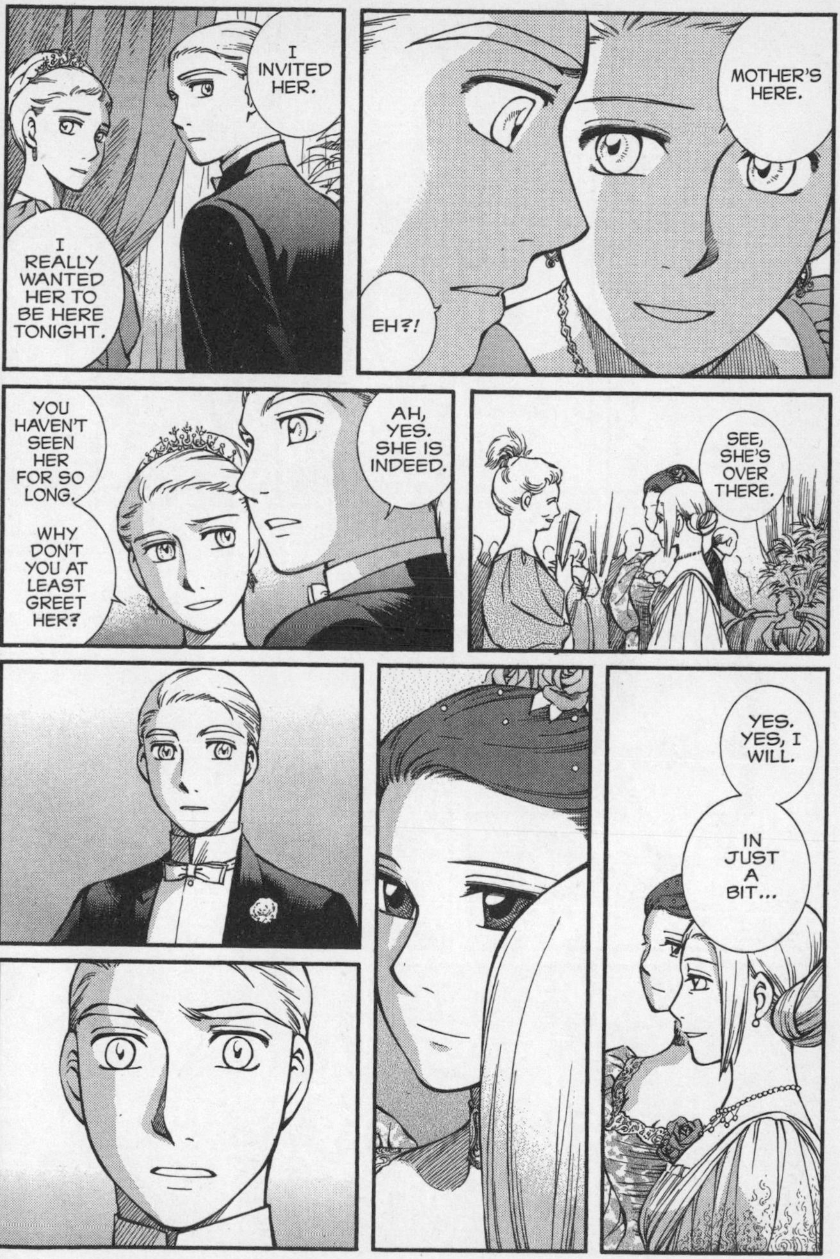
MOTHER'S HERE.
EH?!
I INVITED HER.
I REALLY WANTED HER TO BE HERE TONIGHT.
SEE, SHE'S OVER THERE.
AH, YES. SHE IS INDEED.
YOU HAVEN'T SEEN HER FOR SO LONG.
WHY DON'T YOU AT LEAST GREET HER?
YES. YES, I WILL.
IN JUST A BIT...

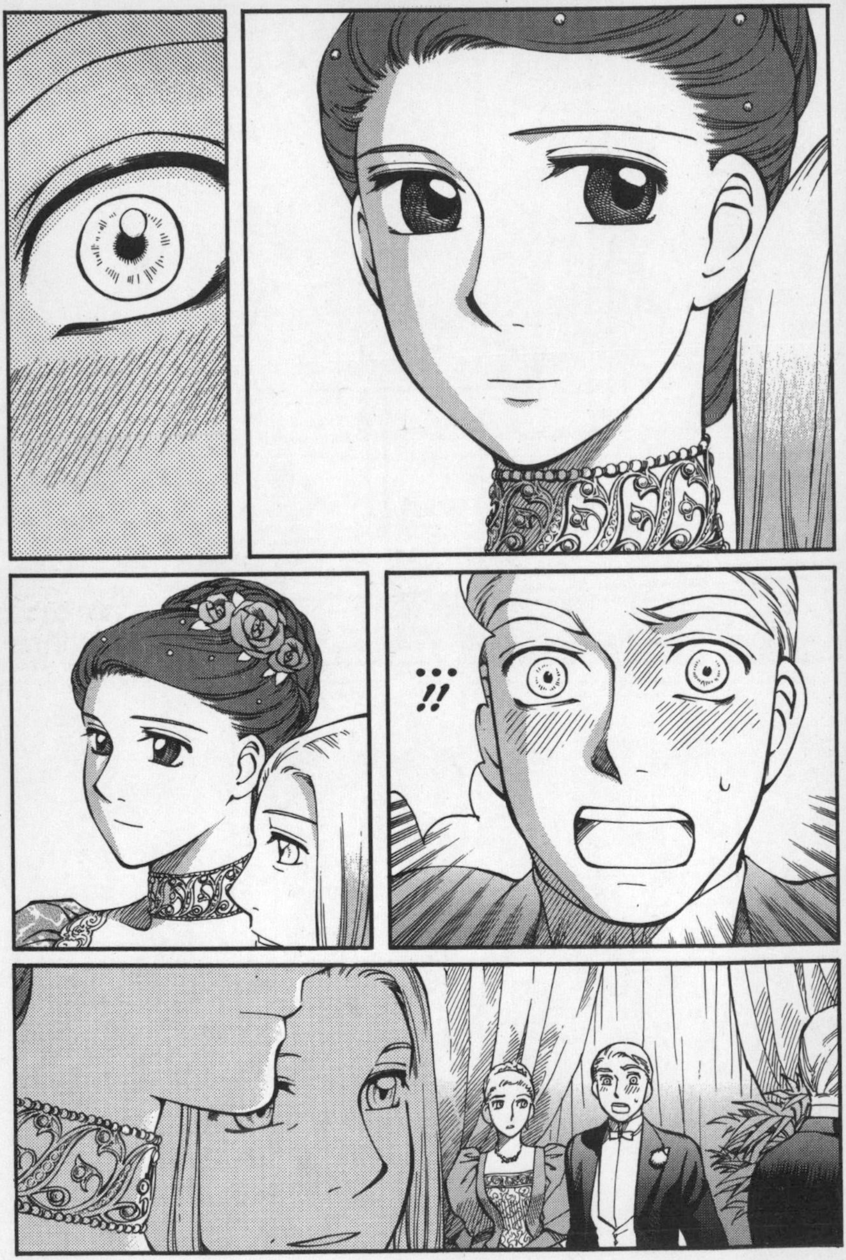
...!!

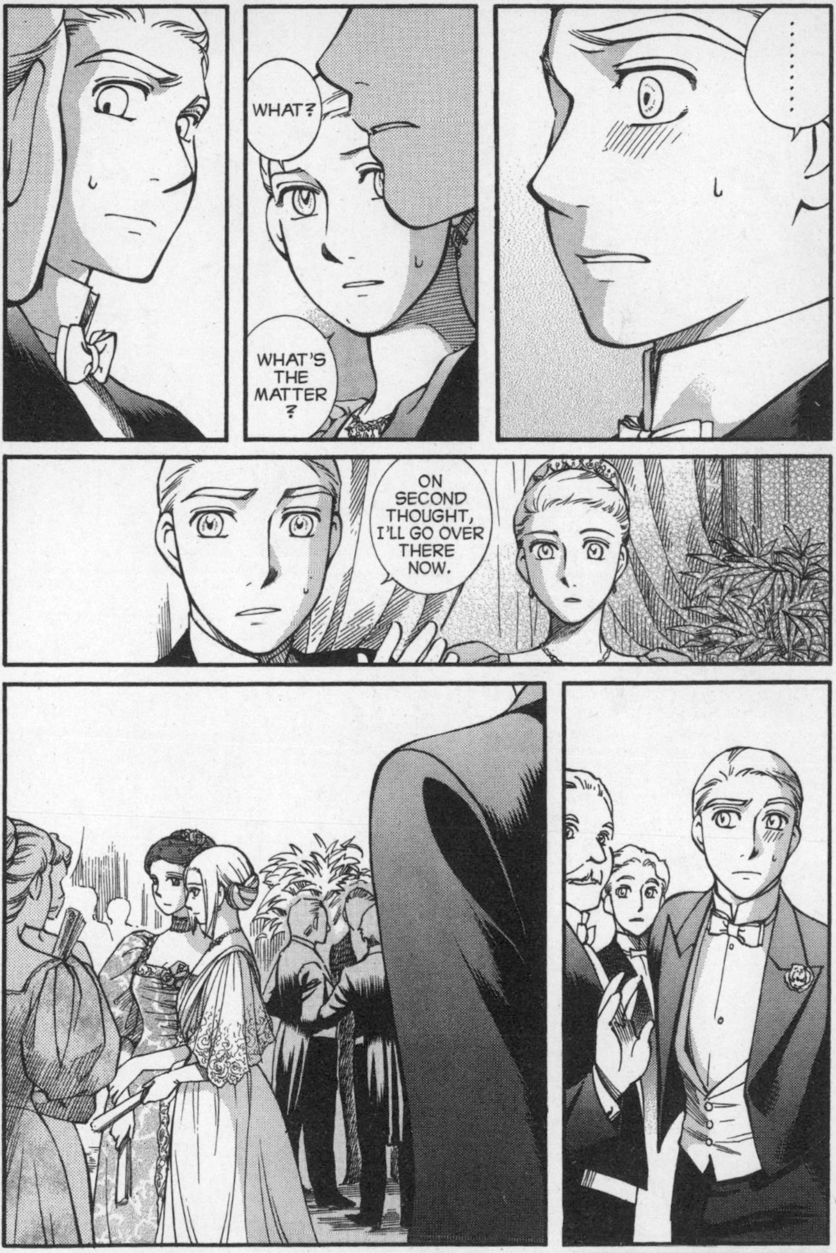
......
WHAT?
WHAT'S THE MATTER?
ON SECOND THOUGHT, I'LL GO OVER THERE NOW.

Chapter Twenty Eight:
The End

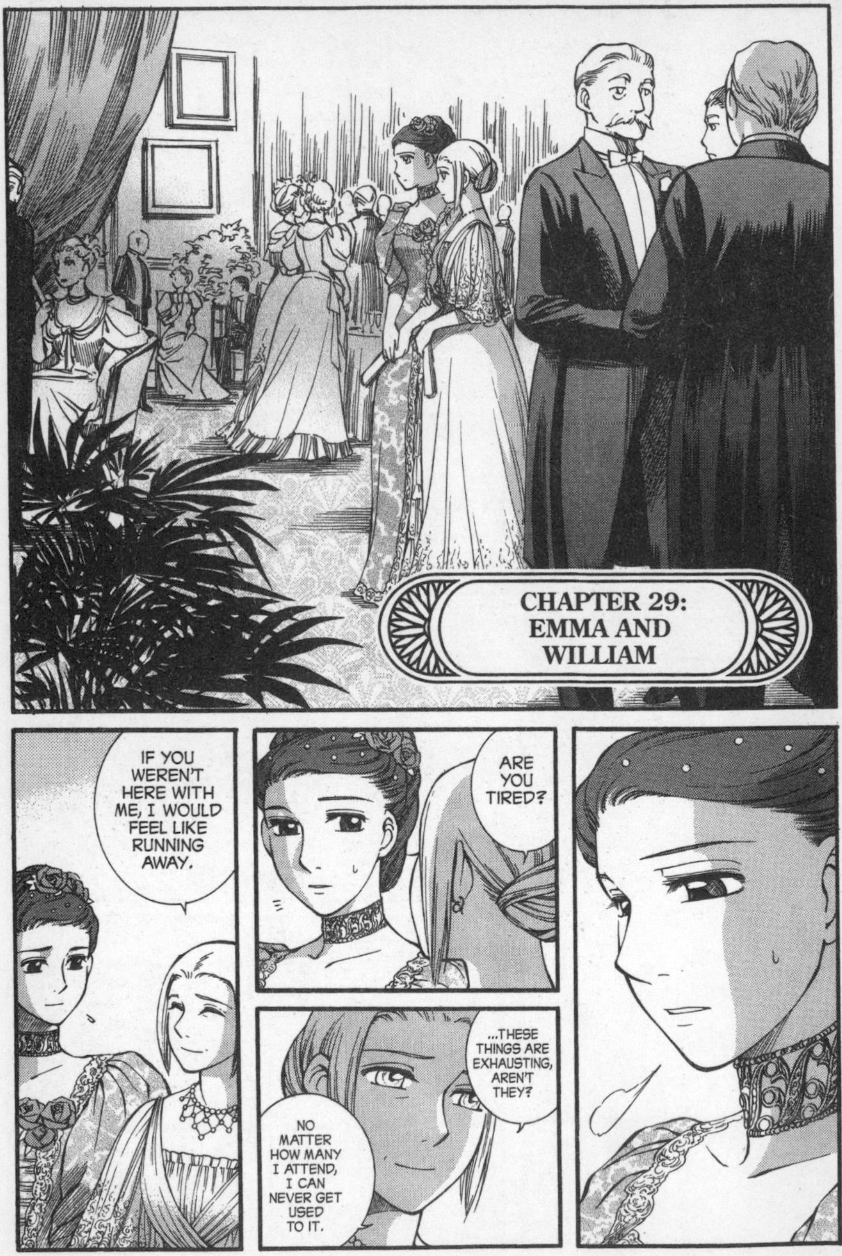
CHAPTER 29: EMMA AND WILLIAM
ARE YOU TIRED?
...THESE THINGS ARE EXHAUSTING, AREN'T THEY?
NO MATTER HOW MANY I ATTEND, I CAN NEVER GET USED TO IT.
IF YOU WEREN'T HERE WITH ME, I WOULD FEEL LIKE RUNNING AWAY.

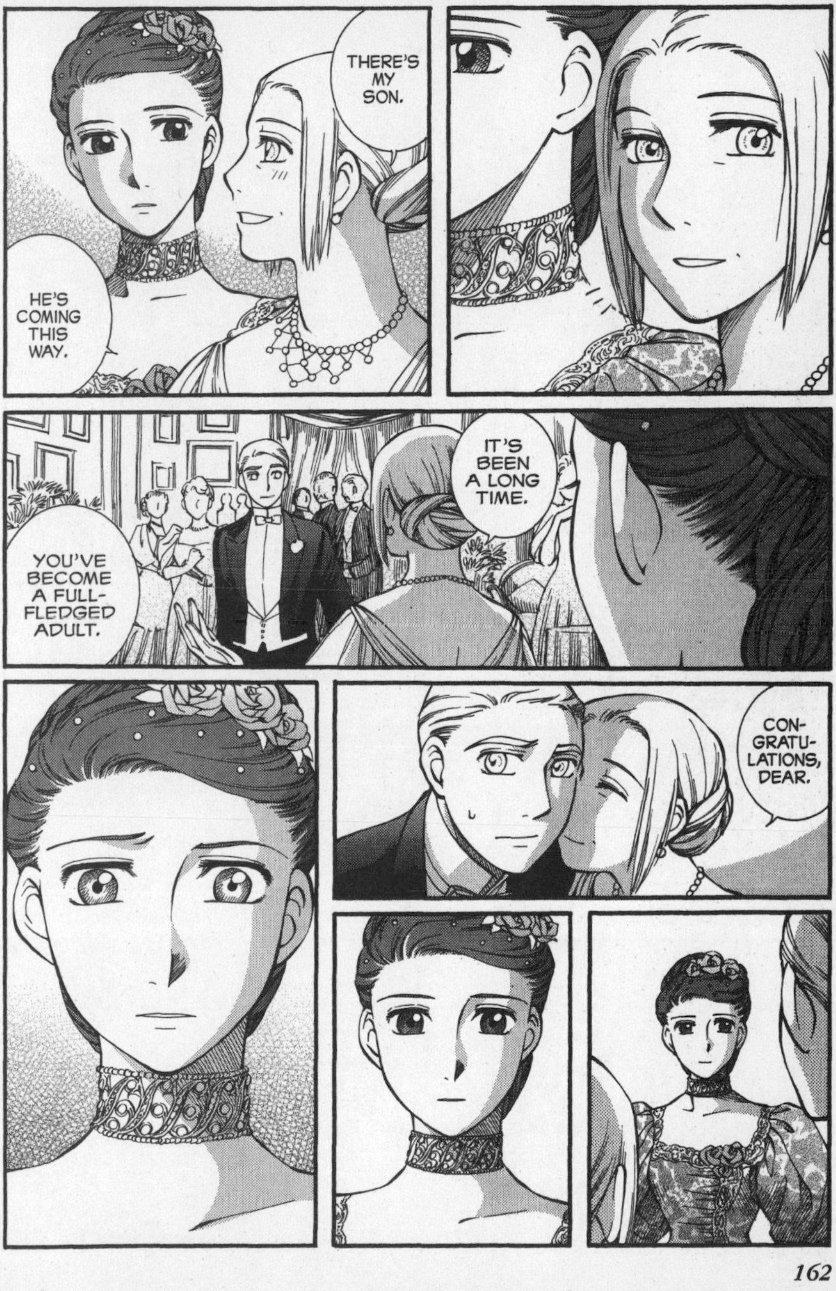
THERE'S MY SON.
HE'S COMING THIS WAY.
IT'S BEEN A LONG TIME.
YOU'VE BECOME A FULL-FLEDGED ADULT.
CON-GRATU-LATIONS, DEAR.

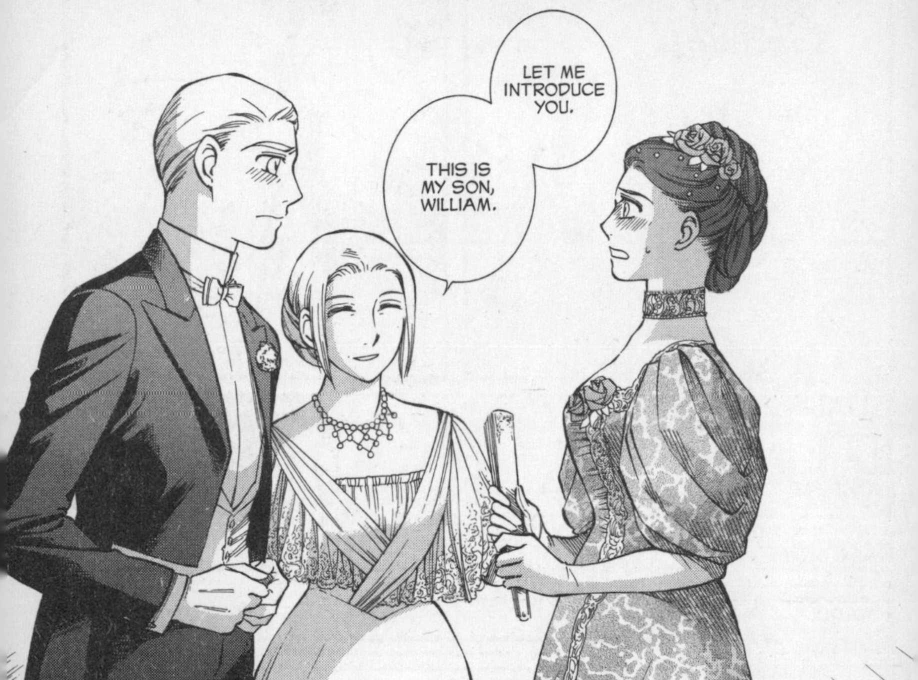
LET ME INTRODUCE YOU.
THIS IS MY SON, WILLIAM.

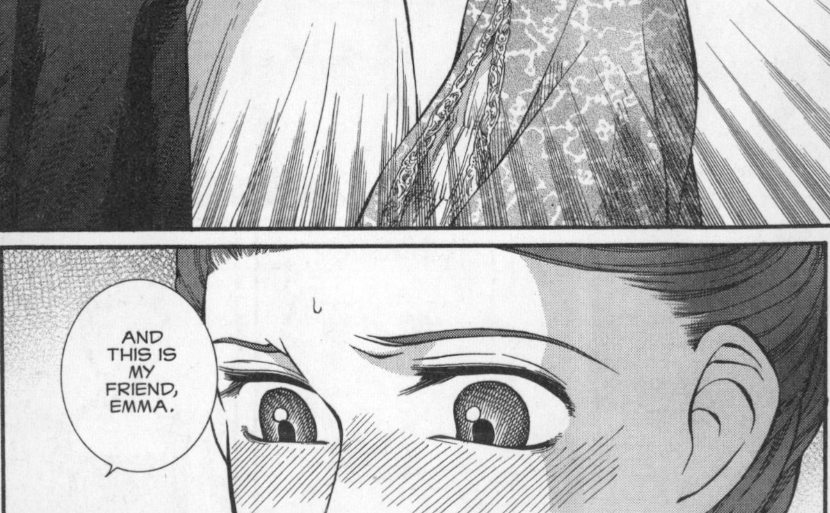
AND THIS IS MY FRIEND, EMMA.

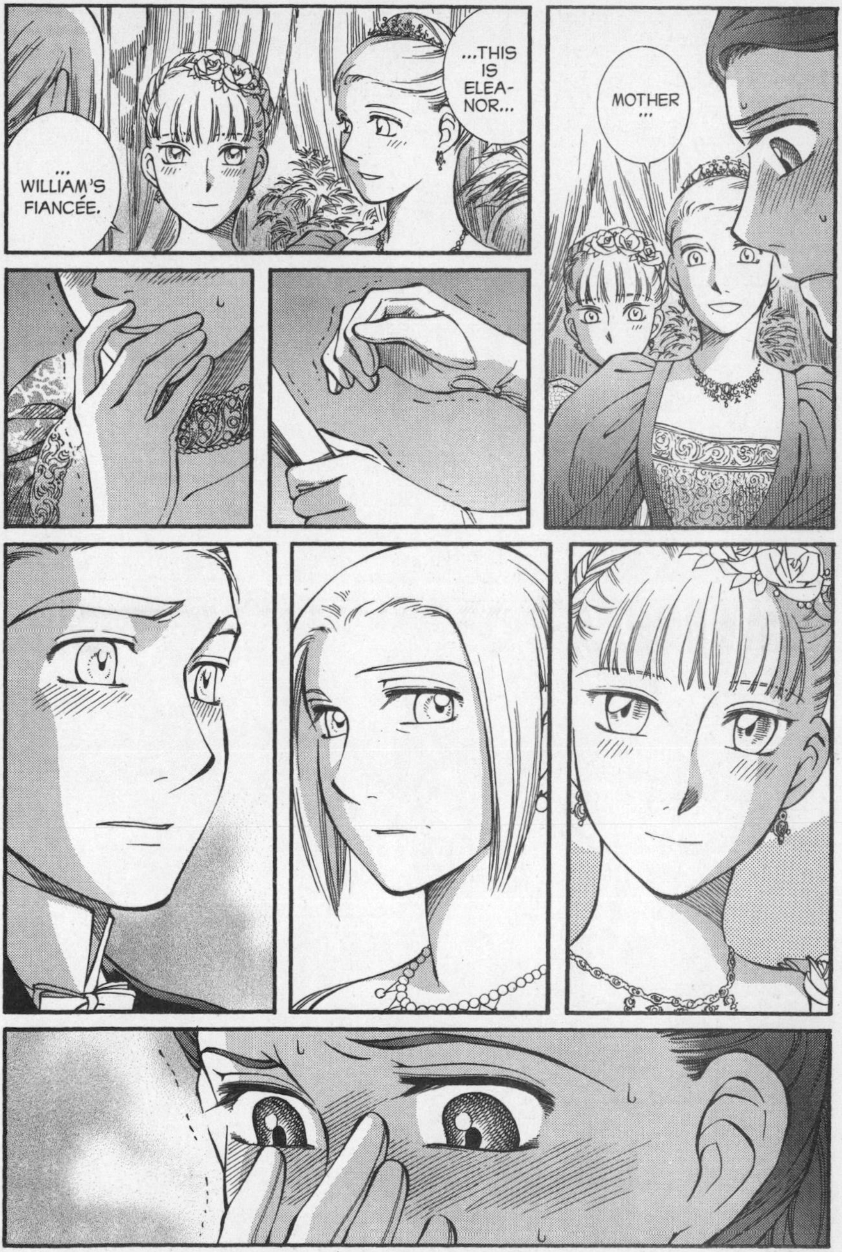
MOTHER ...
...THIS IS ELEANOR...
... WILLIAM'S FIANCÉE.

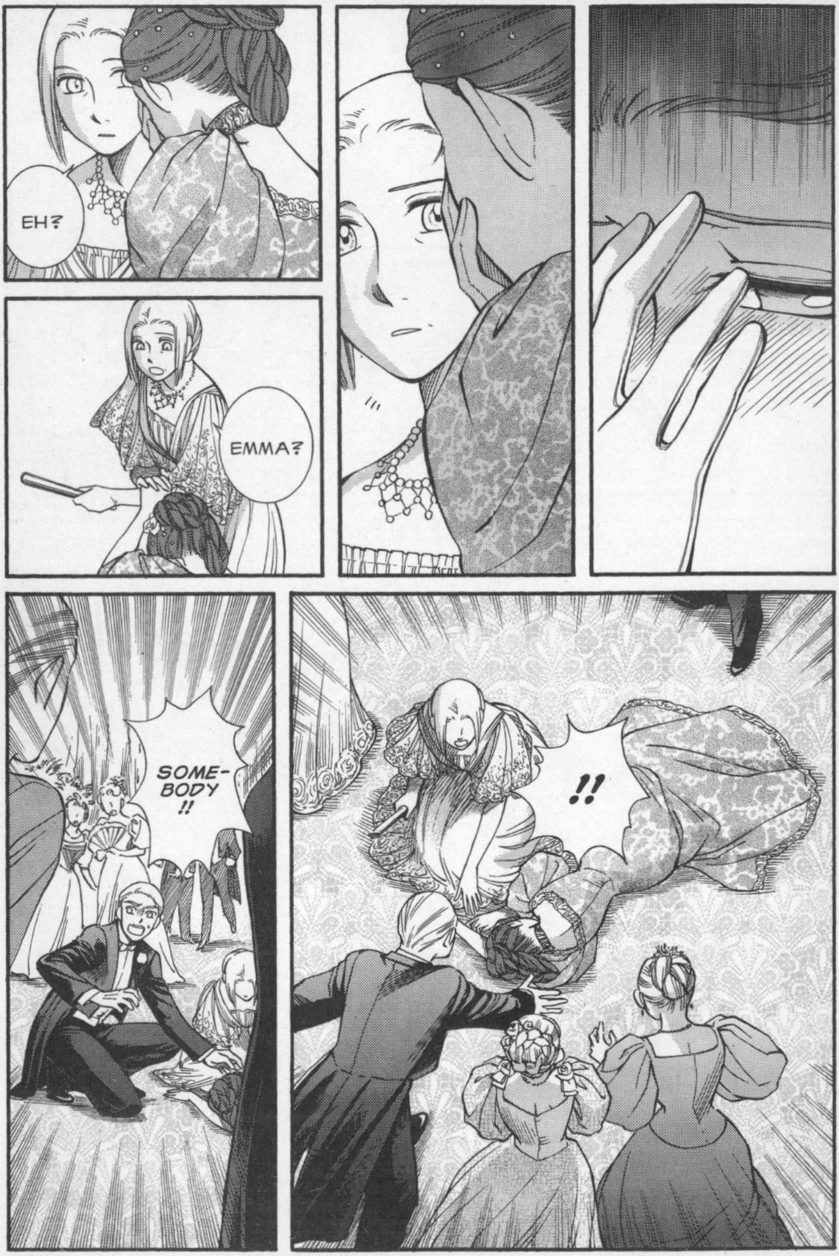
EH?
EMMA?
!!
SOME-BODY !!

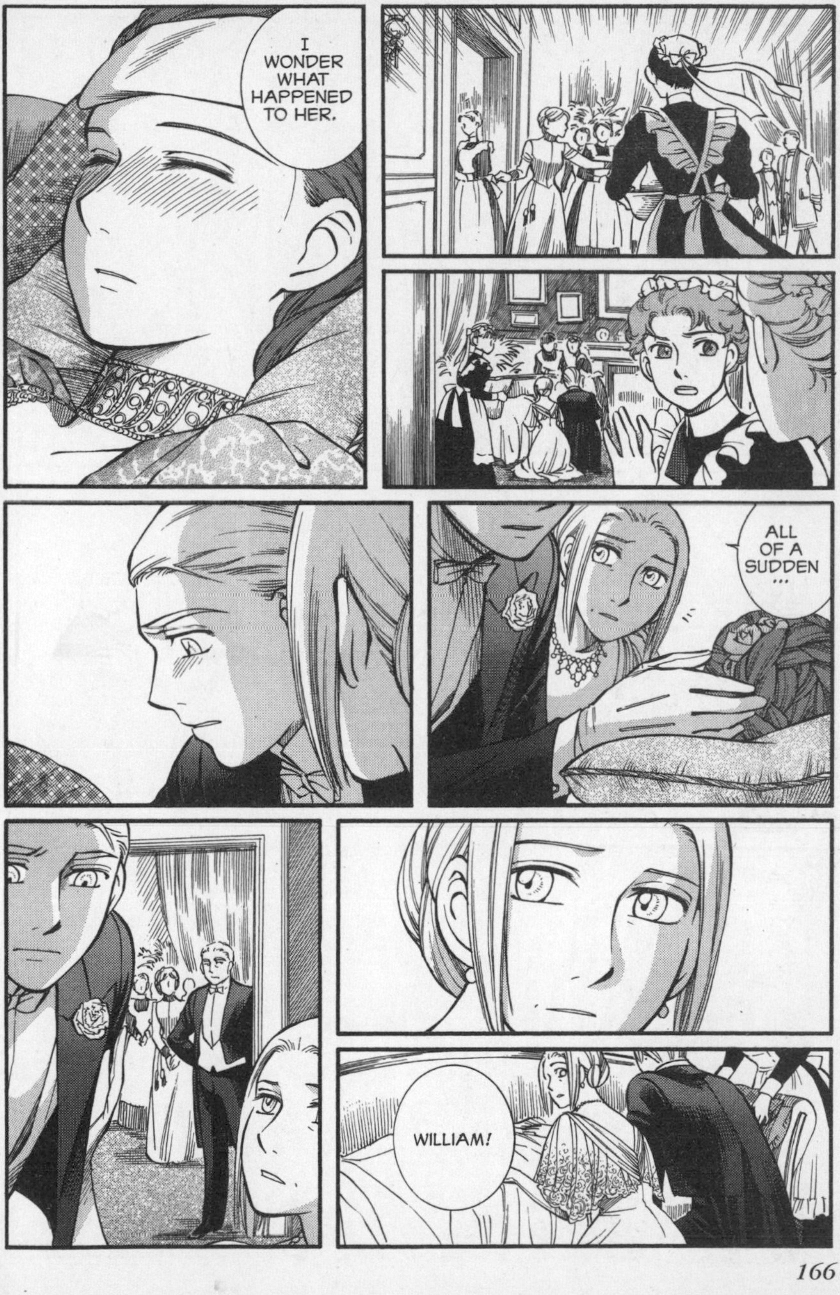
I WONDER WHAT HAPPENED TO HER.
ALL OF A SUDDEN ...
WILLIAM!

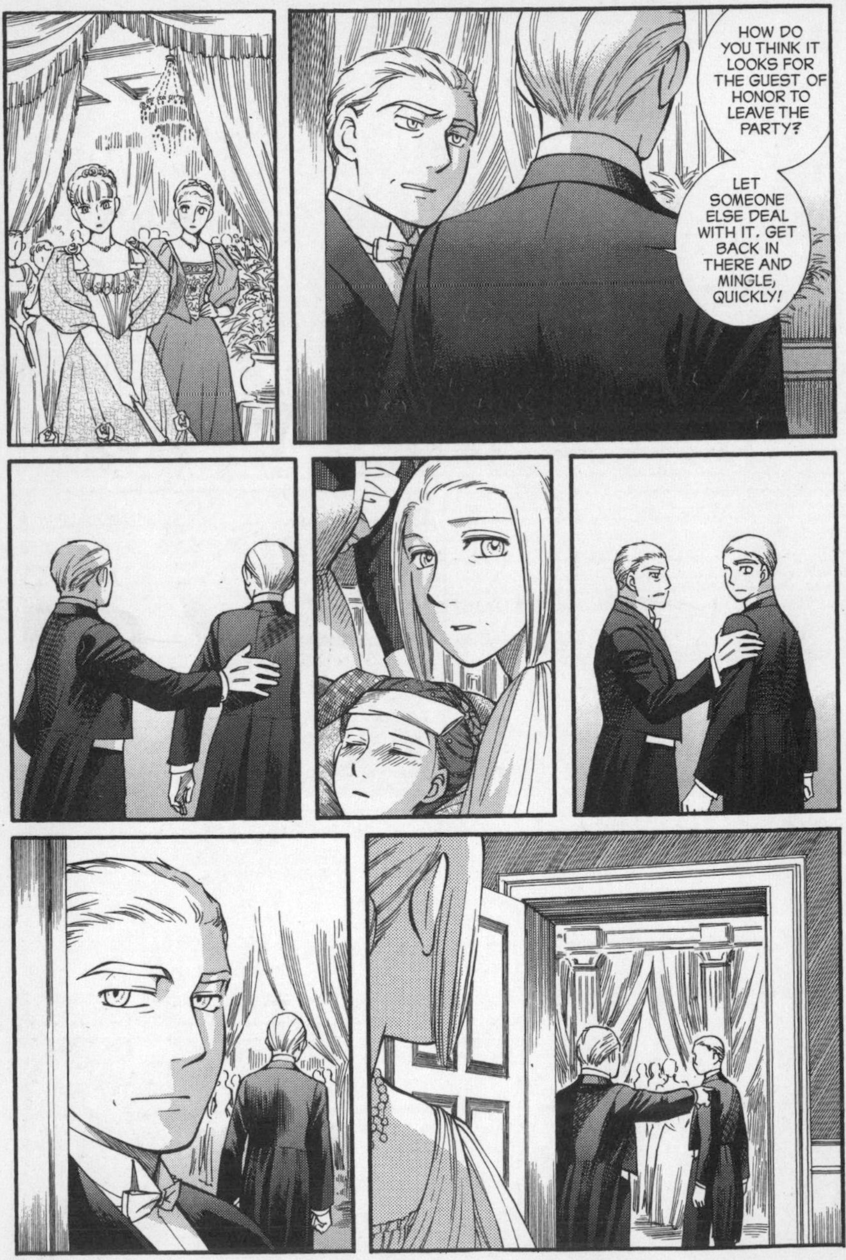
HOW DO YOU THINK IT LOOKS FOR THE GUEST OF HONOR TO LEAVE THE PARTY?
LET SOMEONE ELSE DEAL WITH IT. GET BACK IN THERE AND MINGLE, QUICKLY!

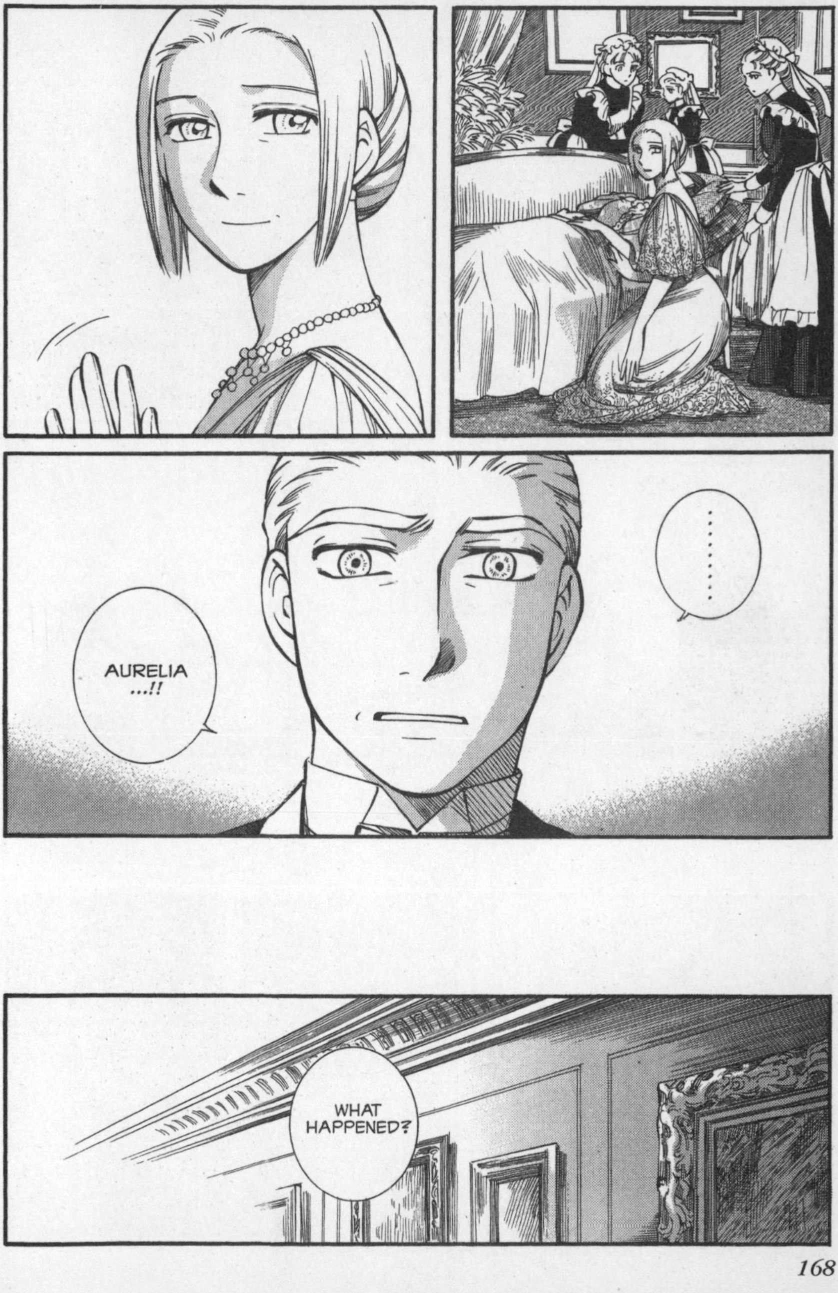
......
AURELIA ...!!
WHAT HAPPENED?

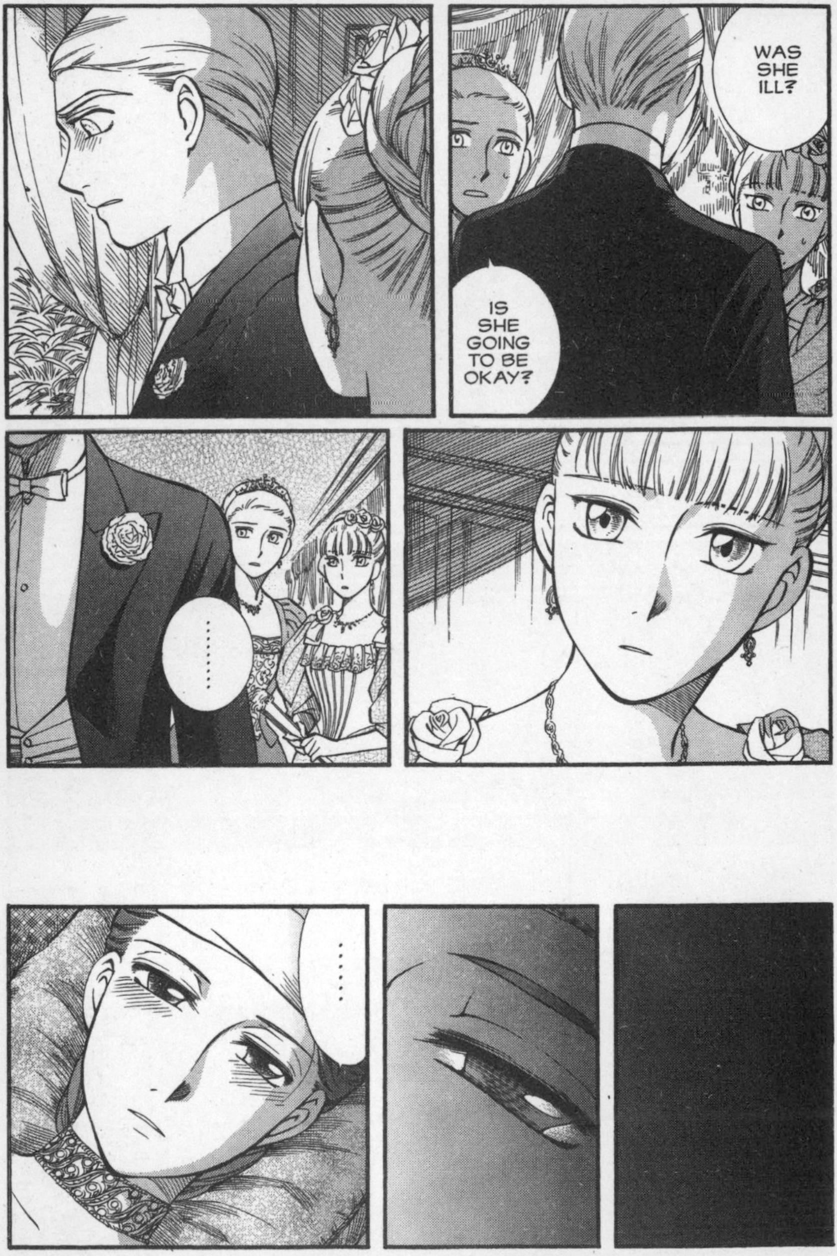
WAS SHE ILL?
IS SHE GOING TO BE OKAY?
......
......

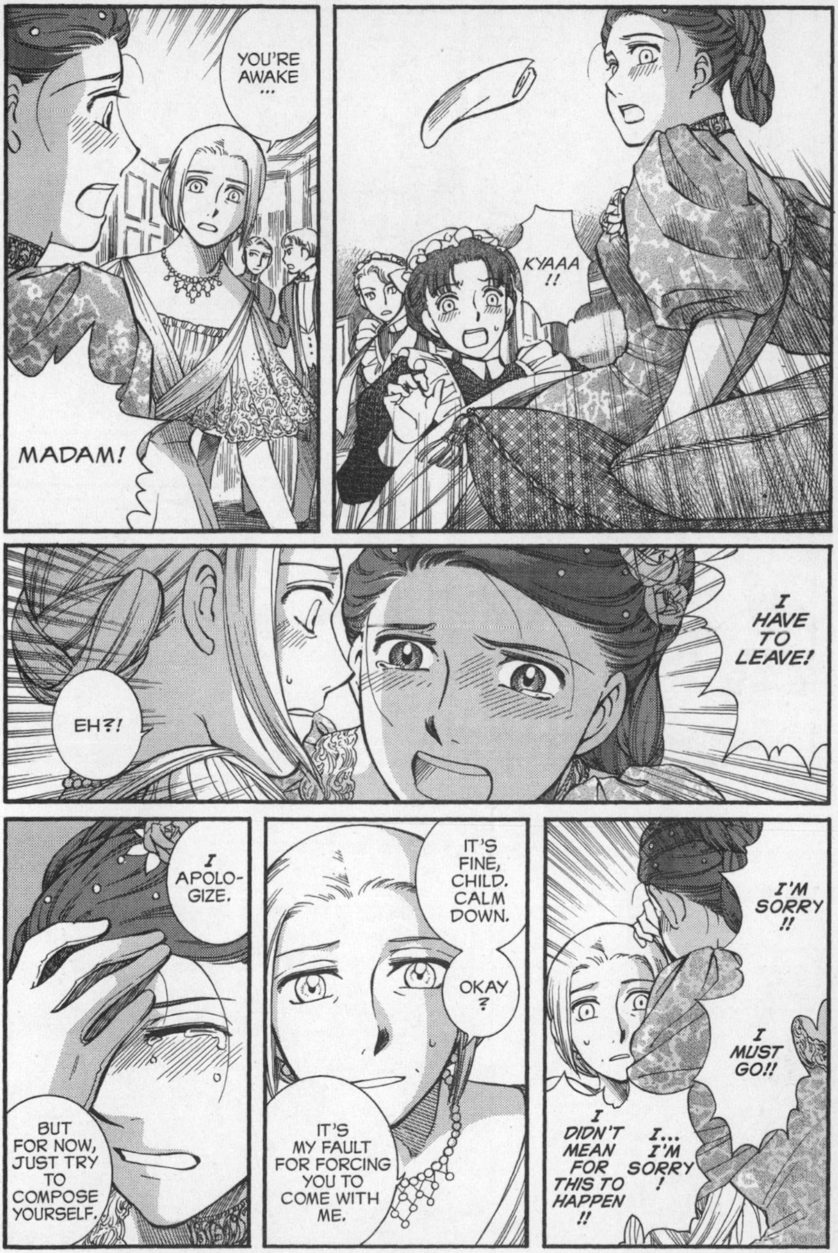
KYAAA!!
YOU'RE AWAKE...
MADAM!
I HAVE TO LEAVE!
EH?!
I'M SORRY!!
I MUST GO!!
I... I'M SORRY!
I DIDN'T MEAN FOR THIS TO HAPPEN!!
IT'S FINE, CHILD. CALM DOWN.
OKAY?
IT'S MY FAULT FOR FORCING YOU TO COME WITH ME.
I APOLOGIZE.
BUT FOR NOW, JUST TRY TO COMPOSE YOURSELF.

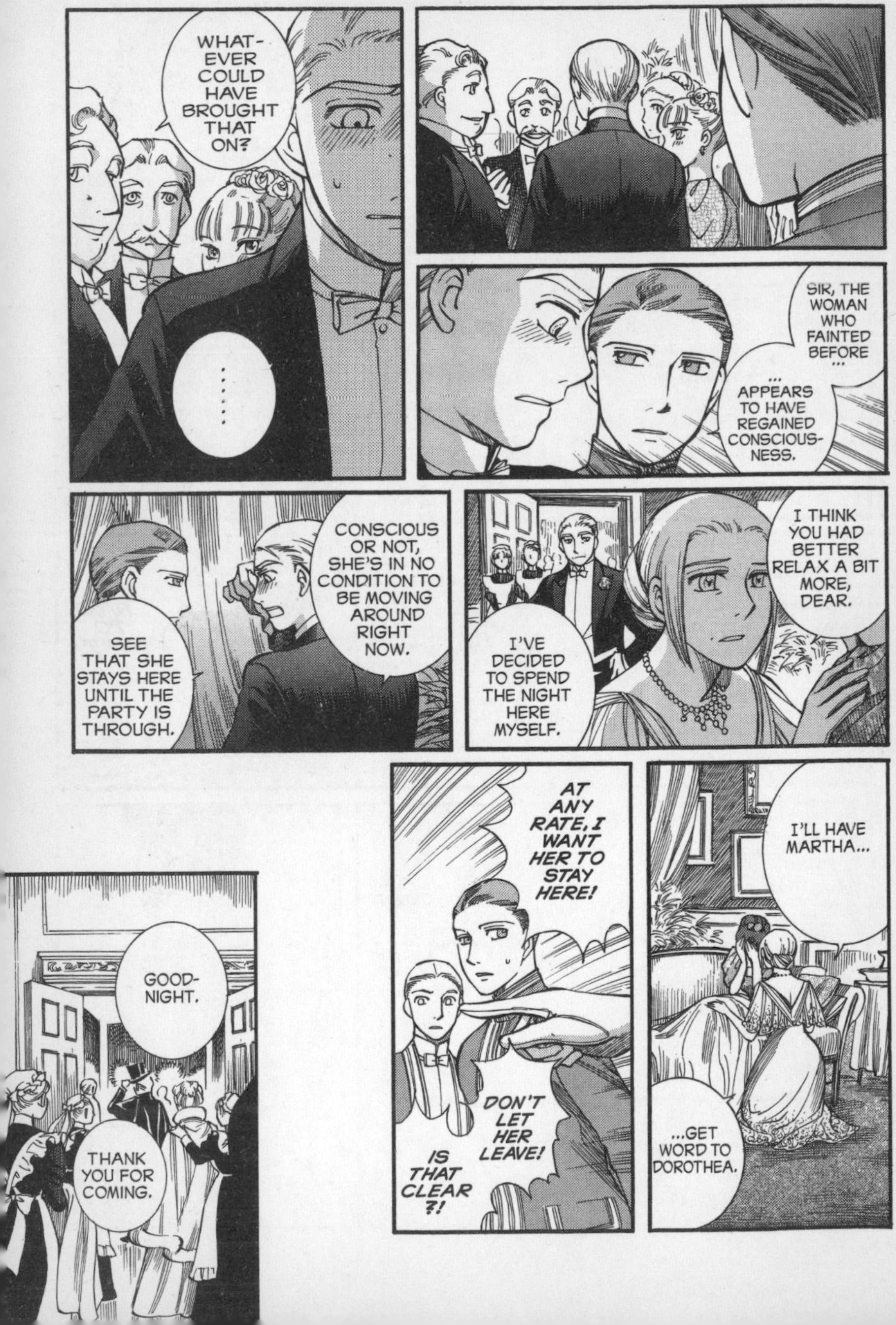
SIR, THE WOMAN WHO FAINTED BEFORE ...
... APPEARS TO HAVE REGAINED CONSCIOUS-NESS.
WHAT-EVER COULD HAVE BROUGHT THAT ON?
......
I THINK YOU HAD BETTER RELAX A BIT MORE, DEAR.
I'VE DECIDED TO SPEND THE NIGHT HERE MYSELF.
CONSCIOUS OR NOT, SHE'S IN NO CONDITION TO BE MOVING AROUND RIGHT NOW.
SEE THAT SHE STAYS HERE UNTIL THE PARTY IS THROUGH.
I'LL HAVE MARTHA...
...GET WORD TO DOROTHEA.
AT ANY RATE, I WANT HER TO STAY HERE!
DON'T LET HER LEAVE!
IS THAT CLEAR?!
GOOD-NIGHT.
THANK YOU FOR COMING.

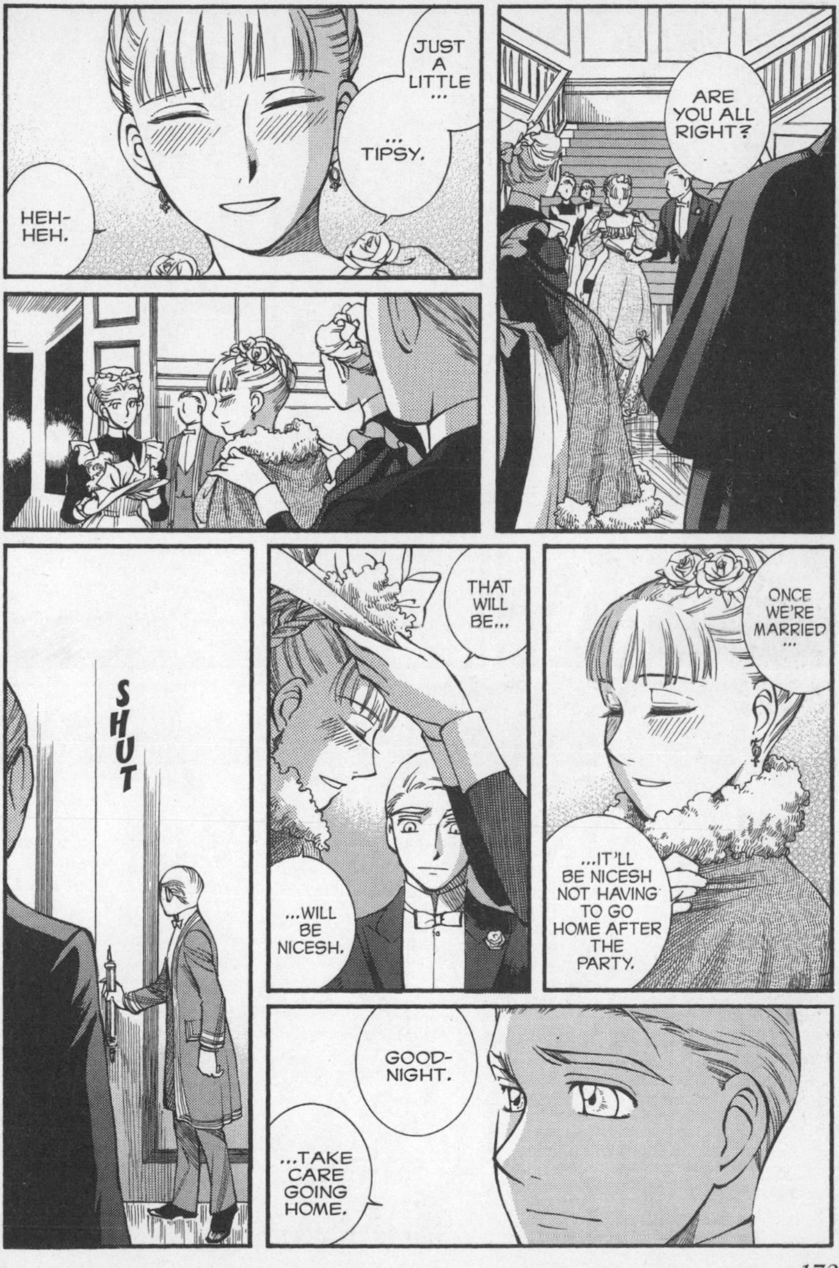
ARE YOU ALL RIGHT?
JUST A LITTLE...
...TIPSY.
HEH-HEH.
ONCE WE'RE MARRIED...
...IT'LL BE NICESH NOT HAVING TO GO HOME AFTER THE PARTY.
THAT WILL BE...
...WILL BE NICESH.
GOOD-NIGHT.
...TAKE CARE GOING HOME.
SHUT

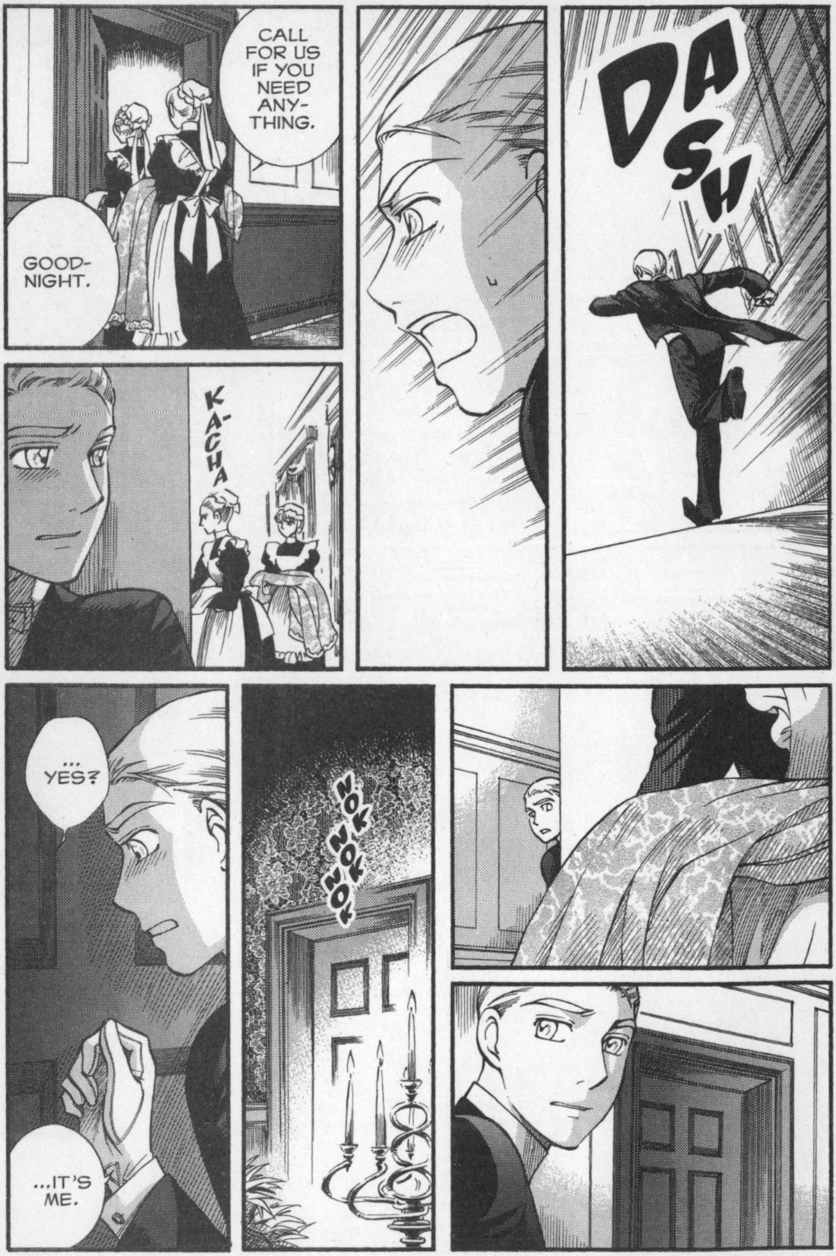
DASH
CALL FOR US IF YOU NEED ANYTHING.
GOOD-NIGHT.
KA-CHA
NOK NOK NOK
...YES?
...IT'S ME.

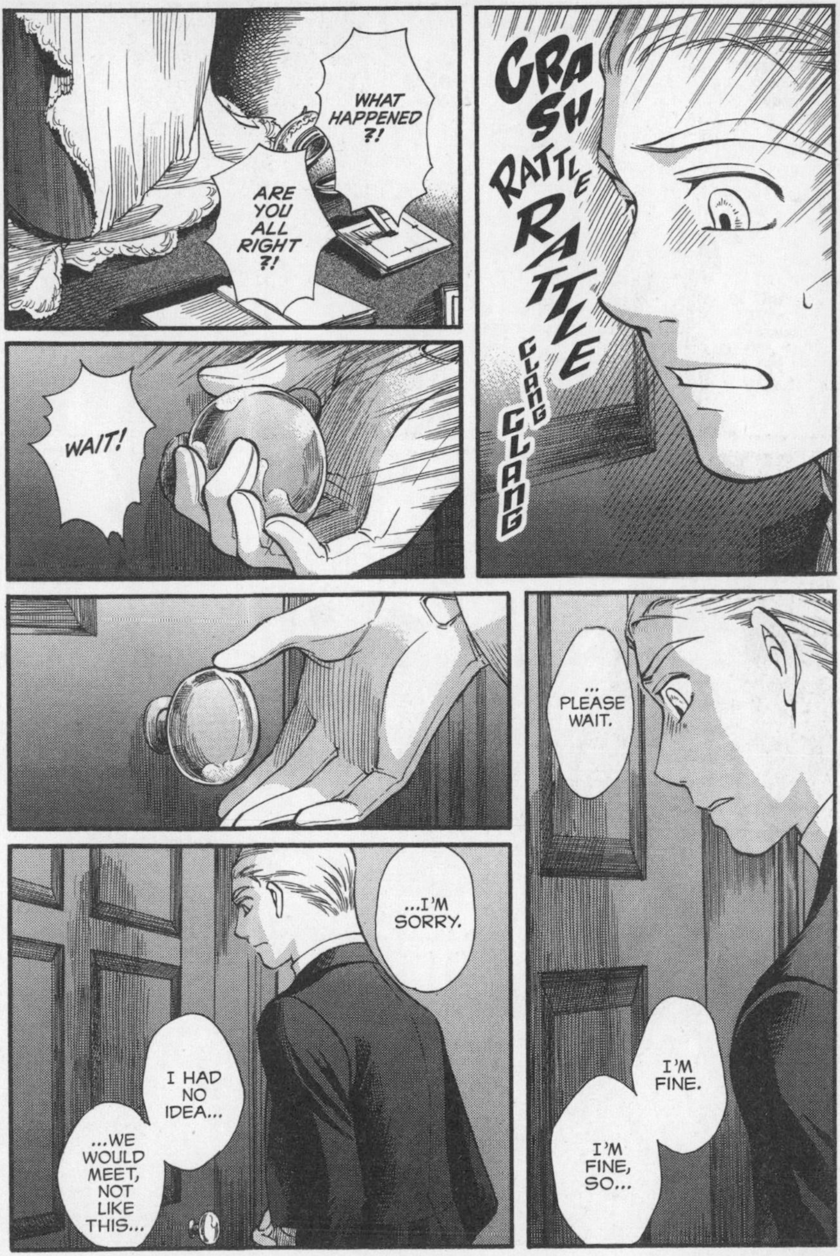
CRASH
RATTLE
RATTLE
CLANG
CLANG
CLANG
WHAT HAPPENED ?!
ARE YOU ALL RIGHT ?!
WAIT!
...PLEASE WAIT.
I'M FINE.
I'M FINE, SO...
...I'M SORRY.
I HAD NO IDEA...
...WE WOULD MEET, NOT LIKE THIS...

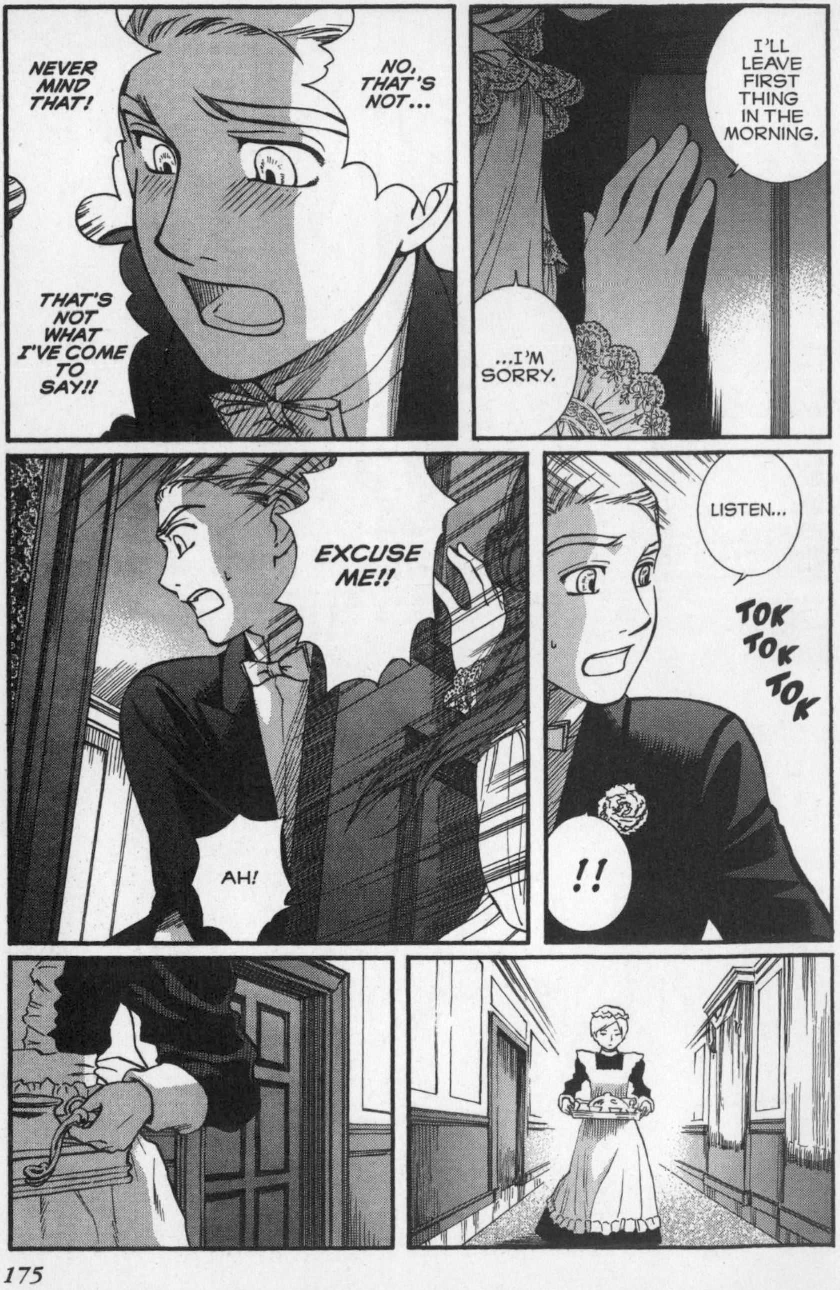
I'LL LEAVE FIRST THING IN THE MORNING.
...I'M SORRY.
NO, THAT'S NOT...
NEVER MIND THAT!
THAT'S NOT WHAT I'VE COME TO SAY!!
LISTEN...
TOK TOK TOK
!!
EXCUSE ME!!
AH!

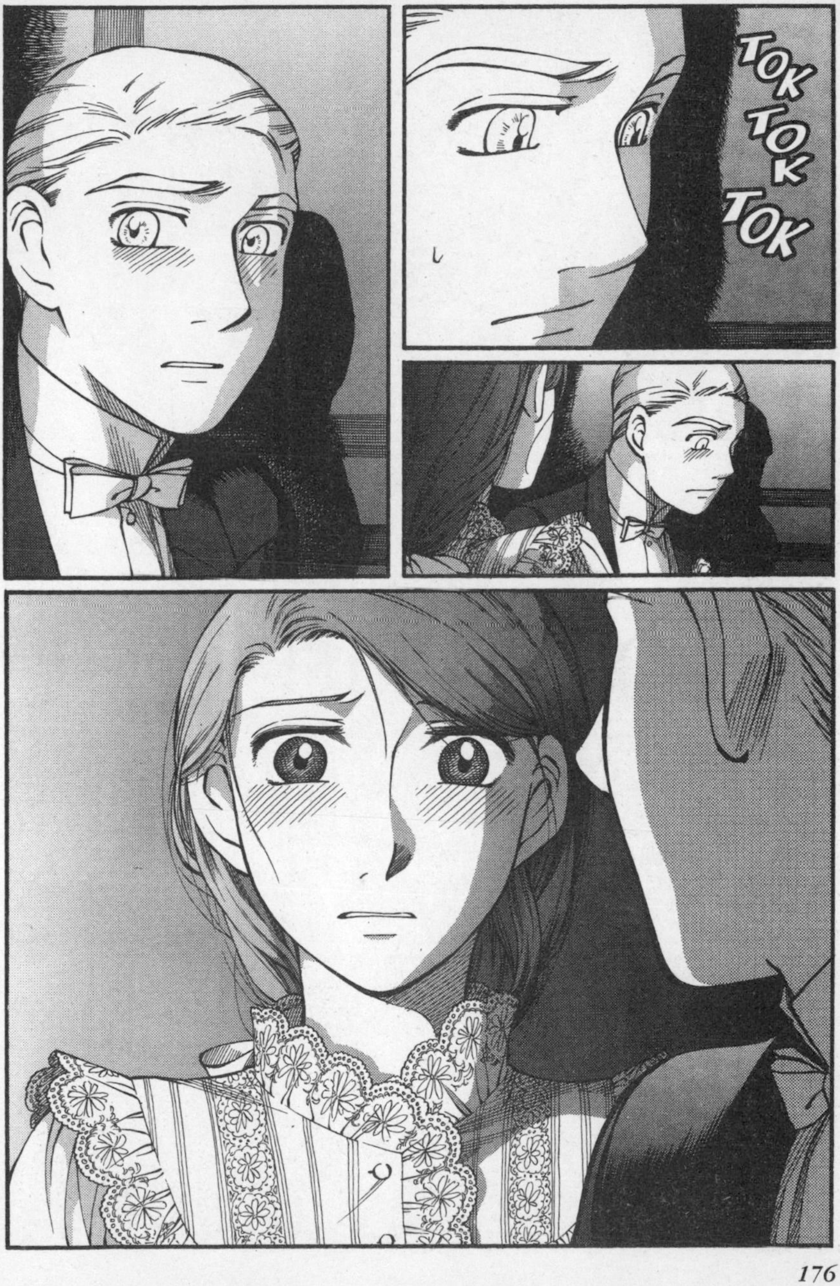
TOK
TOK
TOK
TOK

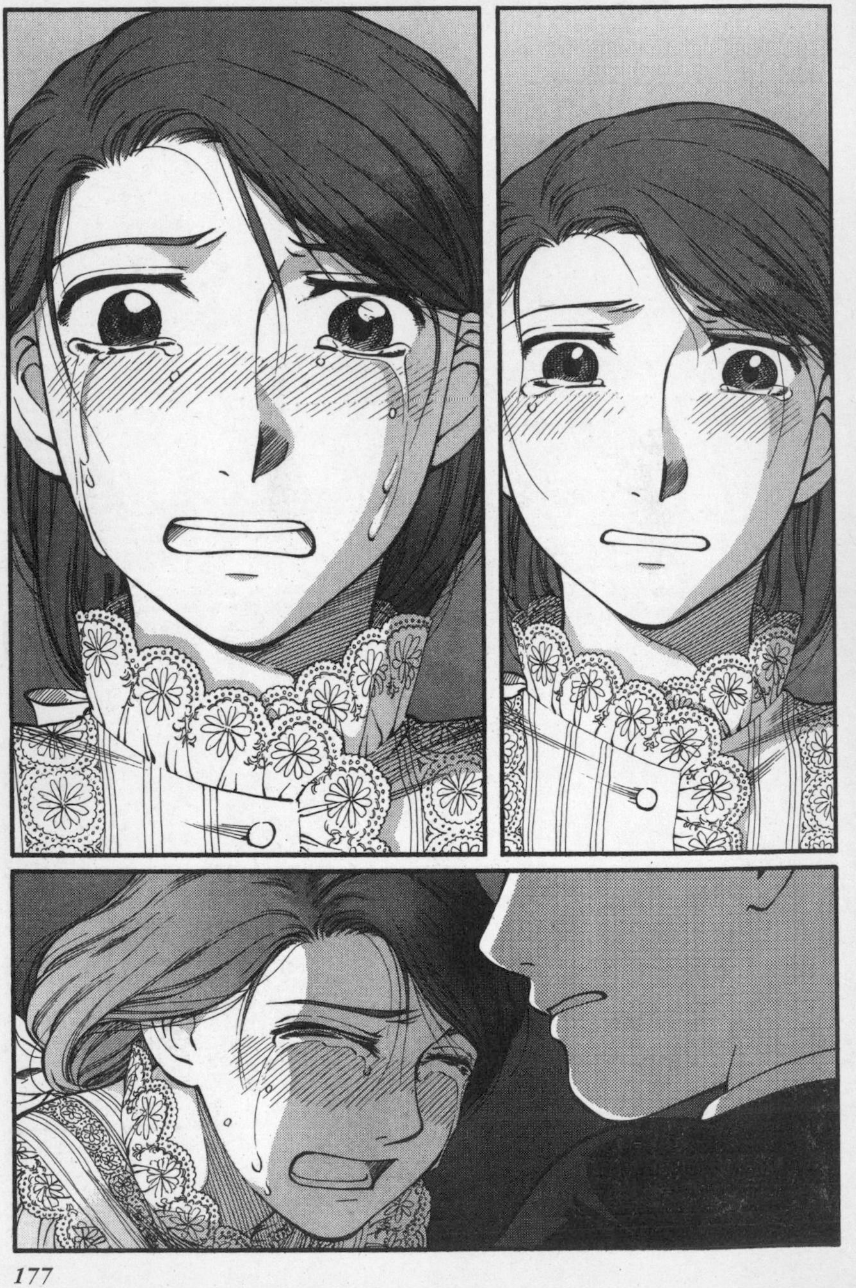

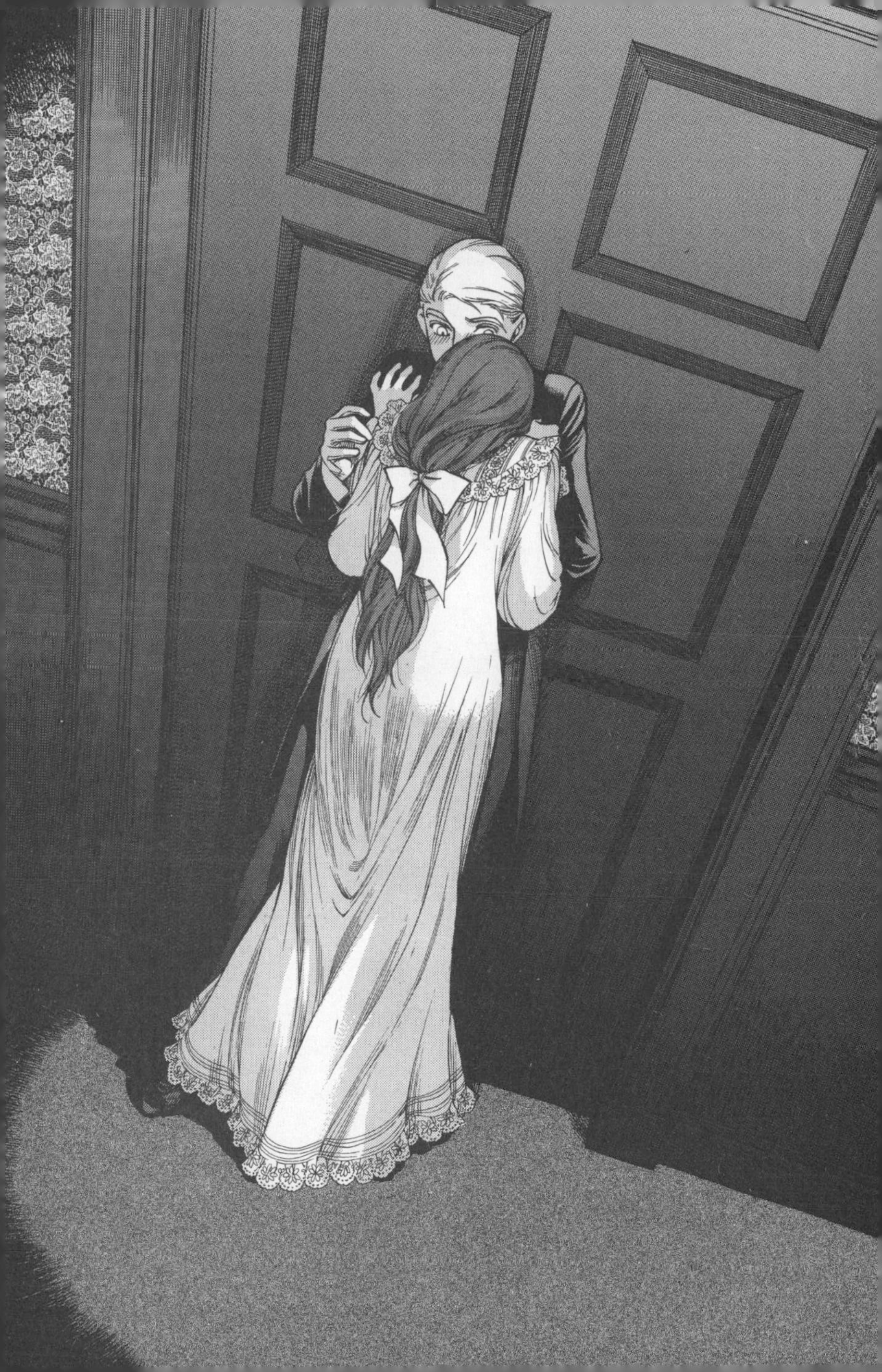

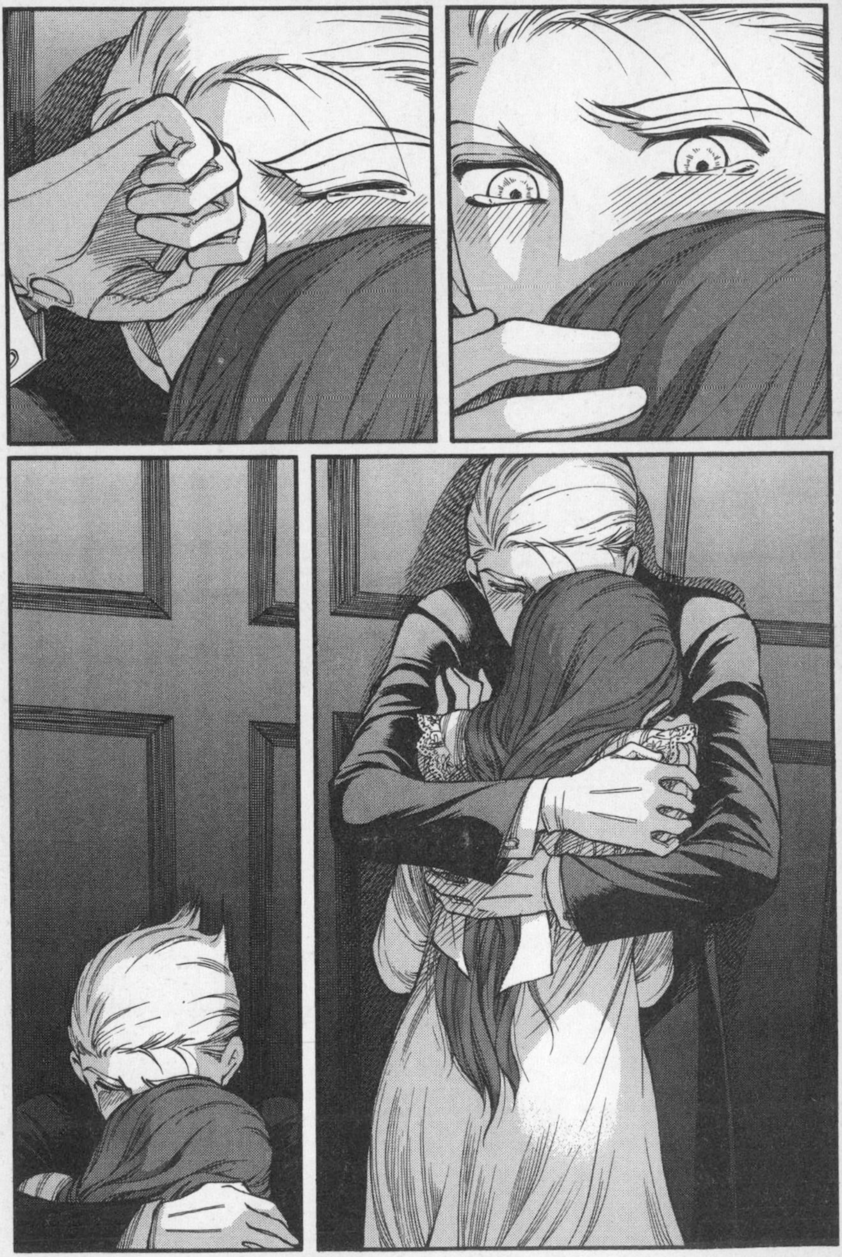

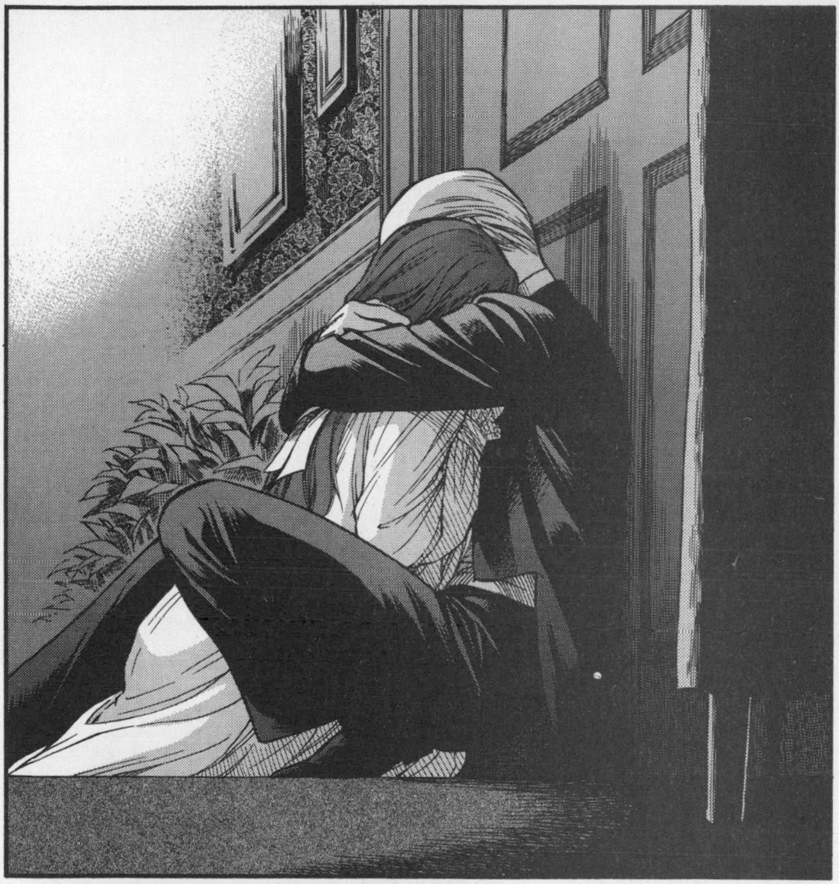

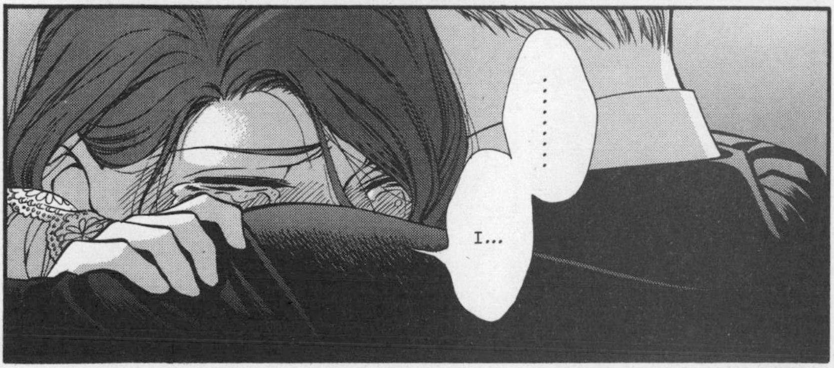
....
I...

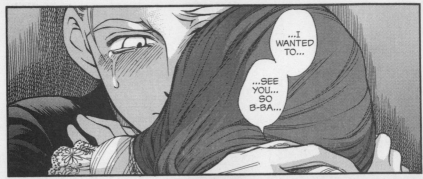

...I WANTED TO...

...SEE YOU... SO B-BA...

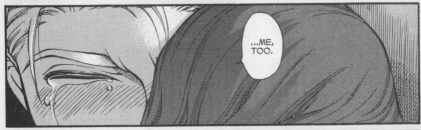

...ME, TOO.

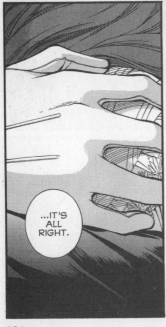

...IT'S ALL RIGHT.

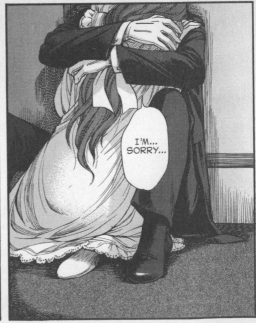

I'M... SORRY...

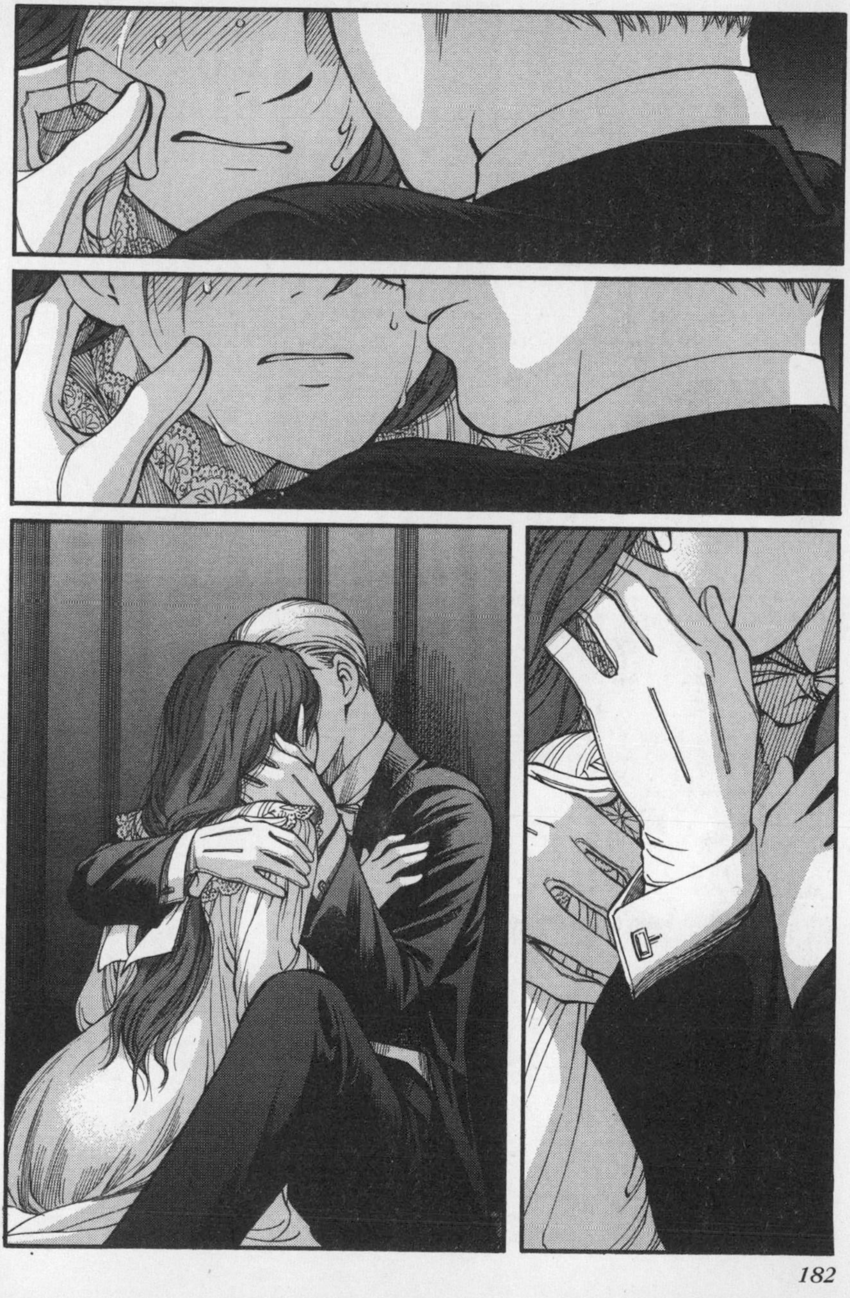

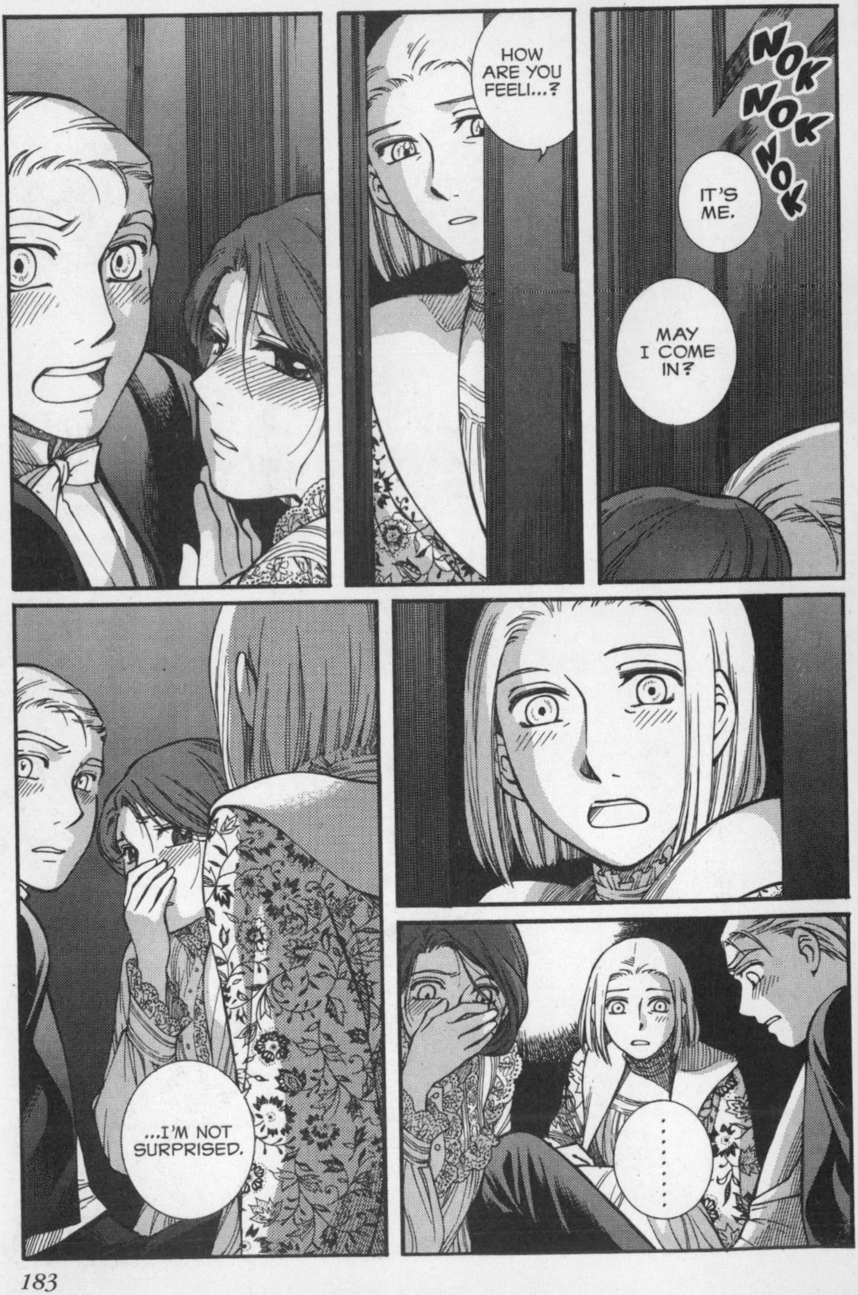
NOK NOK NOK
IT'S ME.
MAY I COME IN?
HOW ARE YOU FEELI...?
...I'M NOT SURPRISED.
......

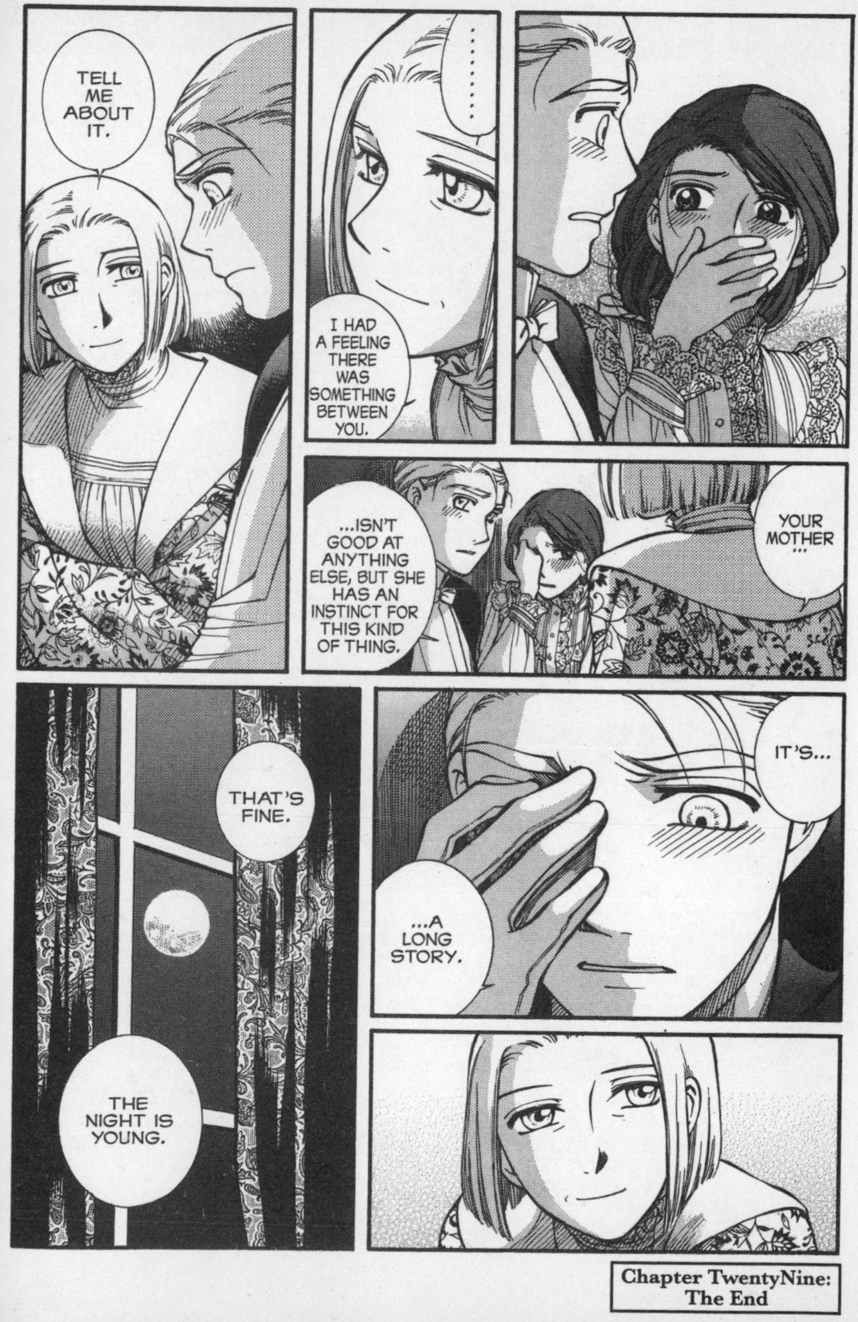
......
I HAD A FEELING THERE WAS SOMETHING BETWEEN YOU.
YOUR MOTHER...
...ISN'T GOOD AT ANYTHING ELSE, BUT SHE HAS AN INSTINCT FOR THIS KIND OF THING.
TELL ME ABOUT IT.
IT'S...
...A LONG STORY.
THAT'S FINE.
THE NIGHT IS YOUNG.

Chapter TwentyNine: The End

SILLY AFTERWORD MANGA

"IS IT FUN PLAYING WHIST* BY ONESELF?"

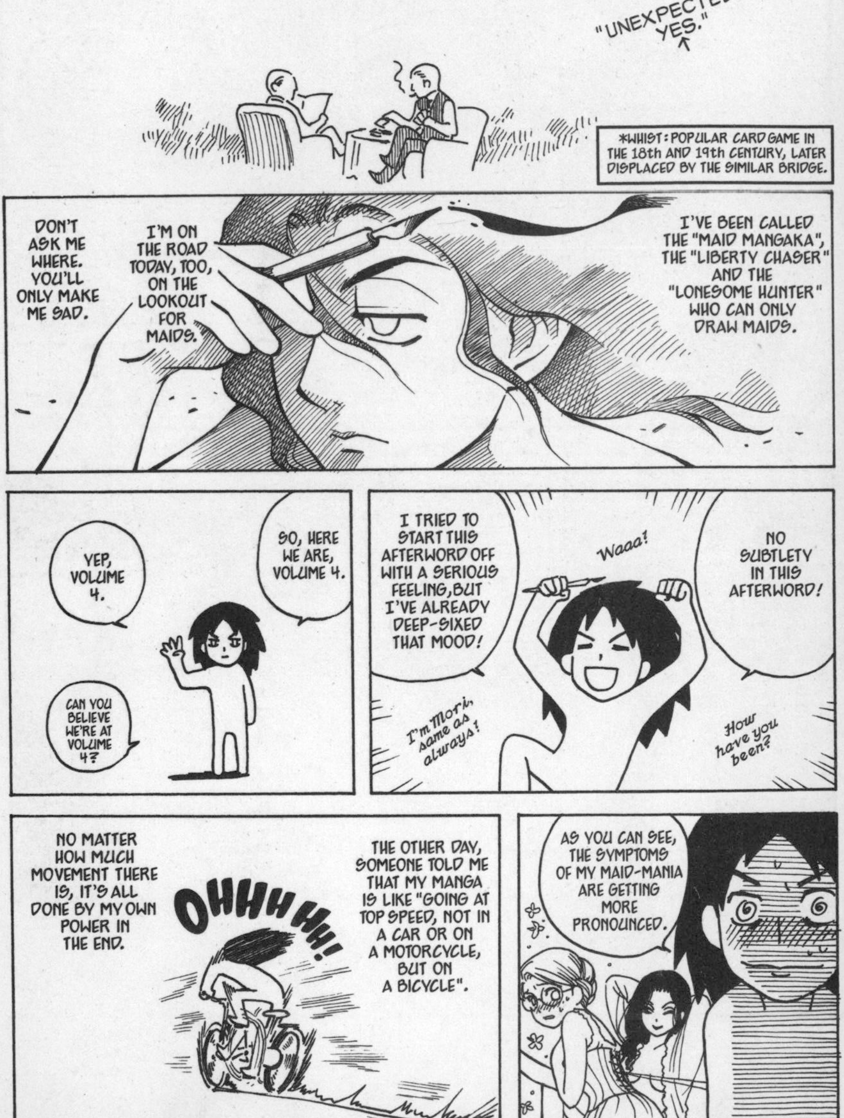
"UNEXPECTEDLY, YES."
*WHIST: POPULAR CARD GAME IN THE 18th AND 19th CENTURY, LATER DISPLACED BY THE SIMILAR BRIDGE.
I'VE BEEN CALLED THE "MAID MANGAKA", THE "LIBERTY CHASER" AND THE "LONESOME HUNTER" WHO CAN ONLY DRAW MAIDS.
I'M ON THE ROAD TODAY, TOO, ON THE LOOKOUT FOR MAIDS.
DON'T ASK ME WHERE. YOU'LL ONLY MAKE ME SAD.
NO SUBTLETY IN THIS AFTERWORD!
Waaa!
I TRIED TO START THIS AFTERWORD OFF WITH A SERIOUS FEELING, BUT I'VE ALREADY DEEP-SIXED THAT MOOD!
How have you been?
I'm Mori, same as always!
SO, HERE WE ARE, VOLUME 4.
YEP, VOLUME 4.
CAN YOU BELIEVE WE'RE AT VOLUME 4?
AS YOU CAN SEE, THE SYMPTOMS OF MY MAID-MANIA ARE GETTING MORE PRONOUNCED.
THE OTHER DAY, SOMEONE TOLD ME THAT MY MANGA IS LIKE "GOING AT TOP SPEED, NOT IN A CAR OR ON A MOTORCYCLE, BUT ON A BICYCLE".
OHHHHH!
NO MATTER HOW MUCH MOVEMENT THERE IS, IT'S ALL DONE BY MY OWN POWER IN THE END.

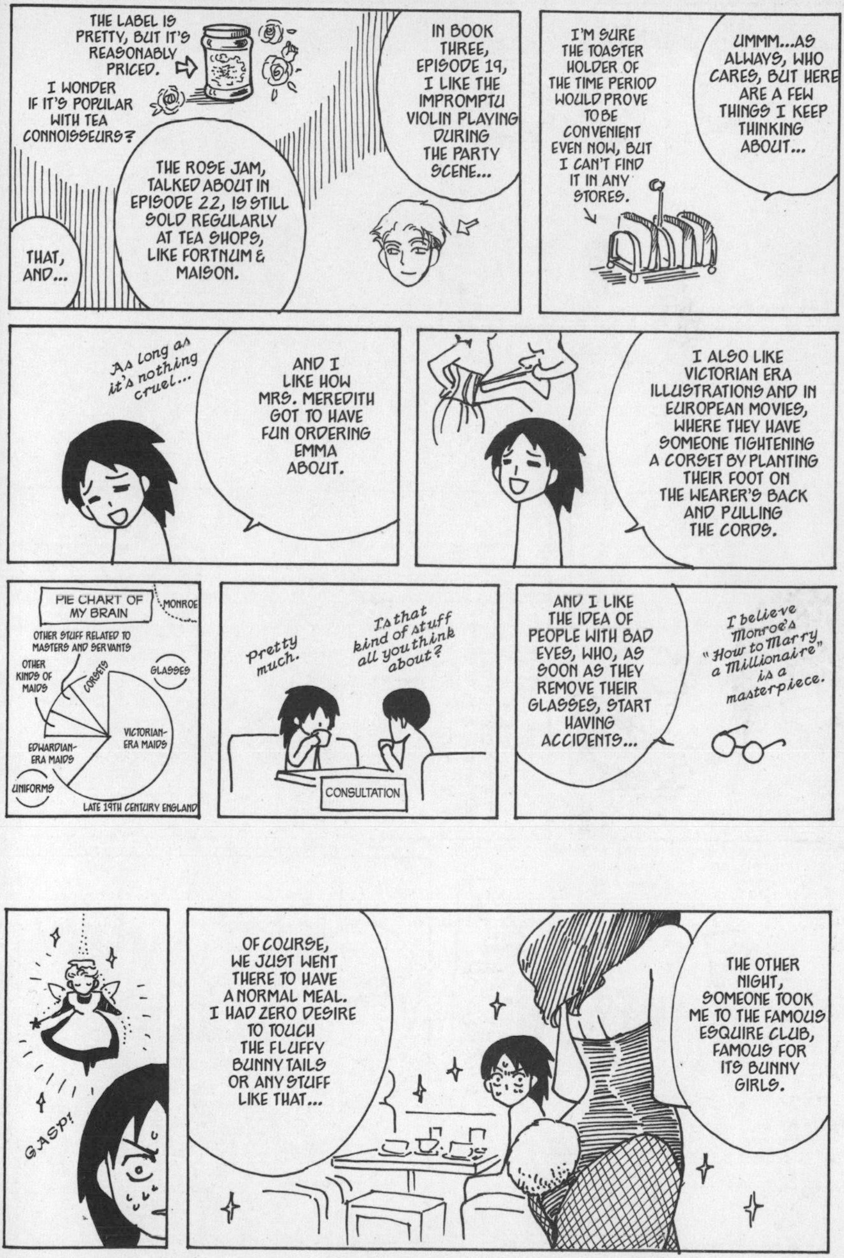

UMMM...AS ALWAYS, WHO CARES, BUT HERE ARE A FEW THINGS I KEEP THINKING ABOUT...
I'M SURE THE TOASTER HOLDER OF THE TIME PERIOD WOULD PROVE TO BE CONVENIENT EVEN NOW, BUT I CAN'T FIND IT IN ANY STORES.
IN BOOK THREE, EPISODE 19, I LIKE THE IMPROMPTU VIOLIN PLAYING DURING THE PARTY SCENE...
THAT, AND...
THE ROSE JAM, TALKED ABOUT IN EPISODE 22, IS STILL SOLD REGULARLY AT TEA SHOPS, LIKE FORTNUM & MAISON.
THE LABEL IS PRETTY, BUT IT'S REASONABLY PRICED.
I WONDER IF IT'S POPULAR WITH TEA CONNOISSEURS?
I ALSO LIKE VICTORIAN ERA ILLUSTRATIONS AND IN EUROPEAN MOVIES, WHERE THEY HAVE SOMEONE TIGHTENING A CORSET BY PLANTING THEIR FOOT ON THE WEARER'S BACK AND PULLING THE CORDS.
AND I LIKE HOW MRS. MEREDITH GOT TO HAVE FUN ORDERING EMMA ABOUT.
As long as it's nothing cruel...
AND I LIKE THE IDEA OF PEOPLE WITH BAD EYES, WHO, AS SOON AS THEY REMOVE THEIR GLASSES, START HAVING ACCIDENTS...
I believe Monroe's "How to Marry a Millionaire" is a masterpiece.
Is that kind of stuff all you think about?
Pretty much.
CONSULTATION
PIE CHART OF MY BRAIN
MONROE
OTHER STUFF RELATED TO MASTERS AND SERVANTS
GLASSES
OTHER KINDS OF MAIDS
CORSETS
VICTORIAN-ERA MAIDS
EDWARDIAN-ERA MAIDS
UNIFORMS
LATE 19TH CENTURY ENGLAND
THE OTHER NIGHT, SOMEONE TOOK ME TO THE FAMOUS ESQUIRE CLUB, FAMOUS FOR ITS BUNNY GIRLS.
OF COURSE, WE JUST WENT THERE TO HAVE A NORMAL MEAL. I HAD ZERO DESIRE TO TOUCH THE FLUFFY BUNNY TAILS OR ANY STUFF LIKE THAT...
GASP!

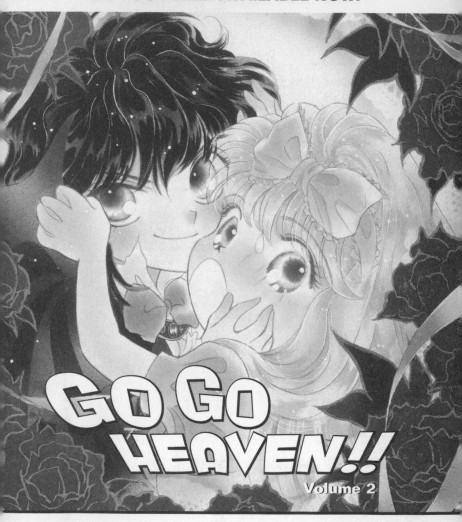

IS THE TIME SHOP CLOSING FOR GOOD?!
FIND OUT IN JUNE!

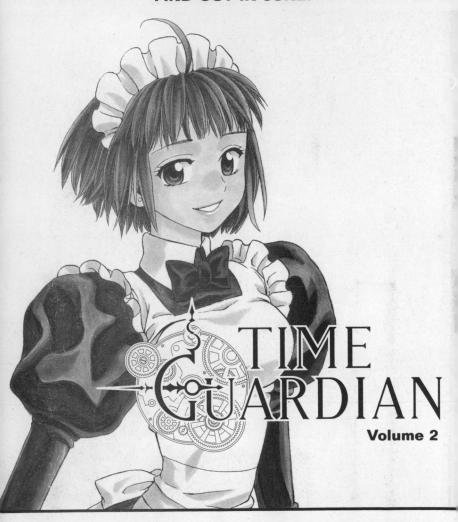

TIME GUARDIAN

Volume 2

By Daimuro Kishi & Tamao Ichinose. In this final volume, two former high school sweethearts trade in all of their memories as a couple in order to forget their relationship...but Miu thinks they still have feelings for each other. Then Mr. Kusaka announces that he's going to sell off all the memories held in collateral and close the time shop. When Miu tries to protest, she can't find him! Is she too late?!

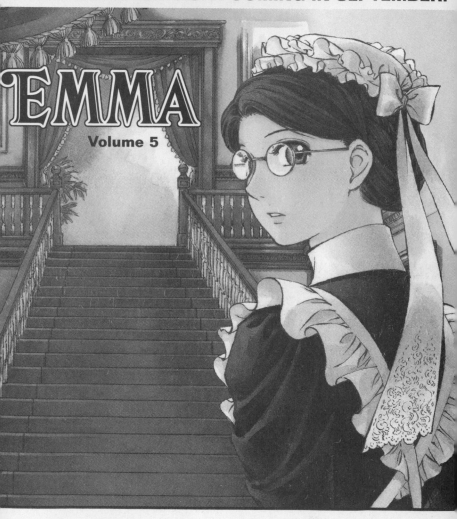

EMMA

Volume 5

By Kaoru Mori. Emma goes back to work at Haworth where all of
the servants notice a change in her behavior. Could it have something
to do with the written correspondence she and William have begun?
Back in London, William also seems to have become emboldened by
his renewed connection to Emma and no one's happy about it. The
forces of society are lining up against them once again and a
reckoning may be coming.

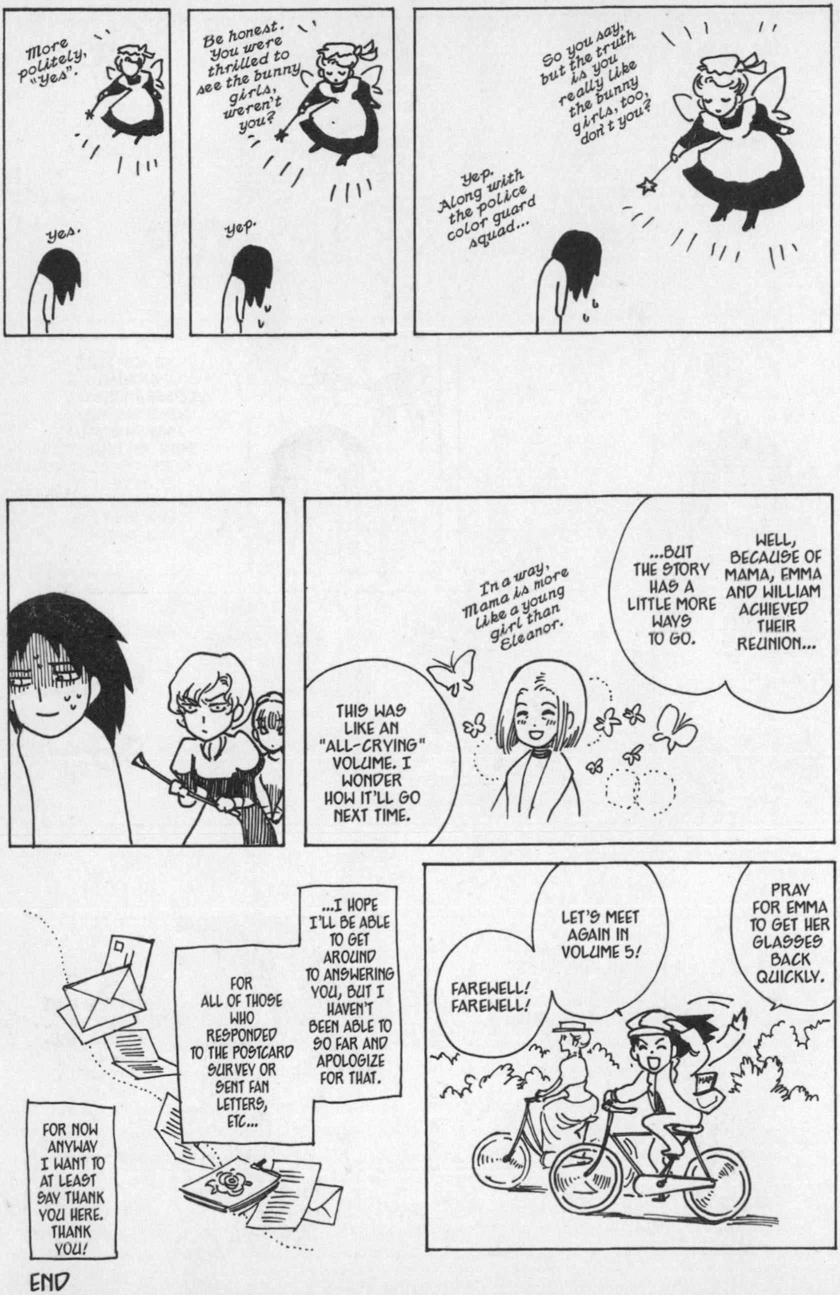
So you say, but the truth is you really like the bunny girls, too, don't you?
Yep. Along with the police color guard squad...
Be honest. You were thrilled to see the bunny girls, weren't you?
Yep.
More politely, "Yes".
Yes.
WELL, BECAUSE OF MAMA, EMMA AND WILLIAM ACHIEVED THEIR REUNION...
...BUT THE STORY HAS A LITTLE MORE WAYS TO GO.
In a way, Mama is more like a young girl than Eleanor.
THIS WAS LIKE AN "ALL-CRYING" VOLUME. I WONDER HOW IT'LL GO NEXT TIME.
PRAY FOR EMMA TO GET HER GLASSES BACK QUICKLY.
LET'S MEET AGAIN IN VOLUME 5!
FAREWELL! FAREWELL!
MAP
FOR ALL OF THOSE WHO RESPONDED TO THE POSTCARD SURVEY OR SENT FAN LETTERS, ETC...
...I HOPE I'LL BE ABLE TO GET AROUND TO ANSWERING YOU, BUT I HAVEN'T BEEN ABLE TO SO FAR AND APOLOGIZE FOR THAT.
FOR NOW ANYWAY I WANT TO AT LEAST SAY THANK YOU HERE. THANK YOU!
END

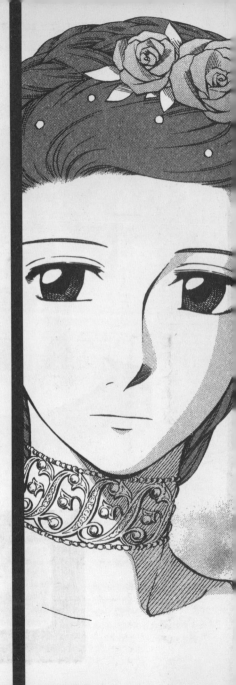

EMMA Vol. 4 © 2004 Kaoru Mori. All Rights Reserved.
First published in Japan in 2004 by ENTERBRAIN, INC.

EMMA Volume 4, published by WildStorm Productions, an
imprint of DC Comics, 888 Prospect St. #240, La Jolla, CA
92037. English Translation © 2007. All Rights Reserved.
English translation rights in U.S.A. and Canada arranged by
ENTERBRAIN, INC. through Tuttle-Mori Agency, Inc., Tokyo.
The stories, characters, and incidents mentioned in this
magazine are entirely fictional. Printed on recyclable paper.
WildStorm does not read or accept unsolicited submissions
of ideas, stories or artwork. Printed in Canada.

DC Comics, a Warner Bros. Entertainment Company.

Sheldon Drzka – Translation and Adaptation
Janice Chiang – Lettering
Larry Berry – Design
Jim Chadwick – Editor

ISBN:1-4012-1135-6
ISBN-13: 978-1-4012-1135-6

All the pages in this book were created—
RIGHT-to-LEFT format. No artwork has
can read the stories the way the crea

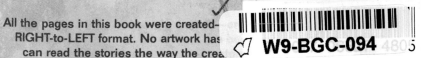

W9-BGC-094 4805

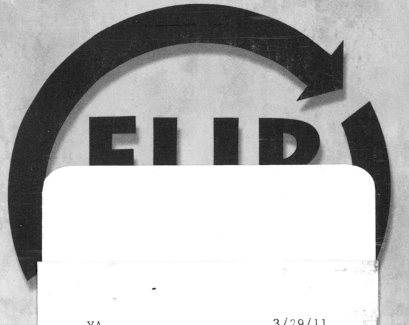

RIG

Traditio
at the
moves
the pag
easy u

For mor
preview
Call 1-8
the near
head to